ARMOR BATTLES

BATTLES

OF THE WAFFEN-SS

1943–45

Kampfpanzer IV, type H

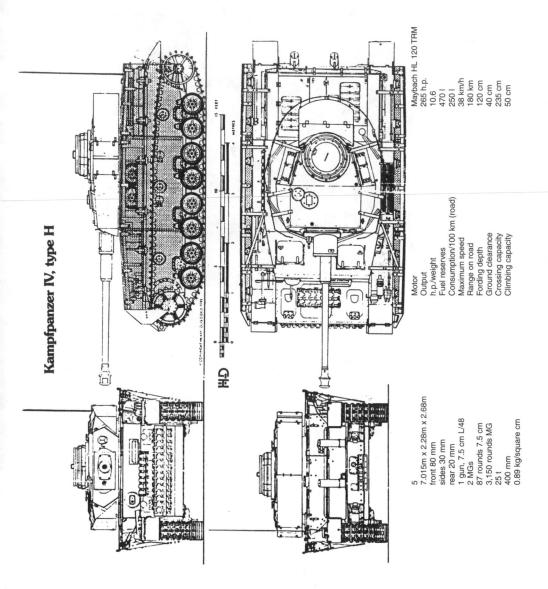

Crew	5
Overall measurements	7.015m x 2.28m x 2.68m
	front 80 mm
	sides 30 mm
	rear 20 mm
Armament	1 gun, 7.5 cm L/48
	2 MGs
Ammunition	87 rounds 7.5 cm
	3,150 rounds MG
Total weight	25 t
Width of track	400 mm
Ground pressure	0.89 kg/square cm

Motor	Maybach HL 120 TRM
Output	265 h.p.
h.p./weight	10.6
Fuel reserves	470 l
Consumption/100 km (road)	250 l
Maximum speed	38 km/h
Range on road	180 km
Fording depth	120 cm
Ground clearance	40 cm
Crossing capacity	235 cm
Climbing capacity	50 cm

Kampfpanzer V (Panther), type G

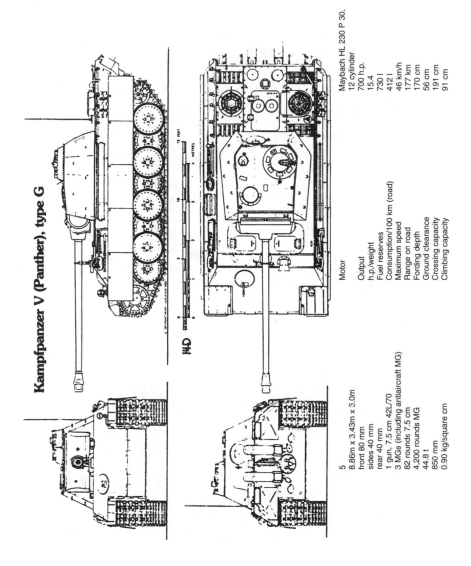

Crew	5
Overall measurements	8.86m x 3.43m x 3.0m
Armcr	front 80 mm
	sides 40 mm
	rear 40 mm
Armament	1 gun, 7.5 cm 42L/70
	3 MGs (including antiaircraft MG)
Ammunition	82 rounds 7.5 cm
	4,200 rounds MG
Total weight	44.8 t
Width of track	850 mm
Ground pressure	0.90 kg/square cm

Motor	Maybach HL 230 P 30,
	12 cylinder
Output	700 h.p.
h.p./weight	15.4
Fuel reserves	730 l
Consumption/100 km (road)	412 l
Maximum speed	46 km/h
Range on road	177 km
Fording depth	170 cm
Ground clearance	56 cm
Crossing capacity	191 cm
Climbing capacity	91 cm

Kampfpanzer VI Tiger

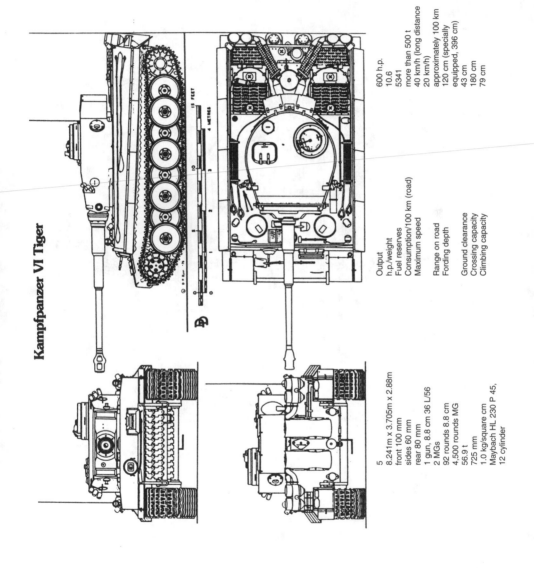

Crew	5
Overall measurements	8.241m x 3.705m x 2.88m
Armor	front 100 mm
	sides 60 mm
	rear 80 mm
Armament	1 gun, 8.8 cm 36 L/56
	2 MGs
Ammunition	92 rounds 8.8 cm
	4,500 rounds MG
Total weight	56.9 t
Width of track	725 mm
Ground pressure	1.0 kg/square cm
	Maybach HL 230 P 45,
	12 cylinder

Output	600 h.p.
h.p./weight	10.6
Fuel reserves	5341
Consumption/100 km (road)	more than 500 t
Maximum speed	40 km/h (long distance
	20 km/h)
Range on road	approximately 100 km
Fording depth	120 cm (specially
	equipped, 396 cm)
Ground clearance	43 cm
Crossing capacity	180 cm
Climbing capacity	79 cm

Kampfpanzer VI Tiger II

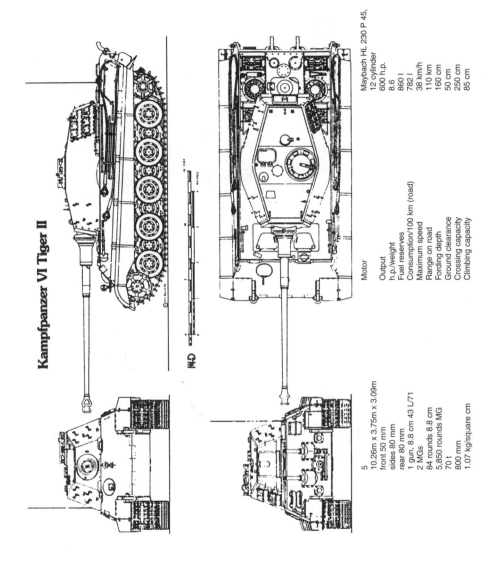

Crew	5
Overall measurements	10.26m x 3.75m x 3.09m
Armor	front 50 mm
	sides 80 mm
	rear 80 mm
Armament	1 gun, 8.8 cm 43 L/71
	2 MGs
Ammunition	84 rounds 8.8 cm
	5,850 rounds MG
Total weight	70 t
Width of track	800 mm
Ground pressure	1.07 kg/square cm

Motor	Maybach HL 230 P 45,
	12 cylinder
Output	600 h.p.
h.p./weight	8.6
Fuel reserves	860 l
Consumption/100 km (road)	782 l
Maximum speed	38 km/h
Range on road	110 km
Fording depth	160 cm
Ground clearance	50 cm
Crossing capacity	250 cm
Climbing capacity	85 cm

ARMOR
BATTLES
OF THE WAFFEN-SS
1943–45

Will Fey
Translated by Henri Henschler

STACKPOLE
BOOKS

English Copyright © 1990 by J. J. Fedorowicz Publishing, Inc.

First published in paperback in 2003 by
STACKPOLE BOOKS
5067 Ritter Road
Mechanicsburg, PA 17055
www.stackpolebooks.com

Originally Published in German as PANZERKAMPF, by Munin Verlag, Osnabrück

www.jjfpub.mb.ca

Printed in the United States of America

10 9 8 7 6 5 4 3 2 1

FIRST EDITION

Library of Congress Cataloging-in-Publication Data

Fey, Will, 1918-
  [Panzerkampf. English]
  Armor battles of the Waffen-SS, 1943–45 / by Will Fey ; translated by Henri Henschler.— 1st ed.
       p. cm. — (Stackpole Military history series)
  ISBN 0-8117-2905-2 (pbk.)
  1. World War, 1939-1945—Tank warfare. 2. Waffen-SS. 3. World War, 1939-1945—Regimental histories—Germany. I. Title. II. Series.
D793.F4913 2003
940.54'1343—dc21

                                                            2003008241

Table Of Contents

Foreword to the English Edition

As commander of a Tiger Panzer and a platoon leader in a Tiger Abteilung, I faced, as did many of my comrades in the uniforms of the Heer and the Waffen-SS, British, Canadian, and U.S. units throughout the tough attacks and defensive battles in Normandy and the Ardennes. The bitterness of the fighting was balanced by the integrity of both sides. Throughout those weeks and months, we faced each other as soldiers at the front, without regard to ideological differences. The chivalry of the fighting, which was not eliminated by the increasing mechanization of the battlefield—more than once did we save wounded and disabled enemy soldiers from their knocked-out tanks—formed the basis for the later understanding that made us into allies.

From the encounters during my service with the Bundeswehr (German Federal Armed Forces) and during gatherings on the battlefields of Normandy with our former enemies, friendships developed, which have, through subsequent exchange of correspondence, remained alive today.

The events described on the following pages are not meant to glorify war, which is no longer a means of politics, but instead to preserve the memory of our fallen comrades on both sides.

Will Fey

Foreword by Otto Kumm,
Major General of the Waffen-SS

To "Panzer Battles" on its way.

More than forty years have passed since those battles of our Panzers, which are being reported here.

And yet, these forty years have not been able to extinguish those memories in each of the then-young warriors.

Too deeply engraved in the soul are these markers:

The Pride
to have contributed to the success of this crucial weapon,
the Rage
when enemy numerical superiority wiped out success,
the Pain
to often helplessly face the suffering of wounded comrades,
the Grief
for the many fallen comrades,
the Fear
of not surviving this inferno—of losing one's young life without having lived,
the Comradeship
—the most valuable good of the soldier—which proves itself when the only one standing between naked fear and the pitiless decision of the fates is he—the comrade.

Love of the fatherland, loyalty to the people, and a firm determination to stand up for the freedom of both—this makes these men into examples for coming generations—even if due recognition is still being denied them.

Otto Kumm
1990

About the Author

Will Fey, Hauptmann a.D. (captain, retired), is a former member of the Waffen-SS and one of the thousands of comrades who contributed to the building of the German Federal Armed Forces.

Fey was born on September 25, 1918, in Lollar/Hesse and was drafted into the Panzerabwehr-Abteilung (antitank) 152 of the 52. Infantry Division (von Arnim) on August 27, 1939. He fought, beginning on June 22, 1941, in the Eastern Campaign's central sector with the same unit. After the 52. Infantry Division was destroyed during Operation "Büffel" (Buffalo), during which he was seriously wounded, he transferred to the Waffen-SS as a Panzer commander in the Schwere (heavy) Panzer-Abteilung 102. After action in Normandy he was ordered to report to the 19th SS officer cadet course at the officer cadet school in Königsbrück from October 1, 1944, to January 30, 1945. He was promoted to SS-Standartenjunker (officer cadet) on December 1, 1944. Beginning in February 1945, he saw action as a leader of quick-response units and in April and May during the final battle in the capital of the Reich as a member of a tank-destroyer team.

On August 1, 1956, Fey joined the Federal Armed Forces and served with troops and staffs of 5th Panzer-Division and Panzer troop school Munster. He was active in the 11th Airborne Division and from 1965 to 1972 served on the staff of the Federal Ministry of Defense.

After his retirement in 1973 until 1980, he was active in the military information services program in the state of Baden. Fey specialized in cooperation with reserve soldiers in Switzerland, Austria, and France, organizing joint military competitions and seminars on defense policy and working with the public. For his active involvement with the French forces stationed in southern Baden, he was awarded the regimental badge of the 12th Cuirassier Regiment and of the 4th Commando-Entrainement.

Since 1978, he is the managing director of the Association of Holders of the Knight's Cross and editor of the magazine *Das Ritterkreuz*. In these capacities, Fey makes use of his powers of persuasion and his drive to promote defense preparedness in the NATO framework and an unbroken tradition of the German soldiers' heritage without any restrictions or exclusions of former soldiers of the Armed Forces.

Introduction

Like a red thread, the journey of young Panzer crews leads through the hot spots of the theaters of war in the east and the west, and ends in the dramatic turmoil of battle during the collapse in the Vienna area and Berlin. We find these Panzer soldiers in the lightning attack on Charkow and Bjelgorod in 1943, in the battles of the retreat in the winter of 1943–44. We experience their actions in the massive tank attacks of the Allied troops in Normandy in 1944 and during the Ardennes offensive in 1944–45, which saw extraordinary results in knocking out tanks. They were in the lead of the breakthrough against the Russian masses between the Oder and Elbe Rivers; they established the link to Army Wenck and thus saved thousands from the fate of displacement and years of imprisonment. Until the hour of the capitulation, a very small number of King Tigers were the backbone of the final battle for Berlin. Panzer soldiers with Panzerfausts, without Panzers, were the last bastion against the T-34 and J.S. tanks of the Red Army.

Many of the soldiers of that time passed on their experiences as teachers and instructors during the establishing of the Federal Armed Forces. The "Leopard," the logical further development of the battle tank, was created by the designers who were involved in the development of the "Tiger" and the "King Tiger."

Despite defamation of the German soldier, the wheel of history has continued to turn. Whoever lived through the past years with open eyes and ears knows that we need an army for the protection of our fatherland. Only within the treaty obligations of free western states in NATO can we have the opportunity to live in peace and freedom.

Messages of greetings were dedicated to the soldiers of the Panzer troops of the Waffen-SS on various occasions. They were from the commanders and leaders of friends and enemies who had commanded Panzer and tank units.

The oldest soldier of the Waffen-SS, Colonel General (four star, retd.) Paul Hausser, wrote years ago:

The experiences of the young Panzer soldiers of the Second World War, described soberly and realistically, date back a long time. An epoch has since been buried. One cannot bypass the negative judgment of history of the supreme political and military leadership. For this political and military leadership, the young soldier cannot be held responsible. He had to do his duty—and carried it out, bound by the old and continuously valid soldiers' virtues.

In particular, the battles of the Panzer soldiers gave daily examples of loyal performance of their duties and their comradeship. They were mostly battles of the most bitter defense without expectation of glory and recognition. The readiness for the same attitude during the danger-threatening tensions of our time must be preserved. The young soldier and our people, too, need it and will use it.

P. Hausser

Hill 112,

Cornerstone of the Normandy Campaign,
Major J. How, MC:

"In comradely solidarity! Bittrich.

The Commanding General of the
II.SS-Panzerkorps, Wilhelm Bittrich"

"In memory of shared experiences.

"To Will Fey, with thanks for his help and as a remembrance of the difficult days of the year '44. Joe How, Infantryman with the 11th Armoured Division"

Weiss. Commander of the Heavy Panzer-Battalion 102, Obersturmbannführer (Lt. Colonel) Hans Weiss."

The Formation of the First Panzer Units of the Waffen-SS

When the grand old man of the former Waffen-SS, Generaloberst Paul Hausser, writes in his introductory note of the "young" Panzer soldiers— and this term "young" Panzer troops of the Waffen-SS is always stressed in numerous publications on this force—an explanation is required for the readers of the postwar generation.

Johannes Rudolf Mühlenkamp, the first commander of a Panzer unit of the Waffen-SS and the last inspector general of the Panzer troops of the Waffen-SS, provided a valid statement. Sturmbannführer (Major) Mühlenkamp was commander of the reconnaissance unit of the SS-Panzer-Grenadier-Division "Das Reich," and found himself at home to recuperate after being severely wounded. At the beginning of 1942, he was directed to gather men and equipment at the Wildflecken training area, where a staff to develop a Panzer force for the Waffen-SS was also located at that time.

The training objective of having a Panzer unit ready for action in the planned 1942 summer offensive in the southern sector of the Eastern Front was achieved.

The required men, noncoms and officers who were particularly suited for this duty, were chosen from the combat units and reserve units of the Waffen-SS. Experienced officers of the Panzer forces of the Heer (army) were detailed as instructors. Representing them all were the leader of the training commission, Hauptmann (Captain) Philipp, who was the last commander of Panzer-Regiment 1 of the Heer and retired from the Federal Armed Forces with the rank of general, and Major Straub, responsible as an experienced engineer for the technical training. This unit was ready for action in the summer offensive of 1942 in the southern sector of the Eastern Front and was attached, as I. Abteilung, to the 5. SS-Panzer-Division "Wiking." Beginning on July 21, 1942, within the framework of the 17. Army, the I./SS-Panzer-Regiment 5 took part in the battle for Rostow, the advance across the Kuban into the area around Maikop, and the fighting in the Caucasus and the Terek area. The three combat units were equipped with the following:

Panzer IIIs with 5-cm long-barrel guns for the 1. and 2. Companies
Panzer IVs with 7.5-cm short-barrel guns for the 3. Company.
Later, the units re-equipped with 7.5-cm long-barrel guns.

Simultaneously, the creation of the first Panzer units for the "Leibstandarte" and "Das Reich" Divisions also took place at Wildflecken and Fallingbostel.

On October 22, 1942 the Supreme Command of the Heer issued orders to the 1.SS-Division "Leibstandarte" for the formation of a Panzer-Regiment to be moved to France into the Evreux area. After the transfer of the 2.SS-Division "Das Reich" to France, the formation of the SS-Panzer-Regiment 2 "Das Reich" was ordered.

In November 1942 both divisions were renamed SS-panzer-grenadier-divisions and were brought into action at the end of January 1943 on the Eastern Front as part of the SS-Panzerkorps.

The formation of the SS-Panzer-Regiment 3 "Totenkopf" began in August 1942 at the training grounds at Suippe near Chalons and La Braconne in France. The regiment, with Panzer IIIs (5-cm long-barrel) and Panzer IVs (7.5-cm long-barrel), received orders in November 1942 to take part in the occupation of southern France: "Unoccupied France, separated from the occupied areas by the demarcation line, will be occupied by German troops. The occupation will extend to the Mediterranean."

On Christmas 1942, SS-Panzer-Regiment 3 moved back to La Braconne. On February 3, 1943, it was shipped to Russia, with Poltawa as the destination and unloading station.

The "Totenkopf" Division together with the SS-Divisions "LAH" and "Das Reich," formed the SS-Panzerkorps Hausser during the fighting in the Charkow and Bjelgorod area (without "Leibstandarte" at the Mius as it went to Italy).

The formation of the 9. "Hohenstaufen" and 10. "Frundsberg" SS-Panzer-Divisions began in January 1943, with the creation of the I. Panzer-Abteilungen (detachments) of the Panzer-Regiments 9 and 10, for the SS-Panzer-Grenadier-Divisions at the Bitsch training grounds in Alsace.

From November 1943 followed the reorganization of these two Panzer-Grenadier-divisions into SS-Panzer-divisions and the enlargement of Panzer-Abteilungen 9 and 10 into Panzer-regiments.

In March 1944, the formation and training of the 9. and 10. SS-Panzer-Divisions were completed. They were fully prepared and ready for combat duty.

When the II. SS-Panzerkorps was dispatched to the Eastern Front at the end of March 1944 at forced march speed, the only element missing was the equipping of the I. Abteilung with the Panzer V "Panther."

The II. SS-Panzerkorps was charged with ending the encirclement of the 1. Panzerarmee in the Lemberg–Tarnopol area (Hube pocket). While the I./SS-Panzer-Regiments 9 and 10 were moved to the Mailly-le-Camp training grounds to receive their Panzer V "Panthers," the SS-Panzer-Regiments with their II. Abteilungen, equipped with Panzer IVs and assault guns, faced their first Panzer action on the Eastern Front as a "fire brigade."

The I./SS-Panzer-Regiment 9 "Hohenstaufen" only joined the SS-Panzer-Division "Hohenstaufen" at the beginning of July 1944 on the invasion front in Normandy. The I./SS-Panzer-Regiment 10 "Frundsberg" had to wait until January 1945 to be equipped with the Panzer V "Panther." It saw action the next month with SS-Panzer-Division "Frundsberg" on the Western Front in Upper Alsace and subsequently in Pomerania. The I./Panzer-Regiment 10 remained in Pomerania to the end.

The 12. SS-Panzer-Grenadier-Division "Hitlerjugend" was reorganized by order of October 30, 1943 into a SS-Panzer-Division. The formation and training of SS-Panzer-Regiment 12 "Hitlerjugend" took place at the Mailly-le-Camp training grounds in France and, from January 1944, at Beverloo in Belgium. Together with the 1. SS-Panzer-Division "LAH," the 12. SS-Panzer-Division "Hitlerjugend" formed the I.SS-Panzerkorps. The SS-Panzer-Regiment 12 "Hitlerjugend" fought in the I.SS-Panzerkorps in Normandy, the Ardennes, and Hungary. It capitulated on May 8, 1945 in Austria.

In spring 1944, three heavy SS-Panzer-Abteilungen, equipped with the Panzer VI (Tiger and King Tiger), were formed and assigned to the I., II., and III. SS-Panzerkorps as Korps units. These heavy Panzer-Abteilungen came from the heavy companies of the 1. SS-Panzer-Division "LAH," the 2. SS-Panzer-Division "Das Reich," and the 3. SS-Panzer-Division "Totenkopf." These companies excelled on the Eastern Front as a force to be reckoned with at the decisive points of major engagements.

The heavy Panzer-Abteilungen carried the numbers 101 in the I. SS-Panzerkorps, 102 in the II. SS-Panzerkorps, and 103 in the III. SS-Panzerkorps. In the framework of a renaming, these numbers were changed in autumn 1944 to 501, 502, and 503 respectively.

Interested readers will find detailed information on the seven Panzer-Divisions of the Waffen-SS in the divisional histories published by Munin Verlag, 4500 Osnabrück, Federal Republic of Germany.

SONG OF THE GERMAN PANZER TROOPS:
Whether It Storms or It Snows

Whether it storms or it snows, or the sun smiles at us,
the day's boiling hot or the night is dark,
our faces are dusty, but our spirits are high:
our Panzer, it races along with the storm.

With thundering engine, as fast as lightning,
toward the enemy, protected by the Panzer;
ahead of the comrades, we're in battle alone,
so we push deeply into the enemy's lines.

When an enemy tank appears in front,
then it's full speed ahead and at the foe.
What value our life in the defense of our Reich?
To die for Germany is the highest honor for us.

With blockades and tanks the foe tries to stop us,
we laugh at him and go around.
And as he shakes his fist in anger and rage,
we seek a path no one else could find.

And if once it deserts us, the faithless luck,
and we won't return to the homeland,
when the bullet kills us, and fate calls us in,
then our Panzer will be our iron grave.

PART I

Panzer Action at the Hot Spots of the Eastern Front 1943–1944

Panzers Between Charkow and Dnjepropetrowsk

WITH THE SS-PANZERKORPS (HAUSSER) IN WINTER ACTION
It was during those fateful days of January 1943 when we found each other. Only a few hours before we knew nothing about each other. Then we were a Panzer crew, a fighting unit, depending on each other for life and death. Five men, more like five boys, but almost all marked with the scars of war: the gunner nineteen years old, but with one year in front action in a Panzer IV company; the radio operator eighteen years old, who came from a Panzer III company and had also been in the east for almost a year; the loader, our youngest at seventeen and a half years old, freshly imported from home, a volunteer, impatient for his first action; the commander twenty-three years old, who was an infantryman for three years and had already marched through Poland and France, been wounded a number of times, and was decorated with everything that makes an infantryman recognizable even from a distance! In battle from the beginning he already had two campaigns in the east behind him and radiated to us a feeling of trust and confidence.

We were to get our Tiger! We were proud of this Panzer, one of the first Tigers to reach the east! For us, from the first day on, it was more than just a weapon. It was not just cold metal, for us it was alive! We nursed and tended to it because we knew how much we would need it during the fighting that awaited us. We slept, ate, and laughed in our Panzer. We trembled and were anxious about it. We cursed it if the engine quit sometimes, but we praised and stroked it when we had another success. We had become a unit, we five men and our Tiger!

Although every tank was urgently needed at the front, our own engagement was stalled for a few days because of a lack of technical parts (ice studs) required for the winter campaign. Since Charkow was just becoming a part of the front, we had to leave our quarters at "filling station west." Our three Tigers took part in the fighting withdrawal while the others were shipped to Poltawa to be winterized by our repair company.

Long since, the endless expanse of the flat country, covered with a dirty-white mass of snow, had taken possession of us. Randomly scattered, isolated villages, above which the cloud-covered sky spread like a shroud.

Before us lay the Donez, a river that, thanks to its heavy ice cover, was no longer an obstacle for infantry units. Day by day, night by night we played fire brigade. We launched a counterattack; then came an alarm from the neighboring sector where Ivan had managed to break through. Defense against tank attacks, violent reconnaissance, and time and again rear guard action for our slowly but steadily retreating infantry units. There was no longer a coherent front line. The Russians drove our exhausted units before them with an unprecedented vehemence. The 8th Italian Army caused us great grief. In full dissolution it dropped everything and could not be stopped! Thus, one day, we too had no choice but to withdraw to the city of Charkow if we did not want to remain a drop in the red flood from the steppe.

We held the eastern edge of Charkow against all tank attacks until, already outflanked in the north and south, we left the city at the last minute. Unforgettable images offered themselves to our eyes. Panic and looting ruled the civilian population, which was about to be reoccupied by the Russians.

Our onboard calendar showed February 10, 1943, when we assembled in Merefa. The remaining Tigers, which were readied for action in Poltava, also arrived there at that time. We mounted local counterattacks and tried to form a main line of resistance. The situation during those February days was very confused. Reconnaissance in force against Russian-occupied villages soon allowed us to form an overall view of the situation. The resulting picture certainly gave us no cause for joy; our communications road was severed and we were cut off from our supply bases to the west. Among the many killed in the fighting to reopen the communications road at the Merefa Bridge was our company commander. Again, with a few Tigers and mounted Panzer-grenadiers we pushed, as so often before, into the endless expanse; silent and cold we sat in the Panzers. No one really knew what was happening. The objective of the attack was a village in front of us. No one knew its name, and it did not matter anyway. We stopped within sight of the place. In the meantime we had learned that a Panzer company of the regiment was to attack from the other side. Scouts had determined that this village was occupied by a scattered Russian unit with tanks.

We wanted to clean up this situation, and the time had come. The Panzer IV company and the assault guns moved in, and wild shooting started. Then it was our turn. The village was surrounded and there was no more escape for the enemy. However, the Russians did not surrender. Night came. We shot up the houses at the fringe of the village in order to keep control, using the light of the fires and thus preventing any attempt to break out.

The Russians did not give in but fought back with the courage of despair. With tank guns, antitank guns, mortars, and machine guns, they fired at us. Our grenadiers crawled under our Panzers since the rock-hard, frozen ground offered no possibility of cover. Losses were inevitable, as some of the Panzers were already immobilized by antitank hits to the tracks. It was impossible to penetrate into the well-fortified village at night! Without cover, our Panzer stood out from the terrain while Ivan was well sheltered. We had to wait for the day. It was a restless night. In front of us we saw the burning houses and heard the constant whistling of the firing of flares and the ongoing rattle and humming of the surrounded Russian tanks. They drove restlessly back and forth, maybe still trying to find a gap for a breakout. So came the morning and with it the end. In the concentrated fire of our Panzers the resistance waned. Very slowly we pushed closer and rolled over antitank guns whose crews lay dead next to them, caught by our explosive shells. The T-34s, then only eight left, fired until they were blown up by our 8.8 shells. The Russians resisted to the last man. The machine guns of the grenadiers reaped a cruel harvest, but the Russians did not surrender. Their losses were unbelievably high. To us, the village was only the "village of death" when we talked about it later. Then the move and refitting of our units was complete. The attack on the Russians who had broken through south of Charkow could begin! With our constant counterthrusts and attacks we did not afford the Russians any rest, and so ensured their confusion and a camouflaging of our orderly, planned encirclement.

But the Panzer IIIs, with their 5-cm guns, also did not allow the enemy, who had broken through, any rest during those winter weeks.

A REPORT BY ERNST BARKMANN, SS-PANZER-REGIMENT 2

In the early morning of February 4 the Panzer commanders of the 2./SS-Panzer-Regiment 2 stood in front of their chief, Hauptsturmführer (captain) Lorenz, who had just returned from the battalion headquarters, and awaited their orders. Among them was young Rottenführer (corporal) Barkmann, commander of Panzer 221.

"Comrades, the company will attack, in unit formation, advanced enemy forces near Olschowatka and take the village. Thereafter we will advance to the next town. Panzer 221 on the left flank of the company, the rest in normal formation. Mount!"

Ernst Barkmann gave the battle orders to his crew via the intercom. "We'll advance to Olschowatka under cover of terrain. Panzer, march!"

The Panzers rolled. Panzer 221 reached a dip in the terrain and followed it, then it swung toward the village where the first antitank gun was already firing on the frontally attacking Panzers of the company. A Maxim machine gun opened fire on Panzer 221. The gunner silenced it with his first shot. At full speed the Panzer raced toward the village. "Watch out! Molotov cocktails!" Bottles filled with gasoline burst on the nose of the Panzer. Burning gasoline ran downward. Emerging from his hatch, the loader tried to wipe off the pieces of broken glass and the burning liquid with an old jacket. Rifle fire repeatedly forced him back into cover. Then the commander saw the flash from a muzzle and recognized a Pak behind a house corner. Opposite, the enemy Pak commander spotted the Panzer, which had closed in to about thirty meters. He brought the Pak around to destroy it. Barkmann saw the blank ring of the muzzle swing toward him. They were still some ten meters apart. "Run over the Pak!" The engine howled. At the moment when the Panzer rammed the gun and pushed its barrel down, the shot roared. Two seconds too late! The shell hit the ground below the Panzer without effect. But the danger was not over, bazookas boomed and their projectiles hit the armor. The engine noise of the Panzers, which had pushed into the village of Olschowatka in the meantime, and their gun discharges echoed between the houses.

"Set up defense in the village" came the order from the company commander. Barkmann heard on the wireless that many Panzers were knocked out. Only three Panzers reported ready for action, among them Panzer 221. The three undamaged Panzers returned to the starting position to fetch fuel and towing vehicles.

Despite constant enemy fire the three Panzers reached their starting position and were loaded up with jerry cans. The young Rottenführer was replaced by an experienced Oberscharführer (sergeant) in the turret, and Barkmann had to move to the gunner's seat. In the middle of the night the three Panzers rolled forward again through the deep snow. Heavy drifting had started, and the visibility was barely twenty meters, when suddenly the Oberscharführer lost sight of the other Panzers. Soon after they were stuck in a deep snow drift in the middle of enemy-held terrain. All attempts to free Panzer 221 failed. At dawn, the commander and the loader set out on foot toward their own lines to fetch help. Barkmann stayed behind with two comrades of his crew. Attacking "Ratas" (Soviet planes) showered the Panzer with fragmentation bombs and machine-gun fire at first light, but the armor withstood the fire.

It only became more ominous when Russian infantry attacked across the snow-covered terrain. Barkmann opened fire with both Panzer machine guns, and the Soviets stalled. Our reinforcements, in the form of horse-drawn Paks, arrived, and a duel with 7.62-cm guns began. The radio operator sent a message to the unit that Panzer 221 had to be towed. Help was promised. In the meantime three German Paks were knocked out, a fourth Pak blew up with its ammunition, and the gunner reported that only ten shells were left. Finally, two eighteen-ton towing tractors approached. The first tractor was stopped by a frontal hit. The responsible enemy Pak was spotted by its muzzle flash in position by a straw stack and was immediately fired on. The straw burned and gave off heavy smoke. Under its cover the enemy Pak scored a hit to the rear of Panzer 221. A bright flash of fire hit the interior, and the three crewmen bailed out head over heels, retreating before the advancing Russians. They were picked up soon after by arriving Panzers of the 5. Company, which was sent as relief by the commander of the Panzer-abteilung, Sturmbann-führer (major) Reichsfreiherr von Reitzenstein. The Panzers of the 5. Company could not save the burning Panzer 221.

A few days later, when Charkow was given up on February 14 and the SS-Panzer-Division "DR" (Das Reich) was pulled back across the river, the I. Abteilung of Panzer-Regiment "DR" handed over its remaining Panzers to the II. Abteilung, and was moved back to German territory for retraining on Panzer V (Panther) tanks. Before Charkow stood an enemy with at least an eight-fold superiority. The red tide overran the Charkow area in wild waves, cutting off our westward communication and supply routes, and broke, where it did not already happen on the same day, into the city from the southeast and northwest on the following day. The encirclement of all our troops that had been brought in for defense was practically complete. Even our last open connection, the road via Merefa to Krasnograd, was cut and had to be cleared again.

Charkow could no longer be held. The troops, whose purpose and major strength was a mobile fighting capability, would have been deprived of all possibility to recapture the initiative. With unparalleled vehemence, the enemy pushed south of Charkow toward Dnjepropetrowsk. The moment appeared as favorable to the enemy as never before.

He had to, at any cost, force the decision. Under heavy tank escort, his horse-drawn sleighs and teams of oxen rushed, without regard for roads or paths, across the open fields and pushed massive wedges up to Pavlograd and Novomoskovsk. The enemy would have moved into a vacuum, as when it broke through the Stalingrad positions, had not the combined force of Panzer-Grenadier-Division "Totenkopf" (Death's Head), which had just joined us, and another division of our Panzerkorps, Panzer-Grenadier-Division "Das Reich," prevented it. While the "LAH" (Leibstandarte Adolf Hitler) pushed with all its force from the area of Krasnograd to the east and northeast, time and again thrusting right into the middle of the enemy deployment and thus taking away his initiative, other Panzer-grenadier-divisions, swinging in a wide curve to the north from Novomoskovsk and Pereschtschepino, closed the circle in a quick pincer movement.

Again, like ghostly wagon trains, teams of horses and oxen appeared on the fields and hills, flanked by T-34s, only this time escaping in the opposite direction. And wherever they showed up, even at night, they were subjected to attacks by our Panzers, armored vehicles, and assault guns.

Thus, an enemy vastly superior in manpower and tanks, the major portion of two Soviet Armies, became the victim of a single Panzerkorps of the Waffen-SS, its flanks masterfully protected by units of the Heer (army). This Panzerkorps was able, during the second push northward, to pin down sizable numbers of the enemy, newly attacking south of Charkow, encircle and, with a few exceptions, destroy them. Two tank corps and three rifle divisions of the Soviets found their end in the encirclement of Paraskoweja.

The wild push to the Dnjepr River was over. However, the enemy was still in and around Charkow. He was able to retreat there with the remainders of his defeated armies, but had already moved up considerable reserves for action. The second move for an encirclement began, the encirclement of Charkow. The LAH attacked the city from its sector to the west and northwest, while other units continued their push from the south. Another attack was directed to the north of Charkow through Krasnograd, Walki, Olschany, and Dergatschi, which cut off the road to Bjelgorod and, swinging southeastward, cut the enemy's last path of retreat, the way to the Donez River. Charkow was doggedly defended, at a time when we had already dug in behind the back of the enemy on the main route to Tschugujew.

**THE ADJUTANT OF THE I./PANZER-REGIMENT "LAH,"
OBERSTURMFÜHRER (FIRST LIEUTENANT) ISECKE REPORTS
ON THE PREPARATIONS FOR THE RETAKING OF CHARKOW
DURING THE EARLY DAYS OF MARCH**

Our battle group stood on the left flank of the division. For the first time
we were to be supported by the Tiger company. Just before lining up, the
commander brought a war reporter named Fernau to me.

"Take him with you in your Panzer. He would like to be in an attack."
Where to put him? After repeated practice with the crew, it turned out
that the best spot was below to the side of the gun.

With sudden concentrated fire we started out. The breakthrough
succeeded. Because of the deep snow, the motorcycle riflemen of the two
companies had mounted the Panzers. The light armored infantry company of the AA (reconnaissance detachment) was only just able to keep
pace. The Schwimmwagens (amphibious jeeps) were towed. Sturmbannführer Meyer led the attack from the Panzer of Obersturmführer Beck
(chief 2./Panzer-Regiment). Sturmbannführer Wünsche held the center.
To the right was the 3./Panzer-Regiment LAH (Hauptsturmführer Lam-
brecht), and the 1./Panzer-Regiment (Hauptsturmführer Jürgensen)
followed some 500 meters behind. Two of the Tigers trailed behind
Sturmbannführer Wünsche. The others were out of action, mostly
because parts and clampings inside the Panzers had ripped loose and
had even injured some of the crews.

Behind and to the left, at the 320.ID (infantry division), we heard
the noise of battle. In a wide line we advanced across the flat snow-covered terrain. On the horizon, at ninety degrees to our direction of
attack, we recognized roofs. That could only be Sneshkoff-Kut. During a
short stop the commander, Sturmbannführer Wünsche, ordered the 1.
Kompanie to swing right and attack the long-stretched village from the
east and move toward us. We were to attack in our present direction. In
front of the village, in particular to its left, there appeared to be a slight
incline. Flashes originated there repeatedly.

We kept going. Our guest Fernau said the scratchy noise in the headset was disconcerting and that it felt somewhat tight in the Panzer but
was quite exciting. In the meantime we had approached to within two
kilometers of the positions on the low hill, which were then more easily
recognizable. Occasionally, the snow billowed in front of us or to the
sides, and we heard a gargling noise go by. We were still eighteen Panzers; behind us came the two Tigers. The infantry was still mounted on
the Panzers in cover behind the turrets.

Fire—stop! On top and ahead of the slight incline, the flashes came on a wide front. Damn it! That looked just like a Pak front. The commander ordered both companies: "Faster, more speed! Let's go!" Half-way to the left Beck's Panzer went out of action. What was the matter with Sturmbannführer Meyer? The Panzer was not on fire, and behind it I could spot some movement. The rapid fire of our Panzers had surely had an effect on the hill. The closest Panzers were 800 meters back. To the left and the right of us, two Panzers were in flames. We were in the phase when most Panzer attacks become critical. None of the Panzers were moving at that moment. Just before, Jürgensen (chief 1. Panzer-Company) called in: "Orion to Merkur (he rolled the R very strongly), village two kilometers ahead, no resistance." Reply of the commander: "Pick up speed." Then quickly: "Commander to all: Follow me!" As his adjutant, fifty meters to the side and behind the commander's Panzer as it raced through the whirling snow, I ordered my crew: "Full throttle, hold tight!" Tensely, I watched through the slits to the sides and the back.

We were already 150 meters ahead when I saw the command Panzer heading for a barn to the right so it could survey the situation from there, covered from sight.

In fractions of a second, I realized that the action was boiling around us. Uncomfortably frequent flashes came from the heights which were then clearly visible. It seemed we had reached a gap in the carpet of fire in the direction of the barn. Then the other Panzers, too, moved.

After reaching the heights, on our right the commander crossed the 100 meters to the barn. I saw the first houses at 200 to 300 meters distance. Immediately there was a flash from the closest house, and we were hit. In the glow of the fire I shouted "Reverse!" Very soon after, another hit. With my shout "Get out!" we found ourselves next to the Panzer in the snow. The cords of our throat microphones dangled from our necks. The heat of the fire had caused burns. Instinctively we buried our heads in the snow. All six of us—luckily Fernau was still with us—crawled some distance from the Panzer. We could not explain why the fire, after it had first started, did not continue to burn.

The Panzer had rolled backward on one of its tracks about twenty meters. We determined later that a T-34 was sitting in ambush in the closest house. Its first hit damaged our left driving sprocket. When we reversed, we had rolled over a mine. We did not have much time to reflect because rifle fire indicated that the positions were still manned.

Where were the other Panzers? Discharges and shell bursts told us that the battle between Panzers and Paks was in full swing. We were unable to make out the command Panzer. Then, a Tiger moved uphill to our side. We wanted to call his attention to the T-34. Of course, he could not spot us. What happened next moved our emotions through extreme heights and depths. Fascinated, we watched the scene to our left through sticking eyelids, all pain from the burns forgotten. The Tiger had barely reached the top when we heard the roar, and flashes and fragments were all around us. When we looked up again, we saw a square meter-size blot on the turret of the Tiger. At the same time we observed the 8.8-cm gun move and point, like a finger, to the target. A flash of fire—we were up on our knees to observe what happened next. Half of the house was blown away, and a burning tank without a turret was clearly visible. We embraced each other with joy. Events then followed at a fast pace. At the edge of the village at least two dozen T-34s came out of hiding.

In the meantime, the second Tiger, commanded by Untersturm-führer Wendorff (the first Tiger by Obersturmführer Pezdeuschek), moved up. Eight enemy tanks were knocked out at Sneshkoff-Kut. After rolling through the village, we managed to get another four while the rest disappeared in the direction of Walki. In the meantime, Sturmbann-führer Wünsche directed the actions of the unit at the Pak front. After the fighting was over, fifty-six antitank guns were counted there. Together with the commander of the AA, Wünsche then organized the mopping up of the village. After receiving medical attention, I was able to return to duty with a bandaged head.

At 7:30 A.M. on March 8, 1943 our battle groups lined up for a further advance to the north.

We were, of course, very interested in how we were to get to Zirkuny. The map showed wooded and marshy terrain north of Charkow. Well, good night! We crossed the other two attack lines, chasing the enemy, and reached the marshes and woods between Tscherkasskoje and Zirkuny. The AA was ahead of us. Sturmbannführer Wünsche ordered: "I will take those Panzers that make it through with me. You mobilize all forces to get going again those that have slid into the bog or are disabled. You know our objective, otherwise just follow our tracks!" Thus started a labor that lasted throughout the night and will forever be remembered by all participants.

Individually, often pulled by two Panzers with extra-long cable, we overcame the worst marshy spots in the wooded area covered by deep snow. We could not foresee the surprise attack by the AA with three Panzer IVs that Sturmbannführer Wünsche was able to pull off. Nor, how surprisingly successful the fighting to open the entrance to Charkow from the northeast was to be. It was still eight kilometers to the vital crossroads in Charkow, the road Charkow–Tschugujew.

The Recapture of Charkow in March 1943

During the first days of March, we rolled in formation with a Panzer battle group toward Charkow for the counterattack. The order from the division had established the objective for our battle group: "In fast pursuit from Walki through Olschany, Dergatscho, you will reach the outskirts of Charkow and there cut the escape route Charkow–Bjelgorod." Just the right mission for us! We moved forward at good speed. Resistance was no longer very strong and was broken by spirited attacks.

A Panzer IV company was in the lead, followed by our Tigers. Behind us were the armored personnel carriers and armored cars of the reconnaissance detachment, which were expected to push through after we opened up a breach.

Ahead of us was a village, where everything was still quiet. The hatches were closed, and we kept in touch by radio. Only 600 meters to go, but no shot was fired. Our Panzer IVs had deployed in attack formation. As the first Panzers approached the dark outlines of the houses, the fireworks abruptly started. The lead Panzer took a direct hit in the turret. Two or three other Panzers gave off smoke, and another rotated around its own axis after a hit to the track! Still nothing was to be seen of the enemy. He sat, well covered, behind the houses and fences. Encouraged by the first successes, the Russians increased their fire, and the light Panzers of our lead company were stuck. They fired as fast as they could but were unable to accurately spot the Paks and tanks. This could not go on. The Panzer IVs couldn't get through. Over the radio came the order: "Disengage, assemble in the gully." Eight Panzers were lost from just one company. The crews of three Panzers were at least able to bail out, but all the others received direct hits.

We reviewed the situation. Our two Tigers were to go into the lead while the other Panzers, spaced, were to follow behind. The vehicles of the reconnaissance detachment were to remain in the gully until ordered by radio to follow. We rolled into the open terrain. An uneasy feeling filled us when we saw our own knocked-out, burning Panzers lying ahead of us. Immediately, the defensive fire concentrated on us but without success at that distance. We were unable to spot any enemy. Then, suddenly, three T-34s broke cover from the houses off to the side, probably planning to attack us from the flank. Short, quick targeting, our turret swung to the left. The Panzer stopped and the first shell left the barrel. Hit and explosion were almost simultaneous! The next enemy tank was already targeted in the sights of the gunner. Fire!—and it literally blew apart; the shell must have hit the fuel tanks directly. The third enemy tank seemed to want to turn back. It showed us its rear when it, too, was hit. Only then did we notice the smacks against the Panzer walls again. The three T-34s had fully occupied our attention. This firing, which must have come from the low cottages, seemed to be a Pak.

We covered cottage after cottage with high-explosive shells and got some breathing space, at least a short pause! We wanted to get closer to the houses. Covering each other, we broke into the village on the wide road. The other Panzers followed widely spaced, while the armor personnel carriers of the reconnaissance detachment rushed to the edge of the village, dismounted their grenadiers and moved forward to the left and right of our Tigers as cover. The houses were smoked out with hand grenades and machine-gun fire. Then we could see from where the defensive fire had come. The Russians had pushed their 4.7-cm Paks from the back into the houses and so could not be spotted.

We pushed across a wide square with our two Tigers and found some more T-34s ahead of us trying to leave the village unnoticed. With a lightning strike our two Tigers destroyed eight more tanks in a short time. We soon realized the reason for the concentration at this spot. Several hundred meters ahead was a bridge that had to be crossed by the tanks.

We were in determined pursuit. Just before the bridge another two enemy tanks faced us. They were probably deployed to cover the preparations to blow up the bridge. This meant their end! We then secured the crossing and advised the commander of the battle group by radio. The Panzer IVs crossed over while the grenadiers of the reconnaissance detachment mopped up the village. During the course of the night we reached the road Charkow–Bjelgorod and cut it off to all attempts by the Russians, which were encircled in Charkow, to break out. But we could not think of a rest. We were to be there again during the counterattack on the desperately fought-for city! A few hours of sleep had to do. Feverishly, we performed the technical chores; oil change, tightening the tracks. We cleaned the ventilation system and waited for X hour.

During the night of March 11, 1943, we rolled into our readiness positions. At dawn, the target of our attack was seen in front of us as if on a tray. We could clearly recognize the skyscrapers of the Red Square across which we strolled only a few days, or was it weeks, ago. We had taken photos of the harsh contrast between it and the slum dwellings, and of each other. The films were probably still in the cameras, not yet developed. Many of the comrades who had then laughingly posed with Russian girls in memory of Charkow were no longer alive.

PANZER COMMANDER MARTIN STEIGER, 1./SS-PANZER-REGIMENT "T," REPORTS ON THE PANZER BATTLES IN THE CHARKOW AREA

The "DR" and the "LAH" Divisions were already involved in defensive fighting. Although the thrust of the "LAH" Division from Krasnograd to the south had demolished the spearheads of the enemy forces advancing westward, there was still a strong enemy to the east of the previous advance route. Further forces were required to wipe out this enemy and to establish contact with the "LAH" to the northwest of Krasnograd.

This was to be primarily the objective of the newly brought-in SS-"Totenkopfdivision," which was subordinated to the SS-Panzerkorps and assembled in the Pereschtschepino area.

For three days we worked untiringly. The Panzers were painted in white, and weapons and equipment were given a last going-over to ensure readiness for action. During the fourth night, the last units arrived. We set out the next morning.

The regiment moved into the assembly area. The I. Abteilung, led by Sturmbannführer Meierdress, and then the 1., 2., 3., and 4. Companies rolled through Poltawa. It passed retreating Italians and Hungarians and German soldiers and railway men who had lost their units or were looking for better cover in the rear. It was an imposing picture, this column of more than seventy Panzers, which soon disappeared from view in the driving snow.

On February 20, at the break of dawn, we began to get ready. During the day it had begun to thaw, but then sudden snowfall set in, and a strong wind blew from the west as we loaded our meager possessions into the vehicles and Panzers. We started out into the pitch-dark night. Since our arrival in Russia, we had not experienced as strong a snowstorm as during that night. We could not see a meter ahead of the vehicles and Panzers. The Panzer crews sat on the track fenders and directed the drivers. Centimeters of snow covered the Panzers and the overalls of the men. Melted snow ran down their backs. Occasionally, we saw the glowing exhaust of the vehicle ahead, the only reference point for direction. The column had long since broken up. Individual Panzers and supply vehicles drove through the ghostly night toward the new morning. When the new day began to dawn, the snowstorm was also over. We were in Karlowka, a larger village on the main road Poltawa–Krasnograd.

More hours passed before the company was able to make camp as a unit. Some of the Panzers were out of service and had to be repaired by the mechanics or, in the case of major damage, towed away. We set out again the next evening. It was a starlit, freezing night. The commanders stood rigidly in their hatches. The Panzers began to slide on the slippery roads. Around midnight we reached Krasnograd, when a major mishap stalled the advance. Several Panzers began to slide on the clear ice at a downhill spot near the exit from Krasnograd and crashed into each other. The Panzers of commander Meierdress and his adjutant and the Panzers of Riefkogel and Siebenkopf collided at a dip in the road and sustained considerable damage. They had to be towed away. It was light already before we got going again. Then we rolled monotonously through Russia's steppes, which were covered with deep snow. If it had not been for the telephone poles on our right, we could not have known that we were following a road.

Enemy forces had closed in toward the road from the right and threatened our flank.

The order to attack went to the first company. "Ready for action— Panzer, march!" The first houses of Pereschtschepino were bypassed before we went in a straight line across the terrain. We encountered Russian infantry and fought it from the moving Panzer. A few antitank rifles went off, but they were quickly destroyed by our concentrated fire. Artillery fire set in; the explosions were without effect and then stopped altogether. Toward evening our objective was achieved. After hours of driving aimlessly because Riefkogel at the head of the company lost his way, we made camp in a village around midnight. At 4 A.M.: Alert!

All of the Panzer-Regiment 3 got ready for action in the area south of Pereschtschepino and attacked the enemy between Orelka and Samara. It was February 22.

In two waves, first by I. and then II. Abteilung, the attack continued southeastward across the ranges of hills in the direction of Werbki fifty kilometers ahead.

The "DR" Division had in the meantime swung north, successfully crossed the Samara River at Pavlograd, with good support from the Stukas (dive-bombers), and captured Werbki. There the spearheads of the two divisions, "Totenkopf" and "Das Reich," joined up. The column on the left flank of our division had meanwhile taken Orelka to the north and thus secured our open northerly flank. The mass of the 1st Soviet Guards Army continued its advance.

Parts of the Russian Popow Group were already cut off by our neighbor army to the right. However, five enemy tank corps were advancing to the southwest in front of Armee Hoth.

The breakthrough group of the "DR" Division pushed into the southern part of Losowaja. The column on the right entered Wesseli. Our Panzer-regiment advanced to the west of them. Other units thrust forward from Orelka to the east and northeast. The enemy had deployed in particularly great strength for defense around Losowaja. Our regiment had to endure severe fighting there. The II. Abteilung pushed into Panjutina and thus created the prerequisite for the further attack.

On February 27, the enemy front collapsed. The SS-Panzerkorps reached the Losowaja–Orelka railroad line. The pursuit on February 28, led further north. The first objective was achieved; the enemy Popow spearhead was beaten. Its mass was destroyed by our division, supported by parts of the "DR" and "LAH," in three days of hard fighting near Jeremejewka. Isolated enemy units that managed to break out made the area behind us unsafe for days before they were wiped out. The commanding general of the Russian XV. Guards Corps was found dead near the field headquarters of the SS-Panzerkorps.

On March 4, we linked up with our other units. The next day the SS-"Totenkopfdivision" completed the destruction of the encircled enemy and thus achieved its greatest success.

On March 6, the attack continued. Road conditions had worsened. The snow cover was deep and slowed down movement, in particular as we were about to attack again farther north. Walki was captured. Olschani became a prey of the "T" Division, and for the third time in this war the battle for Charkow started. We secured the northwest from Dergatschi to Olschani.

On March 11, the "LAH" entered the city in a surprise attack. The enemy conducted relief attacks from the northeast against our division. Our front line was extended to the Charkow River. Parts of our division were set in march toward Tschugujew and Rogan to cut the main road to the southeast.

On March 15, after successful Panzer combat north of Rogan, our division had reached the narrow passage near Tschugujew and blocked it off.

After this success, Panzer-Regiment 3 continued to roll northward to just before Bjelgorod.

On March 18, the company received orders to capture the last town before the Donez River and thus to take the first step to bring about the end of the offensive. At dawn our Panzers were on the hill overlooking Iwanowka. Suddenly, a radio message reached us that Hauptsturmführer Mooslechner was killed in his Tiger. A delay fuse detonated one of his own shells in the interior of the Panzer. After a few hundred meters our attack stalled in a Russian minefield. The first victim was the Panzer of Oberscharführer Wunsch. Pioneers cleared the minefield. Then the offensive continued, and a few hours later Iwanowka was in our hands. The company had only a few Panzers left that were ready for action. A number of Panzers were knocked out and burned out. A few commanders were critically wounded; Riefkogel, his arm ripped open by a grenade fragment, remained with the company despite his wound. With this counterattack against the major Russian winter offensive, the last German victory in the east was complete. Bjelgorod fell into our hands. The SS-Panzer-Division "Totenkopf" began a period of rest and refitting, our company moved into quarters in Nikojanowka.

THE RECAPTURE OF CHARKOW

The Kampfgruppe (battle group) III. (gep.)/2 of Jochen Peiper, because of its surprising attacks, was the spearhead of this operation together with the Panzer-Regiment "LAH."

On March 12 Kampfgruppe Peiper, after establishing contact with the commander of I./Panzer-Regiment 1 (Witt), pushed along the main road, linked up with the commander of II/1 (Hansen) at the Red Square, and formed a small bridgehead along the Staro–Moskowska street. With two or three armored vehicles, Peiper established contact with Kampfgruppe Meyer at the Tschugujew street fork. Kampfgruppe Meyer advanced along a number of city blocks, occupied the important road fork Charkow–Tschugujew and Charkow–Woltschansk, and fought off fierce attacks from all sides.

Sturmbannführer Wünsche led a counterattack with a few Panzers, which led to the destruction of the Russian assault parties that had broken through.

On March 13, Kampfgruppe Peiper expanded its bridgehead across the Charkow River so that the advance along the Staro–Moskowa road to the east could take place at 12:30 P.M.

On March 14, the Division "LAH" pushed forward in hard street fighting and cleared block after block of the enemy.

At 4:45 P.M. the SS-Panzerkorps received the report that the districts of Katschaniwka, Plechaniwkij Rayo to the agricultural experimental station, Jewgerewka, and Pidgorodny, which was all of downtown, had been taken and were firmly in our hands.

With this, Charkow was captured again!

THE ADVANCE ON BJELGOROD MARCH 16–18, 1943

The recapture of Charkow crowned an operation that finally made possible the closing of the 300-kilometer-wide gap, created by the battle for Stalingrad and its consequences. To achieve this objective, three divisions of the SS-Panzerkorps were deployed side by side to attack toward the northeast and north.

On the right the SS-"T" was to take the Donez, in the center was the SS-"DR," and on the left was the SS-"LAH" toward Bjelgorod.

Punctually, on March 16, the two battalions, supported by Panzers of the 5./SS-Panzer-Regiment "LAH" and simultaneous action by dive-bombers, began the attack on the well-fortified positions. In a fast advance, through the deep snow, the objective of the attack was taken at 6:30 P.M.

For the "LAH" the orders remained unchanged on March 17. For the "T" and "DR" Divisions, Bjelgorod was the target.

Kampfgruppe Peiper attacked at 12:30 P.M., and encountered a Pak front which was then broken by the Peiper battalion, supported by the 7./Panzer-Regiment "LAH" under Obersturmführer von Ribbentrop, at the onset of darkness.

On March 18 at 4:15 in the morning, the reenforced Kampfgruppe Peiper commenced combat reconnaissance against the enemy defensive line. The agreed Stuka attack on the line began on time at 7:00 A.M. Ten minutes later the Peiper battalion reported that it had broken through the line and was advancing on the Otradnyj heights. At 10:00 A.M. the Peiper battalion reached Krassnoje. On his own initiative, Sturmbannführer Peiper ordered the advance to continue. At 11:00 A.M., Peiper reported: "Spearhead at eight kilometers southwest of Bjelgorod on main route. Russians retreating to the west. Two tanks knocked out. Cmdr. III./2."

At 12:10 P.M., Kampfgruppe Peiper repelled a tank counterattack on Bjelgorod from the northwest, knocking out several tanks. It received orders to secure Bjelgorod-West, including the northern exit, for the night.

The Division "DR," together with the "Deutschland" Regiment, advanced from the south into the southern section of the city of Bjelgorod.

In the evening of March 18, the Panzerkorps stood in a line from the heights on the west to Murom–Netschejewka–Botschkowa–Brodok–Tawrowo–defensive circle around Bjelgorod and secured the railroad to Charkow to the west.

During the night the enemy continuously pushed against the positions near Bjelgorod-North. In the early morning hours of March 19, the II./2 took over the security line of Kampfgruppe Peiper.

At 1:15 P.M., Kampfgruppe Peiper, reenforced by the 7./Panzer-Regiment "LAH" and two Tigers, advanced. At 3:35 P.M. it reported tank combat with Russian tanks near Strelezkoje. There, seven Russian tanks were knocked out without any losses of our own Panzers, although one of our armored personnel carriers took a direct hit. The bridge at Strelezkoje was destroyed by the enemy, and the battalion returned to the eastern section for the night. On Peiper's orders, Obersturmführer von Ribbentrop drove forward one more time to the burning armored vehicle to determine if surviving grenadiers could have been rescued. He could only collect pay-books and similar items as there were no survivors. The "T" Division and Division "DR," with all their units, reached the Donez on March 19 and they occupied all villages in the attack area.

The Panzer Battle for Kursk—Operation "Zitadelle," July 1943

SS-PANZER-REGIMENT 2 "DAS REICH" IN ACTION DURING OPERATION "ZITADELLE" (CITADEL)

The objective of this operation was to cut off the protrusion of the Russian front line near Kursk. This would have achieved a shorter front, and destroyed many enemy units so that the Russians would not have been able to mount a major offensive during the summer of 1943.

On July 3, 1943, the Tigers were in the assembly area twenty kilometers west of Tomarowka. On the following day, the commander of the regiment read out the Führer order: The Tigers were to be the spearhead of the attack. At 3 A.M. on July 5, the guns of the German artillery opened the battle for Bjelgorod. A fireworks was thrown up, such as the history of war had probably not recorded up to that time. Discharges and explosions could no longer be distinguished from each other. The guns roared, rocket launchers came in, and the steely death hit the enemy positions a thousand-fold. At 3:45 A.M. the sky thundered; German bomber squadrons flew toward the enemy in endless formations. Official reports later confirmed that more shells were fired that morning than during all of the French and Polish campaigns.

At 4 A.M. the Panzer engines howled and the Tigers rolled forward to the attack. We were in the midst of it, having rolled over Bolshevik infantry and blasted and destroyed enemy artillery and Pak positions. Then a six-hour tank battle started during which our Tiger half-company, with the help of medium and light support forces, knocked out, on the record, twenty-three big American tanks and T-34s of a large superior force, and drove back the rest. The dramatic course of the battle, which demanded the utmost from the crews for six hours and which may be regarded as typical of modern tank warfare, is worthy of a few words:

Since the early morning hours the infantry, supported by massive Stuka and fighter-bomber units, had been attacking the closest fortified rear positions of the Russians. These stopped our advance for a while after the initial breakthrough. On the expanse of hills to the northwest, enemy bunkers and trenches abounded. On the back slopes, enemy batteries were in position and their barrages hailed down on our attacking units. Without pause, the Stukas dropped their deadly loads onto the enemy barrier. One battery after the other was wiped out. In the cornfield behind our Panzer position a gun unit had deployed and plowed the enemy positions. Slowly, our infantry advanced. In thin lines, covered by the high grass of the steppe, the groups crawled ahead. They broke into the Bolshevik trenches and bunkers at about 10:30 A.M.

This was the hour of the Panzers. Unnoticed, we had assembled at the bottom of the valley, the Tigers flanked by medium and light companies. Our field glasses searched the horizon, spying into the smoke of the combat that covered the bunker heights like a veil of mourning. The leader of our Tiger half-company, an Obersturmführer from the Rhineland whose calmness enveloped us all, gave the order to attack. The engines howled. We loaded the guns and slowly the heavy Panzers rolled onto the battleground. After 200 meters the first enemy Pak fired. With a single shot we blew it out of the ground. Then, there was quiet for a while. We rolled over the abandoned enemy trenches and waved from our open hatches to our brave infantrymen. They were enjoying a short rest on the heights they had just stormed. We then moved on into the next valley.

Enemy infantrymen ran through the cornfields, trying to avoid us and to reach the village in the next valley. Our machine gun forced them to seek ground cover. As both of our onboard machine guns rattled, approving shouts of the crew accompanied the precise aim of the fire. A heavy truck was spotted in the woods to our right, attempting to get away through the trees. Immediately, tracer shells hit the moss-green wooden walls of the vehicle and it burst into flames.

A white church with five small onion-shaped steeples appeared on the horizon; the first houses of a village then became visible. Soviet riflemen were racing through the gardens and tried to gain safety in the buildings. We hit them with high-explosive shells. The mud cottages half blew up, then burned like weak torches whose brightness was diminished by the bright summer sun.

It was noon, and the sun burned down on us. We had opened the hatches and watched the terrain ahead. An hour later we came under fire. On a dominating hill to the north, a few T-34s lay in ambush. The first shells landed near us, then our front armor was hit. Load, ready, fire! Hit! We pushed ahead. The first T-34 was in flames. Our neighbor's fire had set a second one ablaze. The others retreated behind the hill. After pushing another 500 meters ahead, we spotted twenty, thirty, forty enemy tanks coming over the horizon. They rolled past the two burning wrecks, stopped, fired, rolled again, and fired in quick succession. Hits hammered our front and hull but caused no damage. We moved ahead a little farther into a more favorable firing position and then opened up.

The Panzer battle began. On separate slopes, some 1,000 meters apart, the forces faced each other like figures on a chess board, trying to influence fate, move by move, in their own favor. All the Tigers fired. The combat escalated into an ecstasy of roaring engines. The humans who directed and serviced them had to be calm; very calm, they aimed rapidly, they loaded rapidly, they gave orders quickly. They rolled ahead a few meters, pulled right, pulled left, maneuvered to escape the enemy crosshairs and to bring the enemy into their own fire.

We counted the torches of enemy tanks that would never again fire on German soldiers. After one hour, twelve T-34s were in flames.

The other thirty curved wildly back and forth, firing as rapidly as their barrels would deliver. They aimed well, but our armor was very strong. We no longer twitched when a steely finger knocked on our walls. We wiped the flakes of interior paint from our faces, loaded again, aimed, fired. It lasted for four hours.

Then the moment came to slap our shoulders: The last enemy tanks had disappeared! Twenty-three steel giants were in flames in the terrain before us. We got out, smoked a cigarette, and marveled that we had no losses. Both of our machine guns were shot up. Other than that, we sustained only minor damage. And we had not a shell left. But we were alive. The engines hummed, the tracks rolled, and we were ready to start pursuit in a few hours. The first phase of the Panzer battle, which we had expected after the push through the dual defensive lines, was victoriously completed.

It was midnight when we crawled into the trench we had dug under our trusty Tiger. In it we were to sleep quietly. Our commander ran his hand gently across the underside of the Panzer. We said "good night" to our steely comrade. Finally, we all slept. There was no time to dream. At 2:30 A.M. the sentry woke us. We wanted to roll before sunup.

Routinely, every crew member in the Panzer did his job. The driver started the engine—a calming sensation, this vibration of the concentrated power of the 720-horsepower motor. The radio operator was in receive mode. The commander talked to the driver on the intercom and called the gunner. The radio operators sent the "ready" report to the chief. We waited for the order: "Panzer—march!" Each one of us was deep in his own thoughts. There was a noticeable tension in the air before every new attack—there had been so many already—but the excitement, the unknown, captured us yet again until we were released by the crackling sound in the headset and the radio order "Panzer—march." The sequence, march direction, and objective had previously been determined by the commander. The infantry came out of the fox-holes, waved to us, and deployed for the attack. A railroad line, 1,000 meters ahead, was their first attack objective.

Abruptly, the firing started. Without warning we were in the midst of it.

The duel with three tanks opposite demanded our full attention. After a short while they were on fire. We spotted three or four more T-34s in flames. Then we heard an explosion and had no time to gather our wits. Headfirst, we dove out of the hatch, rolled backward, and pressed against the tracks. The long barrels of the enemy tank platoon sank hit after hit into our maimed Panzer, but miraculously it did not catch on fire.

What were we to do? The commander—still completely calm—looked around, pointed his hand to a wooded area to the right, jumped up first, took three long strides, hit the ground, leaped up again and then crawled on. The gunner was the second one to jump up. The enemy, holding the height along the main railroad Bjelgorod–Kursk in front of us with more than forty tanks, an artillery train equipped with heavy guns, and machine-gun emplacements, spotted the fleeing men and laid concentrated fire on them. The driver and radio operator were the last ones to make the leap.

We ran for our lives. This hell of 150 meters seemed to be endless! How were we to know if the woods were free of the enemy? While scout-ing ahead, we had left our attacking spearheads three kilometres behind. Had the enemy infantry retreated, or were they still in their bunkers in the woods? Although these considerations would have been logical, we did not give them much thought. Our nerves were tense, our legs wanted to give up. But, the whistle of the high-explosive shells and the dust clouds from the rapid impacts of the machine-gun bullets drove us on. After twenty or thirty seconds we let ourselves drop into abandoned enemy foxholes that were dug at the southern edge of the green band of woods. Just there, to where we had run, the woods stopped abruptly and bordered on the green steppe.

We pressed our hot faces into the cool ground and caught our breath for a few minutes. Then the commander ordered observation to the north while he crawled to the edge of the woods and looked back at our Panzer which still sat in the hail of the grenades. Occasional bullets whistled through the trees. It was a blessing that the last of the retreating Soviets did not know how weak we were. The five of us had only one pistol, but had the determined will to get through!

But were we safe? We crouched in the foxholes in the woods and looked up to the railroad embankment.

The din of the Panzer battle echoed across from the village. The Russians had knocked out some ten Panzers when the company chief was mortally wounded. The rest of his crew, the driver badly hurt by six grenade fragments, crawled back. The last two Panzers started to retreat. They turned their turrets, fired their last shells and rolled at top speed back into the valley.

We felt abandoned, but could not wait for the enemy infantrymen to start their hunt for us. On the heels of the commander, we sprinted into the open steppe which stretched a good three kilometers to the vanguard of our infantry. Again, we raced against death. We dropped, crawled, jumped up again, and had some 500 meters behind us when we saw two Panzers coming across the rise. They were to be our salvation! We jumped onto the first Panzer as it stopped and squeezed in behind the turret. Our pulses raced. We flinched as shell fragments from the enemy artillery slammed into the turret and hull. Another kilometer, another 500 meters—finally, we reached the rise and rolled into the flat valley. The shelling could no longer reach us.

Four tanks assembled between the houses of the village. The survivors stood together. They did not think of their own deliverance. Their thoughts were with the dead, with the company commander who paid with his life for his valor.

We were pleased that the repair unit moved in after only one hour. It was to cost one day to bring the Panzers back into fighting shape. We wanted to be back there as quickly as possible to wipe out that blot. But the time was not altogether lost. Stukas appeared in the skies. They headed north and dove onto the tanks on the road, the railroad tracks, and the artillery train which had knocked out our Tigers, but would not reach its home station ever again. We were not alone, we Panzer soldiers. With us moved the infantry, rolled the batteries, flew the Stuka and bomber formations. The next day we were again to be the steel at the spearhead of the attack. Maybe Lady Luck would smile on us!

A REPORT ON THE COMBAT OF PANZER-REGIMENT "LAH" DURING OPERATION "ZITADELLE"

The armored group "Leibstandarte Adolf Hitler" assembled, together with the Panzer group "Das Reich," at 6:00 A.M. along the main route Teterewino–Prochorowka, after preparatory Stuka action.

At 7:10 A.M. the Panzer group was attacked from the north and northwest by more than twenty T-34s. The resulting tank battle, which also involved the Panzer group "DR," lasted until noon. The enemy then withdrew to the north.

Rolf Erhardt, driver of the Panzer of a platoon leader, 7./Panzer-Regiment "LAH," watched the Panzer combat through his observation slits:

> Widely spread, the 7. Company, that is the part of it which was again ready for action after the mine disaster of July 6, assembled on the hill. Somewhere out there was the town of Teterewino. Behind us were the smoking wrecks of the first Russian wave of tanks. Ahead was an impenetrable wall of dozens of T-34s of the main wave, which we would later dispose of in fierce and bitter combat. A wall of steel and fire. In the middle of it, infantry: our overrun Panzer-grenadiers, and Russians, who were mounted on the T-34s or raced forward among them in the attack. The day before, platoon leader Untersturmführer Weiser joined my Panzer as his own was in the repair shop. He returned from marriage leave, still wearing his dress uniform, and did not have an opportunity to get his combat uniform. We looked at the wedding pictures and tried to establish contact. My experience as a Panzer driver in the few days since July 5 consisted of the gigantic bang when I ran over a mine on July 6, and a few meaningless missions. The previous day had not offered anything of great importance. The tank trench had cost us a lot of time, and when the evening came we were glad to leave the night sentry duties to the Panzer-grenadiers of the III. Bat. of the 2. Panzer-Grenadier-Regiment, close to our positions. We had moved to the back slope to spend the night in the usual fox-holes under the Panzers, in the reassuring feeling of the safety which twenty-four tons of steel offered. We ignored the fact that more than one ton of it consisted of high explosives.
>
> After a very early wake-up came shouts, directives, orders: "Start engines—Mount—Ready for action!" We were still stowing our blankets when Untersturmführer Weiser came running

toward us from the command post and shouted only "Speed it up. Enemy tanks!" Then we heard a bang and the first T-34 was in flames, less than 200 meters away.

A Panzer of the staff had caught it with the "5-cm long." No lengthy orders were needed then. We began to roll and a few minutes later had knocked out four T-34s, some at very close range. The other Panzers of the 7. Company were likewise successful. Slowly, the situation became orderly. Radio transmissions again turned into normal orders. For the time, and as far ahead as we could see, we were the masters of the situation. But what was to follow?

The monotony of the numerous orders to change position was suddenly broken. We heard "Georg to Irene" and knew that "Georg" was the leader of the 1. Platoon, Obersturmführer Hoffmann, and "Irene" the chief of the 7. Kompanie, Hauptsturmführer Tiemann. After a few transmissions the following became clear: An infantry messenger had reported that Sturmbannführer Peiper, commander of the III./2, was wounded in the midst of the Russians and asked to be brought out. Anyone who heard this knew what had to be done. The wall of smoke and fire marked the border between friend and enemy. We observed every movement. A T-34 breaking through could not advance fifty meters without being turned into a sieve. How deep was this area of smoke? Would it be possible, under its cover, to reach Peiper's command post? All these were questions which the mind pondered. How did the chief, Hauptsturmführer Tiemann, feel when he had to decide whom to order to go on the mission? We all understood that the attempt had to be made. Then the message came: "Irene to Walter"—that's us—"You are in the best position. Take the messenger into the command Panzer and try to free Peiper. Drive like hell, that is your only chance!"

When I heard "like hell," I realized what the situation was. This soldiers' phrase was normally not in the chief's dictionary and indicated to me that he was greatly agitated. Untersturmführer Weiser confirmed the message, issued orders to the Panzers of our platoon accordingly, and took in the messenger. "Driver, let's go" was his order to me. After a few moments we were enclosed by the smoke. I had to slow down in order not to run into something. As in a silent movie, the pictures moved in front of my observation slits: wrecks, flames, shadowy figures in Russian helmets. Explosion followed explosion. Suddenly, a heavy explosion somewhere. How was I supposed to find the command post in that chaos? The messenger had no way of orienting himself, sitting in the closed turret.

Weiser radioed repeatedly, asked for increased fire cover, and ordered the other Panzers in the group to stay behind. He reported hits and that he was pushing ahead alone with the command Panzer. Then the last radio message: "Am getting rifle grenade and light Pak hits—orientation impossible—will continue anyway." During this feverish activity none of us had noticed that there was no confirmation, no orders from the outside. When had the antenna given up? There was no communication with us, no orders. Were we to give up this hopeless action?

All of this probably took less time than one needs to read about it. The intercom was still working. We were still rolling in the direction of the enemy, amidst the enemy. Was that a German armored vehicle? German steel helmets? Behind us! Ever more Russians! Suddenly, the excited order: "T-34, two o'clock, tank grenade, fire!" "The turret is blocked," reported the gunner. This was really getting serious. The order came: "Driver, take aim with the Panzer, pull right!" I pulled ahead, was in third gear and knew that I should shift but that I did not have the time for it. I pulled the Panzer around. Suddenly, a bang, then quiet. A glance to the rpm indicator showed the engine was stopped. Stalled or hit? Start it! Motor was running. I asked: "What shall I do?" when the radio operator ripped off my headset and yelled at me: "The gunner is dead, the intercom is gone." I shouted back: "Ask through the loader what I should do!" Answer: "The commander is also dead." "Driver, everything depends on you now," went through my mind. In the seconds since the hit on the side of the gunner, I saw Russians storming toward our Panzer. I moved ahead, and suddenly spotted our enemy, the T-34, at no more than 100 meters. Was the gun moving? I pulled the Panzer around 90 degrees, then came the bang. I must have been faster by a fraction of a second. Using sixth sense, I was able to bring a wreck between us. Another 90-degree turn, my feeling told me that should be the direction home. The messenger got out amidst the Russians and the loader was wounded. I had not reached safety yet. I came out of the smoke and saw the Panzer of the leader of the half-platoon, Unterscharführer Harald Stein.

My bulletproof glass had been made opaque by hits. I stuck my head out of the hatch, and Stein directed me with hand signals. Hauptsturmführer Tiemann ordered me to drive back to our positions while Stein covered my six o'clock with his gun.

At the antitank ditch, the radio operator left the Panzer with the wounded loader at the first aid station. I was alone. Later, someone counted the hits on my Panzer. The piece of bullet-proof glass went from hand to hand. My comrades counted seventeen infantry and three antitank hits on it.

PANZER COMMANDER MARTIN STEIGER, 1. COMPANY, REPORTS ON THE ACTION OF SS-PANZER-REGIMENT 3 "TOTENKOPF"

The nights were warm and starlit. Almost always at the same hour, the Russian "sewing machine" (Rata–Russian airplane type) or "UvD" (noncom on duty), as the reconnaissance plane was called by our soldiers, arrived.

Our night reconnaissance planes, as well, became suddenly active and increased their flights in the front area around Kursk and Bjelgorod.

The front was being photographed. Artillery positions, tank assembly points, and all of the trench system with its crew was captured on film, which was developed and enlarged in the analytical office of the army. Based on these photos, our companies received directions. The artillery knew which sectors to cover with its fire. The Stuka units knew their targets, and the Panzers were deployed where the enemy had his own tanks and concentrations of his troops. Thus developed an immense plan, drawn up in the smallest detail. One day, the hour was to come when the whole front would tremble. We waited for this hour. That is why we had moved close to the front and made camp in the woods.

The evening of July 4, 1943 arrived. The first stars flickered in the sky, and a thin veil of fog moved across the dusty ground. Traffic on the main track increased from minute to minute.

The Panzer engines hummed; we were headed for the front. The Russian assault troops had reached maximum strength in the bulge of the front at Kursk. The German command decided on counterattacks with the objective of smashing the enemy preparations and eliminating one of the most dangerous threats of the coming spring even before its planned deployment.

In the meantime, the Russians had built up two strong positions west of the Donez with antitank ditches, Pak positions, and stationary tanks.

The order for the attack was given for July 5. Objective: Break through the strong enemy positions on both sides of the Worskla River and capture the ridge of land near Prochorowka, along the railroad line, which would allow concentrated Panzer action. The attacking corps was reenforced by heavy artillery and a mortar brigade.

The divisions were sent into action in the sequence "Totenkopf," "Das Reich," and "LAH," next to each other. Stuka units supported the attack.

The assembly area was reached around midnight. We rested under the Panzers and awaited the morning.

At 3:10 A.M. the day awakened and the sun sent its first feelers across the hills. As the darkness waned, we beheld an imposing picture: all Panzers of the regiment had deployed in wedge formation and in numbers that we had not seen for a long time.

It was 3:15 A.M. A rustle, a hiss, a whistle! Columns of smoke rose like gigantic organ pipes into the sky. Artillery and mortars opened the battle. A few minutes later, heavy veils of smoke from the artillery explosions darkened the early morning sun.

Stukas came and came, twenty-seven . . . eighty-one . . . we lost count. Stukas, heavy bombers, fighters, long-range reconnaissance planes . . . it was as if the air itself had begun to sing and hum.

Finally, the order came: "Panzer—march!"

Our attack was under way!

Thrusting tanks, diving Stukas, burning Ratas, columns of smoke from the rocket launchers towering into the sky. Self-propelled heavy guns, knocked-out Soviet tanks, the distraught faces of the captured, and time and again the black mushrooms of smoke from countless explosions—that was the battle north of Bjelgorod. For six hours the battle continued. On the sloping steppe, the Panzers, like knights in combat with horse and lance, would not let go. Ten times, twenty times, lightning, thunder, and smoke enveloped the giants. Then they rolled ahead ten meters, swung left or right, and roared anew. The commanders stared at the enemy through the slits; the radio operators sent and received messages and orders; the loaders wiped their oil-stained hands during a quiet second, pushed the hair out of their face, and fed one shell after the other into the massive breech.

The knocked-out enemy tanks stood like torches in the blooming meadow. Some of our Panzers were also knocked out and on fire, having received direct artillery hits. The antitank ditches of Beresesow faced us as an almost invincible obstruction. The artillery pounded the trench ready for the assault and then we crossed it. The Russians defended doggedly, the Paks fired from hidden positions, antitank rifle rounds whistled around our Panzers. Still, our attack pushed ahead despite the heaviest defensive fire. Five days of combat were behind us when we heard the name Prochorowka for the first time. For five days we had battled one position after the other to the ground and wiped them out. We had broken through the heavily fortified positions of the Soviets, and caused the enemy gravest losses. Then, we stood before Prochorowka.

Ahead of us were the "gully of death," the town of Prochorowka, and the Psell River. None of us would forget that assault. The "gully of death," so named by us because of the heavy losses, was to become everyone's terrible memory. The crew of Unterscharführer Prenzl fell victim to a direct hit outside of its Panzer. We had barely crossed the Psell River and conquered its steep banks, barely taken position again above the gully, when the counterattacks by the Soviets began.

They came in battalion and regiment strength. They came with whole brigades and divisions. They moved their guns in battery strength in front of the bridgehead and sent salvo after salvo into the riverbank and the occupied high ground. Tanks charged our lines in numbers that we had not experienced in such a small area during the Eastern Campaign. Prochorowka was not only a bastion at the front north of Bjelgorod, not only the steely tip that broke the floods of the charging Soviet tanks. Prochorowka became the heroes' grave for many brave men; it became the symbol of defense to the last.

Panzer Battles Between the Mius and Dnjepr Rivers, Autumn of 1943

There was a fire at the Mius!

Northwest of Kuibyschewo, near Konstantin, the Soviets had succeeded with eighteen Guards divisions, supported by two tank brigades, motorized and mechanized units, some seventy batteries, and the air force, to force a breakthrough and form a bridgehead on our side of the Mius.

According to Stalin's orders, this bridgehead was to open the Bolshevik summer offensive. It was to be the first step to victory. "The Ukraine must be in our possession! Forward to the west."

The SS-Panzerkorps raced from Bjelgorod to the Mius in four days, a distance of more than 400 kilometers.

What did this mean?

Thousands of vehicles rolled on wheels; tracked vehicles were loaded. Transports by rail had to operate without snags. Immense amounts of fuel were required. Bridges had to be reenforced. Once again, the German talent to organize was the foundation for the success of this operation. We reached our new area on July 27, and moved into the assembly positions on July 30.

We sat in fields of sunflowers, waiting for the morning. Ahead of us lay hill 213.9. It was imperative that we capture it.

Finally, the time came.

At 8:10 A.M. German Stukas attacked the enemy's main front line, and five minutes later our own Panzers rolled out of their positions. We had pushed ahead only a few meters when the fire from a Pak front hit us, from straight ahead and both flanks. Our steel giants moved ahead only slowly, always on the lookout.

Infantrymen had mounted the Panzers, and suddenly, the first Panzers blew up. Mines! Mines! Unterscharführer von Horsten and all his crew perished in the flames inside their Panzer.

When darkness came, two hills that were ahead of the objective 213.9 were finally taken. In the meantime we had captured an important crossroad with considerable casualties. Untersturmführer Moosbrucker died; Quarenghi and other commanders and crew members were seriously wounded.

Night came, and with it a short period of rest. At dawn we continued the attack, supported by Stukas. Every meter was furiously fought for. We made it to within hand-grenade throwing distance of the Russians, but 500 meters still separated us from the top of hill 213.9. The second night fell. Our most advanced line made ready in expectation of enemy attacks. The company had suffered heavy losses. Only two Panzers were still ready for action; the others were knocked out or had become unserviceable from damage sustained in combat. It was depressing as one after the other dropped out. We were without a platoon leader. Untersturmführer Grenzauer was already missing since the action at Bjelgorod. Riefkogel was wounded at Bjelgorod.

The third morning dawned from the ravines. An extremely violent attack by the Russians was repelled. Around noon, the time had come. The division began the decisive thrust. Panzers, Stukas, and grenadiers advanced together. Then we succeeded in breaking through the Russian positions with Panzers and capturing the closest parts of hill 213.9. The way was open for the infantry.

We had barely gotten out of this inferno, had barely said good-bye to our fallen comrades, and had barely enjoyed a few hours of rest, when we were loaded up and rolled, at the beginning of August, into the Charkow sector, which we had left half a year before.

A dangerous enemy spearhead had broken through a paralyzed defense from the Walki area just outside of Poltawa. The threat was severe. If the enemy crossed the main route Charkow–Poltawa, a number of German divisions would have been encircled.

We had to get to the Charkow area as quickly as possible.

It was already evening when we arrived in Charkow and unloaded. That same night, we set out in the direction of Walki. After a few hours of sleep in the Panzer and the vehicles, we were on the move again. Around noon we reached Kowiakj. However, it would only be captured finally by the 2. Kampfgruppe. During the battle, the leader of the Kampfgruppe,

Obersturmführer Burgschulte, was killed when a direct hit to the commander's cupola separated his head from the body. The unit assembled in Kowiakj and was detailed into combat groups. No longer were there companies. The remaining Panzers of the 1. and 2. Companies were ordered to the 1. Kampfgruppe. The remaining Panzers of the 3. and 4. Companies went to the 2. Kampfgruppe. We were full of joy when Obersturmführer Riefkogel returned to us from the hospital and took over the 1. Kampfgruppe. When Kampfgruppe Riefkogel received the order to clear out the area around Kowiakj, we were four Panzers again: Riefkogel in the lead, then Nitschke, Steiger, and Baumeister. Hans Eggert and Helmut Köster had been wounded during the last day at the Mius. After a half hour we faced a Russian Pak front of five guns which, after they had set the Panzer of Oberscharführer Nitschke on fire, were wiped out by us. We returned to Kowiakj.

Two hours later, Riefkogel was wounded for the seventh time. Some of our own fighters fired their onboard cannons at our Panzers, and shell fragments had scraped the left side of his forehead and wounded him in the foot. The commander of the regiment, Sturmbannführer Bochmann, and the commander of the battalion, Meierdress, arrived. Before the lined-up Panzer crews they decorated Riefkogel with the Knight's Cross of the Iron Cross before he was taken by ambulance to the main dressing station. We were without a Kampfgruppe leader once again. There was another change when the leader of Kampfgruppe 2., Obersturmführer Altemüller, was killed during a reconnaissance mission. He was the last company chief of the 1. Panzerabteilung. Both combat groups were then combined and led into further action by the previous orderly officer, Obersturmführer Herbatscheck, a Viennese. Two Russian tanks engaged in an unparalleled bold stroke. As our Panzers sat among the houses of Kowiakj awaiting further orders, two T-34s rattled down the main village street at top speed. Before we could get into the Panzers to chase them, they disappeared in a cloud of dust. During the night, we moved out to secure the village and took up positions 500 meters to the east.

The next day was boiling hot. A major attack was planned for 1:00 P.M. A Russian corps, which was constantly pushing into our flank, was to be encircled by a lightning thrust of Panzers and Stukas and destroyed.

We drove off without accompanying infantry. After only one kilometer, the enemy became noticeable. Russian infantry with light antitank weapons had taken cover in the vast sunflower fields. Driving the Panzers through the sunflower fields was always a tricky undertaking. Visibility was limited and tank hunters often had an easy job.

The enemy was in retreat after a concentrated surprise shelling. Then Russian tanks tried to stop our attack. At the same moment, just ahead of our spearhead, a few Stukas dove on the enemy tanks and destroyed three by direct hits. The other four succumbed to our fire. The main strength of the enemy was broken. We rolled over the Russian infantry, attacked Kolomak, and there, for the first time, encountered a Russian women's battalion in combat.

The enemy resistance increased at Kolomak. After repeated shelling by our 7.5-cm guns, and with the attack of our infantry brought up in armored personnel carriers, this village also fell.

With no further resistance to our attack, we reached Tschutowo toward evening and thus closed the circle.

Thereafter, the direction of attack was toward Kolomak and in a semicircle to Tschutowo where we united with other units of the division.

Distance to the objective was about 40 kilometers.

The complete destruction of the encircled enemy was achieved the next day.

With this encircling attack, a clear front line was reestablished. The unit took up quarters in Konstantinowka, where a few days of rest lay ahead of us. We stayed in Konstantinowka for five days. The Kampfgruppen were reenforced by a few repaired Panzers, before preparations were made for a night march. The fine sand crunched between our teeth. The next morning, when we halted just before Kolontajew, a millimeter-thick coat of dust covered the Panzers. Kolontajew was still held by the Russians.

The lead platoon, together with infantry, took Kolontajew around noon. During this action, our battalion commander, Sturmbannführer Meierdress, was wounded by a bullet in his lung. At 3 P.M. we received further orders to attack.

With eight Panzers, led by Herbatscheck, we moved off against a hill and, without warning, were faced with an invincible enemy Pak front. The Panzers of Unterscharführer Fleuter and Steiger were knocked out, except for two men, the crews managed to save themselves. The attack had to be broken off, mainly due to the darkness that was setting in. Unterscharführer Wehring also badly wounded and lost an arm, and during the evening hours we also lost our Kampfgruppe leader, Obersturmführer Herbatscheck. A grenade fragment destroyed his eyesight. Obersturmführer Strobl, until then the adjutant to Meierdress, took over the Kampfgruppe.

GRUSCHKI GRAVE
Willi Hein, Obersturmführer and company chief, reports on the action of Panzer-Regiment 5 "Wiking" west of Charkow during August 1943.
"The 4. Company of Panzer-Abteilung 5 is being attached to the L./ 'Germania' as mobile reserve, and is to start out immediately."

After Obersturmführer Jessen's injury, I took over the assault gun company during the night of August 31 and received this order one hour later. Four assault guns, in need of a major overhaul, were only conditionally ready for action. Despite all the technical shortcomings (radios were particularly sparse), we rumbled to the directed spot, reported to the commander, and curled up for a short nap.

The morning fog had just lifted when we received the bad news of a Russian tank thrust through the sector in which we maintained contact with the neighboring division. The direction of the attack was aimed at the railroad line Charkow–Poltawa. Immediate action was imperative. Along the railroad line nothing was to be seen of our own troops. We went into a waiting position in terrain that reminded us of a grave mound and was covered with a low growth of trees—the Gruschki Grave. The hills in front of us offered a ghostly target in the morning dawn.

The engines were turned off, so we were able to hear the roaring noise of the Russian T-34 tanks coming toward us. After only a few minutes we saw some thirty-five enemy tanks, loaded like bunches of grapes with infantry, attacking across the hills. "Gun twelve o'clock, distance 1,000, antitank round, fire!" The commanders and the crews reacted with lightning speed. Four shells, four hits, four enemy tanks in flames. Red Army men jumped off in panic. This scenario repeated itself a few times.

Time could not be measured as the enemy lost his momentum. Eleven burning T-34s as well as four other disabled enemy tanks blocked the Russian attack. In reverse gear they retreated quickly behind the hills.

Our men jumped out of the turret hatches, jubilant about the success but anticipating the next attack through the low terrain on both sides of the hills. The new targets were quickly indicated, and the lack of radio communication was overcome by arm signals. Another enveloping attack by the enemy got under way. It went like clockwork—exemplary, as practiced in the sandbox—and the enemy was repelled. Two enemy tanks were stopped in flames; two others were knocked out. A KW II tank rolled its fifty-two tons past us at top speed. "About face!" and after it with my gun. Distance 250 meters; fire, hit, ricochet. This ordeal was repeated four times. Then . . . hurrah! The Russians bailed out! The KW II bothered us. We moved closer . . . the Russians got back inside. Then the turret to six o'clock and we were ready. But the driver turned slowly, the hull faced us. One shot and the antitank shell set it on fire. We moved back into position against the hill and wondered with concern if the Russians had guessed our reserves of ammunition.

Without radio contact to the unit and our last shell fired, we were then chased like a rabbit by some twenty enemy tanks. It was 11 A.M. We reached the cover of the railroad embankment without losses, and there the advancing 3. Kompanie took over the enemy from us. We reported to the unit and had quick repairs made to our assault guns. The radios were fixed with particular urgency, and then, during the evening hours, we moved into new positions in a cornfield two kilometers south of the previous day's area of action.

After a capful of sleep, in our well-camouflaged vehicles, we spotted the enemy tanks at first light through our scissors telescopes, which were camouflaged as straw piles distributed throughout our old positions. We reported by radio to the unit, requesting reenforcements. We waited for further orders; this enemy could have been taken on. We waited, waited. The possibility of attack burned like fire under our feet. The wounded chief of an assault gun battery of the Division "DR" reported to me, and then the sandbox planning began. Together with all the commanders of the nine guns, we climbed the tower on top of the railroad station.

The targets were easily spotted and assigned to seven commanders. Two guns remained in reserve. An artillery observer promised us a smoke screen, and at exactly 11 A.M. on September 1, the attack started.

Under cover of the smoke screen, we reached a firing position some 400 meters from the enemy.

Nine tanks were immediately set on fire. Four T-34s turned their backs to us and were also knocked out. The Russians were wiped out, and only an armored car tried to reach the safety of the hill in a zigzag course. It, too, could not avoid its fate.

We turned away and cleared up an advanced Soviet trench to open the way for a major counterattack of the Regiment "DF" of the Division "Das Reich."

The newly established Panther unit arrived from the west as I./Panzer-Regiment 2 "DR." In March 1943, after the retaking of Charkow, this unit had been moved to Germany. After Panzer IV crews were retrained and equipped with Panthers, the move to the combat arena north of Charkow took place.

RADIO OPERATOR HORST LETZNER, 3. COMPANY/PANZER-REGIMENT 2 EXPERIENCES THE PANZER BATTLE OF KOLOMAK

On September 12, 1943, it was still raining. All of us were encrusted by mud from the softened ground. No movement was spotted anywhere. Despite this, we warned each other to stay alert. The radio squads had not brought any news up to that time.

Then, suddenly, around 1:00 P.M., an excited shout that felt like a salvation came from the driver, Unterscharführer Böck, sitting in the turret: "They are coming! Russian tanks!" The Panzer battle of Kolomak had begun.

Without delay, the driver and commander jumped into their seats. The radio operator and loader got the flywheel starter going with the crank. The gunner got our gear from under the hull. After the third try, the engine finally started. In haste, everyone jumped to their battle stations. The radio was tuned to receive. The weapons were loaded and checked. More and more tanks were spotted some 3,000 meters away. The order came in by radio: "Let approaching Russian tank brigade advance to at least 1,000 meters! Order to fire will then be issued. Do not move!"

In the meantime we learned by radio that the approaching Russians were a complete tank brigade with about eighty tanks. (We had fourteen tanks of our own, two of which were without a serviceable engine). The Russians drove widely dispersed and very hesitantly in their T-34s and a few KV Is and KV IIs. Later, it was determined that there was a total of eighty-six tanks. Ludwig reported from the left that his attempts to start his engine were hopeless. Two enemy tanks were already within 600 meters of his position. The units of the infantry division deployed on the right were already in retreat. A lieutenant with a decimated company passed by and stated that the positions could not be held against the huge Russian tank armada. Schäfer's admonition to let the Russians roll by and then offer a hot reception to the Russian infantry certain to be following behind was shrugged off. He could not hold back his men any more. After a radio message, the reconnaissance unit with the attached 15./"DF" tried to do something for the abandoned sector to its right, in addition to its own fairly wide sector. These great guys, our "old" comrades whom we already knew from previous actions, fanned out farther to the right and let themselves be overrun by the Russian tank brigade across the whole sector.

Hubert Ludwig was back on the frequency. Two T-34s were within 400 meters of his immovable Panzer's position. He received permission to fire and knocked out both T-34s within one minute. The Russians noticed quickly that something was happening on their left flank, and they picked up the pace. The rain had stopped. The majority of the T-34s pulled slightly to the left since they had so far only spotted Ludwig. By doing this, they showed us some of their left broadside and were easy to make out. Even the ones farther away were easily spotted with their typical gray diesel exhaust clouds.

Then, over the radio, we received permission to open fire. The Russians became somewhat disorganized and could not make us out very quickly. Their fire was very inaccurate. Our loader, Ernst Zittla, gave each shell a stroke and a wish on its way. Our gunner, Heinz Schröder, regained his customary calm. While our commander Emmerling got excited in the turret, they aimed without haste and fired.

After only the second shot, the first of the attacking T-34s was in flames. A terrific fireworks began. Then we tried to get our Panzers out of their dug-in positions. After two days of rain, however, this was exceedingly difficult. Our driver Böck was fairly excited at the thought of not being able to get our old crate out of the hole. He let the clutch jump a few times and killed the engine, but after a few tries we managed. Then, Wimmer called from the right. He asked for a tow and needed a new fuel pump.

More and more Russian tanks were on fire. Each Panzer had its share in these victories. Hubert Ludwig reported further successes from the far left flank. At the end of the battle, twenty-three knocked-out enemy tanks were counted in front of his position.

We pulled up our Panzer behind the hole of the right flank Panzer, Wimmer, who had already attached a tow cable and tackle. After many tries, while exchanging fire at the same time, we pulled the Panzer out of the position. Towing it farther was impossible since the pulley and two tow cables broke.

In addition, our ammunition was quickly running out. Then we got a hit in the upper left outside rear engine wall. The shell stuck in the fuel tank, one of five, behind the wall. Fortunately, the tank was already empty and there was no explosion. Shortly after, we received a second hit, in the fourth left running wheel. Again, we changed positions.

Then, we received permission to return to the batalion battle command post. Backwards, march! We moved to the rear over low ground and quickly reached the close-by battle command post. Hastily, we refueled and took on ammunition. Pulleys and tow cables, as well as a quickly found fuel pump, were taken on board. Then we raced back into the steeply rising terrain. As we drove up the slope, we encountered a T-34 about 100 meters away approaching us from behind and to our left. Obviously we had not expected to meet him there behind the front line. After a few seconds of terror, during which the range decreased even more, the commander, Lorenz Emmerling ordered: "Ram and board!"

The T-34 then stopped at about 50 meters and swung its turret to the right toward us. Heinz Schröder yelled: "H-a-a-l-t!" and, making use of the round which was always kept in the breech, hit the Russian tank directly on the turret ring. After two seconds, before our next shot, a flash of flame came out of the Russian's turret, the body of the commander appeared from the hatch and fell forward on the turret.

Once again, our superior weapon, coupled with our experience, daring, and determination, had given us victory over the "comrades with the other field post number." We remembered them later during a silent hour. How easily the result could have been the opposite. However, we had no time to reflect. We had to rush to the waiting immobilized Panzer of Max Wimmer. It was still there and had sustained only light hits.

The battle had long since passed its zenith. Almost all enemy tanks had been knocked out. The driver, Emil Engel, took hold of the reserve fuel pump we brought and, with imperturbable calm, changed it in new record time under occasional shelling.

Even as we approached, our gun fired single shots to detract attention from Max Wimmer. Ahead, we saw Russian infantry trickle in. A T-34 tried to approach to within 2,400 meters. Hans Schröder, who had already loaded an explosive shell, fired and rendered the Russian immobile.

Shortly, earlier than at home, dusk set in. The noise of the fighting faded. The Russians put out the flames in the rest of their burning tanks and began to tow those in front of their advanced lines to the rear. For a long time after dark, engine noise was heard from the Russian side.

THE KNIGHT'S CROSS FOR A PANZER DRIVER

Not much was said during the war about the Panzer drivers. They steered their vehicles dutifully as ordered by the Panzer commanders. However, they, too, took a deciding role in the course of combat as proven by the actions of Unterscharführer Hans Thaler, who was awarded the Knight's Cross for his outstanding courage.

Three medium Panzers of the 6. Panzer-Company/2 "DR" rolled across the steppe, moved up a hill, and were suddenly surprised by fifteen Soviet tanks. Within a few minutes, the Panzer driven by Hans Thaler knocked out three T-34s.

Then, something roared against its skin of steel and shook the Panzer. The heavy hit destroyed the steering mechanism and ripped off the gear box. The commander contemplated the situation and shouted into his throat microphone: "We've had it."

But Hans Thaler had not had it. With a few pieces of wire, and using all his strength, he made the Panzer maneuverable again and got it going. In less than one half hour this Panzer succeeded in knocking out seven more enemy tanks. This success was solely due to the courageous and deliberate actions of Hans Thaler.

Thaler, however, remained quiet and modest, and wore his award on behalf of all the Panzer drivers who silently did their duty. He died a soldier's death on April 7, 1945, as a Panzer commander during the fighting for Vienna.

Battleground Kiev–Shitomir, Winter 1943–44

ERNST STRENG, PANZER COMMANDER IN PANZER-REGIMENT 2 "DR," KEEPS A WAR DIARY
Fighting for Bjelaja-Zerkow.

After the Red Army succeeded in breaking through the German defense front in the Kiev area between November 3 and 11, 1943, the elite of their tanks and infantry columns flooded into the western Ukraine up to Shitomir. Their incredible masses pushed to the south and severely threatened the Heeresgruppe Süd (Army Group South). Again, it was the German motorized units and Panzer troops that were withdrawn from the fronts and transported at lightning speed to be thrown against the tidal wave.

The "Das Reich" Division was placed on alert on November 5. That night Panzer-Regiment "Das Reich," including the Tiger company, was sent ahead as advance detachment to the loading station at Bobruisk. Not only were our tanks arrayed on the street on the cold, foggy morning of November 6, but our division's armored personnel carrier battalion and the alert units were also there waiting to entrain.

Transport was by railroad via Wladislawka and Rakitno, for 150 kilometers, to Bjelaja–Zerkow, an important road and railway intersection. We reached it at eight o'clock at night, in total darkness, and immediately began to unload the Panzer equipment.

The whole city was about to leave. Evacuation trains were rolling out of the station; fires were flaring to burn mountains of files. The headquarters and all German departments were in the process of pulling out. The Russian tank spearheads were expected any hour. Panic and fear drove the people through the streets. Looting and destruction was everywhere.

There was no one to organize the resistance and stop these activities!

That was the situation when we unloaded and moved into quarters at the northern edge of the city. Our reconnaissance platoon was making contact, in the meantime, with the German lines—or the enemy—to the north. While troop transports of our division were unloaded at the station throughout the night, our Panzer reconnaissance platoon was already engaged in combat with advancing Russian tanks eight kilometers to the north. At the beginning, all of us were puzzled how the Red Army managed to move up its immense supplies across the so-called "scorched earth" where all bridges, roads, railroads, and other means of transportation were blown up and destroyed. Only slowly, the reconnaissance results filled in the picture. It showed that the Russians brought their supplies across the Dnjepr on underwater bridges, built twenty to thirty centimeters below the waterline. They were not identified by German aerial reconnaissance for a long time!

In the rear, east of the Dnjepr, German prisoners of war, as well as all of the civilian population, were put into action to keep the required supplies moving. Barrels of fuel were not transported by vehicle but rolled down the roads. Ammunition was carried or loaded on horse-drawn carts, and each village was responsible for moving the supplies to the next village.

In the early morning of November 7, the snow came down in heavy flakes, as a cold northerly wind whipped the plains. Puddles of water and road ditches were covered with a white layer of ice. Our Tiger company, led by Kalls instead of the wounded Tetsch, rolled into the assembly area. After a short halt, it continued forward into action against the Russian tanks rolling in from the north on the road from Fastow and Ksaweriwka. Spontaneous combustion of fuel and oil residues set a Tiger on its way to the front on fire. It burned out completely, accompanied by ongoing and persisting explosions. The crew was thrown from the hatches by the pressure of the explosion and, miraculously, was uninjured.

On the road to Kiev, some five kilometers north of Grebeniki, our Panzer spearhead encountered the enemy and six T-34s went up in flames. After about three hours it had to retreat from the town because of an overwhelming attack by enemy infantry. It blew up the bridge and established a new front line south of the town.

Along the road we picked up eight infantrymen from a construction unit, all that was left of German troops there. They were hopelessly overwhelmed by the Russian tanks. Around noon the snow changed into rain. The weather, which had until then been cold and dry, turned into a continuous rain. While our brave infantrymen, their recovery helped by our rations, dug in on both sides of the road from Grebeniki, the first shells hit the hills ahead of us and threw columns of smoke into the gray noon sky. Without cover, our Panzers and vehicles sat on the back slopes of the hills. We took aim at the road to Kiev where we expected another push by Russian tanks at any time.

When three Russian tanks moved out of the village across the no-man's land in the late afternoon, we opened fire on them at 1,000 meters. Not two minutes later, under the combined fire from six Tigers, they were enveloped in flames and smoke. A fourth Russian tank pushed west of the road in the direction of Slawia an hour later and suffered the same fate as its predecessors. At 800 meters it received a hit and, as a fireball burst skyward, its tank walls broke apart. After these failed thrusts, the Russians concentrated their attacks some eight kilometers to the west and pushed with all their might toward Slawia to break through our strengthening defenses there. For days, Slawia was under fire from Russian tanks and artillery, and the situation there was very critical.

The newly established 25. Panzer-Division, transported from France, was hastily thrown into combat. Because of our critical circumstances, the individual parts of that unit were moved into the fighting directly after being unloaded, without prior assembly. Fastow, which was lost on November 8, was to be retaken by the 25. Panzer-Division. Parts of the division joined the fighting without previous combat experience or knowledge of the front situation. There were undesirable situations when marching columns ran into Russian tanks at night, with the final result: "Severe losses of men and materiel."

In the meantime, other parts of the division, in particular the tracked vehicles, set out from Bjelaja-Zerkow via Grebeniki-Slawia to Fastow. On November 9, Fastowez, located east of Fastow, was recaptured.

Damage to the tracks forced us to pull into the repair company, set up in a large factory hall at the northern edge of Bjelaja-Zerkow, on November 9 and 10. The image of the city had changed completely. Calm and confidence returned! Troops and vehicles rolled through the streets to the front, and the soldiers' club was open and overcrowded. The staff of the Panzerkorps was located in the city.

Meanwhile, parts of the Panzer-Division "Leibstandarte Adolf Hitler," returning from Italy, were unloaded at the railroad station and moved to the front via Grebeniki, Slawia, and Fastow. With this, the critical days at Bjelaja-Zerkow were over. The front began to stabilize. Although bitter fighting still raged day and night, we looked at the combat ahead of us with greater confidence.

In the evening of November 11, we rolled into action toward Slawia. Russian tanks broke through there. Outside the village, among the explosions of the shells, columns of flames rose from burning cottages and enemy tanks. We could hear the Russian tanks milling about. A short briefing by the adjutant followed. We moved out of the village of Slawia, broke through the cover of bushes, and suddenly saw, among the smoke and haze, the black, massive belly of the first enemy tank at 200 meters. Quickly taking aim, we fired and a long lance of flame shot from the barrel. Immediately we saw the yellow-white fireball of the explosion. Smoke and fire mushroomed and obscured the picture of destruction.

Two hundred meters east of Slawia, we knocked out the second Russian tank that had already broken through our lines. Apparently it was stuck in the terrain, or had damage to its tracks, and was pretty well helpless. Around 8 P.M. the enemy shelling slowed down and then stopped altogether. The infantry of the "Leibstandarte" came out of their foxholes in the badly damaged positions. The men warmed up at the glowing exhausts and the engine in the rear of our Panzer.

As we were stomping around our Panzer in the cold of the night, some soldiers walked over to the knocked-out Russian tank and noticed that its walls were still glowing. Even from a fair distance, we smelled burnt human flesh. The whole turret with the gun seemed to have been lifted from its mounting, all its hatches were hanging from bent hinges. We peered cautiously inside: a mess of rods and iron pieces. On the floor and in the driver's seat was a shriveled, crusted, and charred mass; probably the driver and crew of the tank shrunken to the size of children!

Shortly after midnight came the order to get ready. A strong spearhead was to move forward from Slawia. We were to push through in an easterly direction and reach the railroad line to Fastow. There, a break in the front was to be filled again. That was not an especially enjoyable mission. Pale fires and loud combat noises led us on the way through the night. In the southeastern part of Grebeniki, on the other side of the large lake and close to the vast complex of the sugar factory, stood red banks of fire. Discharges flashed and battle noise echoed. No one knew how far the Russian tanks had penetrated into the town, where they were, and where our own troops were on the defensive. When we were finally ready for action among the burning cottages, a new day dawned and threw faint light onto the hazy and smoking streets. Green and red tracer crisscrossed the lake and hit the town. Somewhere the sharp and bright discharges of Panzers bellowed. Who could have distinguished between friend and enemy there? As the day grew brighter, details of the terrain became visible. Slowly, we drove down toward the lake. Again, the bright sound of the discharge of a Panzer gun! Everyone was startled as somewhere a flash of flame brightened the sky. Damn it, where were the shots coming from? Down by the lake, just after the bridge, we came up on a Russian tank enveloped in flames. Dead and wounded soldiers lay around it. Then we finally met up with our own Panzer reconnaissance; its platoon leader briefed us. We drove around the lake, moved slowly up the incline toward the edge of the village, and followed a shallow ditch in the cover of the cottages into firing position. Then three Russian tanks moved into the sight. Barely 100 meters ahead of us, the silhouette of the first tank entered the light.

We pulled hard left. The Panzer turned on the spot and moved closer to the ditch. The gun swung around, a flash of fire, and the first 8.8-cm tank round roared from the barrel into the massive black body of the tank. The impact flashed through the haze of gunpowder, then flames broke out of all hatches and shot sky-high. Suddenly, a second tank farther back came into the sight. Second shot—hit! But it did not burn. Third shot. Finally, the mushroom of fire and smoke grew into the foggy morning sky above the roofs of the far houses. We were feverish; the hoarse voices of the crew overrode the hum and crackle of the inter-com. The exhaust fan hummed and sucked the powder fumes out of the interior. Then another Russian tank came out of a hollow, from the rear, moving across in front of us. Quick aim, a new shell into the barrel! Fire and—hit! What had been a black giant just before, turned into a bright flash of flames with an oily cap of smoke that grew to cover and envelop the whole tank.

A short stop to survey. Then, Panzer—march! The Tiger towered high atop the embankment, then tilted forward and broke a path through the splintering fences, trees, and shrubs with the weight of its momentum to the edge of the town. Only there did the Russians come out of the ditches and hedges, hands high in the air. They threw their weapons to the ground and surrendered. Later, from the right, came the Panzer attack of our 5. Company, which completed the mop-up of the Russian breakthrough. Those who did not surrender and tried to flee across the vast plain northward were mowed down by the tracer salvos of the machine guns. Seen during the light of day, the enemy break-throughs were much less dangerous than they had appeared during the tangled night combat. Our commander drove up and congratulated us. A fire-brigade unit of armored personnel carriers rolled into position for an attack. They could return, as the job was done. Clouds raced across the morning sky. It was terribly cold outside, and the wind brought tears to the eyes.

In the sugar factory nearby, the removal of the stored sugar began. All passing motorized units loaded, as best possible, the 100-kilogram sacks of sugar into the trucks, tractors, armored vehicles, radio cars, and automobiles. Faster than during an alert, vehicles came in from all directions and loaded up. It was incredible how fast word had spread to the sectors of the front close by. It did not matter. Sooner or later the Russians would dig in at the sugar factory, or it would burn down. A transport of the large stores to the rear could not have been considered, much less a removal by rail.

During the second half of November the decision was made to counterattack from the Berditschew area to recapture Kiev and the old Dnjepr line. The Russian offensive from the Kiev area stalled for the time. The unstable situation at the front offered the promise that, given sufficient supplies of German Panzers and motorized divisions, a success could have been achieved. The Report of the Supreme Command of the Armed Forces for November 6 stated: "Between Krementschug and Kiev, our troops drove the Soviets from a number of islands on the Dnjepr and repelled enemy attacks repeatedly in the Dnjepr loop southeast of Kiev. During these battles, the Panzer-Grenadier-Division 'Das Reich' destroyed the 2,000th enemy tank since the beginning of this year." This 2,000th victory, too, was credited to our Tigers.

SHITOMIR

The German counteroffensive, which started from the Berditschew area with insufficient materiel and forces against a Red Army superiority in numbers and material, brought, even in its early days, the recapture of Shitomir. Some sixty kilometers east of Korosten-Radomichl, it slowed when it faced growing Russian resistance and finally stalled in the grim cold of December.

This attack by the Panzer-Division "Grossdeutschland," the 1. and 7. Panzer-Divisions, the SS-Divisions "Leibstandarte Hitler" and "Das Reich," as well as some infantry units was destined to finally stall. But at least, it succeeded in breaking the thrust of the Red Army into the heart of the Ukraine and in stabilizing the front for a time.

Immediately after the recapture of Shitomir, the II. Abteilung moved into positions in the Kornin–Skotschischtsche area, west of Fastowan, along the railroad.

At 3 A.M. the Panzers were loaded onto a ready transport train. The journey led to Shitomir through an area infested with partisans and Red Army stragglers. The Panzers were ready for action. At 11 A.M. huge shacks, warehouses, factories, and sheds appeared out of the haze: Shitomir, captured for the second time by our troops three days ago.

In a short time we unloaded the transport train and took up quarters opposite the railroad station to await the assembling of the unit. Some of the civilian population had already returned to the city. The railroad was being quickly returned to normal operation, the roads were repaired for supply transport, and the functioning of the big city returned to normal.

In the morning of November 24 the regiment assembled in the hangars of the airfield at the northern edge of the city. It took on rations and set out around noon on the main route to the north, direction Korosten-Radomichl.

We reached the sector of the 7. Panzer-Division and the Division "Das Reich" after a march of some seventy kilometers. It was night before we found quarters in the crowded towns. In the morning of November 25 the Tigers formed up for the march to the front. We had to drive around large minefields; blown-up bridges caused holdups. Numerous burnt-out Soviet tanks lined the road. Really amazing, the masses of tanks the Russians operated!

Near the front, German batteries were in firing position on both sides of the main route. Telephone wires were strung across the brown-gray soil and disappeared into a cottage or a foxhole. Motorcycle dispatch riders, ambulances, and cars drove around. For the first time, rocket batteries mounted on armored personnel carriers, mortars, and flame throwers were seen in action there. Above all this hung a foggy sky with low clouds, which darkened the image of the front. The Tigers soon swung off the main route to the left and assembled in a village one kilometer behind the front where the required preparations were immediately carried out. Then, the order for the Panzer attack was issued.

Unrestrained, the Panzers broke through all obstacles, crushed anything that got under the tracks, and rolled, with short pauses to fire, toward the objective of the attack. Our Panzer dropped out. "Engine damage," the driver yelled. The thermostat showed 120 degrees Celsius. The order by radio from Kalls: "Leave the formation and return to our lines!"

For a while, we stopped the Tiger and waited for the engine to cool down. Even then, it moved only very short distances at a time; the fan shaft was broken. Slowly, it drove along the German lines.

Night fell. Fires and artillery flashes glowed among the white and red flares over the front lines. Bullets from Russian sharpshooters and machine-gun salvos smacked against the Panzers. More often than it wanted to, the crew had to ask for the right way through the fires. Around eleven o'clock at night, something happened. Russian tanks began to fire, and explosions echoed from the hollow in the no-man's-land. Whole chains of tracer bullets crossed the darkness.

Suddenly, Russian tank engines roared at the German lines, and a hellish show began. Only 200 meters away, among fresh fires, the bright muzzle flashes from tanks. Russian night attack!

The night almost turned into day, and across the nearby front spread a dim glow of fire. Its gleam showed black shadows dancing past like phantoms. First, three tanks were recognized, then five, six . . . on their way to the firing positions. Another victory. Under a sky-high mushroom of fire, a tank exploded. No one knew where the German or Russian tanks were. The only way to tell them apart was by their different engine noise. However, their exact location could not be made out; an awful situation for our Panzer. Unable to take any action right then, we were condemned to wait.

It was long past midnight, almost 3 A.M., when the fourth Russian tank turned into a bright torch among the fire, smoke, and explosions near the German lines. Then, the noise of the battle died down.

Scattered across the field, fires burned in the dying night. The Russian night attack had collapsed. The enemy infantry had not even succeeded in overrunning the most advanced German foxholes. All of the enemy tanks were destroyed by a Panzer IV company. As our damaged Tiger rolled to the rear company headquarters in the morning of November 26, it was intercepted by the commander of the Regiment "DF." He requested that, despite the damaged engine, we remain at least as added protection in the regiment's sector. Slowly, the Tiger crawled backwards and took up a firing position on a back slope. Gradually, the fog bank lifted from the gulch in which the Russian infantry positions were suspected.

When the fog and haze finally dispersed, our Tiger was unexpectedly faced by two T-34s. The first was apparently immobile; the second was trying to tow it away. Immediately, the crew scrambled into the Panzer, drove into firing position, and opened fire from 800 meters on the seemingly certain prey. But the first shot was too far, the second also went beyond the target, and the third was short. Damn it, what was going on? Then a third T-34 rolled out of the village probably to cover the towing operation. A fourth and fifth shot went in the right direction but either too far or short. This was useless, and it drove us to tears! Three enemy tanks in full view and not a hit. Finally, the problem was located. The sight was loose, not tightened down at all, a problem that could not be fixed quickly. Under the furious stare of the Tiger crew and pursued by its not exactly pious wishes, the Russian tanks disappeared into the far village.

During the night the armorer came by and adjusted the gun in the early dawn using a spot some 1,000 meters away as a target. We were back in business! However, no more enemy tanks were to be seen. The only excitement was a push by Russian infantry during the early morning hours of November 27 that fell apart in the heavy defensive fire of our machine guns and the hellish concert of the explosive shells.

During the night of November 28, enemy artillery action caused some serious injuries. The wounded were bedded down in the company command post, which was covered with tarps and lit poorly by flickering oil lamps. They could only be moved in the morning, if they were still alive then. Having to listen to the moaning of these men pushed us almost to the edge of the endurable. Outside, sentries and scouts moved through the night, which was interrupted repeatedly by short or even lengthy barrages of the artillery. That meant getting one's head down in time. Everyone listened tensely for the discharge and the howling of the rounds. Where would they hit? During the third night we were relieved by our own Panzers. The Tigers rolled back to the rear company head-quarters for repairs and refitting.

Finally, at the beginning of December, the hoped-for frost set in and put an end to the muddy and rainy period. The front lines pulled back to the edges of the settlements, seeking cover from the icy wind between the cottages and hedges. The nights, especially, were already bitterly cold. The company command post was withdrawn to a larger village, where it was easier to reach the front lines.

At noon on December 2, there was an alert. The Russians were supposed to have broken through in the left sector of the regiment. After only 30 minutes, the reserve units assembled at the back slope of the threatened sector near the mortar batteries. They consisted of our Tiger, a scout car company, an antiaircraft machine gun, and some engineers. We had a short briefing on the situation, assuming everything else would fall into place. Swinging to the left across the slope, our small force pushed from the west toward a tiny village of eight or nine cottages that was reported to be in Russian hands. The attack was carried out without artillery preparation. Based on experience, speed and a determined blow were the only promising actions in such cases. We almost reached the edge of the village without a shot. That was strange. Then, suddenly, unkempt and uniformed shapes jumped out of some cottages to the right. The turret machine gun opened up, and almost too late we recognized that they were German soldiers who had resisted to the last. In their brown camouflage jackets, they were difficult to tell from the Russians, especially since we had been told there were no more German soldiers in the village. Two were wounded, and the third hit the ground at lightning speed.

Then our Tiger rolled into the village, turned right at its center, and broke through the growths of hedges and gardens between the cottages into the open. There, an amazing spectacle came into view. Across the fields, all the way to the Russian lines at the village some 1,000 meters away, large numbers of brown-clad infantrymen rose from the ground when the armored German force broke through. Our Tiger raced into these brown masses, leaving them no time to think, and swerved about among the perplexed jumble. The armored personnel carriers moved into firing position, and the machine guns began to clatter. An incredible, chaos then started!

The masses of Soviet infantry jumped up, raced about, and ran backwards, forwards, and backwards again. They ran in all directions, without a thought or a plan, threw themselves on the ground, were caught by the tracks of the Tiger, and crushed. Faces surfaced, like ghosts, frozen into grimaces of fear and rage. After a few salvos, both machine guns jammed. Our Tiger then fired explosive shells, but suddenly the firing stopped altogether. It had become completely senseless anyway. The Tiger chased the Ivans across the fields in big bunches toward the German lines where large groups of prisoners were already forming.

Suddenly, the Tiger was only some 200 meters away from the edge of the village and well inside the Russian lines. A metalic burst hit the left side of the hull. A bolt of lightning flashed through the interior. Pak hit at short distance!

It was getting dangerous. The Russians had moved a Pak into position from somewhere, under cover of the gully. Or maybe they had manned one of the scattered and abandoned guns. We hammered a few more explosive shells into the confusion at the edge of the enemy-held village. Some more cottages went up in flames, before, in reverse, the Tiger reached the German lines unscathed.

REPORT OF UNTERSCHARFÜHRER SIEGFRIED MELINKAT, 2./SS-PZ. RGT. 5

SS-Panzer-Regiment 5 "Wiking," November 17, 1943—Attack on Swid-owok on the Dnjepr River as gunner in the Panzer IV of Kampfgruppe Leader Jessen.

In the dawn of the morning, the Panzer IVs, Panzer IIIs, and assault guns made ready for the attack. Later, 10.5-cm assault howitzers of the army joined the group. The gun of the leader of the Kampfgruppe, Obersturmführer Jessen, malfunctioned almost immediately. He trans-ferred to our Panzer IV, and we approached the edge of the town of Swidowok. The grenadiers of the Regiment "Westland" advanced on both sides of the path through the woods. The Russians raced backward and took up positions at the edge of town. Suddenly, a 4.5-cm Pak opened up from there. Our driver's viewing slit blind was hit. Another hit destroyed the fuse box and caused an electrical short. Fire broke out in the engine compartment, but it was quickly extinguished. I sent off a few explosive shells but had difficulties aiming because of the smoke from the burning cottages. Our driver was wounded in the head and could not see any more. The radio operator and loader took him to the rear.

Jessen and I stayed close to the Panzer IV, which was under constant fire from the Pak. Then the Russians attacked and pushed back our grenadiers. Both of us had to run backward with them, or Ivan would have grabbed us. At the edge of the woods, Jessen assembled the strag-glers for a counter push. A Walther pistol in his hand, he encouraged the grenadiers. I grabbed an MG 34 with belt magazine. With hurrahs, we stormed out of the woods and the Russians raced back. I saw the Ivans run ahead of me and fired the MG from the hip. Soon after, we were back at our Panzer IV. Jessen wanted to have it towed. In order to achieve that with an assault gun III, I was to get into the driver's seat and use the steering brakes to help. I glanced around the corner of the house and counted the seconds between the explosions of the Pak shells: eight to nine seconds. During this span I had to make it into the driver's seat. Let's go. Discharge, explosion. With one leap I was on the hull and dove into the hatch above the driver's seat. Immediately, another hit on the gun mantlet followed. In the meantime, Jessen had brought in an assault gun. But before it was in position to tow, the Pak caught it in the side, seriously wounding Unterscharführer Günter Ploen.

Only a second assault gun was successful. It crossed the open spot and moved into position, under cover of a house, in front of the Panzer IV. It then pulled our Panzer IV in a wide circle through the village, right through the Russians who were gathering, ready to attack again. I concentrated completely on the towing operation and the steering brakes. The Pak fired wildly on our Panzer, which was inevitably showing its side. Hit to the hull, hit to the turret, hit to the motor, explosions were all around me. My forehead was covered with sweat. At any moment, the Panzer could have caught on fire and blown up. A ripped-off part of the commander's cupola viewing port rattled down and hit me in the shoulder. Damn it, that hurt. I pulled down the lid of the driver's hatch to prevent anything else from flying in. Then, an immense roar bellowed below me, on the side of the radio operator. The Panzer was lifted up, and I hit the lid of the hatch with my head.

I only saw stars in front of my eyes. The assault gun had pulled our Panzer onto a tank mine. The track was ripped, two rollers gone; that was it! On top of it all, the Russians had gone around us and were attacking on the flank. No choice now but to get out. I grabbed the coding documents and took the electric firing pin since there was no time left to blow up the Panzer. The Russian infantry, with "urras," attacked only sixty meters away. Two assault howitzers had pulled up and fired high-explosive shells with impact fuses into the approaching masses. I ran so as not to be cut off, racing for my life, when I heard an explosion behind me.

Glancing back, I saw our Panzer in flames. One of our howitzers fired on it so that it would not fall into Russian hands. Rage almost made me cry. So much bad luck all at once! All efforts were wasted and only brought us losses. Silently, I ran backward to report the loss of the Panzer. Soldier's luck was not always on our side!

ACTIONS OF THE TIGERS WITH THE 1. SS-PANZER-DIVISION "LAH" IN THE EAST

The SS-Panzer-Division "Leibstandarte" was put on alert in the morning of November 5 while being transported by rail to the east. After arriving on November 11, it was attached to the XXXXVII Panzerkorps the next morning to attack in two spearheads the road Kiev–Shitomir to the north. The division had only one Tiger company, the 13. Heavy Panzer Company in the SS-Panzer-Regiment 1, and these Tigers went into action in the morning of November 13. At noon of that day they reached the Kamenka River, and SS-Obersturmbannführer Schöberger, commander of the SS-Panzer-Regiment, had them ferried across the river east of Potschnikij. South of the Unowa creek the Panzers encountered massed enemy forces for the first time. Initially, the Panther Battalion was put into action and rolled directly into an enemy tank spearhead. When the

Tigers, under their company chief Hauptsturmführer Kling, began to roll ahead, the enemy was already in motion before it was decided that Brussilow would be the next objective of attack since the enemy had assembled the 1st, 5th and 8th Guards Tank Corps there.

During the battle that followed, the two platoons of Untersturm-führers Wendorff and Wittmann fought in feverish actions.

By noon, Wittmann's Panzer alone, with his gunner Balthasar Woll behind the 8.8-cm gun, had knocked out ten T-34s and five Paks. Wittmann then went on reconnaissance and spotted another Pak and several T-34s, which he attacked with his platoon. Wendorff's platoon took part in the fighting during which all eleven enemy tanks and the Paks were destroyed.

By the evening, Wittmann's crew had wiped out another ten T-34s and seven Paks. Only after several days of fighting was the 1. SS-Panzer-Division able to capture Brussilow on November 24. The divisions of the 4. Panzerarmee were redeployed. The 1. and 7. Panzer-Division and the 1. SS-Panzer-Division "Leibstandarte" (LAH) were to attack the flank of the 60th Soviet Army from the area of Kamenka–Federowka. The Tigers started out on December 6. The Pak barrier between Kortyky and Styrty was broken, and numerous Paks were knocked out. Then, Wittmann's Tiger destroyed a Russian assault gun, and shortly thereafter Styrty was reached. The enemy was in retreat in a long column of vehicles. The Tigers destroyed the column with high explosive shells. The Panzers kept rolling toward Golowin. When Russian tanks opened fire on them, they returned it and hammered the enemy into the ground. Michael Wittmann, who knocked out his 66th enemy tank in the east during those days and bagged almost as many Paks, had a saying: "Each tank counts, but each Pak counts double." Other tank commanders would agree with this. The Pak, well entrenched, was hard to spot. Because it generally fired at a high rate before the Panzer commander was able to make it out, the Pak was among the most dangerous enemy weapons.

When the enemy ripped open a hole in the sector of the 4. Panzer-armee in the Berditschew area, the three Panzer-divisions, among them the "LAH," rolled south to close the gap again. At Christmas, the SS-Panzer-Division "Leibstandarte" took up positions at the northern edge of Berditschew. The Tigers of the "Leibstandarte" received support from the 1. Panzer-Division, and Russian tank units, attacking from the north, were stopped and wiped out.

In the early morning hours of January 9, Wittmann rolled forward together with two other commanders, Lötzsch and Warmbrunn, to conduct a reconnaissance. The three Tigers were directed by the infantry and rolled into a shallow gully. When enemy tanks appeared at the facing incline, all three Tigers fired simultaneously. Lötzsch and Warmbrunn knocked out two T-34s each, which Wittmann got six. On January 13, Michael Wittmann received the Oak Leaves to the Knight's Cross for a total of eighty-eight knocked-out tanks.

The Tiger company was put on alert again during the evening hours when Russian tanks had broken through the lines of the SS-Panzer-Grenadiers. When the Tigers reached the area of the fighting, two regiments of the Red Army had already advanced behind the T-34s. The Tigers encountered the tank pack, which had advanced the farthest, and the battle began in the falling darkness.

The enemy was stalled, and there was a short period of quiet.

During the next morning, the entire Panzer-Regiment and the grenadiers attacked anew. The battle lasted for hours. During this action, Hauptsturmführer Kling, chief of 13. Company, knocked out his thirty-seventh and thirty-eighth tanks.

Wittmann's Tiger, with the reliable gunner Woll, was unquestionably the most successful during these battles. No fewer than sixteen enemy tanks were added to his list of victories. In the afternoon of the second day he reported an additional three tanks and three assault guns as destroyed.

On January 15, 1944, the day after the SS-Division "Leibstandarte," which had destroyed more than 100 tanks and assault guns, received mention in the Armed Forces Report, the gunner of Wittmann's Tiger was handed the Knight's Cross by his divisional commander, Theodor Wisch, for his contribution to eighty-eight tank victories.

When the Tscherkassy pocket was closed, encompassing an entire German army corps, the "Leibstandarte" left the area Shitomir–Berditschew to aid those beleaguered divisions. With it rolled the 13. Company and its Tigers.

During the meeting of the commanders in the early morning of February 6, Gniloi Tikitsch was identified as the first objective. Half an hour later, the Tigers of 13. Company were slogging through the mud, with Hauptsturmführer Kling leading the heavy company with two platoons. Untersturmführer Wendorff rolled on the left flank; Obersturmführer Wittmann with his five Tigers was on the right. They encountered enemy tanks of the Russian 5th Guards Tank Corps, and during the fighting that followed, Wittmann and his crew knocked out nine enemy tanks.

Other Panzer commanders, too, achieved successes. The attack continued the following day. Two Tigers that had been rendered unserviceable by enemy hits were recovered and readied for action during the night. By the evening of February 8, the Division "LAH" had fought its way to Gniloi Tikitsch. Two days later a ferocious battle occurred in which the Panzer group "Bäke" and the heavy Panzer-Abteilung 503 of the army took part. On February 17, three groups were formed inside the encirclement ready to break out. The attackers alone were unable to smash the ring, and they pushed with all their Panzers towards those breaking out. The 13. Company took part in this attack, and its company chief, Hauptsturmführer Kling, was wounded. Michael Wittmann took over the leadership of the company and continued to lead it during the following weeks after some 35,000 soldiers had been freed from the encirclement. Seven Tigers were lost during these actions at Tscherkassy.

While the 1. Panzerarmee was encircled in the Kamenz–Podolsk area, the Tiger Company fought its way backwards. The Division "Leibstandarte," at the end of its stamina, was withdrawn for refitting and transported to Belgium. There, the Tiger Company provided the nucleus for the setting up of the Korps-Tiger-Abteilung 101 of the I. SS-Panzerkorps.

Michael Wittmann was ordered to the Führer headquarters to receive the Oak Leaves to the Knight's Cross. His new responsibility was to be the chief of 2./heavy SS-Panzer-Abteilung 101. At the same time, the Korps-Tiger-Abteilung 102 of the II. SS-Panzerkorps was being set up. The heavy 8. Company of Panzer-Regiment 2 "Das Reich" formed its nucleus.

CHANGE OVER TO DEFENSE IN THE SECTOR OF PANZER-REGIMENT "DAS REICH"

There was no question that the Russian side was gathering strength. While the Soviets were able to assemble new forces, regroup, and refit them, we had to pull out our fully operational Panzer-divisions to put them into action at other endangered sectors of the front. In numerous leaflets, which they dropped from aircraft on the front, the Russians openly spoke of their near-term goals. They spoke of how they would water their horses at the Bug, Weichsel, and Oder Rivers!

Meanwhile, the land was freezing, and even if the thermometer did not register minus 40 degrees Celsius at the beginning of December, the cold temperatures were an additional load on the German troops.

Waves of snow raced across the wintery landscape of plains and gullies. Snowflakes covered the ripped-up fields, the destroyed cottages, and torn paths like clean white linen. Bright points of light shone from the villages and cottages farther back during the cold and dark nights.

Rocket launchers, artillery positions, and light and heavy Flak lined up north and eastward of our quarters. They blended into the slopes and gullies around the villages. Smoke from the stoves in the bunkers rose gaily and whirled in the wind. For days, the front was silent and rested, dug into the ground.

One day, as the December sky spanned the glittering fields of snow with a cloudless blue, the howl and roar of Soviet combat aircraft approached in the morning and at noon. Not just once, but five and six times, Soviet aircraft attacked the village. There were dead and wounded, destroyed cottages, and burning vehicles. The danger of the air attacks was the surprise factor. The crews sat in the cottages and could not dive in time into cover under the Panzers. Of course, the red bombers recognized the Panzers sitting next to the cottages and concentrated their attacks on them.

Like long strings of pearls, fire from super-heavy machine guns hit the ground among the exploding bombs dropped on the cottages and vehicles. Fires shot sky-high, and columns of flames and smoke stood in the clear winter day. Often, it was a race for life. The Panzer crews were washing, half-dressed, inside the cottages when they heard the howling of the combat aircraft followed by gunfire and the diving and climbing of the planes. Soon after, the rockets danced around the Panzers. Especially during these seconds, as death approached with such din that one could hear him whistle, almost believing in seeing him in person, all begged silently that death would race by again—just one more time. Meanwhile, Christmas 1943 came closer. The soldiers wrote letters and were, in their thoughts, with their distant loved ones. Generally, the morale was good. Shortly, the division was to have been withdrawn to the training grounds of Stablack and Arys in East Prussia for refitting.

During the night of December 5 and early morning of the 6th, a Panzer attack in the sector of Regiment "Der Führer" was ordered.

When all usable Tigers of the unit were lined up at 6 A.M. on the slopes behind the German lines, the attack order was abruptly canceled. At exactly 6:30 A.M., an overwhelming fire attack was planned to hit the tanks and artillery of the Russian lines. Up until then however, the front was still quiet, while everyone kept glancing at their watches. The individual companies, which had been briefed on their attack sectors, waited for the order to attack. Then all guns began to roar and shells left the barrels with bright jets of fire. A glance through the gun sight showed a terrible, even if appreciated by our own infantrymen, picture of battle. All of the enemy lines were covered by heavy artillery fire. Wherever one looked, there were the bright flashes of explosions, black, yellow, or white smoke and columns of dirt as high as houses. Salvo after salvo howled across and dug in among the rows of cottages. In between there was a deep howling, growing ever higher, huge and unnerving, hitting the enemy positions with a tail of fire: our rocket launchers. Much later, after the Tigers had long returned to our old positions, hesitant enemy gunfire set in. For the following few days the Russians probably had their share!

An attack on Radomichl, a city on the upper Teterew River some twenty kilometers north of the main route from Shitomir to Kiev, took place. Portions of a paratroop division brought in from Germany, supported by Panzer-Regiment "Das Reich," were to take the city in a localized counterattack and thus straighten out the front line.

On December 9, at 5 P.M., departure for the assembly positions had begun. Five Tigers and a Panzer IV company were the fighting force of an entire detachment, which was to support the attack by the paratroopers. Then the Tigers were on the move, and we saw the wintery world from the perspective of the Panzer men, through the hatches of the steely, moving fortresses.

It was difficult to find the way in the morning dark. Approaching a creek in the dangerous swampy terrain, the first Tiger missed the path by a few meters and bogged down in the treacherous ground together with the following two Panzers. The leading Panzer broke through the frozen crust of earth, brought the dark dirt to the surface with both its tracks, and just managed to reach firm ground at full engine power. The second Panzer stopped and sank that much deeper into the wet and ripped-up tracks left by the first one.

The third Panzer also stopped, tried to swing to the left, and dug its rear deep into the swamp. Half of its tracks were covered with mud and dirt. Everyone out! With each minute, the Panzer sank another few centimeters into the bog. Flashlights were turned on. Feverishly, the men shoveled the tracks clear, attached tow cables, and had the first Panzer free after ten minutes. Despite the grim cold of the morning, their shirts stuck to their bodies wet with sweat. The Panzers were freed and, even if a good hour late, reached, the assembly area still in time.

At exactly 7:30 A.M., together with a company of paratroopers, they commenced the attack on Russian positions in the woods. The company leader directed the action. Out of the smoke and flames in the woods came the first wounded. Broken tree trunks, dead Russians, and the noise of battle showed the path of the Tigers, which had pulled ahead and were engaged in fighting. Radio communication was established, and orders were received. Ahead, in the dark green of the snow-covered firs, the first tanks dipped up and down like prehistoric animals. Flames shot up from earth bunkers; smoke and gunpowder gasses drifted through the woods. Limping horses raced about and in the tangle of the uprooted firs hung dead and wounded Russians. Tracer salvos danced closer and drilled into the tree trunks. A chaos without equal, it was most difficult to find one's way in. Fighting in the woods was something else. One had to be damned alert to get out of there unharmed. Behind the snakes of fire from the 8.8-cm guns, the assault teams of paratroopers pushed ahead, preceded by the blue balls of smoke of their hand grenades. Son of a gun, those were elite soldiers! They kept going despite the high losses of the fighting in the woods and the determined resistance of the enemy. Knocking down trees with their bows and tracks, the Tigers broke a path through the tall trees. The crews had to watch out for the tracks and guns more carefully than for the Russians to avoid damage to the Panzers. We pulled off to the right of the Panzer column, drove up a slope, and found ourselves facing a wooded gully. At its edge was a fully manned trench. Our machine guns began to rattle simultaneously, hammering into the earth bunkers which soon gave off flames and clouds of smoke. A few meters ahead, we saw the Russians break out and disappear into the undergrowth.

Two explosive shells ripped the bunkers and fortifications apart, throwing planks and beams into the gully. Then the Russians tried to attack us from the cover of the dense young growth surrounding the Tiger. We hurled hand grenades into the bushes and hoped they would have the desired effect. Still, it was an uncomfortable situation when one could not see anything.

Suddenly, we spotted a Russian racing down a path from the opposite edge of the woods into the gully with an antitank rifle in his right hand. That was not courage, it was madness! Thirty meters ahead of the Panzer, he jumped into a foxhole and slowly pushed the antitank rifle above the edge. To us, it looked like imagination gone wild! Slowly, we wound the gun down and pushed the electric firing mechanism: a hefty smack and simultaneous discharge. Through the veil of flames and smoke, we saw an explosion in front of the foxhole. A man was hurled skyward together with clumps of dirt and fell back to the ground. Amazed, we let him crawl back along the wooded path. One more time we let our machine gun work down the trenches and the gully as branches fell earthward among the smoke and flames before we left toward the rear. Swinging left, we quickly linked up again with the company that had fought its way to the opposite edge of the woods and sustained considerable losses. There, it too was stopped at "our" gully, which cut across the direction of the attack at the edge of the woods. The first Tiger rolled into a low sandy depression in order to capture the plain ahead of us for the breakthrough to Radomichl, but soon it was completely stuck in the ground. The attack stalled. The Russians hung on to both sides of the trenches we had overrun and began strong counterattacks into the flanks of our spearhead.

It may have been noon when we received the radio order to come to the left flank of our attack. We drove between the high trees and the gully into firing position, swung 90 degrees on the narrow, sandy ground, and let the Panzer roll back a few meters. The gun was then only just above the ridge of the gully. In the sand, dug up meters deep, the track tightened to the extreme and ripped off the left driving wheel. We were the second Panzer unable to move! We felt boiling hot, our hearts beating in our throats.

Immobile, we sat in the middle of the Russians pushing on around us. They could have blown us up, or we could have been taken prisoner, which might have meant death! Not a stone's throw away we saw the brown-clad Ivans creep between the firs and undergrowth—whole hordes! Still holding back, they disappeared into the gully into a blockhouse in the woods. Although we were able to swing the turret, we had almost no field of fire.

Orders by radio came from Kalls to prepare the Tiger to be blown up, so that it would not fall into enemy hands under any circumstances. On the other side of the plain, we watched the tank and vehicle columns of the enemy roll through the village, but we no longer had a field of fire in that direction either. Then we saw new reserves moving in across the hazy plain above which artillery salvos danced like will-o'-the-wisps. Inside the Panzer we held council on how to salvage the Tiger. It had to be possible to drop off the track and shorten it! Normally, it would have been cut with a blow torch or an explosive charge, but neither of these was possible in our situation. So, outside, the driver and radio operator tried to overcome the tension of the track. And there, using all their strength, they were unexpectedly able to throw off portions of the track. Then, another difficult piece of work waited: the loosening and knocking off of the driving wheel. In the meantime the Russians had begun to pay attention. The hammering and knocking by the Panzer made them listen up. Bullets smacked against the left side of our Panzer! We dropped into the sand as machine guns opened up. That was not going to work. They would have picked us off one by one; they were already throwing hand grenades! We jumped back into the Panzer from the other side, sent a few explosive shells into the tops of the trees without aiming, fired the machine gun, and got out again. But, a few minutes later, the same performance all over again. As soon as the heavy hammering started, bullets whistled around our heads. It was a miracle that not one of us was hit. Back into the box. Because of the lay of the terrain there was little we could do. The Russians cunningly used its features for cover. Thus, we asked for help from the infantry. Soon, our chief Kalls showed up with a platoon of paratroopers, led by world record-holder Harbig, and pushed the Russians back into the depth of the woods. In the meantime our commander recognized that the violent fighting in the woods would have decimated his company and that we might have been cut off. In the course of the afternoon it was therefore decided to disengage the Kampfgruppe from the attack area with the arrival of darkness and to return it to its old front line.

We toiled for hours to get our Panzer back on its track. While the hazy dusk and the fog of the late afternoon made the plain in front of us dissolve into marvelous forms and smoke from the fires and explosions mixed with the fog at the edge of the woods, the din of the fighting in the woods continued during the falling darkness. Finally, the driving wheel came off; the track was shortened and connected. We made it at the last minute!

The entire Kampfgruppe was only waiting for our "ready" report to finally get out of that impossible situation. Not enough that we had to retreat, a counterattack by the larger Russian forces was expected at any moment.

Night had fallen when, pulled by another Tiger, we finally got free of the slope and joined the other Panzers in the middle of the battleground. All the wounded and dead were loaded onto the Panzers. At the same time, orders were issued to all units to slowly retreat toward the Panzers. We hoped it would work! Finally, everything was ready. The order was given to get going. The engines howled. In a long line astern the Panzers broke through the woods, backward on the path of the attack. The pale red of the fires from the battlefield disappeared among the dark trunks of the trees. Several wounded on our Panzer smoked in hasty pulls on the cigarettes and gossiped with their comrades next to them to take their minds off what happened and to overcome the fear and tense nerves of the previous hours.

We could not have been all that far from our own main front line when the column suddenly stopped. What was going on? Somewhere ahead another Tiger had gone unserviceable. Its crew was to remain with the Panzer in the woods through the night, and it would be towed the next day. Using headlights we loaded the wounded and dead into the ambulance and trucks. The platoons and companies assembled on the path in the woods and returned to their old positions.

The crew of the Tiger left behind had an uncomfortable night. While they were silent inside the Panzer, they heard the Russians come closer and walk around the Panzer, do pull-ups on the gun barrel, and converse in their hoarse throat sounds. Only with the dawn could our own be brought out by a tracked towing vehicle. They would never forget that night.

Across, in the small clearings dotted by snow, eighty meters from the path, the number of fresh earth mounds grew. More and more rows of birch crosses: the graves of fallen German soldiers. Finally, on December 15, 1943, the division was ordered to be relieved. All serviceable Panzers were assembled into a Kampfgruppe under the leadership of Endemann, a large, blond Rhinelander. Men, equipment, and spare parts started out for Shitomir on December 16 for loading on transport. Those comrades who had not had any leave during the previous year were handed leave forms on December 19 with the order to return to Stablack in East Prussia afterwards. What a blissful thought, to spend Christmas and New Year's at home!

The German Armed Forces Report stated on December 24 that the expected Russian major offensive in the area west of Kiev had broken out. The holidayers from the heavy Tigerkompanie were ordered back to the unit by telegram.

But where were they to find the unit? Shitomir had long been taken by the Russians who pushed irresistibly forward. Indescribable chaos reigned behind the front lines! All roads were blocked by supply units flooding backward, by wounded and refugees. Military installations were blown up. Some of those returning from leave received orders to report to Stablack, East Prussia, from command posts at the front. The heavy company had lost all its Panzers. A detail was sent on its way to Germany to pick up new Tigers.

RUSSIAN SPRING OFFENSIVE 1944

The armored battle group of Division "Das Reich" was ready for action after a quick overhaul of the vehicles.

The Panzer commander of a Tiger, Ernst Streng, reports: Finally, on February 10, 1944, the Panzer transport, led by Tegthoff, arrived at its quarters in Prokurow with five Tigers and ten Panzer IVs. Together with one company of Panthers this was then the total equipment of Panzerkampfgruppe "Endemann" and the Division "Das Reich." These leftovers deployed southwest of Schepetowka.

Despite their superiority, the Soviets had been unable to force a decisive change up until then. It was not expected for the coming months either. Our troops in the north stood at the Narwa River at that time.

In the central front sectors the Russians had not been successful in breaking through to the Beresina and Pripjet Rivers. Thus, a sudden push by the Red Army toward central Poland was not likely there either. On the southern front a pincer movement against a German bulge in the line west of Tscherkassy had begun. On January 30, an assault on the German bulge east of Kriwoi Rog started. Thanks to the deployment of unbelievable masses of men and tanks, both Russian attacks were successful.

Only during the second half of February did a certain calm settle on the southern sector. The fronts began to stabilize. The Crimea was still firmly in German hands despite incessant attacks by the Russians near Kertsch during the previous twelve weeks.

Around the middle of February, the weather changed from day to day. One day, the supply routes to the front consisted of mud with no foundation, which almost no vehicle could dig its way through. The next day, the valleys and slopes glittered in the light of the freshly fallen snow, and a rising wind covered everything with wavy white veils. Northern storms then raced across the heights into the valleys, howled around our miserable cottages on the slopes, and dumped clouds and snow on the Panzers outside. Masses of clouds rolled through the quiet Ukrainian nights. The fires in the stoves were kept going at all times. Only rarely would a star flash through the broken cloud cover. Airborne and ground reconnaissance daily reported the continued strengthening of the Russian lines. Strong tank and infantry formations were moving in. Every time that the divisional general, Hasso von Manteuffel, visited the heavy companies, he explained that a Russian attack was to be expected soon.

On March 1, the Tigers advanced into the assembly area east of Semjalintzy. The civilian population had already evacuated the area. The animals were still grazing in the meadows; large herds of horses trotted between the villages. No one was there to take care of them. Extensive reconnaissance was carried out during the following night since most of the forward routes could not be used by the Tigers because of the large areas of swamp.

The attack by the whole detachment began on March 2. More than thirty Stukas circled above the battleground when it started and dove down on the enemy targets with their distinctive whine. They dropped their bombs, making the earth shake for many kilometers.

Blue clouds from the explosions drifted across the horizon. A violent artillery battle broke out in which the light, echoing sounds of the Panzer discharges could be heard.

As the early dusk of the winter evening dropped on the land, the German Panzers, stuck in front of the enemy Pak and infantry positions, had to withdraw with considerable losses. Two Tigers and three Panthers were rendered unserviceable by enemy fire and returned to the repair company. During the night the division ordered a repeat of the attack for March 3.

A gnawing unrest was felt in the morning of March 3. Was it the coming massive attack, which we knew could not take place without losses? Was it the reports from the prisoners of the previous night that indicated strong concentrations of enemy troops and tanks? Russian deserters, who arrived at the German infantry positions shortly after midnight, confirmed the concentration of strong Soviet forces at the front. They stated that the expected massive attack was scheduled for that morning. Until then, little credence was given to these reports on our side. The planned German counterattack was to have taken place under any circumstances. But what tragic confusion was to result from this! Even the Report of the Supreme Command of the Armed Forces of the previous day had soberly reported that there was only limited German fighting activity going on in the southern sector of the Eastern Front, and that units of combat aircraft had successfully attacked Soviet troop concentrations in the Polonnje and Schepetowka area. Violent combat against superior enemy units had been raging for days in the area of Newel, Witebsk, and Pleskau.

It was 6:15 in the morning. Ahead of us, the first Panzer IVs with their weak armor careened in uneven curves across the hard frozen road to assemble for departure. The cold made us tremble all over. The village echoed around us with the roar of the engines and the rattle of the tracks.

Then it happened damned fast. We were still directing the driver as the massive Panzer pushed slowly forward between the clay huts when Russian harassing fire suddenly hit the long stretched-out village. A deep howl whistled above us. Somewhere between the cottages stood a rising mushroom of smoke and flames. It collapsed to make room for the next explosion. Nervously, the Russian artillery felt its way into the village. No wonder, the noise had enveloped the front throughout the morning.

Then, Endemann in his command Panzer started out, followed by the leader of the Panzer IV company, the holder of the Oak Leaves, Kloskowsky. We all got going and put on our headsets and microphones. With an immense noise our column roared through the abandoned village across a narrow wooden bridge, past the village pond, to the north exit. Another short stop followed. Low humming and crackling came from the headphones; the crew was briefed on the intercom about the target of the attack. Minutes later, it was hard to recognize anything in the slowly approaching dawn, our Panzer behemoths pushed across the edge of the village on the frozen ground onto the dark plain. With every shift of the gears the engines threw meter-long snakes of fire out of the exhaust pipes, blinding the eyes of those behind. The Russian artillery fire had fairly accurately targeted our attack sector and moved toward the front at an even speed. The cold of the morning crept through all the cracks and into the open commander's hatch through which, using field glasses, we were trying to search the terrain for the attackers. Ahead of us the light Panzers formed into a firing line. A Panzer slid into the ditch and was stuck. If only we could have seen something! Suddenly, massive artillery fire hit among the Panzers. We had been spotted by the enemy without being able to make out his positions. The Russians let go from all barrels and with all calibers into the German Panzer attack. The gurgling explosions threw mud, fragments, and clumps of earth sky high and against the walls of the Tiger. Daylight came slowly and the visibility improved. Thank God, we could at least orientate ourselves and were able to determine the enemy positions. Our light company was already involved in heavy fighting. Their guns fired without pause.

Then we were on the way! Still, the commander held us back. Only then did the incoming radio messages make it clear to him that the Russian major offensive had begun! Masses of Soviet infantry, which we could then spot with the naked eye, flooded the plain to the right of us. As far as one could see, the brown spots were in motion. Thousands and thousands of them. German infantrymen, like drops in the ocean, left their positions at this spectacle and ran backward for their lives.

Flares rose among the buzzing and whistling and the "tack-tack" of countless machine guns. On the radio, one piece of bad news chased the other. The last veils of fog dissipated on the plains. The morning of

March 3 brought a ghostly gray light, a day like any other, but for many it would be their last. Then the order came to bring the Tigers into action on both sides of the railroad station. In a hopeless attempt the commander tried to save anything he could in the face of the enemy superiority. It was bitterly tragic that this same order simultaneously determined the end of the German Panzer detachment.

About face, march! After 300 meters we swung right toward the station. The bombed-out ruins and sheds stared back at us without solace; the German infantry had left. Craters, debris, pieces of masonry as well as the fear of close combat kept us back from the ruins.

Then we reached the embankment and saw disaster approach across the vast bald plains. Thousands and thousands of Russian soldiers! All the way to the horizon, Russian infantry was on the march, among them horse-drawn Paks and Flak. Frightening, these masses! But then, beams fell, walls crumbled, snow whirled and the ground turned into dust under the massive Panzer tracks. Our Panzers climbed across all that and pushed into the ruins to take up firing positions. Immediately, our machine guns began to hammer. Salvos of tracers hailed into the brown lines, which turned in bewilderment and then hit the ground, and 8.8-cm explosive shells were sent into the fields. With every shot, clouds of gun powder dissipated across the embankment and obscured our vision. The ventilation system hummed away quietly. One container of ammunition after the other was emptied, the cartridges thrown through the hatches. The Panzer shook and vibrated. We watched the destruction on the other side. The fever of the hunt had gripped us as surroundings and danger were forgotten. Any Russian soldiers who were spotted were destroyed without mercy. But, time and again, they got up. Fanatical, determined fighters despite danger and death! We did not know whether this fighting had been going on for one or two hours. Hundreds of MG salvos knocked on our steel walls. Once, men of the Red Army tried to get to our Panzer under cover of the ruins and crumbled walls to knock us out at close quarters, but our shells slammed into their lines and destroyed their plan.

With the help of our three Tigers this massive Russian wave was finally wrestled to the ground and the attack stopped, if only temporarily.

At the very moment of this pause in fighting, the radio order arrived to go into immediate action against enemy tank forces in front of the fire line of the Panzer IV company. With this, our defensive fighting had changed into a race with death. At full throttle we broke out of the ruins into the open fields to the left.

Russian tank attack! Those were not three or four Russian T-34s. By the dozens they pushed their dark bodies across the horizon onto the plains. Distance 1,400 meters! The closest enemy tanks burned brightly. Next to us and behind, our own Panzers blazed like immense torches. It was unnerving to see the white glowing bodies of the Panzer IVs sitting in front of the flaming, smoking, blood-colored sky. All around us were haze and billowing smoke, drifting banks of gun powder, deafening explosions, discharges and impacts, roaring engines, the shouts of the wounded and the burning. . . .

That was the morning of March 3, 1944. We were in a firing position next to knocked-out and still firing German Panzers. Shell after shell left the barrel and drilled into the bodies of the enemy tanks. Across, oily smoke from torches rose vertically. Ten . . . twelve, ever more fresh T-34s broke apart. That was the Russian tank attack! Then it had visibly stalled; they had probably no longer expected such resistance. We were not sure just then how many German Panzers had been lost. Six serviceable Panzers pulled back behind the fire line of the Tigers. Twenty, thirty enemy tanks were on fire. Then the Russians recognized that a breakthrough there was impossible. The Panzer battle appeared to be over, and we believed victory was in our pockets.

Through our field glasses, however, we began to watch another spectacle and foresaw the drama that was about to begin. We, and all the others, watched the long tank columns of the enemy go around the German Panzer group, swing to the right and advance under cover of the bald heights into the flanks and deep into the front line. Under no threat, the Soviets rolled into the gullies behind us. We saw their black bodies, miniature by then, dive across the horizon and disappear again. There had to be 100 tanks. Powerless, we felt our end approaching!

At this very time the commander could be found in the village. It had been the known Russian tactic that we had practiced years ago: break through at the point of weak resistance, then encircle and destroy. A little too late the commander recognized this danger and ordered the immediate withdrawal of all Panzers to our original positions. Not knowing that it was too late already, we believed that we still had an opportunity to break through and out. In vain. A message arrived from Tegthoff: "Secure the withdrawal!"

Swinging to the left, we drove up an incline into firing position. Suddenly, we spotted Russian tanks racing across the heights. Quick decision and order: "Antitank shell—800 meters—fire!" A cloud of powder gasses from the gun, outside and inside the Panzer, obscured the field of observation for a few seconds before we saw the hit explode on the broad side of the enemy tank. A white flash of flame, and then black smoke developed into a giant mushroom. A terrible explosion ripped the tank apart.

The order to pull back finally came. Swinging wide, we approached the burning German Panzers at top speed to save what could be saved, against all reasonable thought of our own safety and our hopeless situation. In between the shells that howled and whistled across the plain came the hacking, staccato salvos of the Russian machine guns. We stopped the Panzer and loaded all of the bloodied, maimed, and moaning wounded who were able to move and who made it to the Panzer. Very quickly, the hull and turret were covered by those unfortunates, and we had to get going. "Full throttle—march—let's go!" The wounded on the ground were still yelling loudly, and we saw them waving weakly. "Comrades, help us. Take us with you!" It was useless and without hope. It was too late, not only for them, maybe for all of us. Every minute could decide on life or death. This was their end. Maybe the end for us all. Only a few had any idea that the way back had been cut off by the masses of enemy tanks that had bypassed us and that the fate of the German Panzer group had thus been sealed.

At full speed we raced through the gullies, broke across the trenches, and bobbed like a canoe on the high seas across the bloody battlefield, chasing the other German Panzers ahead of us.

On the radio we received word that our assembly area and quarters at Semjelintzky, whose bridges offered the only possibility to cross the upper, winding, Horyn River, were already occupied by the enemy. We kept the town some 500 meters to our right. An incline obstructed the field of vision toward the edge of town. Smoke and flames rose through the haze into the gray sky.

Hundreds of enemy tanks had ripped open the brittle German lines with their ten- or twenty-fold superiority and rolled toward Tarnopol without resistance. There was nothing left to be thrown against these masses! Swinging to the east, our column broke through the Russian infantry attack in order to follow the lower run of the river and, somewhere, to find a crossing. To the left and right our hand grenades exploded among the surprised and perplexed clumps of Russian infantrymen. Submachine guns and machine guns let go at them before they had a chance to take cover. We were just as perplexed when we finally arrived at the bank of the Horyn River. A swamp to the north prevented the Tigers from driving on behind our back enemy tanks. Up until then, the Russian riflemen who were all around us did not dare to fire. Quickly, the commander jumped out and ran over to Tegthoff, who was consulting with Kloskowsky. No one knew what to do next. Finally, they decided on a forceful push through Semjelintzky while Kloskowsky would follow the river downstream with his light Panzers. Soon after he was hopelessly bogged down in the swamp. In the meantime we had received authorization from command to attempt the breakthrough with the Tigers. The faster, the better! Only speed and the element of surprise could have helped. As he was turning, von Einböck got hopelessly stuck in the swamp and even the belly of the Panzer was touching the mud so that the tracks dug ever deeper into the mud and water. Time was running out. The order came: "Crew—get out! Blow up the Panzer!"

All the wounded able to walk were ordered to cross the river and adjoining height on their own and to try to reach the main German line to the south. Hastily, as dictated by our plan, we swung the guns around and knocked out von Einböck's Tiger at a short distance with two rounds.

Amazing, how these engines were able to perform! We drove in eighth gear.

Tegthoff was in the lead, racing back along the same path, taking no notice of the enemy scrambling out of the way. The tracks threw the frozen dirt high into the air and hauled us across the plain. A little later, Tegthoff swung left, crossed the gully, and raced up the slope toward Semjelintzky right through the middle of a horse-drawn battery. Teams and soldiers took off in immense panic and fell to the ground. Seldom had we seen such fear-stricken faces and begging eyes, as if the devil himself were after them. Like shadows, we saw them in the corner mirror jump about and fall. Then, something else happened that almost took our breath away. The rpm of the engine started to drop. Fink shifted down from one gear to the other. Our speed fell off, the distance to Tegthoff increased. No doubt, we had engine problems. Fink reported that he could not pinpoint the cause. And this on the way to break out in the middle of an enemy column! Our faces were probably as white and drawn as those of the enemy before. Instinctively I yelled at the radio operator: "Radio Tegthoff to stop! Our engine is quitting!" Twice we sent the call for help. During these anxious seconds, without answer, Tegthoff headed up the height toward Semjelintzky. His Panzer was a ready target for the waiting enemy tanks . . . direct hit! Immediately after, another one! Explosions and smoke, flying pieces of human flesh, parts of the tracks, spare parts! We watched as they ripped open the hatches and some of the crew came out. Tegthoff, his loader, and gunner jumped off while the driver and radio operator were killed as they were getting out. The injured lying on the hull were also killed, or wounded again.

"Driver, pull hard right and turn around," the order went to Fink and we succeeded without taking an enemy hit. We stopped for a few seconds to take on Tegthoff, then rolled back down the slope at full speed, with other men hanging on to the front and the rear of our Panzer. Then, the Russians noticed their chance and fired into the wounded and helpless men on our Panzer from the chaos of their overturned, entangled horse-drawn guns.

Tegthoff lay across the driver's hatch and waved at us. Unfortunately, a piece of his coat was hanging over the driver's vision port so that he could not see. We heard him swear and complain on the intercom, a bad situation.

One more time we saw Tegthoff signaling: he wanted us to go faster. That was the last we saw of him. During these seconds, when the driver was being directed, orders were issued to the radio operator and the gunner. Everyone who could still find room crawled into the Panzer through the loader's hatch. They moaned, blood streaming from under their coats. Some were half-naked, their uniforms ripped off their bodies by explosions. Others had bloody faces, while those who were uninjured were driven by overwhelming fear. During these seconds a new disaster hit the last German tank, something which had not been experienced before!

All enemy tanks and Paks fired and concentrated on our Tiger. We heard a ringing around the armor plates in front and rear, saw the flashes of explosions! Hits to the sides, front, and rear. All around us we saw the muzzle flashes but had no idea of their positions. A hit to the front lifted Tegthoff's body and threw him against the gun mantlet. With his death, the field of vision was opened for the driver again! For the second time we pulled into the swampland on the shore of the Horyn. For how long would the engine take this? Suddenly, a hit set the engine on fire, as flames broke through the firewall into the interior! We yelled at the driver and loader to activate the automatic extinguishers. Thank God! The fire died, and the motor kept on roaring. The farther we moved east, the fewer hits we seemed to take. But then, we had the feeling that was the end; an immense hit ripped open the loader's hatch. A bright flash raced through the interior, ripped Mateika's left forearm into pieces, severing his hand. Groaning with pain, he pointed the stump of his arm at us, while another man collapsed onto the swivel of the gun, and a third had blood dripping from his skull. Among the gunpowder smoke, misery, and pain, we put temporary dressings on the wounds.

For the second time we stood at the shore of the Horyn and could not go any farther. Any retreat was cut off by the swamp and the river. The Panzer was lost, but the commander wanted to save as many men as possible. When flames shot out of the engine compartments into the interior for the second and third times, the commander issued the order to bail out.

Escape across the river and the height toward the retreating German lines, well back already, was all we had left. At lightning speed we jumped out of the hatch, dropped to the ground, and ran to the right side of the Panzer, facing away from the enemy. We waited until all the wounded had left the Panzer, then ran across the incline toward the south.

Running, we could see the heads of the Russian soldiers watching us from forty and a hundred meters off to the side in the frozen swamp. The first of the injured had made it across the river and up the bank already, as we raced, without weapons and in cover of the Panzer, to the shore, slid across the ice, and waded through the knee-deep icy water. On the other side we pulled the badly limping von Einböck onto the shore. We were the last across! All around us there was silence, an unreal silence after the terrible explosions and the engine noise. The next few seconds were to decide whether we would succeed in crossing the height. The Ivans knew that and saw what shape we were in. They could have picked us off like rabbits. Panting, we ran uphill, pulling the moaning von Einböck along. The blood hummed in our ears, and we gasped for air. The others had already run ahead quite a distance. Why didn't the Ivans fire? If only we could make it to the top! The wet winter overalls clung heavily to the legs. No belts, no hats, no weapons! Then, an icy shock of realization hit us. We turned our heads and knew why the Ivans were not firing. Barely thirty meters behind our backs, we saw them closing in. They wanted to capture us! Then, von Einböck realized that there was no escape for him with his injury. Time and again his lips murmured: "Don't leave me. Take me with you!" The slope was climbed. Behind it there was a drop into a small treeless valley, some two kilometers wide, in which a herd of cows grazed peacefully. No German soldiers were to be seen anywhere. We heard the Russians' yelling come closer, saw them twenty meters away, and had to let go of von Einböck who could hardly stand up. Our own naked lives were at stake. Immense fear put a cold clamp on the heart and produced unbelievable strength. We raced for our lives into the valley, toward the cow herd. Afterwards, we would not know any more whether the noise was bullets whistling by us or the blood humming in our ears!

We dropped to the ground among the grazing cows, gasping for air. Looking back, we saw the Ivans standing around the fallen von Einböck. We heard pistol fire; they probably shot him dead. That brought us back to our feet. Racing ahead through the cows we used their bodies for cover, raced in zigzag across the valley, and heard the disgusting chirping of rifle bullets around our heads. Out of breath, panting from exhaustion, we fell, jumped up again on shaking knees, and crossed the valley. Looking back, we were thankful for the tough training of our bodies whose endurance and mobility had saved our lives here. If the enemy did not advance any further, we would be safe!

After two kilometers we caught up with the last of the wounded who had fallen well behind the others. Taking turns, we carried our wounded, and stumbled across a second height, searching for our own troops.

Only at the edge of Semjelintzky, on the road from Isjasslaw to Jampol, did we find our reserves lined up. There we also met up with our command car and reported back. We claimed thirty-one enemy tanks knocked out but had to pay for it with the loss of twelve of our own Panzers.

The Russians drove their major spring offensive forward with full force and wild energy. It was impossible to stop the Russian steamroller. Therefore, the German high command decided on a withdrawal to the Dnjestr River. The weather had changed, and the grim cold appeared to have finally broken. Staro-Konstantinow had fallen. Preparations were under way to defend the edges of Proskurow. Thousands of German vehicles had to be blown up on the road to Staro-Konstantinow. The remains of the heavy company moved into quarters at Proskurow. Everywhere the question was asked: What was to happen to us? Would we be returned home or given another refitting? Only a few Panthers and two Tigers remained in action north of the city. Finally, during the night of March 15 and early morning of March 16, the order arrived to move those portions of the detachment not in action to the south. After a nonstop drive, led by Kloskowsky, across occasionally treacherous terrain, the detachment reached Kolomea, which was held by Hungarian troops, on a good road, on March 21.

Amazed, the men of the Tiger company marveled at the peaceful sight of the city. Hungarian officers in dress uniform, sabers, and gloves, who were promenading with Hungarian nurses and girls at their arms, seemed to feel that the fast-approaching war did not exist for them. The unit took up temporary quarters in the city of Stanislau. After the long, hard time in frost and cold, dirt and mud, the soldiers had a chance to reacquaint themselves here with the achievements of civilization. Soldiers' clubs, movie houses, front theaters, cafes, and restaurants were visited; the men of the heavy company began to enjoy themselves. But then word soon came that Russian tank columns had moved to south of the Dnjestr and the city was already threatened. The evacuation of Stanislau began, and that seemed extremely disquieting.

In accordance with the detachment orders, all its members, except the indispensable drivers of the motorcycle squad and the supply vehicles, were to be sent on leave and then to report back to front headquarters in Paris. This was an order appreciated by all. Everyone was glad to escape the hell of the Eastern Front. Even the trip to Przemysl on a freight train was nothing, a small episode. The wheels rolled without pause, but this time toward the west, toward home. And a holiday at home awaited!

During the journey in the train, which took back those on leave from the front, many other comrades from our unit were met. Among them were eyewitnesses who reported that the highly esteemed world-record holder, Harbig, found a soldier's death.

THE I./PANZER-REGIMENT 5 "WIKING" IN THE NOWO-BUDA BRIDGEHEAD—A BATTLE REPORT OF FEBRUARY 13–14, 1944

So that the units encircled at Czerkasy would join up with the relief forces that had been set in march from the outside toward Liss-Janka, the town of Nowo-Buda was taken in a night attack that started out from Steblow. This brought about the later relief of the encircled corps in the Schanderowka area.

It was impossible to secure the newly created ten-kilometer-long front since only minimal forces were available at the time. This gave the enemy the opportunity to attack Nowo-Buda once from the west and once from the east.

The Russians attacked the southeastern sections of Nowo-Buda with two battalions on February 13. They succeeded in breaking into some of our positions, which were only reinforced at intervals.

When Schumacher started a counterassault with two Panzers and dislodged the Russians from the eastern section, the enemy attacked the southwestern section of Nowo-Buda with fifteen tanks.

Untersturmführer Schumacher decided to stop the tanks' breakthrough with his two Panzers and to destroy the enemy who had already pushed into the town with eight T-34s. After the enemy tanks had been cut off inside the town, Schumacher was able to reach the southwest exit of Nowo-Buda and to knock out two more enemy tanks there.

The following day, the Russians attacked with eleven tanks. Schumacher decided to push into the enemy-held southern section with two Panzers in order to attack the enemy from the flank. The gun of the second Panzer was damaged by a Pak hit. Thus, Schumacher's Panzer was initially the only one ready for action. After successfully knocking out seven enemy tanks, he had only seven high-explosive shells left. With these he forced the crews of three more enemy tanks to bail out.

It was then possible to send Schumacher another Panzer as support. The three enemy tanks were sent up in flames and another, which pushed from the south toward Schumacher's rear, was knocked out.

Schumacher's actions enabled us to hold the bridgehead of Nowo-Buda and help with the retreat of the encircled corps from the areas of Korssum and Schanderowka. The independent decision by Schumacher to stop, initially with just two Panzers, the tank breakthrough by the enemy made it possible to prevent a further Russian advancement past Nowo-Buda to Schanderowka. Schumacher played a major part in the knocking out of thirty-two T-34s during this action.

The tanks were knocked out by Panzer IIIs and IVs.

The Encirclement Battle for Kowel

BATTLE REPORT ON THE BREAKTHROUGH OF THE 8./SS-PANZER-REGIMENT 5 TO KOWEL, FROM MARCH 27 TO MARCH 30, 1944, BY OBERSTURMFÜHRER NICOLUSSI-LECK

1. Enemy forces of four rifle divisions with approximately twenty tanks had encircled the city of Kowel together with Kampfgruppe Gille inside during March 17 to April 5, 1944. The enemy was defending against the 131. Infantry-Division attacking from the west along the line from a wooded area two kilometers northeast of Nove-Koszary to one kilometer east of Stare-Koszary, to the western edge of Kalinowka, and to the height west of Kliewieck. The positions were reinforced with strong Pak fronts, artillery and Flak, particularly in the wooded area three kilometers southeast of Stare-Koszary and a range of hills west of Czerkasy.

The 131. Infantry-Division with attached III./SS-Panzer-Grenadier-Regiment "Germania" and an assault gun detachment had advanced from the west eastward to the edge of Nove-Koszary and Stare-Koszary. There, it had stalled due to the growing resistance. Repeated attacks were unsuccessful.

On March 27, I was transported by rail with the 8./SS-Panzer-Regiment 5 and attached to the 131. Infantry-Division for the further attack on Kowel. Strength of the company: seventeen Panzer Vs (Panther), one recovery Panther and ten Maultiere.

2. Following a feinting attack on Targowiecze after unloading at Maciejow on March 27, my company and I moved ahead to Tupaly.

On March 29, at 8:30 A.M., the company was unexpectedly alerted. The commander of Grenadier-Regiment 434, Oberst Naber, issued battle orders to me at his command post at the same time. I was to be ready at 11 A.M. near Stare-Koszary to reach Moszone Kowel, by way of Czerkasy, with mounted volunteer assault teams of thirty men.

At the same time a frontal attack by the forward units was to take place. Artillery support from a detachment into the wooded areas northeast and southeast of Koszary and on Czerkasy and Moszone was also planned.

I drove immediately to the command post of III./SS-"Germania" and was briefed there by Sturmbannführer Hack on the terrain.

The terrain on both sides of the railroad line was deep swamp. I agreed with Sturmbannführer Hack to initially attack the heights and the woods one kilometer east of Stare-Koszary. After destroying the Pak front, I was to push ahead through the woods along the road with all Panzers and all of the Hack battalion and to reach Kowel. Sturmbannführer Dörr and the commander of the assault guns also agreed with this plan.

After the arrival of Obersturmbannführer Mühlenkamp at the Hack command post, a final decision was made at 10:30 A.M. I was to attack Czerkasy first, along the railroad line, and then, after scouting the terrain, to push ahead via Moszone to Kowel.

On the right flank, the Hack battalion with assault guns was to take the heights and the woods. To the left, the Bolm battalion was to follow the attack of the Panzer company with seven assault guns and secure the left flank.

Because of the lay of the terrain, I decided to assemble at the crossroads at the southeast edge of Stare-Koszary to attack initially to the east and break through the advanced enemy positions. Then swing to the north, reach the railroad line in the only swamp-free stretch of terrain, and attack the defensive positions west of Czerkasy to the right of the railroad line.

3. I started out at noon with sixteen Panzer Vs (Panthers) and thirty mounted assault team volunteers, broke through the forward enemy lines under heavy artillery, Pak, and mortar fire, and reached the railroad line with all Panzers as planned. Those of the enemy infantry not destroyed left their positions in the direction of the wooded areas.

During the further advance to the right of the railroad line, five Panzers got stuck in the swamp. They were ordered to secure the right flank with their guns against the wooded areas since our own infantry was not yet to be seen there. With the other Panzers, I attacked the heavily fortified positions, which were equipped with ten to twelve Paks, 600 meters west of Czerkasy. Three Panzers were disabled by enemy fire. The planned artillery support was not provided since the accompanying observer was unable to establish radio contact.

After knocking out all of the enemy guns, I reached the height at
2:30 P.M. and destroyed, with the help of the volunteer assault teams, the
infantry that had remained in the positions.

Because of heavy blowing snow and reduced visibility I remained on
the height for some forty-five minutes. At 3:30 P.M. I started a further
attack toward Czerkasy with the intention to circle the town to the right.
Since three more Panzers got stuck in the swamp, I crossed the railroad
line just north of Czerkasy and attacked the town, circling to the left.

After a short exchange of fire, the guns stopped firing. The western
edge of town was set on fire by our shells. Enemy infantry of approximately a thousand men left the town in northerly and easterly directions.
A reconnaissance assault was then executed in the direction of Moszone,
during which five Paks were knocked out and two Panzers got stuck in
the swamp. Around 4 P.M. the infantry of the Bolm battalion reached my
forward forces and asked for fire support to clear out the town. The
occupation and clearing was completed at 5:30 P.M. without encountering any significant resistance.

At approximately 6 P.M. I received the following radio message:
"Company to remain in Czerkasy and secure to the north, east, and
southeast." I then ordered the mobile Panzers to set up defensive lines to
the north and east and those stuck to the right of the railroad line to
secure the south. At dusk I ordered the towing of the stuck Panzers. In
the town we captured two abandoned Flak guns and four 7.62 infantry
guns as well as a number of mortars, antitank rifles, and horse-drawn
vehicles. Judging by the flares, the infantry to the south of the railroad
stood a fair distance to the west.

4. Calm set in around 7 P.M. At that time I judged the situation to be
the following:

> The target of attack, Czerkasy, has been reached as ordered by
> the regimental commander in his last radio message. At this
> time I have six fully serviceable Panzers; another three to four
> can be towed from the swamps within the next three to four
> hours. Because of the swamp, I cannot count on supplies of fuel
> and ammunition by Maultiere. Our own infantry has reached
> the height to my left and occupied Czerkasy. To my right, flares
> indicate our infantry far away.
>
> My scouting and reconnaissance sortie in the direction of
> Moszone has indicated that a further advance in this direction
> toward Kowel is almost impossible: 1.) because of the swamp, 2.)

because of fuel shortage and 3.) because of the strong resistance, which has begun to show there and which indicates that the enemy is expecting us in this direction.

The terrain to the east is also completely impassable, the same south of the railroad line to the edge of the woods. The enemy does not appear to have set up a further antitank defense to the south and east after the destruction of his three-line Pak position of sixteen guns west of Czerkasy. None of my stuck Panzers were fired upon despite a favorable firing distance.

It is not probable that the Paks could be towed during the night to block the railroad embankment because of difficult terrain. In addition, the enemy is not expected there because of the scouting sortie in the direction of Moszone where the enemy retreated from Czerkasy.

Thus, the embankment is the only passable way, and least obstructed by defense, to Kowel but only if it is still used tonight. I have been made aware of the situation at Kowel by radio; it is so ominous that provision of heavy weapons has become imperative.

I will set out at approximately 10 P.M. and push along the railway embankment toward Kowel. Doing this, I will not be abiding by the last received order to defend Czerkasy. But I will be acting within the intent of the original plan of attack, to reach Kowel.

Around 7:45 P.M. Hauptmann Bolm made contact and advised me that he had sent patrols in the direction of the wooded areas east of Czerkasy. So far they had not reported enemy contact. Hauptmann Bolm inquired about my intentions and advised that he would set out with me at 10 P.M. along the embankment.

At approximately 10 P.M. the regiment discontinued contact. Radio communications would be reestablished on March 30; we were to be ready to march then also. At the same time I was told that my company would not see any action March 30.

Since the salvaging of the Panzers was greatly delayed, I sent word to Hauptmann Bolm's infantry that I would set out only at 4 the next morning.

At 3 A.M. on March 30, I had available nine mobile Panzers. With these I started out in a column at 4 A.M. along the embankment.

The infantry of Hauptmann Bolm followed to the left of the embankment and deployed toward the wooded areas behind the Panzers. Two kilometers east of Czerkasy we received fire from two enemy tanks in the woods to the right of the embankment. After destroying them, we lost two Panzers to mines during the further advance. The infantry, which had stayed back during the firefight, then moved ahead of the Panzers to form a safety net that included the railroad station and woods to its east as well as the ammunition dump to the right of the railroad embankment. Enemy resistance was minimal.

A mine barrier was cleared up at 6 A.M. by an assault team of pioneers. Hauptmann Bolm advised me he had orders not to advance any further. I explained to him that I could not stop and continued on, the accompanying assault teams riding on the Panzers. I had ordered the two Panzers rendered immobile by the mines, under the command of Oberscharführer Fass, to commence preparations for repairs and to defend the Czerkasy railroad station at the same time. This was to keep the railroad embankment open for the Panzers following behind. Hauptmann Bolm provided me with infantry for the close-in defense of the Panzers.

When my Panzer spearhead had approached to within 2 kilometers of Kowel, I received the following radio message: "Order from the battalion commander, stop the Panzers." This message had been shouted to the commander of the trailing Panzer by a messenger sent by Hauptmann Bolm and was relayed to me by radio. My leading Panzers were already engaged in battle with enemy infantry and antitank riflemen who cut off the northwest exit of the city. Shortly thereafter, a violent firefight developed with ten to twelve Flak and artillery guns from a line roughly Kowel-Moszone. For these reasons, it was impossible for me to stop and I disregarded the message from Hauptmann Bolm. Apart from that, he was not my superior.

The threat to our left flank was temporarily neutralized by heavy blowing snow. At the same time, the enemy positions, blocking the way ahead of the advanced position of Strecker, were destroyed. Again, the accompanying assault teams performed excellently.

The contact with the infantry of Hauptmann Bolm was lost.

At approximately 7:30 A.M. we reached the loop in the railway and linked up with Hauptmann Strecker. After acceding to some special requests regarding support in fighting the enemy's defensive forces in the northwest of the city, I pulled into Gille's command post and reported to the group leader (Generalleutnant) at 8:15 A.M.

UNTERSTURMFÜHRER RENZ, LEADER OF THE PANZER-AUFK-LÄRUNGSZUG (RECONNAISSANCE PLATOON) OF THE II. ABTEILUNG, DESCRIBES BREAKTHROUGH OF PANZER-REGI-MENT "WIKING" TO KOWEL ON APRIL 4 AND 5

In the afternoon of April 4, I was ordered to report to the commander of the Abteilung, Obersturmführer Pätsch, and received directions to join the attack with my two reconnaissance Panthers, as my other Panzers had not yet arrived. I was to be the adjutant, since Obersturmführer Förster had dropped out due to a sudden illness. We started out at 4:35 P.M. behind the 6. and 7. Companies and reached, at good speed, Moszone, which was the starting point of our major attack.

Initially, the two companies had to break only minor enemy resistance and reached, with the staff of the Abteilung, the area of Moszone in the evening hours. There, we set up positions and prepared, at the same time, for the breakthrough to Kowel. I received authorization from the commander of the Abteilung to join the spearhead of the attack by the 6. Company under Hauptsturmführer Reichert with the Grossrock platoon. It was hoped that my detailed knowledge of the terrain would make it possible to determine the best route for the southern Panzer spearhead to the northern edge of Kowel. The commander of the regiment succeeded, even during the night, to break through to the northwest of Kowel with two command Panzers and without enemy contact. However, the Panzer of the commander was damaged by mines and had to be secured. In the early hours of the morning we started out at dawn and tried, along the dirt road Moszone-Kowel, to secure terrain in southeasterly and easterly directions toward Kowel.

"Adler (eagle)—Adler—come in . . . Falke (falcon) moves to the point together with Sperber (sparrow hawk)!" With this radio message I joined the attack of the 6. Company.

The skyline of Kowel was indistinct in the distance. The river Turja runs through the city, which is located in flat swampy terrain, from north to south. The river's many tributaries and branches create the large swamp around Kowel, which is bordered by wooded areas.

In between the swampy areas, large tracts of woods formed an almost insurmountable obstacle for a large-scale Panzer attack.

Kowel was one of the most important railroad junctions in White Russia and as such an important strategic point for all military operations. The railway line Lublin-Kowel, with its elevated embankment to the north and northwest of the city, formed a natural protective wall. At the same time, it offered firm ground to drive on. The barracks installations in the northern part of the city were barely recognizable in the morning haze. They stuck out of the city's skyline and formed a natural defensive position. The height, located in the northeast area of town, controlled the northern and some of the eastern approaches to the city.

My men sat tensely in the Panzer, observing the battleground and the road. Radio communications between the individual units of the regiment were excellent, and the progress of our Panzer spearhead succeeded, almost by the book, without great difficulties on its way to Kowel in a southeasterly direction. In the meantime, I had moved to the center of the company in order to be able to reach the point as quickly as possible. The terrain did not allow speeds of more than twenty to thirty kilometers per hour in particular as the drivers pushed ahead only with the greatest of care, using any light and dry-looking spots as more secure ground. Luck was with us, and, to the detriment of the Russians, all of the terrain was still very solidly frozen and partially covered with snow.

"Bussard (buzzard) to Falke . . ."

What's happening now, I thought. Hauptsturmführer Reichert sent an emergency call on the radio. He was stuck in the swamp right up to the tracks. All the Panzers ahead of me did not stop but pushed on carefully, like waddling ducks, in first gear across a very soft-looking swampy spot. Their chief got stuck to the right of the path and could not free himself without help. Gunner Bahrmann and another crew member ran wildly around the Panzer, carrying a tow cable. I stopped on a dry-looking patch of ground at a safe distance and ordered my driver to back up slowly in order to pull out Reichert. Our 700-horsepower engine howled wildly, and regrettably much too loud, as we began to move, again under enemy fire.

The tow cable snapped with a violent noise, and the forty-four tons of Reichert's Panzer slid backward again into the churned-up ground. We were lucky. My deft driver had given our Panzer full throttle, and we jumped ahead with a jerk so that we were safe from sinking in at that time. The dear "Ivans" then steadily fired on us from the northern edge. I directed two more Panzers by radio to come closer, and then Bahrmann, two other crew members, and I, on our stomachs, crawled over to bring in two tow cables. Just as we were crawling, the crew of one of the Panzers of Grossrock's platoon threw us another cable. The men were quick as weasels and, amazingly, succeeded in attaching the cables. We had suffered no losses until then, despite the ever-increasing fire. We were lucky. The rising terrain somewhat blocked the enemy's field of vision so that his fire went rather wildly into the blue. The second attempt, employing three tow cables, succeeded, accompanied by a stream of insults from the laughing Bahrmann who, despite the somewhat ticklish situation, watched the entire show from his turret hatch. In any case the company commander was once again in on the party. The terrain had improved somewhat. I was able to catch up with Grossrock, who had moved his Panzer into the point position after a few hundred meters. Grossrock had noticed that something had gone wrong and slowed down. We agreed on our tactics with a few words. In accordion formation, offering covering fire to each other, we pushed at fair speed, always at full throttle and carefully overcoming the difficult terrain, toward Kowel. I drove ahead of the five Panzers of Grossrock's platoon in my "chain-dog." There was full daylight then, and the gun barrels were never silent. The Russians had recognized our intentions and seemed to have moved all available forces to the northern edge of Kowel. They tried, with all their weapons blazing, to prevent their final destruction. Heavy Pak forces were in position at a cluster of buildings at Dubowj, located on the road Kowel-Brest-Litowsk. From there a sustained barrage originated. These buildings were the main defensive positions of the Russians at the northern edge of the city. It appeared they had set up several Pak fronts there to stop our breakthrough. The Pak fire was quite accurate.

During our next forward move, we took a hit, which, luckily, only rattled our Panzer. My gunner reacted with lightning speed. I directed him, patting his shoulder with my right hand, exactly to the target. With "Explosive shells—800 meters—cluster of buildings, Pak position in front—fire!" we began the firefight. Our first shot was dead-on. A huge cloud of dust, mixed with fragments of trees and building material, rose into the sky. Being the point Panzer, I directed the fire of the whole 6. Company by radio. Grossrock followed my gunner with the fire from his five Panthers, and within a few minutes we managed to stop the fire from the Paks and tanks. Afterwards it was determined that we had destroyed several tanks, approximately ten Paks, and numerous heavy and light machine guns.

There was no holding me back. "Sperber, Sperber come in . . . request fire cover for a push to the northern edge of the barracks across the road Kowel-Brest-Litowsk!" Grossrock agreed and immediately gave fire cover to my "chain-dog." At full speed I tried to get across the dangerous road as the first Panzer. The "Ivan" had not yet been silenced completely. Several Pak shells hit the ground somewhere in front of my Panzer. All of the 6. Company, listening in, then fired shells and smoke grenades from all available barrels. Suddenly, there was a terrible explosion and an immense cloud of smoke rose at the northern edge of Kowel. A fuel and ammunition dump had blown up. Taking advantage of the situation, we pushed ahead even faster. Just before the road embankment, we were hit. Our armor withstood this hit, too. There was no choice but to join the firefight; my gunner did not need orders for that. He had accurately spotted the Pak position. Within a few seconds, the enemy, 400 meters away, was destroyed with the first shot. In order to cross the road without being fired on, we deployed smoke. We succeeded in crossing the elevated road and reached a position on the other side of the embankment. The Russians were on the run. Their infantry tried to withdraw to the east. Grossrock, under covering fire from the other Panzers, then dared to jump across the road. Within fifteen minutes we had knocked out six enemy tanks east of the road.

After another half hour the remaining enemy resistance along the whole northern edge of Kowel was broken. We could deploy to secure the northeastern edge of the city, north of the barracks. From these excellent positions we were able to, for quite a while, lay fire on the enemy fleeing to the woods located north of Kowel, achieving good results.

The company received orders to remain there until the arrival of the 7. Company. Suddenly, an armored reconnaissance vehicle showed up on the road. It had a strange-looking pedestal built inside. Our most forward Panzer first took aim at it from 500 meters. Promptly, our own signal flares were fired. It turned out that it was Oberstleutnant Hoffmann of the 4. Panzer-Division with a film reporter. He was on the way to the Gille command post in Kowel. Toward evening we pulled into Kowel, where the liberated garrison offered us an enthusiastic welcome.

Defensive Fighting
East of Warsaw, 1944

MARTIN STEIGER, PANZER COMMANDER 1./SS-PANZER-REGIMENT 3, REPORTS

Our transport arrived in Warsaw without difficulties. It was already midnight when we began the unloading. The rest of the Abteilung also arrived during this night and was again incorporated into the "T" Division. The division had been in action without a break for a full year and was urgently expecting the new "Panther-Abteilung." Battle orders to the Abteilung were issued around midnight of the next day.

We had to get to Siedlce as quickly as possible. There, a strong thrust by the Russians threatened to break through the German lines protruding to the east.

It was about eighty kilometers from Warsaw to Siedlce. We rolled just after noon, in burning heat, and reached the edge of the city of Siedlce around 3 P.M. What we saw during this race to the front describes the situation more accurately than the most detailed report. Fleeing soldiers, female communications operators, civilian workers of the "Organisation Todt," and railway personnel crowded the retreat route. Some of the shouts from the masses flooding backward hit us like whips: "Warmongers—we're going home—we've had enough." Others, however, were more encouraging: "Drive them back, the Russians . . ." etc. As we rolled into the center of the city, heavy Russian artillery fire came down as a greeting to welcome us. The city appeared to have already been deserted by German soldiers. Enemy tanks were reported.

We halted in the town center, and the platoon leaders were called to the chief of the company. Orders were issued:

"A German Army staff is encircled in Brest-Litowsk, our mission is to free them. The Abteilung, with the 1. Company at the point, will advance in a southeasterly direction at 8 P.M. Obersturmführer Schramm will command the point platoon; Oberscharführer Ober will be in the point vehicle. The enemy is holding positions with strong forces behind the railroad line."

We had barely crossed the railroad line at dusk when, at very close distance, destructive defensive firing started. The lead Panzer was knocked out, while two T-34s were also left burning on the road. Chaos seemed to set in. In the bright light of the burning tanks, we were clearly visible targets. The leader of the 2. Platoon, Untersturmführer von Rennenkampf, was critically wounded when he left his Panzer, as were some commanders and crew. The attack had failed; we had to return to Siedlce. A breakthrough succeeded only during the next day via Mordy to Losice, with heavy losses. Oberscharführer Kessler's crew was reported missing. Unterscharführer Massarei and Sturmmann Koser were killed, and Sturmmann Robel was killed by a shell fragment while under his Panzer in Siedlce.

When we joined up again with the company three days later, the noncom in charge had the sad duty to write off a large part of the company as dead, missing, or wounded. On July 28, our chief was given the office of tank defense commander of the almost-lost city of Siedlce. During the afternoon of the same day, the sad news reached us that Riefkogel had been critically wounded by a grenade fragment and died a few hours later at the main field dressing station. His noncom in charge, who had still seen him alive there, conveyed his last words to the company:

"Take my greetings to my proud company. Obersturmführer Schramm is to lead it from now on in my spirit."

Siedlce fell into Russian hands on July 29. The Russians pushed with strong forces, and violent battles occurred again near Stanislaw. A concentrated attack by the "Wiking" and "Totenkopf" Divisions among Stanislaw, Okuniew, and Radzymin made it possible to destroy the enemy.

The "Wiking" and "Totenkopf" Divisions were assigned to the newly established general command IV., SS-Panzerkorps Gille, on August 10.

The Korps was put into defensive action east of Warsaw. Enemy artillery fire hammered for days as, attack after attack, the Russians rolled against our already very weak lines. The superiority of the enemy was immense.

The gaps along the front grew larger, often a grenadier only every 100 to 200 meters.

Once again, we played the firefighters of the east.

We lived from one attack to the next, from one shortening of the front to the next. Withdrawals of a few kilometers were followed by counterattacks to relieve neighboring units.

We stood thrity kilometers east of Warsaw and held off the Russian masses with only a few Panzers left.

Enemy tanks, growing in numbers like flies, broke through, destroyed supply units, and kept fighting well behind our lines. We were thrown at them, knocked them out, and lost some more of our Panzers in the process. When we returned again to where our main front line had been only the day before when we left it, we found it captured already by the Russians. This happened almost every day. The losses of men and Panzers were staggering.

A new order awaited us at the Abteilung command post.

ATTACK ALONG THE MAIN ROUTE WARSAW-BIALYSTOCK

We looked at each other and suppressed a curse. During that counterattack Schramm was wounded in the head but was able to continue to lead the company.

Still, during the same night, we moved out to secure the wooded area near the fork in the road Radzymin-Wola. The next day Russian tanks attacked us. All of them were knocked out by us at 200 meters away. Then, commander Meierdress called us back to Radzymin to take over securing the rear for two days. But another tank alert came from the front.

Russian tanks were preparing for an attack in Guzowattka. We advanced and reached the town around 3 P.M. without having seen any enemy tanks. Instead, we were welcomed by strong defensive fire, during which our comrade Hans Baumeister was killed in the loader's hatch by a shell fragment. The front was retaken toward evening. Obersturmbannführer Säumenicht, who had led the Abteilung for the past year, was killed during the night of August 25 to 26. The losses of the other companies were equally high. The 2. Company had only five commanders left, the 3. Company had six, and the 4. Company had only three. Obersturmführer Lumitsch, chief of the 4. Company, was wounded seriously.

Only three commanders were left in the 1. Company: Schramm, Lizjewski, and Schäfer.

For two days we secured the exit of the city of Radzymin. Then came an urgent alert from the neighboring Division "Wiking" on our left.

The enemy had broken through in its sector.

During the night we rolled to the main front line of the "Wiking" division.

Several salvos from the "Stalin organs" (rocket launchers) hammered into our assembled Panzers.

Zeitler's Panzer had to be returned to the repair company. Because of this, the 1. Company was split into two Kampfgruppen: one Kampfgruppe under Schramm, the other under Herbatschek. It fought near Nadma for several days until the commander, Obersturmbannführer Lachmann, united the company again after one week.

A forced march of forty kilometers brought us close to Serock on the Bug River. The Russians had again broken through the "Wiking" division.

In unit formation, together with the supply vehicles, we started out on the march during the night. During that night we lost another one of our Panzers. The Panzer of Unterscharführer Köster burned out completely, caused by fuel line damage. At dawn the attack began in the area where the enemy had broken through. In the evening, the front was straightened again. The company knocked out several enemy tanks during this action and brought back the tractors that had been captured by the Russians. The short night hours were spent in a small wooded area. Another forced march of eighty kilometers to the gates of Warsaw was scheduled for 4 A.M.

The enemy had occupied the suburbs of Warsaw. We moved again toward the south.

We rolled through Jablonna, along the paved road, then through smaller towns whose names were almost unpronounceable, and reached Zapky in the late afternoon.

We refueled once more in great haste and took on provisions. The supply vehicles were barely out of sight when the Russians opened up a barrage. Meierdress, the Abteilung commander, ordered the 1. Company into the suburb of Praga to an important fork in the road. There, we experienced a veritable hell for hours. The heaviest calibers of the Russian artillery hammered away at the fork in the road. We had received the strictest order to hold the position. The front was once more in retreat. German troops flooded backward along the arterial route, and the Russians pursued them in regimental strength, accompanied by several tanks. Because of the restricted visibility, we could fire at them only from a very close distance.

The grilling heat had made staying inside the Panzer a real torture until an evening thunderstorm roared over the city. Very soon it turned pitch-dark, and a few Russian assault guns, type SU 85, dared to break through. At a distance of only thirty meters, the first one was knocked out and the second turned back immediately. At about 3 A.M. we received orders by radio to return to Zapky. The Russians had broken through there in the meantime and threatened us from the flank. Demands for Panzers came from everywhere—but we had so few of them. The entire Abteilung was scattered. It operated in company or platoon strength in the various sectors, and no one knew the whereabouts of the others. Only the Abteilung commander, Sturmbannführer Meierdress, had control and the total picture.

We had to change radio frequencies almost every day. The Russians were interfering and broadcast many false orders and directives.

We started a counteroffensive near Zapky, straightened the front once more, and knocked out some tanks. There we discovered that a new type of tank, the "Stalin 1," had made its appearance. It was to cause us severe problems.

REPORT BY HAUPTSTURMFÜHRER HANS FLÜGEL ON THE PANZER ACTION WITH SS-PANZER-REGIMENT 5 "WIKING," EAST OF WARSAW IN AUGUST 1944

With our withdrawal in August 1944 via Stanislawowo, we reached the area east of Warsaw in the middle of August. Our Panzer-abteilung was positioned between the neighboring "Totenkopf" and "Wiking" divisions.

On August 16 the Russians laid barrages of artillery and mortar fire on the whole sector of the Abteilung. The location of our positions was extremely unfavorable. At our back was a river which, by itself, was a formidable obstacle to Panzers. The enemy succeeded in pushing past us and breaking into the neighboring positions of the "Totenkopf" division.

The Abteilung was stretched out. The 7. Company with the Abteilung staff was located in a wooded area. The other companies were positioned in the open to secure the divisional sector behind the river sector. From there, they were to conduct individual assaults and defensive movements against the attacking enemy.

The pressure by the enemy grew stronger and stronger. We noticed that we had been outflanked after our neighbors had withdrawn. The artillery, which had been to our rear, had also pulled back. The enemy thrust had grown so strong that we could no longer disengage.

All company chiefs had been ordered to report to the Abteilung command post to receive important orders. With me were Nicolussi-Leck, Grossrock, Schneider with Olin, and the Abteilung's medical doctor, Dr. Kalbskopf. The meeting began prior to the subsequent barrages that the Russians laid on our sector.

My Panzer had received damage to the back gears and was out of action at the repair shop. There was no time for goodbyes at the briefing. The sudden onset of a Russian barrage denied me any possibility of an effective organization. The chief of 8. Company received a shell fragment in the right thigh, was unable to go on, and was taken into my Panzer. The chief of 6. Company, Martin, died as a result of enemy action. He had been transporting prisoners to the command post for identification in an armored vehicle when a prisoner blew himself up with a hand grenade, fatally wounding Martin in the process. The company was then taken over by Grossrock.

During this total confusion I only had the chance to say to our Dr. Kalbskopf: "Doc, look after the removal of the staff units. Try to cross the river by the bridge."

The Abteilung immediately began a counterattack against the attacking enemy.

The Russians carried out one air attack after the other. They dropped aerial mines among our Panzers, severely damaging the transmissions of some. We took losses and with the infantry no longer with us, were completely on our own.

The enemy attacked across Hill 99 with infantry and tanks. The 7. Company, under Schneider and Olin, deployed to hold our hedgehog position for as long as was necessary to establish clearly what had happened in the meantime on our left and right flanks.

Thank God, we had scouted the terrain some days previously in order to be prepared for any contingencies. We did not plan to withdraw across a river that was impassable to Panzers.

The Russian infantry pushed into the wooded areas to our rear after the enemy had established a bridgehead across the river, which should have been held by our neighbor "Totenkopf." We were exposed to pistol fire and were able to move our Panzers only short distances. Large-scale attacks or relief actions were out of the question.

Fortunately, good radio contact with the regiment and the division still existed. I was able to brief them accurately on the situation. The regiment and the artillery both promised relief, but all was without success!

In the afternoon we were almost in Russian hands. I ordered:

"No one leaves the Panzer; no one is to get out of the Panzer."

We stopped all scouting activity by the Panzer crews. Our only objective then was to protect each other.

Around 2 P.M. we heard an explosion from the direction of my immobile Panzer. Immediately, we set out with two Panzers to determine what had happened. We found that the crew, having fired its last shell, had blown itself up along with its Panzer.

We were totally preoccupied with remaining in some kind of firing position and with holding our positions. Using our last battery power, we were able to arrange with the division that we would begin withdrawing in the evening around seven o'clock. We were to try to join up with the regiment and the main body of the division which had dug in at a new sector fifteen kilometers behind us.

Time went by very slowly. Our supply of ammunition dwindled quickly, and the fuel supply shrunk. We agreed to fire only when absolutely necessary.

The Russian columns marched past us along a railroad embankment. Everyone marching on the embankment used whatever he had, hand grenade or submachine gun, and threw it or fired it at us. Our crews had to endure it and just watch, firing back was allowed only as a last resort.

Dusk set in around 7 P.M. The division had promised a surprise concentrated fire across, onto, and in front of Hill 99 to support our first attempt to break out in the direction of Tluscz. I had decided that there was no choice but to drive along with the Russian tank forces at attack speed toward our own division.

We drove through a railroad underpass to our left. Zugführer Grossrock had orders to push two Panzers through the underpass, knock out a few Russian tanks in their column, and thus enable our Panzers to get through. Thereafter, we wanted to deploy and join the Russian attack in the direction of our own lines.

Dusk had fallen. Grossrock himself, as could have been expected from him, was at the point. He had barely left the underpass when his Panzer was knocked out by a direct hit. I assumed that it had been a high explosive shell with high penetration power. The Panzer was almost glowing. Badly burned Grossrock managed to get out of the Panzer. The crew was also able to save itself and was taken into other Panzers.

Our attempt to break out had failed. The remains of my Panzerabteilung stood, Panzer next to Panzer, to discuss the next attempt by radio. We were well camouflaged but there was no rush in any case. was No one was in a position to offer us help. Our own sudden fire attack did not materialize. As it turned out later, the artillery had been forced to leap its position once again.

The second attempt to break out went in the direction of our former neighbor, the "Totenkopf-Division," toward the bridge. Russian tanks had already crossed the bridge and were to our rear, on the other side of the river. I thought to myself: "What they can do, we can do as well!"

Schicker, my adjutant, took the point position. I drove closely behind him. Schicker had barely driven for a hundred meters when his Panzer dropped headfirst into a large bomb crater. The turret mount jammed. Schicker's hand was caught in the mount, and he was severely injured. It was impossible to salvage his Panzer. It had to be blown up and Schicker was taken on board my Panzer, which was getting quite crowded with Grossrock, Schneider, and their crews as well.

This attempt to break out also failed. We had no other choice but to push across the river in the direction of Tluscz to reach our own lines. Radio contact had been lost.

The decision for the final attempt to break out was made around 2 A.M. and discussed in detail. Our Panzers were equipped with side skirts, consisting of armor plate, to protect the tracks. They were to play a special role during our breakout action. We agreed to sink the side skirts in the river to provide the tracks with a firm surface to travel on. Two four-barrel Flak guns were to secure the crossing of the river.

During the course of the night, strong enemy tank activity took place in close proximity. The Russians fired flares of all colors above us, and we were glad when some of the fog, caused by the river, moved in. Under its cover we were able to conduct some close-up scouting. This, of course, had to be done on foot. With great care we felt our way through the Russians in order to locate a spot where the river could be forded by Panzers. I took a few platoon leaders and company chiefs to the river to determine the exact spot where to cross. We did not get very far. On the opposite bank of the river a Russian battalion had made camp. They were preparing to follow the Russian spearhead which, as I was to learn later, was already in the process of taking Tluscz.

The four-barrel Flak guns were moved up and positioned side-by-side. Then we sank some of the side skirts in the river. It was really a scene of great confusion. The Russians did not know who was friend or foe. At the firing of a previously agreed-on flare, our two four-barrel Flak guns fired to clear the crossing spot. The element of surprise, and the panic of the Russians, helped us greatly as we forded the river with the first Panzers, which were hooked up to the ones behind by cable.

When the first Panzers had reached the opposite shore, they first cleared the area and then pulled all the other Panzers across. We were left with nine Panzers. We halted for a while and then decided to try to cross the railroad embankment alongside which there was a good path in the direction of Tluscz.

The Panzer of commandant Förster was brought ahead to run a scouting sortie across the embankment. Everything happened very slowly and carefully; we had a lot of time until dawn. When Förster had reached the embankment after about 300 meters, looking to locate the path to Tluscz, his Panzer exploded with an immense bang. Virtually thrown into the air, it crashed down the embankment headfirst and remained there, immobile. Without regard to what might happen next, we advanced and covered Förster's Panzer. It looked terrible. Several explosive charges had been thrown at the Panzer, which had run off its tracks. Förster had lost his legs; they were mangled and torn. He said to me:

"Hauptsturmführer, I've had it. I'm reporting off duty!"

With only eight Panzers left, we were forced to scout in the direction of Tluscz. The order of the commander was to check out the capacity of a small bridge across a river close by. At first light, the 7. Company pushed its Panzer ahead. When the Panzer reached the bridge, Russians suddenly jumped out of the bushes and immobilized the Panzer by using explosive charges. The crew was able to bail out under cover of the other Panzers and get back to us. Our ammunition was running out. All I had left were a few flares. We watched from our position as the Russians advanced toward Tluscz with several tanks on which infantry had mounted. We had no choice but to drive across the terrain, covered with bushes and small trees, in the same direction to reach our own lines again. My last flare was meant to show our comrades that it was not Russian but our own Panzers approaching. Our remaining seven Panzers were overcrowded with wounded and the extra crews. I decided to drive at high speed toward our own lines in the same direction as the Russians.

Starting out, we noticed the noise of battle some two kilometers away.

I immediately ordered our signal flag hoisted. Luckily, our own infantry recognized us right away, and we were able to rejoin our main front line without further losses. We had sustained terrible losses of materiel, and all company leaders had been lost, some wounded. Fortunately, we had been able to bring back all the dead and wounded with us.

Only two hours later I was on my way again with new orders. The 5. Company under Karl-Heinz Lichte was experiencing heavy pressure. My own Panzer had given out and was at the repair company for an overhaul. Thus, I took a Panzer of the regimental staff and helped create some room to allow our own troops to withdraw to new positions.

THE DEATH OF PANZERS AT THE NAREW RIVER

A battle report on the action in the "Wet Triangle" on September 6, 1944, north of Serock, during the defensive battle for Warsaw:

SS-Obersturmführer Ola Olin, a Finnish volunteer, was ready for action in the assembly area at Gut Male with three Panthers; his own 711, Panther 714 under its commander Hans Wolf, and 734 with its commander Willi Bückle.

After the collapse of Heeresgruppe Mitte (Army Group Centre) the Soviet tank units pushed with all their might toward the attack objectives of Warsaw and the Weichsel River. The pressure at the Narew River increased daily, and strong tank units were attempting a deep penetration there. During these bitter battles, accompanied by barrages and heavy fighter-bomber attacks, 240 enemy tanks and assault guns were destroyed in the two previous days. Dramatic scenes of defense and attack took place there at the steep shores of the Narew and further downstream where the Russians tried to cross the stream and form a bridgehead. Grenadiers, armed with panzerfausts and antitank mines, waited in their foxholes and repeatedly inflicted heavy losses on the enemy. In the fields and in the woods along the Narew sat the wrecks of tanks, T-34s, Shermans from the United States, and the new Stalin tanks. Some still smoldered, burning out slowly. These wrecks formed an iron front behind which the grenadiers found welcome cover from the barrages of the artillery. But the Soviet units continued their attacks with newly brought-in tanks.

Soviet tanks had broken through our lines in a village in front of us and were assembling in a wooded area from where they threatened our supplies and heavy batteries. At that moment our three Panzers received the order to counterattack. We counted fifteen enemy tanks, rolling toward us across the adjoining fields. When the last of the enemy tanks had left the cover of the woods, the time had come for the Panthers of the "Wiking."

Shell after shell howled out of the 7.5-cm guns, and within a short time six tanks stood in flames in the terrain ahead of us. The Russians were in a panic. Their engines roared; they wanted to save their remaining tanks from destruction. This flight succeeded for only a few meters before the next tank sat smoking in the open fields. The wrecks obscured the field of fire, so we had to leave our cover. "Full throttle—march!" Three more were knocked out by the Panthers, and three others fell victim to the valiant grenadiers and their antitank mines. They had arrived on the battlefield from the flank. Two Russian tanks were stuck. Abandoned by their crews, we captured them.

The result of this September 6 battle north of Serock on the Narew: Ten T-34s knocked out and two captured by three Panthers of the 7. Company of Panzer-Regiment 5 "Wiking."

PART II

Panzer Actions in Normandy and the Ardennes

On the Battleground of Caen

The young Panzer soldiers of Panzer-Regiment 12, SS-Panzer-Division "Hitlerjugend," earned everlasting glory during their heroic battle against the numerical superiority of the Allied invasion troops. . . .

Only parts of Panzer-Regiment 12 reached the assembly area southwest of Caen on June 6. This was due to the initial transfer of the 12. SS-Panzer-Division "Hitlerjugend" into the assembly area at Bernay-Lisieux-Vimoutiers and the subsequent move to the area southwest of Caen. Additional delays were caused by constant fighter-bomber attacks and the extra spacing required between the vehicles because of these attacks.

The II. Panzer-Abteilung, equipped with Panzer IVs, arrived during the night of June 6 and morning of June 7. The I. Abteilung, equipped with Panthers, was still far behind at that time.

Brigadeführer (major general) Witt, commander of the 12. SS-Panzer-Division, issued orders in the afternoon, after a briefing by the I. SS-Panzerkorps, to the 12. SS-Panzer-Division for the attack on June 7 at 4 P.M.:

"Attack the enemy on the left of the railroad line Caen–Luc sur Mer and drive him into the sea!"

Panzer-Regiment 12 received orders to support the attack along a wide front together with those parts of the II. Abteilung that had arrived in the meantime. The battle command post of the commander of this Kampfgruppe, Standartenführer (colonel) Kurt Meyer, was set up in the Ardennes Abbey.

Around 10 A.M. on June 7, the first Panzer IVs of the II. Abteilung arrived. Sturmbannführer Prinz reported some fifty Panzers ready for action and rolling into their assembly areas. In the meantime the enemy had assembled for the attack on Caen. The first engagements took place, and the first Panzers were lost. Untersturmführer Porsch was on reconnaissance with four Panzer IVs of the 5./Panzer-Regiment 12 along the road Franqueville-Authie when he suddenly encountered Shermans of the Sherbrooke Fusiliers at approximately 2 P.M. They knocked out three of his Panzers during a short firefight. It had become impossible to wait for the planned start of the attack at 4 P.M. The commander of Panzer Regiment 12, Obersturmbannführer Max Wünsche, ordered the attack by radio from his command Panzer to all Panzers of the Panzer companies of the II. Abteilung. "Panzers—march!" The 6. Company and the 5. Company, immediately to the left of the Ardennes Abbey, set out without delay. Their fire caught the surprised enemy in its left flank. Within a short time, several Shermans were in flames and exploded.

The 6. Company knocked out more than ten enemy tanks and lost five of its own Panzer IVs.

STURMMANN HANS FENN, GUNNER IN THE I. ZUG (PLATOON) 6./PANZER-REGIMENT 12, REPORTS ON THIS BATTLE

In the meantime, Obersturmführer Gasch had joined us with the rest of the company and took over the lead of the point platoon. We took a lot of prisoners, whom we sent back to the grenadiers without getting out of our Panzers. We advanced farther through gently rolling terrain and suddenly entered a plain with the I. Zug and came under fire from Canadian Paks. Four Panzer IVs of my platoon caught on fire immediately. Ours, the fifth Panzer, took a direct hit between the side of the hull and the turret when we made the mistake of trying to turn around under Pak fire after we had been unable to knock out the Canadian Paks firing from 1,500 to 2,000 meters. The shell ripped a leg off my commander, Oberscharführer Esser. As I heard later, he managed to get out of the turret. The incendiary shell immediately set fire to all parts of the Panzer. I lost consciousness. The rubber bag at my gunner's hatch prevented me from getting out immediately since it had melted and jammed the hatch. Somehow, I managed, without being fully conscious, to crawl over to the hatch of the loader. I could only remember clearly the moment when I dropped headfirst out of the hatch to the ground. With bad, third-degree burns, I walked back toward our advancing grenadiers. They looked at me as if I were a ghost, which was how I must have looked. Our medic took me back to the field hospital in the chief's car.

In the evening, the Kampfgruppe of Panzer-Grenadier-Regiment 25 with II./Panzer-Regiment 12 held defensive positions stretching from the railroad line Caen–Luc sur Mer to the Rue Nationale (national road) No. 13 from Caen to Bayeux. It had been possible to stop the attack by the British and Canadians north and northwest of Caen, and to drive back the tank spearhead, which had pushed right through to the Carpiquet airdrome, with heavy losses to the enemy. The war diary of the "North Nova Scotians" reported twenty-seven lost tanks. Our own losses were fourteen Panzer IVs.

Two companies of Panthers of the I./Panzer-Regiment 12 arrived on June 8.

The divisional commander, Witt, had ordered an attack on Bretteville by Panzer-Grenadier-Regiment 25, supported by two Panther companies, for the night of June 8 and morning of June 9. Because of the increasing Allied air superiority, and in order to surprise the enemy, the Kampfgruppe assembled in the falling darkness around 10 P.M. The 1. and 4. Companies of Pz. Rgt. 12, with mounted motorcycle riflemen, drove at high speed across the flat terrain of le-Bourg. The area was free of enemy forces and could be crossed without any delays. When the first Panthers reached the edge of Bretteville, they encountered strong Pak fire, which set one of them on fire. Max Wünsche ordered the 1. Company to swing left, bypass the town, and push into the town center from the southwest. The leader of the I. Platoon of the 1. Company reports on this night action and close combat:

> I received orders by radio from Hauptsturmführer Berlin to push into the town from the west. Some houses at the town's southern edge and the railroad station were already on fire. I ordered the breakthrough as fast as possible in order to offer only a short-time target in front of the burning buildings. Despite this, all three Panthers took Pak hits almost simultaneously from the edge of town to our right. The Panther on the right burned like a torch, probably a hit to the engine compartment. The crew managed to bail out. My Panzer took a penetrating hit to the turret. The loader was badly wounded; he was blinded. The electrical system failed. The Panther on the left only took a hit to the track fender and stayed mobile. I reported to the chief of the company, Berlin, by radio and was ordered to return. In the center of town stood a Panther of the 4. Company, burnt out and still glowing.

Gunner Lengheim of the second Panther, III. Platoon of the 1. Company, experienced the night attack in this way:

> We fired from all barrels. The second platoon, under Untersturmführer Teichert, attacked south of the town. We were more to the west. Zugführer Dittrich, in Panzer #135, ordered us by radio to follow his vehicle. Teichert was immobilized inside the town, surrounded by enemy infantry. His Panzer had received a hit to its tracks. We followed Panzer #135 to get Teichert out.

Panzer #135 took a hit from a row of bushes some 100 meters away and the crew had to abandon it. All of them, except for the radio operator, made it.

Obstructed by the heavy smoke from the knocked-out Panzer, we fired a few shells in the direction of the bushes. Untersturm-führer Dittrich and his crew came running toward our Panzer and waved us back out of the range of fire of the Canadians. Through my sight I saw a veritable wall of fire moving toward us from about 900 meters away. There was no time to think, load—fire, load—fire, as fast as possible, until it was all over for us as well. Hits to the slanted front armor and the gun ruined its adjustment; our fire lay way short. The next hit went exactly below the commander's cupola. The cupola and the head of our commander Hohnecker were gone. The order came by radio to take our useless Panzer back to the repair company. Our nerves were tense as we drove to Martinville with our dead comrade in the Panzer. There we were able to bury our comrade Hohnecker.

Kampfgruppe Meyer/Wünsche broke off the attack which had caused such heavy losses, in the morning of June 9. Untersturmführer Chemnitz reports:

The Panzers were returning from the attack. Since the road there ran on top of an embankment, the Panzers had to be directed in order to get onto it. Initially, the commander of the Panzer-Regiment, Max Wünsche, did this himself until I took over from him. One of the Panzers had turned around on the road. I stood in front of it directing the driver. Wünsche stood behind me to the right. The orderly officer of Panzer-Regiment 12, Untersturmführer Nehrlich, stood behind me to the left. At that moment, the Panther took a shell hit from a Canadian tank to the front armor. Wünsche was wounded in the head by a fragment. I took a shower of small fragments from my head to the knees. Nehrlich was so critically wounded by a fragment that, although he was immediately put into the sidecar of a motorcycle to be driven to the dressing station, he bled to death during the drive.

The 3./Panzer-Regiment 12 had arrived in the evening of June 8, too late to take part with its Panthers in the night attack on Bretteville. On June 9 it was ordered into action to prevent the pending Allied attack. It was planned to take Norrey, a town of great importance for the resumption of the attack to the north. Before noon on June 9, the commander of the Panzer-regiment, Max Wünsche, was still at the main dressing station to have his wounds looked after.

The order for the action of 3./Panzer-Regiment 12 was probably issued by Standartenführer Kurt Meyer. We quote from the report of half-platoon leader Morawetz:

> The commanders were briefed in the vicinity of Villeneuve and received orders for the attack on Norrey which was held by strong enemy forces. The attack began at 1 P.M. Hauptmann Lüdemann led the company, since the chief of the company Obersturmführer von Ribbentrop, had been wounded.
>
> The twelve Panthers were lined up next to each other at a right angle to the railroad line Caen-Bayeux. It was 12:30 P.M. Unlike most other days at noon, there were no fighter-bombers in the air, and it was fairly quiet in front of us. We set out and reached open terrain, meadows, and fields. The whole company moved, well spaced, at high speed and without stopping. When our left wing approached the town of Norrey, half-left ahead of us, the order came by radio: "Wartesaal (waiting room) swing left!" (Wartesaal was our code name). I was driving some thirty meters ahead of the company to the left when my Panzer came to a stop after a loud bang that shook the vehicle. I thought I had driven onto a mine, and glanced to the left to determine the situation we were in. As I did, I saw the whole turret flying off the Panther on the left wing. At the same moment, after another explosion, my Panzer started to burn. The MG ammunition caught on fire. Before pushing into the town, I had closed the hatch. Now we could open it only partly, not completely. My gunner was badly wounded by fragments. I managed, after many tries, to open the hatch. I jumped out, fell to the rear, and, after a short period of unconsciousness saw a flash of fire hiss out of the open hatch as from a blowtorch. I lost my balance and hit the ground headfirst. Later I saw other burning Panthers along a line with my own. Members of the crews of the other knocked-out Panthers, all with burn wounds to the face and hands, came toward me. Of the twelve Panthers in the attack, seven stood burning in the fields. When I was being looked after at the main dressing station, I found out that fifteen of the thirty-five crew members had been killed. The others, with very few exceptions,

had been wounded. The remaining five Panthers had, firing constantly, withdrawn to the starting position.

During the attack, this sector was under heavy artillery fire, some of it from ships' guns, and constant MG fire, which greatly hampered the rescue of the wounded.

On June 11, SS-Panzer-Grenadier-Regiment 26, under the leadership of Obersturmbannführer Wilhelm Mohnke, requested Panzer support against an enemy tank and infantry attack near Le Mesnil. Obersturmführer Hans Siegel, chief of the 8./Panzer-Regiment 12, was in ambush position behind the II./26, about one kilometer south of Le Mesnil. When he noticed the noise of battle growing in this sector, he moved forward with three Panzers of his Panzer IV company to "check things out." He reported:

During a stop in the advance to scan the area, the gestures of our own grenadiers, who were pointing their spades in the direction of the enemy, indicated that acute danger existed. With my order "Ready for action" the hatches of the three Panzers closed as by themselves. The barrels were brought into firing position, and antitank shells loaded on the move. A hedge was still obstructing the field of vision toward the enemy to the left. When we got clear, I was in the midst of our own infantry and spotted several Shermans approaching through an orchard at a threatening distance. We had driven in front of their barrels and were exposing our vulnerable flank.

"Enemy tanks on the left—nine o'clock—200—open fire!" That was all I could do as chief and commander of the point Panzer. The month-long drill and battle experience of the crews paid off. The driver yanked the Panzer to the left and thus brought it into firing position. Even before the crucial air exhaust fan got up to full speed, the closest Sherman was knocked out. Within a few minutes, four or five enemy tanks were on fire. The last one, however, was only spotted when it had worked its way to within about 100 meters from us and swung its turret toward us. "Enemy tank hard left—ten o'clock—100!" Barrel faced barrel, almost close enough to touch when seen through the periscope. Then, a bang, fire from our 7.5-cm gun. The other tank exploded. Only then could the other two Panzers move closer. Before the grenadiers got up to advance, the three Panzer IVs rolled past the burning wrecks. The command Panzer succeeded in knocking out two more Shermans. During the further advance I received Pak fire from the right flank and brought my Panzer into firing position.

A duel started during which, after exchanging five shots, my own Panzer took a direct hit from the Pak. The crew had to bail out, regrettably without the radio operator who had fallen victim to the hit to the right front. My Panzer burned, covered by fire from all weapons. The other two Panzers, which had driven behind me, stopped to fire and were immobilized with damage from hits.

In the meantime, Sturmbannführer Prinz, commander of the II./Panzer-Regiment 12, had moved in other units for the counterattack on Mesnil. He led their attack west of Mesnil and through the town.

The "Hussars" lost thirty-seven Sherman tanks and counted considerable losses among the officers, noncoms and soldiers of the B and D squadrons as well as the D company of the "Queen's Own Rifles." Our own losses at Mesnil were 189 men. Three Panzer IVs were knocked out, one of which was later salvaged and repaired. Obersturmführer Siegel, company chief of 8./Panzer-Regiment 12, reported on the final phase of this battle:

"When I had reached our own lines again, together with a Canadian corporal who had surrendered, we observed an unusually impressive picture. The Canadians drove onto the battlefield with ambulances; a man was standing on the running board waving a large Red Cross flag. Medics jumped off with stretchers, the flag carriers continued to wave their flags. For about half an hour they searched for and collected the wounded and dead as if it were an exercise during peacetime. Not a shot fell to disturb their activity."

ON JUNE 12 S. SS-PANZER-ABTEILUNG 101 FINALLY REACHED THE COMBAT AREA AT CAEN

The June 11 attacks by the 50th British Infantry Division and the 7th British Armoured Division, supported by parts of the 3rd Canadian Infantry Division, on the left wing of the 12. SS-Panzer-Division "Hitlerjugend" and the sector of the Panzer-Lehr-Division of the Heer, from the north, with the objective of Villers-Bocage, had been without success. When the attack failed again in the morning of June 12, the 2nd British Army was ordered to take advantage of a gap that had developed further east. This action was described in a report of the 22nd Tank Brigade of the 7th Armoured Division:

"Based on the difficult terrain and the resulting slow advance, it was decided that the 7th Armoured Division would by-pass the left flank of the German Panzer-lehr-division to the left of the American sector. The Americans were reported just to the north of Caumont and there was a good chance to take advantage of this success by pushing in the direction of Villers-Bocage and, if possible, to take hill 113."

If this assault was successful, the division was to advance to Evrecy. Portions of the 50th Infantry Division were to follow, and reenforcement by the 1st British Parachute Division was planned. Evrecy is located in a valley of a range of hills between Odon and Orne, only three kilometers southwest of hill 112, which was to become of great importance during the subsequent fighting.

A battle group of the 22nd British Armoured Brigade formed the advance group in the following sequence:

- 8th King's Royal Irish Hussars (reconnaissance battalion)
- 4th County of London Yeomanry "Sharpshooters" (tank battalion)
- 5th RHA (artillery unit)
- 1/7 Battalion The Queen's Royal Regiment (infantry battalion)
- 5th Battalion Tank Regiment (tank battalion)
- 1st Battalion The Rifle Brigade (armored infantry battalion)
- 260th Antitank-Battery

This battle group assembled on June 12 at 4 P.M. Its advance units encountered Pak and infantry near Livry. When the situation was cleared up at 10 P.M., it was too late for further advance.

The battle group rested in Livry before assembling on June 13 at 5:30 P.M. for further advance.

This threat was recognized by the I. SS-Panzerkorps. But none of the three Panzer-divisions in action at the front had available reserves to protect the flanks. The General Command found itself forced to move those parts of Tiger Abteilung 101, which had arrived during the night of June 12 and 13, behind the Panzer-Lehr-Division. The Abteilung had left the area of Beauvais, some seventy kilometers northwest of Paris, during the night of June 6 and 7. The 3. Company and the repair company had suffered substantial losses during a night air attack in a wood near Versailles. In addition, the long march across country had caused a great number of technical breakdowns. Thus, the companies arrived at the front with only a portion of their Panzers and had no time for repairs and maintenance. The 1. Company, under Hauptsturmführer Rolf Möbius, had rested in the morning of June 13 some ten kilometers northeast of Villers-Bocage after the night march. Seven to nine Tigers had arrived by then. The 2. Company, under Obersturmführer Michel

Wittmann, had made camp, at the same time, in a small wooded area immediately south of the small village of Montbrocq, which was located directly south of the Route Nationale and two kilometers northeast of Villers-Bocage. The vanguard of the 22nd Armoured Brigade, in the meantime, had reached Villers-Bocage and passed through it without encountering any obstacles. The main column, driving on the road Livry–Amaye-sur-Seulles-Villers-Bocage, made no contact with the enemy. A company of "Sharpshooters" and a motorized company of the 1/7 "Queen's" marched along the Route Nationale to hill 113 to set up covering positions there. The further developments of this day, which were to bring about the great success of Obersturmführer Michel Wittmann, were detailed in the request of the general command of the I.SS-Panzerkorps for the awarding to him of the Knight's Cross with Oak Leaves and Swords of June 13, 1944:

SUBMISSION FOR THE AWARDING OF THE OAK LEAVES
WITH SWORDS TO THE KNIGHT'S CROSS.
(Awarded on June 22, 1944, as the 71st soldier)

Generalkommando I.SS-Panzerkorps Battle command post,
June 13, 1944

Leibstandarte

SS-Obersturmführer Wittmann received orders on June 12 to secure the left flank of the Korps near Villers-Bocage. It was to be expected that English tank forces that had broken through would advance to the south and southeast.

Wittmann arrived at the exact time as ordered with six Panzer VIs.

During the night of June 12 to 13, 1944, extremely heavy artillery fire forced Wittmann's company to change positions three times. In the early morning hours the company stood at Point 213 north of Villers-Bocage with five Panzer VIs ready for action.

At 8 A.M. a sentry reported to SS-Obersturmführer Wittmann that a strong column of enemy tanks was marching on the road Caen–Villers-Bocage.

Wittmann, sitting in cover 200 meters south of the road with his Tiger, recognized an English tank unit followed by an English armored personnel carrier battalion.

The situation required the fastest possible action. Wittmann did not have time to issue orders to his men in the distant positions. Instead, he pushed immediately, firing on the move, with his Panzer into the English column. This quick action initially broke up the enemy column. Wittmann destroyed four Sherman tanks from eighty meters, then moved his Tiger into and parallel to the column, and drove along the column at ten to thirty meters, firing in the direction of the march. He was able, in a very short time period, to knock out fifteen heavy enemy tanks. Another six tanks were hit, and their crews forced to bail out. The accompanying battalion in armored carriers was almost completely destroyed.

The other four Panzers of the Wittmann company, following behind, took some 230 prisoners. Wittmann pushed ahead, while well in front of his company, into the town of Villers-Bocage. In the center of town his Panzer he was immobilized by heavy enemy Pak. Despite this, he destroyed all vehicles within reach and routed the enemy unit. Thereafter, Wittmann and his crew bailed out and made their way on foot some fifteen kilometers to the north to the Panzer-Lehr-Division. There he reported to the Ia, turned around with fifteen Panzer IVs of the Panzer-Lehr-Division, and pushed again toward Villers-Bocage. He was able to reach the 1. Company, deployed along the main road to Villers-Bocage, in his Schwimmwagen, which had since been brought forward again. Based on his knowledge of the battle and situation, he used the company to attack the enemy who was still in the town with tanks and Paks.

By his determined actions with his Panzer, Wittmann single-handedly destroyed the enemy, the English 22nd Armored Brigade, which was already well to the rear of our own front. His immediate decision, carried out with greatest personal valor, averted a critical danger to the whole of the front of the I. SS-Panzerkorps. At that time, the Korps did not have any other reserves available.

With the count of today, Wittmann has achieved a total number of victories over 138 enemy tanks and 132 enemy Paks with his Panzer.

Signed: Dietrich

SS-Obergruppenführer and
Panzer-general of the Waffen-SS

Tiger-Abteilung 102's Battle for Hill 112

The Baral platoon, of which we were part, had orders to scout the situation at Maltot in order to ensure that we would be safe from all surprises from the flank during our attack on Hill 112. Our four Tigers reached the edge of the town of Maltot after a high-speed drive across open fields. Without hesitation, we pushed our Tiger through the hedge and had four Shermans in front of our gun. "Panzer—stop!—Tank furthest left 200—fire!" Two shells were enough. Then the second one on the left, same distance, suffered the same fate. In the meantime, platoon leader Baral had moved in next to us and knocked out the third Sherman. The fourth was looking for safety in hasty retreat and got away along the road in the direction of Eterville. The objective had been achieved; there was nothing to be feared from this flank for the next few hours.

This first action in the west meant a proud success for our young crew! After arriving at St. Martin, we could still see the burning Shermans like torches in the evening sky.

There was no rest for us. An attack in a wide front on Hill 112 had been ordered for 10 P.M. Grenadiers of the "Hohenstauffen" Division were to accompany the Tigers.

The enemy artillery fire grew to suffocating intensity. With the movement we had practiced almost too often, each of us slid into his seat. Within a few minutes our company was assembled for the attack. Radios ready! The operator adjusted the two VHF receivers on his left and connected the headphones and microphone. The frequency scales were dimly lit, electricity hummed in the speakers. 8:10 P.M. The hatch covers closed with a bang, and we locked them. The driver started the Panzer with a gentle jerk. Through the slits, we watched the tree branches we had used for camouflage, slide off in front. The tracks gave off a screech as we turned half right.

Our company approached the road, on which arm-thick branches were lying in a long column at an angle. We could see only the trees to the left and right and the rear of the Panzer ahead. Then there was a short halt; we had arrived at the back slope. The 1. Company formed a wide wedge with fourteen Panzers. Halfway to St. Martin, an area of thick bushes stretched across the gentle slope of Hill 112. There, we had to take up firing positions. From the top of the hill, the Canadians could see past us into the valley of the Orne River, from where our supplies came. Under cover of concentrated fire, which had woken us up in the morning, the enemy had reached the top of the hill. They began to dig in up there and showed no desire to fight. We waited impatiently for a chance to test our strength against theirs.

On July 10, the heated, desperate struggle for the hill began, which, soon after, was given the name "Calvary Mountain." There was not a meter of ground that was not dug up by shells. During this inferno of the heavy weapons, we left our cover in order to draw out the enemy. Soon, half a dozen enemy tanks appeared on the horizon. A part of the 1. Company pushed a little farther ahead to scout. The commander glanced across his four men in the dark interior below.

There was the gunner, as young as all the others. He had come from the motorcycle riflemen of the "Das Reich" Division and was as experienced at the front as anyone. He had a soft soul inside his huge body and a partiality for anything edible. His home was Kiev, and his father had lost a leg as an officer with the Afrikakorps. Below left sat our driver, nineteen years old. He had been driving the Tiger already on the Eastern Front, knew everything about the Panzer business, and could count himself among the old guard of the company. And then there was the radio operator, who also was in charge of rations and of firing the bow MG. His path, too, had led him in Russia from Panzer III to Panzer IV and then to the Tiger. These, then, were our boys who had asked themselves only a week ago in Holland: "What will it look like, the war in the west?"

Our chief, Kalls, was in the command Panzer. Deliberately, he issued his orders, which were heard immediately in all the other Panzers. The crew did not notice the heat developing in their small interior space. The driver at the steering wheel calmly checked his instruments, the tachometer, oil pressure, engine temperature. Throttle—shift—throttle!

We had advanced quite a bit when the Shermans opened fire. They seemed to concentrate on the lead Tiger. Explosions threw up dirt between the dispersed Panzers. Despite the order from the company chief, Soretz did not pull back one meter. He was enveloped by a spectacle that made our blood run hot and cold. (This valiant Soretz, an old comrade in arms from the days in the east, would later die in a car accident). Three enemy tanks were already silenced; the others kept on firing without pause. Then we finally had the most eager one in our crosshairs. The two farthest to our right had already been knocked out by us with five antitank shells, when light bombers showed up above the battleground. Like eagles, they fell out of the sky, dropped their loads of bombs, pulled up, and climbed away again. They came at us like a swarm of hostile hornets and covered us with a hail of medium-heavy bombs. At the same time, smoke shells landed among us and covered everything around with an impenetrable white fog within minutes. This was a new way of fighting to us, something we had not encountered on any battleground before. We withdrew to the starting positions where at least the infantry was able to keep the enemy close-assault teams away from us.

As soon as the white curtain lifted or was blown away by the wind, new smoke shells hit almost without sound. There was no question, we had to give up for the day. We spread out across the terrain and waited for the morning. Throughout the night, constant artillery fire kept us awake and gave us some idea of what all was awaiting us behind that hill. . . .

In the dawn of July 11, we pushed our attack in a northerly direction, determined to capture the hill this time! On the side of Hill 112 facing Aunay, we tried to drive up the hill through a narrow ravine. A reconnaissance aircraft, similar to our Fieseler Storch (stork) aircraft, flew above us in a wide spiral, returned, and pulled up in a steep climbing turn to the west. This was a bad sign for us, for these aircraft were equipped with excellent radios. It probably was less than ten minutes later when the storm turned into a hurricane. High-explosive shells landed on the turret and the front; shells ripped the crowns of the trees apart. Our Panzer-grenadiers did not dare to lift their heads as many a valiant comrade died on the hillside. Our Tigers knocked out a few Churchill tanks in quick succession. The small wooded area, a square cattle pen surrounded by hedges, contained quite a bit of hardware!

When Knecht was being squeezed from both sides, we raced across trenches and earth mounds at 20 kilometers per hour to his aid and took aim at the Tommy while on the move. After our third shot had drilled its way into his gun mount, his turret was half lifted from the tank body. At the far left of the cattle pen, the enemy brought Paks into position. The crews were pulling apart the gun supports and suffered their first losses even then. They were brave, the Anglo-Saxons! We slowly closed in and made the setting up of the dark brown guns superfluous.

The enemy again set up a heavy smoke screen, which stopped our Panzers shortly before reaching the hill. In this milky soup our Tiger took several hits to the rear and the turret. Our commander ordered the driver: "Ahead, full speed—march!" Somewhere, this fog had to end—and then we were through! "Panzer—halt!"

We had a spectacle in front of us that any Tiger would have wished for—less than 100 meters ahead the Tommies were evacuating their position. Trucks and personnel carriers swerved to and fro loading crews and equipment. Our commander reacted quickly: "Radio operator, open MG fire! Antitank shells, open fire!" Two Churchills, securing the terrain covered with low growth immediately ahead of us, were set on fire even as they aimed their guns at us. Then, we aimed high-explosive shells and the turret MG at the numerous targets offering themselves to us. The fog had lifted in the meantime.

A repeated order by radio arrived from our chief, Kalls: "Withdraw immediately to the line of the company." We would have much preferred to chase the fleeing enemy! During this day, during the same attack, Endemann and his crew found their fate. Maybe it was the fog that proved fatal to them.

Hill 112 was in the hands of the Tigers since the evening of July 11. It would be in the center of the fighting for twenty days and nights. It would change ownership repeatedly; its slopes would be soaked by blood. There would not be a day when Hill 112 was not mentioned in the armed forces report until it was given up, as ordered, by the undefeated Tigers at the end of July.

During the night of July 11 and July 12, the Tommies occupied the hill again. Our grenadiers were unable to reach the position of the Tigers in the constant concentrated fire.

Our Tiger had to return to the main base. The numerous hits of the afternoon had not been without effect. Our tanks leaked, the air conditioner had failed. At slow pace we reached St. Martin. Our gunner and the driver were wounded during maintenance when a surprise artillery attack took place. The gunner had to leave us and the driver, Hermann Schmidt, returned to his place at the wheel after medical attention. A new gunner joined us; he had proven his ability already in the east with a heavy company. It was always a good feeling when more soldiers than we could use volunteered to serve with our Panzers.

At four o'clock in the morning, on July 13, we rolled again against Hill 112, which was lost the day before. We stood among the wrecks of the Paks destroyed on July 11 and the burnt-out vehicles. The wooded area of the cattle pen, crowning the top of this hill as its prominent landmark, was recaptured during a forceful attack.

Since then, the heaviest possible concentrated fire centered on the hill. The grenadiers could no longer hold on; there were losses after losses. On July 15, the Tigers were again alone up there, without any help from the infantry. It seemed the night from July 15 to 16 would never end. Our commander Weiss and chief Kalls came to the top in the chief's Panzer during the evening hours. We were to hold the present positions under all circumstances! In the morning of July 16, the grenadiers of the "Frundsberg" Division again took possession of their old positions. The small wooded area had completely changed its face during these five days. Without leaves, naked tree trunks reached, as if accusing, into the sky, and the countless craters created the impression of a moonscape.

WE CLEARED "POINT 42"!

Throughout the night there was activity in Maltot. Through the binoculars we clearly determined motion, and, repeatedly, we heard the sound of tank tracks in the valley. Some Tigers received the order to clear Maltot. "Panzers, march!" our commander ordered. We had hardly left the bushes when we went on the attack. The humming of the radios in the headphones and the noise from the engine and tracks muted the inferno outside. The small space of the radio operator received only dim daylight from the cupola above. To the left one could make out the face of the driver on the other side of the power train. When the operator leaned back, he could watch our commander up there in the cupola, his hatch open most of the time regardless of the fireworks.

The village, occupied by the Canadians, came ever closer. We could already spot individual foxholes among the trees and bushes in the yards of the houses. The artillery observer over there, who had been watching our approach, had long since reported our coming to his batteries. They did what they could to offer us a proper welcome. Explosions threw the dry ground into the sky, took the roofs off the houses, brought down walls. When the dirt settled for a moment, we caught a quick glimpse of the church steeple where a battered Red Cross flag flew from the uppermost window. Then, a whole salvo of hits rained down on us. Our commander moved uneasily about in his seat, threw a quick glimpse on the surroundings of our position, and gave, with his usual calm and accuracy, target directions to our new gunner: "Half-left—500, flashes of muzzle fire!" Albert brought the turret about. On the road angling toward us, four enemy tanks were moving up.

Long-body, small-massive turret: Churchills! Our commander ordered to initially "scratch" only the first and last of the olive green monsters. Open fire! The first Churchill swung around on its own axis, immobilized! While the radio operator opened up with his MG on the crew bailing out, the last tank was set on fire. Oily black clouds of smoke darkened the sun. The two tanks in the middle swerved around each other wildly, knowing they were caught on the open road and that they had to get down the embankment. Quickly, however, their fate was sealed: number three took two hits to the body above the tracks—no one could have gotten out of that! The last one was finally knocked out by two hits to the rear. Thin white smoke rose from the hatches after several seconds before the heavy armor plates were ripped off the rear with a terrible bang. A flash of fire came from the engine compartment, igniting the ammunition.

Suddenly, clouds from small explosions appeared on the ground in front of us. At the same time, a radio signal: "Watch out for Paks at the edge of the woods!" We reacted with lightning speed: "More to the right, more to the right, speed it up!" Then: "Pull up left—halt!" Humming gently, the turret turned. Bang! The jerk of the recoil threw our heads backward. Two more shots, then we started out again.

Slowly, the fire died down. Then, fighter-bombers appeared and plastered us with their rocket fire. "Close hatches!" We had been on the move for three hours by then. Some Tigers had bypassed Maltot in the meantime. The radio traffic made it clear that we could not go any farther. A Tiger had taken a few Pak hits, and two men of the crew were wounded. We had to wait until the wooded area on our flank was cleared. Finally, the order came to continue. In the last light of the day we rolled back onto our hill. Our rations arrived on time. Either by VW or captured carrier, without regard to weather or enemy fire, the "soul soothers" made their way across mangled terrain in the darkest night. Mail had been added to the canisters of rations. Most of the time, master radio operator Stetter or our medic Nausester was with the party. Often enough, their bones trembled and we admired them. At the time, there was no "rear." We remembered well the pudding with added grass and sand! The vehicle had driven into a bomb crater, and the containers emptied. Nausester filled them again, but in the dark he had dug a little too deep. Our medic was all right. "Bring out the dishes!"

Oh, man! Goulash, noodles with chicken, fist-sized meatballs, hot tea, etc. Mail! Leni is about to deliver, little Herbert had eaten green soap, Walter next door has been killed, they have gone to get a shoe ration card, Mrs. Mickering on the second floor had another new lover. . . .

During the next night we were "blessed" for about four hours when well-aimed mortar fire decimated our infantrymen. Damn it all, that could not be coming from too far away! Three corporals came crawling in after midnight and reported that something was happening at the far left corner of our hedge. No one could make out anything in the dark. There was no question of imagining things! We waited tensely for an hour and determined, based on the timing between the firing and the explosions, that the Tommies had to be very close indeed. A few MG-42s laid fire on the suspected position. When the machine guns stopped, the mortar began to spit again. When our commander ran out of patience, he pulled slightly to the right, rolled ahead a few meters, and covered the corner with explosive shells to the extent that, during a pause in the fire, some hands were hesitantly raised. These Tommies had set up their mortar no more than thirty meters from our left wing!

Three tall Canadians crawled from their foxhole. "Hands up!" They pulled out four badly wounded men, six dead remained behind. In rubber boots, with camouflage nets over their uniforms, blackened faces, sharp knives not unlike our field hatchets, they had tried to roll up our positions. They stared at us unbelievingly. "So that is what these devils look like who keep beating us about the head," is what they may have thought to themselves.

In the bright sunshine of the morning of July 24, another eight Churchills came out of Maltot in the direction of St. Martin. We were in position, together with another Tiger, commanded by Schwab on this day, far to the right on the open flank toward Maltot. Before the other Tigers had spotted the enemy, our commander had already directed the gunner to the targets and opened fire. "Distance 400 meters—trailing tank—open fire!" None of the tanks at the point would be able to escape their fate as they drove straight into the fire front of the Tigers. And none of them would be able to escape through fast retreat to Maltot. The commander directed the gunner methodically from target to target, every shot a hit!

In the meantime, the other Tigers had opened fire. Only a few Churchills had a chance to fire. Soon, heavy clouds of smoke enveloped the end of this tank assault.

THE END OF THE WORLD DID NOT TAKE PLACE!

On July 25 we were still up there. Daily, we heard the "trumpets of Jericho" and the songs of the angels in heaven. Some choirs, they were! And then it was time again. The English appeared out of the fog banks, jumped from crater to crater, and tried their best not to leave the covering fog. But we had already spotted their "antitanks," weapons that looked like stove pipes, and were in no mood to let ourselves be wiped out. Anxiously, the driver checked the fuel gage. The needle dropped steadily. In addition to all that, the starter did not work. The only way to get the engine going was with the big hand crank. It started, but the fuel reserve was visibly sinking. We turned off the motor to save gas. Whenever we had to change positions, two of the crew jumped out, put in the crank in the rear between the big exhaust pipes, discolored by the heat of the gasses. They turned the crank until we finally heard the soothing song of the Maybach HL 200 engine again.

"Close hatches!" someone yelled, and already the first hits rained down on us. We heard the howling, a mighty bang, a crater spewing fire. The Panzer shook and trembled! Immense air pressure pushed smoke and dust through the cracks to the inside. Overhead were silver-gray Bristol bombers. Fighter-bombers circled around them, giving them air cover. They dropped on us like hornets. Bombs came whistling down, bursting to the left and right, in front and behind. They unloaded on us and all the way to St. Martin some 1,200 meters behind us. Still, the well-orchestrated end of the world weakened, and the humming of the bombers disappeared slowly into the distance. We opened the hatches and surveyed the chaos. This was what it may have looked like after the big earthquake in Tokyo. The bomb carpet stretched all the way to St. Martin-Vieux; luckily the infantry unit had been pulled back the previous day. Our "friend Adebar," the skinny, long-legged reconnaissance aircraft, circled overhead, weaving left and right. Probably taking pictures, we thought, of this remarkable duel ground near the Atlantic.

We barely had time to wave at the neighboring Panzers to let them know "All are alive here," when there was a howling in the air, a high whine and whistle. "Strafers—Strafers!" The ground around us turned into an inferno, and black clouds grew into the sky like a wall. More and more destruction came from above, then the on-board weapons hurled their tracers at us. . . .

In the evening we were relieved by the 3. Company. Our Tiger limped back with a shot-up radiator, the engine turned glowing hot, and the loader got the fire extinguisher from its mount. The first house of the village—only its walls were still standing—served as the company's field command post. Our chief, Kalls, sat at a table made of a splintered door, a flickering candle giving off dim light. Through the open ceiling we could see the stars. Kalls asked us to sit and in a tired voice, quickly explained the situation, listing the losses. Our base was now at Cropton. We found some water in an almost-empty canister and poured it into the radiator. It sounded hollow. We made our way through the village in the dark. Debris and walls of houses lay across the narrow streets, and parts of roofs hung from other houses in a bizarre manner. Wires, torn from telephone lines, whipped our faces. Cows, without food or milking for days, bellowed the pain of their over-full udders into the night! A stray dog disappeared into the dark. Some ducks paddled in the fountain in front of the destroyed church. In long, silent columns, Panzer-grenadiers with MGs, hauling boxes of ammunition, moved forward along both sides of the street. Which unit? "Hitlerjugend." How many of them were to come back? Late the previous afternoon, German rocket launchers had been put into action together with artillery against concentrations of enemy tanks and other vehicles.

Then, there it was again, the old, well-known howling, seeming to last an eternity. A heavy shell from a railroad or ship's gun came howling in and exploded at Feuguerolles, probably blowing up one of the village's houses in whose cellars a reserve battalion was housed. For a moment, the whole village and the surrounding terrain trembled, then, more incoming shells. Deafening explosions followed.

Somewhere over there a house was blown into the sky. A few minutes later, at an exact interval, came another roar, louder even than the other explosions, from shells ahead at the slope which were giving off a constant whistle. As if there had not already been enough destruction and madness, all for a few frightened, miserable humans . . .

German reserves disappeared faster every day. German defectors to the other side were no longer an exception. Seventeen and eighteen year olds had been sent to the front, together with old, gray men, fathers of families. The day was to come when the depleted homeland could no longer provide anything else, neither people nor materiel. . . .

Day after day the Allied invaders landed new divisions and war materiel. A lack of raw materials? Unsatisfied needs? All these were unknown over there.

Throughout the night we rotated guard duties every two hours to secure the position of our Panzers. Then we followed the changing of places for the sleeping crew from the canon to the turret mount to the driver's and operator's seats and vice-versa.

The early hours of the morning, when night was replaced by the slowly dawning day, gave us the only restful period of the entire day. Fog and smoke on the ground were slowly blown off by the gentle winds of the morning. The light of the early morning from the east replaced the darkness in the ravines and valleys. Dewdrops sparkled on blades of grass in the first rays of the sun, while birds, awake already for a long time, chirped their morning songs from the branches of the fir trees.

July 26 also began as a clear midsummer day, with blue skies, ideal for air attacks, in which the fliers of the RAF enjoyed themselves. A further order came from the Abteilung: "Attack the enemy movements on hill 67 and the northern exit of St. Andre. Take up securing positions west of Feuguerolles!"

And every morning, we found the enemy defenses strengthened by artillery and antitank guns brought in during the night!

Despite all this, we succeeded again in knocking out or setting on fire four Paks, three tanks, and ten other vehicles from our standby and ambush positions. At 11:30 A.M. we relieved Oberhuber at our old defensive position and pulled up our own Panzer right next to his. He motioned excitedly toward Maltot where he suspected Pak fire originated in the woods. His first shot exploded over there among the trees and left a gray-white cloud of smoke.

Attentively, we watched for a possible reaction and searched the edge of the woods for any enemy movement. Nothing! Suddenly, a meter-high cloud of dust appeared from the sand behind our Panzer. Where did this shell come from? We continued to search in all directions for a well-camouflaged enemy. There—another explosion, another cloud of dust, which quickly disappeared again in front of our stopped Panzer. It was getting serious! The words "Attention—Pak fire—driver, start engine—load explosive shell!" came through the intercom, informing and alerting the crew at once.

There was a sudden flash of explosion on the right side of the hull of Oberhuber's Panzer and then the recognition hit us like lightning; the enemy fire was coming from the right! A round, black hole at the height of the radio operator indicated the deadly hit whose force had thrown Oberhuber from the command cupola onto the rear deck. Clouds of smoke streamed from the hatches, ripped open by those who were not wounded and who then scrambled out with fear showing in their eyes.

I yelled into the throat microphone: "Backwards—march, let's go!" Only speed could have prevented a catastrophe! Immediately, the engine roared at full throttle, the tracks started to move and propelled the Panzer backward out of range of the enemy guns. We swung our turret toward the enemy, still not yet spotted, even as the Panzer began to move.

The driver of the knocked-out Panzer wildly waved the bloody stump of his arm from which his hand was dangling, held by some pieces of skin and flesh, and sought cover with the other survivors to the side. The radio operator had been killed by the direct hit. Our other Panzers then advanced from their standby positions to the ridge of the hills. Across from us, there was no more movement. Everything remained quiet.

It appeared that the Canadian attempt to break through, which began with such high hopes, had been stalled by the valor and determination of our grenadiers. Its brutal force spent, it faltered.

An order by radio assembled our Panzers in the late afternoon in an orchard behind Feuguerolles to continue to fight enemy forces to the right of the village. The crews were still busy with small technical duties. Some were topping up the radiators, others were adding oil, yet others were working on the tracks. Just then, the adjutant of the infantry battalion in the advanced lines came running toward us from Feuguerolles. He told us to expect an air attack on our assembled Panzers in a few moments. Heavy armor plates fell onto the rear deck plates with a clang. Tools, oilcans, pieces of clothing, everything was blindly thrown onto the hull, and we disappeared through the hatches at lightning speed. Engines roared, and across tree trunks, debris, and trenches the Panzers rolled into the safety of the woods.

Even as we moved out, English fighter-bombers buzzed above us and into the area already marked by streaks of pink fog. The diving squadrons resembled a dark star disintegrating into fireballs and shrapnel! Behind us, engine noise, explosions of bombs, fountains of dirt, rocks, trees—waves of hot air formed and enveloped the Panzers. We raced across earth mounds, wide trenches, and craters as if the devil himself were after us. Fighter-bombers dove behind us, darted past us at low level before they pulled up, and took another dive with a great howl toward the earth. We broke through small and tall firs and decidious trees into the dark center of the wood. Under the cover of the roof of leaves we waited, breathing deeply, until the enemy squadrons had flown off.

We had held this hill for sixteen days. The enemy attacked constantly, and we had to prove our determination every day. One time the enemy attacked from Maltot; another time he came racing across the fields from the direction of Evrecy! His advance was regularly accompanied by smoke screens, which meant that the Panzer crews were on their own. The Panzer-grenadiers no longer left their foxholes, which they had covered with branches against shell fragments. Every hour gnawed on our nerves and those of the infantrymen. Whenever we were not changing positions, soldiers sought cover under our Panzer. The constant artillery fire on our hill, which the enemy had accurately targeted for days, stopped any movement. Some of the Tigers were temporarily at the repair company because artillery hits had ripped off their ventilators.

After a drive of twenty meters, the red warning light lit up on the indicator panel of our driver: Engine temperature 100 degrees Celsius. Halt!

Shell fragments ripping through the damaged rear armor had caused leaks in the radiators. Despite its 700-horsepower engine, despite weighing sixty tons, the Tiger had to be treated like a raw egg. Even such giants had their Achilles heels. From time to time, enemy ships' artillery sent us their heavy "pieces of luggage." They always threw a few cubic meters of dirt high into the air. And almost every night, on this plateau without any cover, comrades in black overalls appeared. They were our repairmen who had come to fix the worst damage done by the shells to the tracks, the ventilation, the antenna, etc., or to exchange the bow or turret MGs. We were short too many tanks already!

The Supreme Command of the Armed Forces reported from the Führer headquarters in a terse statement for July 31 and August 1: "Enemy attacks south of Caen, supported by tanks and heavy artillery, broke down with heavy losses."

Those at home were never to know how much heroism and willingness to sacrifice, what suffering and deprivation lay behind these sober words. Daily, for years, one had become used to this language, which, although militarily brief, reported on the attacks and defensive fighting by the sons out there at the front. "Heavy combat involving advancing enemy tank units is taking place south of Avranches." With these words, the same Supreme Command report gave an indication of developments in the southwest sector of the German encirclement front.

Heavy combat developed there and continued to grow in intensity and extent, the beginning of the largest and bitterest combat actions in Normandy!

The worst danger threatened our front at that time in the southwest sector, south of St. Lo.

Battleground Carentan–
St. Lo–Avranches

ACTION OF SS-PANZER-REGIMENT "DAS REICH"
A Report by Panzer Commander Ernst Barkmann

When the invasion began on June 6, the 2. SS-Panzer-Regiment remained initially on alert in southern France since further landings were expected there. Finally, it was set in march to Normandy.

U.S. forces, the 30th and 9th Infantry Divisions, had crossed the Vire-Taute canal on July 7 and pushed ahead to Lé Desert. Taking advantage of this success, the 3rd U.S. Armored Division attacked northwest of St. Lo. The "Das Reich" Division attacked the enemy with a Kampfgruppe on July 8 near St. Sebastian–Sainteny. The 4. Company, with its Panthers, formed the spearhead. For the first time, Ernst Barkmann encountered Sherman tanks. Accustomed to the steppes and wide open spaces of Russia, he experienced the first of many bitter battles in this landscape crisscrossed by hedges and gullies, the fighting at short distances and the great value of the individual Panzer. There were no longer any Panzer battles on a large scale at Abteilung strength, let alone at that of the regiment.

Action took place only at company or platoon strength. Often, the Panzer commanders were all by themselves and had to master the situation without help from the infantry.

On July 8, Ernst Barkmann succeeded in knocking out his first Sherman, just before the company stalled under murderous artillery fire.

On July 9, he took part in the counterattack in the area of Périers and the attack by the 3rd U.S. Armored Division faltered. From then on, the Panthers and Tigers exchanged fire daily with the U.S. tanks, which were desperately searching for an opening, and caused the enemy heavy losses.

On July 12, Barkmann succeeded in knocking out two enemy tanks and immobilizing a third one. On July 13, the company stood in ambush positions, camouflaged against fighter-bomber attacks, in Bocage when the first enemy tanks appeared from the bushy area. Six Shermans were clearly spotted at a range of 400 meters. After two tanks had been knocked out, the other four withdrew. Then, a grenadier came running and reported that the Americans had broken through behind us and cautioned that they had half-tracks with Pak. Barkmann swung his Panther around and raced through a small wooded area until he saw the enemy spearhead in front of him.

The Pak was being set up. Barkmann immediately opened fire on this enemy with his gun while the radio operator fired on the infantrymen with the MG. Suddenly, Pak fire ranged in. A shell whistled past the turret. The Pak was silenced with a direct hit. Then came a bang from the right; our Panzer took a hit only centimeters below the optical sight in the front armor. Flames began to leap from the Panzer. "Bail out!;" the commander ordered. While the driver, radio operator, and loader managed to get out, the gunner remained unconscious in the interior. Barkmann ran back through the shelling and pulled the gunner out through the commander's hatch. "Extinguish the fire!" was the commander's next order. They were successful and managed to start the engine again and take the Panzer back to the repair company.

Barkmann received a replacement vehicle, with an order to take three Panthers and break through to the four Panzers of the 4. Company, which had been encircled by the enemy. As he entered the Panzer, he could still see the blood of his predecessor who had been killed by a shot in the head—the "affliction" of the commanders. This mission was completed without losses. Barkmann took over the positions of the four damaged Panzers.

During another attack by Sherman tanks, Barkmann scored three more victories. Around noon, the commander of the regiment, Obersturmbannführer Tychsen, came to the position. It was planned to free wounded men of the division who were being held prisoner in a house some 800 meters away. The three Panthers crossed the terrain at high speed and took the wounded prisoners back from the retreating enemy.

That was Tychsen, the commander, who had proved his mettle in many Panzer battles in the east and then in the west and who died, only a few days later, at the spearhead of his regiment during a Panzer attack. On July 20 and 21, Barkmann added four more victories over Shermans before artillery fire damaged the tracks of his Panther and he had to take it back to the repair company under great difficulties.

The "old" Panther 424 had been repaired in the meantime, and Barkmann and his crew took it over again. When the breakthrough of the VII US Corps near Marigny, directed toward Avranches, became evident, Panzer-Regiment "DR" was withdrawn from its sector to close a gap in the position of the Panzer-Lehr-Division. This was successful despite enemy air superiority. This division had been decimated in a two-day bombardment by strong Allied bomber units. During a change in position, Panther 424 suffered carburetor damage. The repair group attempted to fix the problem right there.

To save time, it was decided not to take any special precautions, a decision that turned out to be disastrous. Four fighter-bombers attacked. The first rounds whistled through the open engine hatch into the Panzer.

Cooling hoses and the oil cooler were shot up. The engine caught on fire. The crew managed to extinguish the flames and worked throughout the night. Its hard labor was rewarded. At dawn on July 27, Panther 424 was able to follow the company into its new combat sector. It reached Le Lorey near the main road Coutances–St. Lo. On the curving road, at the exit of the town, Panzer-grenadiers and supply soldiers came running to the Panzer. "U.S. tanks are advancing on Coutances," they yelled at us. But that was where we were going! From the distance Barkmann could hear the noise of battle and aircraft engines, then fire from submachine guns and rifles. Spiess and Schirrmeister, both wounded, approached his Panzer. They reported American tanks driving on the road to Coutances, together with a long column of vehicles. "Ready for action!" ordered the commander. Panther 424 rolled ahead slowly until the crossroads were in view. It was an ideal firing position, 100 meters to the crossroads, covered at the side by an earth mound with bushes.

"Tanks coming from the left, we will fire on the two point tanks." Gunner Poggendorf had the first tank in the crosshairs, and the first shell ripped the turret off the enemy tank. Then the second tank at the point was in the crosshairs, and it was set on fire. With this, the crossroads were blocked for the following tanks. They turned back, and even those vehicles which had already passed the crossroads retreated.

"Open fire!" The Panzer gun fired shell after shell into the personnel carriers, jeeps, and ammunition trucks. Within minutes, the crossroads resembled a burning auto graveyard. Suddenly, Barkmann spotted two Sherman tanks driving off the main road and approaching from half left. A duel of Panzer against tank began. The first Sherman burned brightly after the second shot. Barkmann took two hits from the second Sherman before it, too, caught on fire after a hit to the rear. Fighter-bombers then appeared over the Panther; the first bombs howled earthward but did not hit. But with each dive they came closer. A violent explosion made the Panther tremble and shake. Fragments ripped apart a portion of the tracks, and explosive rounds hit the turret and hull. A number of Shermans closed in and opened fire. Barkmann managed to knock out two more before his Panzer sustained heavy damage from hits. A shell ripped apart the weld and dovetailing of the Panzer hull. Another shell blew the track from the teeth of the driving sprocket, and the ventilation system in the interior failed. There were more hits to the rear as the crew tried to move the Panzer back into cover with the track blown off and a damaged driving sprocket. This maneuver required the highest concentration, but it was successful. Another Sherman, which had pushed ahead the farthest, was also knocked out when the Panther limped back to a farmhouse in the village of Neufbourg where the most critical damage was repaired. Barkmann's battle at the main road to Coutances had stopped the advance of the U.S. troops in the rear of German units long enough to allow many units, which had already appeared lost, to save themselves from threatened encirclement. As the last one to break off contact with the enemy, Barkmann's Panther, with two others in tow, reached Coutances on July 28.

Enemy tanks had already broken into the city, and one of the Panzers in tow was knocked out by a Pak. As he drove around enemy-held sectors of the city, Barkmann experienced another fighter-bomber attack. He was wounded by a fragment in the calf, and the loader was also wounded. During the night of July 29 to 30, Barkmann drove his Panther in the direction of Avranches and had to cross the path of moving U.S. units. The next morning, he was forced to blow up the second Panzer he had in tow. His own Panther 424 burned out a little later after its ammunition had exploded. The crews, fourteen soldiers altogether, made their way on foot to the coast and reached their company again on August 5. They had walked through U.S. lines and crossed the Gulf of Avranches at low tide. In the justification for the awarding of the Knight's Cross on August 27, 1944, one reads:

"During the fighting at the invasion front, SS-Unterscharführer Barkmann with his Panzer was left behind to cover two of our own immobilized Panzers. Due to a withdrawal movement by his division, he was separated from our own forces. Barkmann blew up one of the Panzers and took the other one under tow. He repeatedly crossed American troop movements and knocked out fourteen enemy tanks. During the nights he joined the U.S. columns and managed to reach his own lines two days later. . . ."

DEFENSE AND RETREAT IN NORMANDY 1944
Fritz Langanke, Platoon Leader and Panzer Commander in Panzer-Regiment 2 "DR," Reports

We had been relieved from our position east of Carentan during the night and were in St. Sebastian as reserves. However, we had to get going again the following day before noon. At top speed, I had to drive to the northeast edge of Périers with my platoon of four Panzer Vs and report to the commander of the regiment, Obersturmbannführer Tychsen. Since the order demanded "Drive without regard to enemy aircraft activity," it was clear to us that the situation had to again be most desperate. We were lucky on our way and were hardly bothered by fighter-bombers. However, the area of assembly was most inhospitable. It was under considerable artillery fire, which quite impressed us, as we waited for the regimental commander. When he arrived, he drove his open car very close to my Panzer, stood up from his seat, and began, without wasting time, to brief me on the situation and objective in his precise, military manner that was known well beyond our unit.

Right at the beginning, a series of explosions closed in on us and interrupted his explanations. Without noticing, I slid deeper into the Panzer so that I could just look out. The regimental commander did not move at all. He stood erect in his car and, without saying a word, looked up at me without batting an eye.

Nothing in his behavior was meant for show or to impress. It was, as in all armies of the world at all times, the duty of the outstanding leader to be the focal point, to set an example during difficult or even desperate situations, to display confidence, calmness, and maximum self-discipline. These are requirements that often cause the spark to jump across to the followers in such situations, causing actions and behavior from units and individuals, which could not otherwise be explained. Such circumstances are difficult, if not impossible, to describe in the sober words and context of usual language. They open a field of vision onto an area that describes the difference between the nonsoldier and the real soldier. Here, at the outskirts of Périers, this had an uncomfortable effect on me. The impact of such exemplary behavior is much stronger than reason, it overcomes fear and pettiness. Suddenly, I could no longer look down from the height of my turret on my regimental commander who was standing, without cover and stoically calm, in his car. Despite the fact that it would have made more sense to remain in the turret, I felt compelled to jump from the Panzer and stand at attention close to his car, thus restoring the proper military relationship. People who are not born soldiers may never fully appreciate that strict military formality. Drill and ceremonies are not, in themselves, of great value. Without the proper context they may appear useless and superfluous, possibly even ridiculous. But these factors, which are integral parts of a soldierly life, are expressions of mental attitudes, of moral and ethical commitments, and, as such, vitally important and necessary. Without them, an army is only a group of people equipped with uniforms and weapons who, in the best of cases, can be expected to satisfactorily do their job. But they could never be expected to perform supreme efforts of military and soldierly requirements, let alone outstanding heroic acts.

As soon as I stood in front of the car, Obersturmbannführer Tychsen got out and briefed me, using the map, in detail on the situation.

During all this, shells continued to fall around us. The urge to get down into cover was almost overwhelming. But this strong combination of strict military training, soldierly mental attitude, the experiences of the difficult war years, and the behavior of the commander was much stronger. I stood there and noticed how calmness and self assurance can overcome and replace human natural fear.

After the briefing was completed, I saluted correctly and waited until the commander had departed. Then I entered the Panzer in the usual fashion, despite the fact that I would have liked to jump like a kangaroo. Of course, the crews had followed the encounter in detail, and breaking its style at the end was out of the question.

The Americans had increased their pressure from the north and threatened Périers. They had almost advanced to the small river Sèves. Some Panzers of our regiment had been knocked out. My platoon was ordered to stop the enemy at the road that led straight north, west of Périers, from Route N 800. I remember it as the "Roman road." The heavily damaged Périers gave a ghostly impression as we drove through. We reached the route by dirt roads, accompanied by an American artillery observation aircraft that circled lazily above.

As we pulled up on the right side of the road, not far from a farm, we immediately received heavy fire. We spotted fairly strong mixed American units on a slope across the river, some one kilometer away. I was still contemplating how to best set up our position when our company chief, Obersturmführer Schlomka, showed up in his Volkswagen. He was visiting the widely scattered platoons of our 2. Company in order to form his own picture of the situation. I had just shouted at my driver to pull into an orchard to the right of the road for better cover, when the company chief came running to us across the street to inquire whether we could set up a better position in a field surrounded by hedges to the left of the road. We had barely arrived there when a salvo of heavy shells came sailing in. I wanted to hit the ground, but it was too late.

As I was dropping, I received a large shrapnel in my right upper arm. There were people during the war who were followed by luck in an almost unreal way and lived, unharmed, through one campaign after the other and always with the fighting troops. I was one of them. The shrapnel was already at the end of its trajectory and hit flat with its rounded inner side on my upper arm. Only one of its jagged edges pushed deeply into the flesh—unbelievable luck once again. Obersturmführer Schlomka easily looked after the damage with his first aid kit.

We had established that the left side of the road was not preferable to the right, and ran back across to our vehicles. There, minor chaos reigned. While looking for a good firing position, my Panzer got stuck in the ditch. The driver, Renatus Seeger from Lör-ach, jumped out and hooked up tow cables so that another Panzer could pull us out. During this, he had taken a shrapnel to the mouth area that knocked most of his teeth out and caused a bad wound. The shock and loss of blood mixed up his mind. He stumbled, unnoticed by the crew, out of the orchard and ran back along the route we had come in on. Someone pulled him into a vehicle, provided first aid, and took him to the company supply base. Luckily, the noncom in charge, recognized the situation immediately and sent us another driver, Sturmmann Heil. In the meantime, we had become quite angry at our friend Seeger whom we were searching for under heavy artillery fire. After a while we had to give that up, with no success. I climbed into the orphaned driver's seat as the other Panzer, hooked up in the meantime, pulled us out of the ditch. It was a fairly difficult maneuver due to my badly swollen upper arm.

We found the most advantageous firing position and, together with the others, fought the American units with good results. The concentrated fire of all our weapons brought them to a halt before reaching the small river, and at dusk we had achieved our objective of blocking the road. All our ammunition, except for a small reserve for defense, was used up.

With the falling darkness we received orders to withdraw to St. Sauveur Lendelin. We pulled back slowly, facing the enemy to prevent our exhausts, which often threw out flames, from giving us away. After the first curve, we returned to our normal way of driving. Périers was behind us when we rolled past an infantry unit of the Heer, also marching to the rear, which made an excellent impression on us.

Shortly thereafter we reached a bridge, which pioneers were preparing for demolition. They did not want anyone to waste time crossing it so that they could carry out their order to demolish it at midnight. Time was running out. Then, one of those dramatic scenes occurred which had happened a hundred times on all fronts of the war during all retreats. Pioneers, with firm orders, had to destroy a bridge. They all knew of occasions where delays, for whatever reasons, had caused severe, sometimes fatal, consequences. On the other hand, retreating units had not been informed in time or had been unable to disengage from the enemy because of heavy fighting. We explained that we had to wait for the infantry. We begged, threatened, and yelled at each other. Nothing helped; the pioneers were as determined as we. Finally, I drove onto the bridge and ordered the others in the Panzer to take their stations and get ready for action. I yelled at the commander of the pioneers that we would fire on anyone approaching the bridge. I could have cried out of frustration for being in such a situation. It was one of the bitterest moments in the war, one in which a soldier had no choice. When reporting on situations that occurred in the war, one has to be careful not to use words and phrases that are too strong or emotional. I believe, however, that there are not many situations that can be termed "dramatic" with the same justification as the violent encounters at bridges, in particular during a dark night when passion meets passion, one order faces another order, and reason battles reason in hopeless entanglement. Luckily for us all, our grenadiers appeared in time before the worst, any shooting, occurred.

Following our arrival in the St. Sauveur Lendelin area, we were made part of the corps reserves.

After refueling and taking on ammunition, we bedded down under the Panzers. Not much later we were awakened again. Wild rumors and bits of information that we caught were contradictory, but one thing was clear. The withdrawal, conducted in an orderly fashion up until then, was turned into a catastrophe by an American breakthrough. I received orders to block the road St. Lo–Coutances with my platoon. The Americans were reported to have reached the area of Campron/Cambernon in the meantime.

The route of march to Cambernon offered us good cover at most times so that we were able to move at good speed. Some battle noise was heard from the town. I talked with the leaders of different units, sometimes already quite mixed, who reported that the Americans were standing close to the town to the east and northeast, and that our defenses were holding firm. Hearing this, we raced down the road to the left of the railroad line from Cambernon to the south and reached, still at high speed, the road St. Lo–Coutances. As soon as we turned onto it, in the direction of St. Lo, we were engulfed in the heaviest fighter-bomber activity I experienced during the war. The only thing similar occurred during the break-out from the encirclement at Falaise/Trun. The light-colored ribbon of concrete of this road was littered, as far as we could see toward Coutances, by wrecks of vehicles and other military equipment. Some of it was burning, smoking, entangled, or just abandoned. Here and there we saw dead or wounded soldiers. Once our small unit had been spotted driving on the road, fighter-bombers dove on us from all sides, dropping bombs and firing onboard weapons. To catch our breath, we pulled off the road to the right for a while into an orchard. That did not help very much as that area was being hammered as badly as the road. During such heavy fighter-bomber attacks, there were different ways of reacting. Most of the crews bailed out and sought cover, if nothing better was available, under their own Panzer. Others remained inside. It was questionable which was more effective. I have always followed the second avenue with my crew. We sat there for a while and then decided that the attack would not stop in any case, and we had been ordered to halt the American advance along this national route.

Therefore, I waited for a pause in the bombing and then issued the order by radio to get going again. We pulled the vehicle back on the road and drove at high speed in an easterly direction. Like crazy, the fighter-bombers dove down on us again. We were afraid only of the formations that attacked in a straight line along the road from the front or rear. We paid almost no attention to those attacking from the sides.

The sky was covered with broken clouds. On our radios we could hear the exchanges of the Americans, probably from the aircraft. Whenever one noticed the transmitter coming closer, as an old reconnaissance radio operator I had an ear for that, a group of fighter-bombers came hurtling out of the clouds. Off and on I thought I could understand a word, but that was maybe only my imagination. Some aircraft flew so low that we thought they would touch the trees along the road with their wings. Frequently, we made out the faces of the pilots. After a while we noticed that we were the only ones moving on the road, but we kept going at full speed. Later, we found out that one of the Panzers of our platoon, whose crew had stayed inside as well, had lost its antenna during the fighter-bomber attack and could not receive, while the other crews had remained under cover of their Panzers. We were outside each other's field of vision.

After some four kilometers we reached a group of houses and farms and pulled sharply right off the road into the usual orchard to catch our breath. There we noticed that the fighter-bombers, which had even previously attacked us somewhat less violently, were no longer looking for us along the road. That meant that we had to be very close to the Americans. So, we drove back onto the road and carefully on toward the east. The fighter-bomber attacks had stopped completely. We were quite certain then that the American tank spearhead was immediately ahead of us, probably units of the 3rd Armored Division or the 1st Infantry Division.

A bend in the road ahead completely blocked our vision. We slowed down even more and rolled into the bend ready to fire; an antitank shell in the barrel and the distance set at 500 meters as always when the situation was not known, the gunner pressed to the telescopic sight, fingers on the triggers, even the radio operator's, the loader ready with the second shell.

We continued at walking speed and drove by a Panther facing in the direction of our travel at the left side of the road. It was a vehicle from our regiment. The rear turret hatch was open. But when we inspected its front we saw the hole at the lower right of the forward armor made by a direct hit. Its caliber had obviously been greater than 7.5 centimeters, but the Panzer had not burned. This sight dried our throats and caused knots in our stomachs. The gun that had knocked out this Panther had to be still ahead of us somewhere. We were all tense and ready as we rolled on. Then, all of a sudden, the view was open again on the road, which stretched straight ahead of us. It offered a spectacle that belonged to the pictures of the war one would never forget. As far as we could see along the road, there were German and American vehicles of various types, cars, trucks, half-tracks, tanks, some of them burning and entangled. In between, German and American ambulances were driving back and forth, flying Red Cross flags, recovering dead and wounded who were strewn on the road or still in the vehicles. I had the impression that a German unit, probably from our regiment, was stopped there and caught by surprise when the Americans advanced, without enough time to make it back to the road. To my left was a fairly open field, bordered further back by bushes or trees. Just ahead of us and to our left was the road from Campron. Along our road and off to the side in the open field stood quite a number of American tanks and, probably, tank destroyers. We thought we could also recognize guns. Not a shot was fired when we showed up, probably so as not to disturb the activities of the ambulance units. We did not fire either, despite the fact that the gunner was nearly going crazy with excitement. The whole situation was completely unreal, especially when one thought back to the war years in Russia. It was a picture that could have come from another world. Time passed incredibly slowly. The tension rose to the point of being unbearable. We could feel drops of sweat forming on the skin. We wanted to do something, anything, but had to sit there, concentrating to the utmost, and wait—but for what?

Some 200 to 300 meters away stood an American tank behind a pile of wood or rocks on the same side of the road as we were. We could only see half of it. That seemed to be our most dangerous enemy. When the last ambulance was loaded and started to move out, we began to take aim at the turret of this tank. That was our first movement since we had entered the field of vision of the Americans, and it broke the spell. It was likely that the Americans had been sitting there as tensely as we. Our aiming maneuver, in any case, brought an end to this unreal, undeclared cease-fire. The multitude of guns ahead of us opened fire, and we were badly shaken about inside our Panzer. Almost simultaneously we fired on the targeted tank but did not manage to set it on fire.

We took hit after hit, and I kept thinking with fear of the hole in the armor of the Panther. Then, I issued the order "Backwards—march!" There was no way we could have remained there by ourselves. Constantly firing on various targets, we drove back, much faster than when we had come in, through the bend, past the knocked-out Panther and were pleasantly surprised not to have such a hole in our front. What results, if any, our fire had was impossible to tell with the heavy fire directed on our Panzer.

We pulled back a little further behind the bend and took cover, as best possible, on the right side of the road, ready to welcome the Americans should they decide to advance. Because of the surrounding terrain they would have had to use the road at this spot which meant that only two or three tanks at a time would come into view. But on that day, July 28, 1944, they did not resume their advance on Coutances.

In the late afternoon a group of grenadiers from the "Deutschland" regiment showed up. The men took up positions close by but were pulled back in the evening and marched off in the direction of Savigny. It was a bad feeling to be all alone in this situation as the night began to fall. I had no radio contact and did not quite know what to do. Was my order still valid or was it outdated?

Just when I thought we had been forgotten in the general confusion of the retreat, my company chief, Obersturmführer Schlomka, suddenly showed up. He was in his VW, which was badly damaged by then; one of the tires had been shot out and was stuffed with hay. He led us back to the regiment, in the same direction the grenadiers of the "Deutschland" Regiment had taken. During the night I met up with the other Panzers of my platoon. After the usual refueling and taking on of ammunition, I was assigned to Sturmbannführer Schreiber with my four Panthers. In the meantime we were in the encirclement of Coutances, and Schreiber's mission was, together with the III./SS-"D," to open an escape route to the south. So we drove into the morning of July 29, a day on which the Division "Das Reich" would lose most of its heavy equipment and many of its men. I was luckier. During a bitter night battle, July 29 to 30, I was able to break through the ring surrounding us with three Panzers, two assault guns, and several wheeled vehicles and open the way to freedom for some 100 members of battered units of various divisions.

Inside this encirclement we also learned that the commander of our regiment, Obersturmbannführer Tychsen, was killed shortly after he had taken over from the wounded commander of the "Das Reich" Division. Near Trelly, he encountered an advanced American tank spearhead and was shot in his car.

The briefing by the regimental commander under heavy artillery fire at the outskirts of Périers, which had so deeply impressed me, thus became my last memory of Obersturmbannführer Tychsen, who was surely one of the outstanding members of a group of younger Waffen-SS commanders.

PANZER BATTLES WITH TANK UNITS OF THE U.S. ARMY

During the last days of July 1944, the fighting at the base of the Contentin peninsula entered its critical phase. Repeated breakthroughs, encirclements, and breakouts made the situation almost impossible to grasp for the fighting units and supply troops. Large-scale combat was replaced more and more by individual actions. The leaders tried desperately to keep a grip on their units and to direct them in an orderly fashion through withdrawal movements to new defensive positions and assembly areas. Failure and determination, panic and loyal performance of duty, self-deprivation, and growth beyond one's limits in a desperate situation were the outstanding occurrences of those days that would remain firmly in the memories of all who took part.

During that dramatic period, I was a platoon leader in the 2. Company of the Panzer-Regiment of the SS-Panzer-Division "Das Reich." We had broken through the American encirclement in bitter night fighting northwest of Percy, and spent the following day wandering between German and American columns in the area of Villedieu/La Haye–Pesnel. During the next night we finally found our regimental command post not far from Villedieu. Although the regimental commander, Enseling, had promised to let us get plenty of sleep after two days and nights of fighting, it was not to happen. After refueling and taking on ammunition, we left some three hours later by ourselves for a crossroads to cover the withdrawal there. After two days there under heavy artillery fire and fighter-bomber attacks, we started the next withdrawal move to the east. We passed through the Forêt de St. Sever, and in the early hours of the following day I received orders again to set out alone and secure another road. Reportedly, paratroopers were setting up positions before noon to the right of the road, and to the left of it were units of the Heer from Vienna, which I already knew from the previous day.

I pulled up to the right side of the road, in line with a fairly large farm to the left of the road, under good cover. Without perfect cover one fell prey easily to the fighter-bombers, which had made vehicle movement during the day almost impossible. Some time later, the Viennese infantrymen arrived, a badly decimated battalion. I had a hard time convincing them to take up positions in the terrain, which was quite favorable for infantry, some 100 to 150 meters in front of the farm. Soon after, a second Panther, the vehicle of my company chief, Obersturmführer Schlomka, arrived as reinforcement. Both of us drove into the large orchard, located to the left of the farm and offering good cover. I sat in its right forward corner, very close to the farm, and Obersturmführer Schlomka was some forty meters away in the left corner of the orchard. I could see down the road about 200 to 300 meters. Approximately 100 meters ahead of us, a dirt road led from the road toward our side at a shallow angle and passed close to the orchard.

During the course of the morning, fog moved in and the visibility deteriorated. It was almost impossible to make out the beginning of the dirt road. Suddenly, a Sherman tank appeared on the road, driving at a slow pace, its commander standing in the open turret hatch. We moved our turret around by hand as quickly as possible. Since the engine was not running, we could not use the hydraulic system. We fired just before the tank disappeared from sight behind the building, but we did not manage to hit it. In the meantime, we had hastily started the engine, reversed, and drove as fast as possible through the farm entrance to the road, which was at a noticeably higher level. During this, we turned the turret to three o'clock and drove up the embankment in such a way as to break down a tree with our left track in order to gain some cover against the other Shermans. We could not see in the fog, but we knew they had to be there. We did not really expect to get on to the road unscathed, but somehow we made it.

As soon as the Panzer had leveled, we knocked out the tank sitting some fifty meters away. Its commander had still been looking out of the turret hatch but had not noticed us. The tank took a hit to the engine and immediately caught on fire. Then we pulled our Panzer around sharply on the road, swung the turret to twelve o'clock, and drove around the crown of the tree we had knocked down in the direction of the other tanks. They had pulled up, individually, on the side of the road to fire. We were able to make out only the first two about 150 meters away and set them on fire with one shell each. Then we saw soldiers running around between them, and we were about to fire when I just barely made out raised hands and did not issue the order to open fire. I assumed that they were Americans surrendering to our infantrymen who were dug in at about this line to the left of the road. We learned afterwards that they were our own men who had left their positions and surrendered to the Americans farther back who had then again withdrawn. I continued to wait for a while at the right side of the road for further advances of the Americans. Shortly after, the commander of our regiment showed up. He was checking on the various Panzer positions of the Panzer-Regiment "Das Reich." Of course, he was happy with our success.

When the fog had lifted around noon and the visibility was good again, I returned to my previous position next to the farm. Artillery fire set in. It increased soon after and concentrated almost totally on the orchard in which our two Panthers were sitting. For one or two hours, my gunner, Rottenführer (corporal) Meindl from the Sudetenland, and I exchanged seats. The seat of the gunner was more comfortable than that of the commander. In addition, one could lean one's head against the turret telescopic sight and sleep in a relatively relaxed position. We were all dog-tired and worn out.

We had just changed around again, each sitting in his own seat, when a Sherman suddenly came into view. It turned onto the dirt road and came toward us, its gun aimed at our Panzer, at high speed. The Americans had to know our situation in detail. Until then, we were used to American tank advances against fortified positions only after previous heavy fighter-bomber attacks.

Since the fighter-bomber activity in our sector during that day had been only "normal," this dashing attack completely surprised us. The same was true for the other Panther. Its gun was aimed somewhat more favorably, and it fired immediately but without stopping the American. Using the highest concentration and greatest possible speed, again by hand since the engine was not running, we tried to take aim at the Sherman. Fortunately, we were at the right elevation by chance, and the lateral correction was also achieved quickly, since the American entered into our target range with his high speed drive along the dirt road. The Sherman had to lower its gun a little, but we were a touch faster. By the time we were ready to fire, I thought I could look directly into the barrel of the enemy. The tank caught on fire immediately and its daring attack, the most spirited American maneuver I personally observed during the war, and which had almost been successful, found its end forty to fifty meters in front of us. The commander just managed to bail out and, as far as I could make out, got away uninjured. The artillery fire, which had slowed down before this attack, became heavier again and left us no time to pay any attention to our tense nerves. The heat inside the vehicle became almost unbearable. It was a very hot day, we had nothing to eat or drink, and the hatches had to remain closed due to the heavy enemy fire. We were all overtired, and time and again we nodded off only to jerk awake with a start and bump our heads against one thing or another. The worst of it was that I could no longer observe the outside. Shell fragments and machine-gun fire had rendered all observation periscopes in the commander's cupola useless. Time dragged slowly. We knew something had to happen, and would happen soon. It made no difference what was awaiting us. In such situations we only desired it to happen soon, to end the ever-growing tension. This tension expressed itself in finding every movement, every word of the comrades aggravating and making it more and more difficult to maintain self-discipline. Occasionally, paniclike waves of emotion flowed through the vehicle. We felt closed in, hopeless, finished.

Quite suddenly, one just wanted to get out and run off, one was close to going crazy. Almost worse, one had to fight one's self when this feeling of indifference set in, when one did not care about anything and just sat mutely and waited for some kind of end. It was most difficult to stay away from this condition.

I had just dozed off once again when we all were suddenly jerked back into wide-awake reality. Very heavy machine-gun fire hammered our Panzer. We heard the other Panther start up and begin to move immediately, then we experienced a heavy bang. We thought we had taken a direct heavy hit. I had to risk opening the turret hatch a crack and saw our sister-Panzer driving toward the road at high speed, knocking down fruit trees. One of these trees was lying across our rear; it had been the cause of the loud bang.

I thought that the other Panther had spotted enemy tanks on the road and driven out of the orchard to attack them. We started the engine immediately and followed as quickly as possible to assist. Then we were under constant heavy fire from infantry weapons. The radio communication with our sister-Panzer no longer worked. We could still hear the men but could not understand a word. Our antenna with its mounting had been shot off.

I realized that there was a crucial need to see more and opened the turret hatch fully despite the increased danger it caused to our Panzer. I followed the motto: "A field of fire is more important than cover," and in order to fire, one had first to be able to see. We drove onto the road with great momentum, crossed almost to the other ditch, pulled the vehicle to the left, fired immediately and received, simultaneously, a horrible blow, a whole salvo of hits. The driver and gunner yelled immediately that they could not see anymore. Then I recognized what had happened. The Americans were acting very cleverly. Between the two, still smoking, knocked-out tanks on both sides of the road I could make out a whole row of Shermans.

They were staggered in such a way that only the barrel of the next tank behind was sticking out alongside the turret of the one in front, and they were firing simultaneously.

The events of the previous few minutes had driven off all feelings of tiredness and weakness, all hopelessness. The need for action hit us like a drug.

The crew was again cool and self-assured; we functioned like a well-oiled machine. Such moments of greatest possible demands freed strengths and abilities in men that clearly surpassed normal levels.

I recognized immediately that we could not have achieved anything more there, and if we stopped, we would have been wiped out in no time. So I quickly said on the intercom: "We will drive at a sharp angle toward the left side of the road and wait in cover of the knocked-out Sherman until the Americans come driving around it one by one to get to us. We will keep the turret aimed at the tanks at all times." That meant that the driver who could not see outside had to be directed on the intercom, while the gunner, also unable to see out, turned the turret right and left, guided by taps on his shoulder. All this happened at lightning speed. While I was saying "Pull to the left" for the second or third time, we took another salvo of hits. This time, the impacts were even more severe than before. The welds on both sides of the upper front plate were ripped partially open, we could see daylight from the outside. Stubbornly, we kept the turret aimed and fired on the tanks, but I could not tell if we had any success.

I ordered: "Straight ahead, straight ahead!.," but the vehicle kept turning until the hull was almost at a right angle to the road, close to the left shoulder. The intercom had failed during the heavy fire and the last thing the driver had heard was "Pull to the left." I realized at once that our position meant the end. Immediately, there was a bang inside the Panzer, not overly loud, and I saw the loader, Sturmmann Fähnrich from Duisburg, completely engulfed by flames. It looked as if a large number of sparklers were burning on a tall Christmas tree. It was obvious that we had been hit and were on fire. I could only yell: "Bail out!" and leaped out of the turret hatch into the ditch. I turned a somersault and stayed on my back for a moment while the gunner and loader also bailed out. Surprisingly, the loader had received only small shrapnel to his back, and his uniform was a little singed in that area, but he had no burns. We realized only then that we had been knocked out not by the tanks but by a bazooka from the right side of the road where the terrain was higher than the road.

Then we noticed that Americans were all around us.

After the turret crew had jumped out, our Panzer came under such heavy machine-gun fire that it would have meant certain death to the driver and radio operator to open the hatches. Both Sturmmann Heil and Rottenführer Pulm had the nerve to remain in the burning Panzer for a while longer, drive it closer to the ditch, and only then to rip open the hatches simultaneously and jump out. Personally, I doubt very much if I could have done that.

As all five of us, luckily uninjured except for the loader, lay panting next to our burning vehicle, we had the burning desire to get out of there as quickly as possible before our Panzer blew up. However, just as soon as we lifted our heads, we received fire from various sides. Then we found time to think of our sister-vehicle and spotted it sitting some 100 meters behind us. Its gun was damaged and it was defenseless against the Shermans, but it was somewhat outside their field of fire. Despite being in grave danger, it did not abandon us and held its position. Both its machine guns kept the Americans away from us. When we realized what was happening, we used our last energy and began running toward the

Panther. We ran first in the ditch and then on the road, while the Panzer, firing its machine guns, slowly crawled backward until it reached cover behind a low rise in the terrain.

It was not too difficult to underrun the salvos of the turret MG, but one had to be almost an acrobat while running crouched and at high speed not to get hit by the bow MG of the radio operator. But when it was a question of survival and one was determined to continue living, the tired body was able to offer reserves one could not normally expect. We reached the Panzer of Obersturmführer Schlomka, dropped to the ground, and caught our breath. We heard repeated explosions from our Panzer, which by then was totally in flames. But it did not blow up, and, as long as we could still see it, the turret stayed on the hull.

Our sister-Panzer remained in its position to continue observing, as the road was blocked by our burning vehicle.

The five of us set out for the command post of the "DF" Regiment not very far away. Only a few kilometers before we reached it we had to cross a small hill without much cover. There a group of fighter-bombers, probably already on the way home and looking for a chance to get rid of their remaining ammunition, caught us. We were fortunate that narrow and deep draining ditches had been dug in the field we were just crossing. We dropped into them and the fighter-bombers began a target practice on us, which was probably quite enjoyable for them. They flew along the ditch we were lying in, or at right angles to it, split into two groups and headed for each other, with us in the middle, like aerobatic pilots. The bullets hit the walls of the ditch just above our backs; dirt and pieces of the clay pipes lying next to the ditch rained down on us. This was really the last torture our nerves could take. Two or three times the fighter-bombers stopped for such a long time that we thought we would be able to make the run to the next small wooded area. But each time it was a ploy, and we barely made it back into our ditch before the first salvos from the onboard weapons hit the ground around us again. They came down so low that we could have easily reached them with a thrown rock. It was late afternoon before this ordeal finally ended. One of our fighter-bomber friends was hit by a 2-cm Flak before he pulled away. The pilot was able to parachute down near the "DF" command post.

Soon after, we reached the "DF" command post near Mesnil-Clinchamps. We received rations and started out, after a short rest, for our repair company. After two or three days, we took over another Panzer, which had just been repaired.

With this vehicle, which was regrettably not fully ready for action as we found out soon after leaving the repair shop, we then drove to the assembly area for the counterattack on Mortain.

This is my report on the action on the invasion front. I should add that only the driver and I survived the war. The gunner and the loader drowned next to me during the attempt to swim across the Seine in Elbeuf.

We had broken out across the Seine with a Kampfgruppe from the SS "D" after the end of the fighting in Elbeuf, and the Americans had already occupied the city. Both comrades were poor swimmers, and we had reached the limit of our physical strength.

The radio operator, who later became my gunner, died just before the end of the war from Russian artillery fire as a Panzer commander and the last member of 2./Panzer-Regiment "Das Reich" at Spratzern near Sankt Pölken. We buried him in the cemetery of Erlauf.

Defensive Combat in the Vire–Chenedolle Area

**ERNST STRENG, PANZER COMMANDER IN THE
2. COMPANY/102 REPORTS ON THE ACTION OF SS-PANZER-
ABTEILUNG 102 (TIGERS) IN THE VIRE BATTLE AREA**

An order from the corps arrived in the afternoon of August 1:

"The heavy Panzer-abteilung is to be withdrawn under cover of darkness to the south to assist the 9. SS-Panzer-Division "Hohenstauffen," whose armored reconnaissance is already involved in heavy offensive and defensive fighting with advancing English/Canadian tank units. Starting at 8 P.M., the individual Panzers will disengage from their firing and reserve positions, unnoticed if possible, at twenty-minute intervals. They will march via Lacaine, Hamars, and Campandre during the night, reach Roucamps, and make themselves available to the Abteilung."

Even as we began the march, English batteries lay down heavy fire on the dust and limestone clouds caused by our tracks and accentuated by the setting sun, but a dark night soon set in.

Suddenly, enemy armored cars encountered our moving vehicles and opened fire. But Schroif returned a concentrated covering fire with explosive shells. As quickly as the enemy had appeared, he disappeared.

Loritz and Streng took the lead, closely followed by Schroif who announced each fork in the road and decided the path to be followed. At the first houses of Vire, some paratroopers waved at us from the ditch. Schroif made contact with them and scouted into Vire while Loritz covered there with the company. If there was fighting, we were supposed to follow. The city itself was completely destroyed by air attacks, and only ruins and mountains of rubble could be seen.

A narrow path crisscrossed the rubble, dropping suddenly toward the northern suburbs and the railroad station there. When the scouting part reached the height, battle noises and fire from tanks were heard from the suburb to the north. There had to be some forces left down there! We quickly crawled on through the debris while ferocious fire from tanks hit to the right and left of the road. Soon we reached the railroad embankment and a group of paratroopers defending themselves there. The enemy fire slowed down and soon stopped altogether; obviously, a tank attack was to follow. Our arrival brought new hope to the comrades, in particular as they were without heavy weapons. We had already determined how we were going to act after this enemy scouting attack. Vire, located at major crossroads, had to be turned into a defensive position, with special concentration on the main arterial routes. One or more Tigers were to be placed at each position with paratroopers for close defense and scouting between the individual positions. Some paratroopers came along immediately as guides to lead our Tigers through the shot-up streets to their positions. The scouting party had barely returned to the Panzer company when orders were issued. After a short briefing, the Panzers rolled out with the paratroopers mounted on them. Loritz's platoon took up position at the railroad station in the northern suburb while the others moved to the various arterial routes. The company command post was located on the northern slope from where the whole area could be observed. Half an hour later, all Tigers reported being in position.

During the night a motorcycle dispatch rider reported that the objective was reached, and in the morning he again arrived, with new orders for the 2. Company. They read:

"At 10 A.M., the company, together with the reconnaissance Abteilung 'Frundsberg,' will start an attack with the objective of the northern exit of La Bistière. 1. Company will start out from Estry and link up with 2. Company to encircle enemy tank units that have broken through to the south."

The company took on supplies during the morning hours. It assembled just before ten o'clock in the northern suburb for a short briefing. Everyone was surprised to see that the reconnaissance Abteilung consisted only of its commander and some twenty, lightly armed infantrymen. A rifle company with an antiaircraft MG of the paratroopers joined it.

At exactly 10 A.M., Schroif lifted his arm, gave the sign to start engines, and then the column began to move with Loritz's platoon at the point. We reached the fork in the road north of Vire fairly quickly. The Panzers drove laterally staggered so that at least two in front had an open field of fire. The infantry advanced to the left and right of the hedges to secure against surprises from the flank. The commander of the reconnaissance Abteilung had announced that some of our own scouting par-

ties were still in the terrain ahead of us. We had barely reached the fork
in the road when we spotted a tank and several men in a group of bushes
near the road, about 500 meters ahead. We could not determine defi-
nitely whether it was the enemy. Suddenly, a light scout car drove out
from behind the tank and raced off to the north. It could only be seen
for seconds, not long enough to knock it out. Immediately, the order
came: "Open fire! Destroy!" While the first shells hit the enemy tank, a
howling could be heard in the air above us. The infantrymen jumped
into cover. Our sector received enemy artillery fire. Schroif ordered to
continue the advance. Despite the hits the tank had received, it did not
blow up. Close behind it in the bushes and at a crossroads stood four
more Cromwell tanks. We knocked them all out. Then we halted for a
moment until the infantry had caught up with us. The terrain ahead of
us dropped off, then rose again. The last three Panzers provided covering fire while the others quickly rolled down the hill and up the other
side. The rest then followed, the infantry mounted on them. The objective of our attack, a small village, was seen 600 to 700 meters ahead. The
infantry advanced through the meadows right and left of the road,
before the Tigers began to move again and the first houses were
reached. There hell broke loose. Close to the road, covered from sight
by houses and high hedges, sat the enemy Sherman tanks. But our two
point Tigers, Loritz and Streng, cooperated excellently and knocked out
one after the other. We, too, had our hands full. We received fire, in particular from the height to the left which was covered all over with
hedges, obviously from tanks. We informed each other of hits so that we
could move out of the field of fire.

We took many hits to the tracks. Schroif ordered again and again to
fire on this bush or that. Slowly, we found our targets, as flashes of flame
rose here and there. The enemy fire slowed down. The road then rose.
When we reached the last house, the center of the column came under
heavy fire while the point kept moving. Shells whistled by like bright
flashes of lightning. We took more hits to the tracks. The chief ordered
fire from all barrels to the left. Again, concentrated fire on a group of
bushes half-left, two more tanks exploded. This was close combat at fifty
or a hundred meters. Schroif took a number of hits from a house in
front of him until explosive shells ended this enemy defense as well.
Then the advance continued, the road kept rising, and the objective of
the attack was reached.

We knew it was important to move into favorable defensive positions
in the terrain. Our spearhead had reached the top of the hill when we

got more fire from the left flank. We were hit. Although the radio failed, the engine still ran. Through hand signals and loud yelling, the gunner was directed to fire into the direction from where the fire came. We had barely fired the first shell when the other Tigers also opened up. They recognized immediately what was happening and supported us with violent fire. The spearhead rolled unconcerned down the hill and up the other side. During this most important moment, the radio failed. What were we to do next? Schroif waved Harlander closer and took over the relay of orders to the company.

"Stop immediately, objectives reached! Jupiter 1, take up position on this hill to cover to the north! Jupiter 2, secure at the crossroads 100 meters back to the right and left!" The Tigers rolled back into the positions indicated. Rosowski was about to turn into the position when he took six heavy hits from about thirty meters, which left deep dents in his turret. The seventh shot was his own, aimed into the hedge from where the fire came. A high flash of flame and a loud bang showed the result of his shell; the enemy tank blew up. Shortly after, a reconnaissance aircraft flew over our position. The 2-cm Flak-MG (antiaircraft machine gun) took aim at it, but it pulled away sharply and directed a fire attack by artillery on our area.

At about 3 P.M., the commander of the reconnaissance Abteilung drove back to Vire with the armored personnel carrier and the Flak-MG to report to the Abteilung that the objective of the attack had been reached and that twenty-two enemy tanks had been knocked out without any total losses to us. We had only sustained heavy damage from the hits. Regrettably, there was no radio contact, and the distance was too great.

The captured area was then systematically searched by smaller groups, mostly two Panzers and some infantrymen. Several nests of resistance were wiped out. Until evening, several trucks were set on fire, and two armored reconnaissance vehicles and a motorcycle dispatch rider were captured. We were blocking a route of advance of the English Guards Armored Division and captured its orderly officer, a captain, and his armored reconnaissance vehicle. The radio in this vehicle was very loud, and we could hear all of the enemy radio traffic. For this reason, the vehicle was immediately sent to the corps. Loud noise of fighting on the right flank was heard; that was Kalls who was working his way toward us, supported by mortars. For a while, we heard him very faintly on the radio. Schroif sent a scouting party to the right to determine enemy positions, terrain, and Kalls's whereabouts. A Panzer started out with the party but could accompany it only for a short way, as the terrain was too rough for Panzer movement. After one-and-a-half hours the scouting party returned with heavy losses. It was caught in an ambush in the broken terrain. We felt sorry that we could not spare anyone to go and assist Kalls, but we were getting strong pressure from the north ourselves and had to fight off assault parties along the road, especially after dark. Supplies arrived during the night of August 2 to 3, and rations were brought in at dawn.

At 10 A.M., Kuhlmann's Panzer just out of the repair shop, joined us, and was immediately given a mission. From the left of the road, enemy tanks were trying time and again to move in on us. Expertly directed by a few infantrymen, Kuhlmann moved into a favorable firing position and knocked out three tanks in a short period of time. We achieved the same success a little farther back, to the right of the road, where five enemy tanks sat in a ravine. Three of them were knocked out by us, the others caught on fire and burned out.

Toward evening, the enemy tried again to get our Panzers with assault parties, advancing from the north on both sides of the road. The Tigers were only waiting for the right moment. Our shells ripped trees out of the ground that fell across the road. The assault party jumped up, and our MGs and antitank shells hammered among them. Despite all this, the enemy got closer, as the terrain offered excellent cover. Our few infantrymen could not provide close cover to the semicircle of the Tigers, so the Panzers worked together in groups of two and kept the terrain around them clear through occasional bursts of fire.

Everyone was extremely tense, as we listened into the night. That helped us in holding off the enemy. Around 9:30 P.M., Schroif sent a Panzer to the fork in the road south of us with the order to observe the withdrawal there, to secure to the northwest, and to hold up the advancing enemy and safeguard the march back.

When the order to pull back arrived at 11 P.M., the vehicles with the worst damage from hits to the tracks set out first, the infantrymen mounted on them. The serviceable Panzers followed last.

The withdrawal was completed in total order. Around midnight, we reached Vire, where strong units had been concentrated. While we had held out, far ahead, for two days, they had set up a new front line there.

The company made camp next to the road three kilometers south of Vire and had a chance to repair the considerable damage from the hits; two teams from the repair company had been provided.

Hard days of fighting were over, and they had been successful. Without losses, the company achieved considerable success. Twenty-eight enemy tanks were knocked out, more were damaged, fourteen trucks destroyed, two armored scout cars and crews captured, and two motorcycle dispatch riders taken prisoner with their bikes. Greater, still, was the tactical success. Because of the energetic assault by the 2. and 1. Companies, the enemy felt its flanks threatened and his advance on Flères stalled.

The British reported:

"When the VII. British Corps attacked in the direction of Flères on August 2, it had to turn and face tank reserves coming from the west bank of the Orne River. While the 11th Armoured Division was advancing to its right in the direction of the road Vire-Vassy, the Guards became involved in heavy fighting southeast of Beny-Bocage. The Germans did not bring in strong forces but created this erroneous impression by operating in a very aggressive and adroit manner. Small battle groups, each with two or three tanks, an infantry company, and a team with rocket launchers, infiltrated into the widely staggered British columns and threatened their flanks. Through these methods, the Germans brought the Guards to a stop near Estry and forced the 11th Armoured Division to halt its march toward the road Vire-Vassy. This German tactic could have been answered by determined assaults against the enemy centers of resistance. The German battle groups were extremely exposed; they did not have infantry available to form a continuous front line and could not spare any motorized forces to secure their supply lines."

INSIDE TIGER 134 (FEY) OF THE 1./102 ON AUGUST 6 AND 7, SECURING THE ROAD VASSY-VIRE NEAR CHENEDOLLE AGAINST THE INCREASING ATTACKS OF THE 11TH BRITISH ARMOURED DIVISION

After a thorough overhaul and repair of the damage from hits sustained in the fighting in the Vire-Chenedolle-Vassy area, we received the order to return to the Vire combat area. In a roundabout way we reached Vassy, a small town on national route 812, connecting Condé and Vire. A few kilometers from town, signs "WE 1" finally indicated that we were close to our destination. Our noncom in charge, F. Schreiber, gladly welcomed us at the command post, as every Tiger was urgently needed there! Two more comrades, Tresemann and Taschl, were killed on the previous day. We were attached to Egger's platoon and immediately received combat orders that took us to the front into a reserve position the very same day. Things were happening there; houses were on fire, and constant harassing fire was concentrated on the abandoned town, which could be seen on a hill against the evening sky. There was a certain anxiety in the air, a

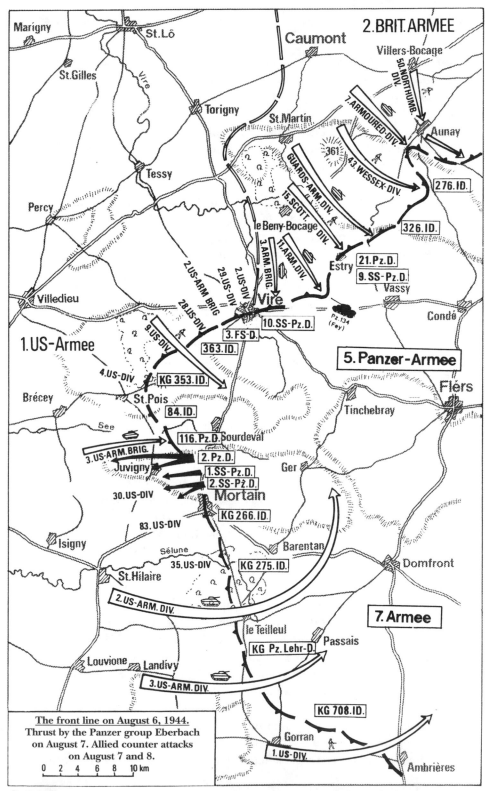

Marigny
St.Lô
Caumont
2. BRIT. ARMEE
Villers-Bocage
50. NORTHUMB. DIV.
St.Gilles
7. ARMOURED DIV.
Aunay
Torigny
St.Martin
361
43. WESSEX-DIV.
276. ID.
Tessy
GUARDS-ARM.DIV.
15.SCOTT. DIV.
326. ID.
Percy
le Beny-Bocage
3. ARM. DIV.
11. ARM. DIV.
Estry
21.Pz.D.
9. SS-Pz.D.
Villedieu
2.US-ARM.BRIG.
29.US-DIV
2.US-DIV
Vassy
28.US-DIV
Vire
Condé
9.US-DIV
10.SS-Pz.D.
Pz.134 (Fey)
1. US-Armee
3. FS-D.
363. ID.
5. Panzer-Armee
4.US-DIV
KG 353. ID.
Flers
Brécey
St.Pois
84. ID.
Tinchebray
See
116. Pz. D. Sourdeval
3.US-ARM.BRIG.
2. Pz. D.
Ger
Juvigny
1.SS-Pz.D.
2.SS-Pz.D.
30.US-DIV
Mortain
KG 266. ID.
83. US-DIV
Isigny
Sélune
Barentan
Domfront
35. US-DIV
KG 275. ID.
St.Hilaire
2.US-ARM.DIV.
7. Armee
le Teilleul
Passais
KG Pz. Lehr-D.
Louvione
Landivy
3.US-ARM.DIV.
KG 708. ID.
Gorran
1. US-DIV.
Ambrières

The front line on August 6, 1944.
Thrust by the Panzer group Eberbach
on August 7. Allied counter attacks
on August 7 and 8.

0   2   4   6   8   10 km

© H.E. Furbringer

premonition that we were to have our hands full there. After a short briefing of the commanders came the order of all orders:

"Get ready! Panzers, march! Advance to the farthest infantry positions!"

This was meant to take us into the most favorable starting position for the attack planned for the next morning. As always, we arrived just in time. Our grenadiers were no longer able to withstand the enemy pressure. They were running back across this terrain without cover and suffered many losses. We could not stop them. Their casualties were too high, and too intense was the mental pressure caused by the steamrollers of enemy fire that preceded all attacks. An armored car, travelling at full speed and well ahead of its troops, was blown up by a shell from our gun at a short range at the last light of day, just before it could take cover behind the first houses. Then came a radio message from Egger: "Panzers, halt! Hold your positions!" It put an end to the activities of that day. We had advanced the farthest with our Tiger and sat on the left, open flank. Despite the fact that our position was critical, we never thought of pulling back. A long, threatening night lay ahead of us, and the next morning was to bring the continuation of the attack. Without cover from the grenadiers, we stood close to, if not already among, the advancing enemy, about 100 meters away from our own closest Panzer. There was no thought of sleeping. All five men sat at the open hatches and listened into the night. It was filled with the noises of enemy vehicles moving about, the rattle of tracks, and the clearly audible orders and conversations of the assembled Amis (short for Americans) and Tommys.

In between, we heard other sounds, the shouting, moaning, and whimpering of wounded German grenadiers. It cut one's heart to hear the often repeated call: "Mother!—Help!—Take me with you!—Get me out!" We could not take that for the entire night! The loader was given the necessary instructions, and we crept into the dark, carrying a tarpaulin and first aid kit. We soon found the critically wounded man who had been calling all the time among a group of dead soldiers. It was almost impossible to calm him down, his wounds were too serious for us to offer substantial help. He clung to us and did not want to remain alone among his dead comrades. Time and again he moaned: "Why did they leave me here? Where is my company chief?" What could we answer to that? We had to be near to a path with the wounded man. Repeatedly, enemy soldiers walked by so close that we could hear their carefree talk and laughter and could see their burning cigarettes.

When we finally had the wounded man on the tarpaulin, we carried and dragged him, as best possible, back to our Panzer and bedded him down on the rear deck. Without much hesitation, we raced backward at high speed until we reached the first infantry positions where we handed over the wounded man for further transport. Then, forward again to our old position, at high speed! The noise of the engine had caused uneasiness everywhere. Flares lit up the night, and MGs opened up until, finally, calm returned.

But there was no calm for us. In the light of the flares during the rescue, our radio operator, Trautmann, spotted a Pak position. It was half-right from us and must have been set up during the darkness. We quickly formulated our plan, clipped a few hand grenades to our belts, grabbed the explosives that were really meant for our own Panzer if something went wrong, and set out for the Pak under cover of darkness. Then, several hand grenades, a few salvos from the submachine gun, and the Pak sat all by itself in the terrain. It turned out, at closer inspection, to be the feared 8.5-cm gun. We quickly attached our explosive charge to its breech.

The radio operator had, in the meantime, taken a look at the foxholes. He jogged toward our Panzer with a ration box containing sandwiches, cans, chocolate, and cigarettes and with a map-case. We lit the fuse on the five-kg charge and raced after him. Such fuses were not long, ten to fifteen centimeters, which translated into ten to fifteen seconds. That meant we had to really move our legs. The Pak was blown to pieces with an immense bang. We reached our Tiger unharmed, glad of the sumptuous booty of food.

The front had woken up again and was in turmoil. Exhausted by the tensions of the last few minutes, we explored our catch more closely. What we found made us doubly glad. It contained, in addition to the welcome provisions, a valuable map of our combat sector.

Radio messages from Zugführer Egger and the company command post came in, demanding to know what was happening with us. But it was all over, we had only rescued a badly wounded comrade, possibly saving his life, and destroyed one of the most dangerous enemies of the Tiger, the 8.5-cm Pak. For this, we thought, prior permission or report on success was not necessary.

OUR MOST SUCCESSFUL DAY

Then the morning of August 7, 1944, dawned. It ushered in a day that was to bring to our Tiger and its crew the greatest proof of worth and outstanding success.

We were still waiting for the grenadiers who were to join the Tigers in the attack that morning; it was to start after a preparatory artillery fire.

The platoons and groups of Pionier-Bataillon 600, comrades from a division of the Heer, had arrived at our Panzer. They spread out and sought cover in trenches and behind bushes. We waited and waited, but still there was no artillery salvo to indicate the start of the attack. Hour after hour passed, and then it started but not on our side. Some pioneers to our left gave us a tank alert. Shortly after, we surveyed the situation from our Tiger. The Shermans rolled out of a wooded area, down the hill. We spotted ten—twelve—fifteen enemy tanks, between them scout cars, armored personnel carriers with mounted infantry, and wheeled armored personnel carriers. The whole slope came to life. The distance was approximately 1,200 meters. Until then not a shot had been fired. The scene looked like a tank attack as taught in military schools, everything that was required was there. The grenadiers watched us. What would we do? They, and their company chief, started to show a certain nervousness. An Oberleutnant (first lieutenant) climbed onto our Panzer, asking us to open fire. But he had to leave that to our commander. The radio operator was given a message to send to all: "15 Panzers will attack, with infantry, from the left flank. Open fire at 600 meters!" Immediately, the order by radio came from commander Weiß "Ruderboot" (row boat) to Ofenrohr 3 (stove pipe): Start out immediately. (Ofenrohr 3 was the code name for our Tiger in radio traffic). That was all we needed. The commander ordered the operator not to acknowledge and to turn off the receiver immediately, and from then on we only transmitted.

The enemy tanks arranged themselves and rolled toward us in a wide wedge formation. The distance was still approximately 800 meters. Long before, the loader had readied antitank shells. The driver was told, when so ordered, to immediately let the Panzer roll back over the left track for a few meters while pulling up on the right track. In this way we brought the front of our Tiger into a favorable defensive position within a few seconds. The comrades with the other field post number had something in store for us, and the side of our Panzer, facing them, was too sensitive for that.

Then the time came, 600 meters. We maneuvered our Panzer into the desired direction for firing. The gunner had already had his first target in his sight for some time. It was the tank at the point, exactly in the center of the attacking pack, probably its leader. The second and third targets were also determined, first its neighbor to the left, then the one to the right. After that, it was to be the Shermans at the extreme left and right. They could have been dangerous if they were able to come around on our flanks; even a Tiger was vulnerable inside the 400-meter range.

Finally, the relief-bringing order came:

"Antitank shell—600—Fire!" The first shot was wide, and realizing this froze us only for a few seconds. "Gun sight 400—Fire!" That was a hit. A second shell followed immediately, another hit. Then, the next target: "Tank on the left—Fire!" It, too, took two shells. Within a short time, four Shermans stood in flames on the slope. The enemy then overcame its first confusion, stopped, and opened fire. We took hit after hit, on the turret, to the front, the tracks. Nuts, bolts, and rivets whistled through the interior. The Oberleutnant of the grenadiers, who had been inside the Panzer until then, jumped out head over heels, and withdrew with his soldiers. There were to be no more attacks started that day! The radio operator reported constantly on the development of the battle, and in between he found plenty of work for his machine gun. The commander radioed again: "Withdraw to own lines!" We counted six burning and smoking tanks by then; there had to be an awful confusion over there! Its infantry dismounted and ran about, looking for cover. Vehicles ran into each other as they tried to turn around. Then, the seventh and eighth tanks were knocked out. As they were tangled up, our 8.8 had taken aim and brought about their quick end. They burned out, close to each other.

Was it minutes that had passed, or hours? We did not know. Our loader, the Volga German, strong as an ox, sank to his knees. Standing the closest to the breech, he had inhaled too much gunpowder gas and passed out. And our Panzer took more and more hits. The loss of the loader caused our operation to stall. The gunner manned the turret MG, while the radio operator had already worn out the fourth barrel. By then, all the Shermans had zeroed in on us, and we had to try to get out of their range, otherwise they might have found one of our weak spots. "Driver, backwards, march! Halt!" We took another hit, the Tiger jerked backward. That was a different caliber, that was a Pak! Smoke drifted inside through the hatches. The shell had come from the left. We had to act; a second hit landed between the driver's and radio operator's sights and wiped out the bow MG. The driver took the place of the unconscious loader, but there was nobody left to drive! The left track was ripped off, and the Tiger was no longer mobile. Then we spotted the Pak by its muzzle fire at the far left near a bush. The turret was turned to nine o'clock, Albert received quick and accurate directions, a high explosive shell was loaded, and then: "Fire!" We spared three shells for this enemy, then explosions and whirling parts of metal testified to the end of this well-positioned Pak.

The tank battle continued. We felt neither hunger nor thirst; the fighting demanded all of our concentration. Dripping sweat, our eyes reddened, we gasped for air in the thick fumes of saltpeter. With every shot from our gun, a gray-blue cloud of smoke came from the breech. The ventilation system was unable to keep up. Paul lay between Hermann's legs on the turret mechanism, his eyes turned up. We still faced a few Shermans; it was really not easy! While we were firing at the Pak, the Shermans took aim at us. When we took on the Shermans, the antitank guns gave us hell. It was a real chore, having to fight two enemies at once. In the meantime, twelve burning enemy tanks were witness to our battle.

Then the commander radioed, having received the report on our Tiger's inability to move: "Blow up the Panzer, fight your way back with the crew!" But that was impossible for us. As long as we had one shell left, one round of MG ammunition, we would not quit this battle and our Panzer! Once more, we remained silent and forgot to acknowledge receipt of this message.

And the tank battle went on. We took more hits to the turret, the front and the right track, but knocked out two more enemy tanks.

Then, both MGs failed, and we were running out of antitank shells. Fourteen Shermans gave up their ghosts and ended their march toward Berlin prematurely northwest of Vire at noon on a beautifully bright August day. And the whole engagement took only thirty minutes! But there was more fighting to do! We could not spot any more Shermans on the move or firing, but we thought there had been fifteen attacking Shermans! A gully just ahead of us, covered with trees and bushes, demanded increased attention. We fired one high explosive shell after another; there were enough targets. Abandoned armored reconnaissance vehicles and other supply vehicles went up in flames. Half-tracks at full speed, some of them with mounted antitank weapons, so-called stove pipes, were knocked out. The whole slope was covered by dark blue smoke, which gently covered the recent drama. From time to time, tanks blew up with sky-high bursts of flames and deafening noise. The smoke from the burning vehicles enveloped the battleground and allowed a number of enemy soldiers to escape this inferno alive.

Since we did not know how much longer we would have to stay with our Panzer and our ammunition had been used up except for a few shells, we wanted to add to our supplies during the developing break in the fighting. The commander quickly slid down from the Panzer and ran and crawled to get out of the enemy field of vision. Harassing fire had set in. The enemy slowly zeroed in on our position, having recognized that his attack had faltered at this point.

Completely exhausted, the commander reached a Tiger of our company and tried to attract attention at the driver's and radio operator's hatches, both locked because of the steady artillery fire.

Finally, a lid was lifted, and the commander was able to make his request for a few antitank shells, but without success. Without an explanation why we could not get anything, the hatches remained closed and any further requests remained unheard. He continued on to the next Tiger, again crawling, running, and jumping a few hundred meters. This effort was not in vain. With an antitank shell under his arm, the commander crawled back to his Panzer.

The artillery fire constantly increased in strength. Unfortunately, we sat in the middle of a meadow without cover and took the first artillery hits to the hull and turret. We learned from one of the last radio messages of the day that Schwab's platoon with three Tigers was to pull us out with the coming of darkness. But it was to be a long time before night fell. On top of everything else, our radio packed in under the constant fire. Fighter-bombers circled above us, diving and firing from all barrels on our brave Tiger, which sat, immobile, as if for target practice. Their bombs were too damn close! Was that to be the end? But just before the next formation flew in, we had a saving thought: smoke candles were placed on the rear and front, and we played the role of a knocked-out, burnt-out Panzer! We had enough of these smoke candles on board and managed to remain unnoticed for some time. Suddenly, we were wide awake again, ripped out of our half-sleep. We heard the familiar rattle of tank tracks, but not from one of our comrades. It came from half-right ahead of us, where the gully flattened into groups of trees and bushes. We slowly brought our gun around, almost unnoticeably. We aimed it, with the lowest possible elevation, at the cluster of bushes. We only had two antitank shells left, one of them already in the barrel. Our nerves were tensed to the breaking point. Was it one tank, or two? There were only 100 meters between us and the gully. The driver and radio operator sat in the open hatches, ready to bail out. Paul, who had recovered, was holding the second, and last, shell ready in his arms. If these two were fired and missed, it would have meant bailing out as quickly as possible. The rattle of tracks and engine noise came ever closer. Seconds turned into eternity! Maybe, the others did not know that a German Panzer, ready to fire, was sitting there? Our other Tigers had long since pulled back, and we had been giving off smoke all afternoon. But enough of these thoughts!

Ahead of us, the bushes parted. A long, smooth barrel without muzzle brake came into view, no doubt, a Sherman. Then the curved hull and the turret appeared. "Fire!" Our first shell glanced off, and we saw it rise steeply into the sky. Surprising, the details one noticed even during such a tense situation. "Aim lower—Fire!" We roared loudly as the shell disappeared precisely under the barrel, at the base of the turret. As if gripped by an iron fist, the tank stopped with a jerk. A fine column of smoke, growing increasingly denser, rose vertically into the sky. It was the fifteenth tank kill of that day. Counting the tank knocked out the previous evening in the same area, the total was sixteen, a whole tank company not even counting the armored cars, reconnaissance vehicles, half-tracks, and other vehicles that were impossible to tally. Despite all these successes, would we be able to hold off the enemy?

It had suddenly turned quiet. We quit talking. We were suddenly indescribably tired as we waited for the Tigers to pull us out.

We were thankful and reassured when, suddenly, rocket launchers threw a wall of fire, with an immense roar and whistle, into the gully and onto the adjoining slope. We thought no one could live through that.

Just as the last salvos of the rocket launchers had whistled by, exactly as per plan, the three Tigers of Schwab's platoon showed up and pulled us out. Two Tigers did the pulling, the third provided cover. So we rolled, pulling our tracks behind, into the dark night. After a short stop at the company command post where our chief, Kalls, congratulated us on our success, we reached Vassy the next morning. But what condition our Tiger was in! Holes, big enough to put one's head in! The drive wheel with steering mechanism was cleanly shot through. The shell was still stuck in the hull, which would give the repair company a few days of welding and patching! But we felt all the more proud and close to our Panzer. The more holes and scars it had, the more precious it was to us! It was much more than cold metal to us, it was a part of us!

Panzer Battle on
Route Nationale 158
Between Caen and Falaise,
August 1944

**THE CANADIAN-BRITISH OPERATION "TOTALIZE" BEGAN ON
AUGUST 8 WITH THE OBJECTIVE TO BREAK THROUGH TO
FALAISE ALONG BOTH SIDES OF ROUTE NATIONALE 158**

At 11 P.M. on August 7, the shelling of the villages on the flanks of the
battleground where armored units were to break through began as per
plan. Half an hour after the start of the shelling, the armored groups of
the enemy assembled east of the road to Falaise. The 51st Highland Division, together with the 33rd British Armoured Brigade, drove in three
columns with only one meter distance between them. Each attack column had a heavily armored spearhead with two platoons of Sherman
tanks, two platoons of mine removal tanks, and one platoon of tank pioneers. The latter had the objective of marking the attack area through
use of tape and lights. Behind the spearhead followed the main body,
consisting of a great number of tanks and an infantry battalion mounted
on armored vehicles.

These three columns consisted of some 1,900 men and 200 tanks.
They were followed by a group of tanks as support, which were to secure
the terrain so that the armored groups could deploy and ensure favorable starting positions for the infantry.

The 2nd Canadian Infantry Division and the 2nd Canadian
Armoured Brigade attacked, in four columns, in the same direction to
the west of Route N 158.

To facilitate orientation, searchlights illuminated the cloud cover
from below. In addition, directional radio beams and use of compass, as
had been practiced, were supposed to help in maintaining proper direction while driving. At 11:45, 360 artillery guns began laying a moving wall

of fire, 3,700 meters wide and advancing at ninety meters per minute, along both sides of the N 158 in the direction of Falaise. Altogether, 720 artillery guns were available for the various tasks.

The artillery fire reached all the way to the command post of the 89 Infantry-Division near Bretteville-sur-Laise. During the course of the night, the 51st Highland Division managed to capture the towns of Garceslles, St. Aignan, and Grasmesnil. The woods immediately south of St. Aignan were occupied in the morning hours of August 8.

The infantrymen of the 89. and 272. Infantry-Divisions bloodily fought off the first attacks but had to pull back their positions after Hill 75 and St. Aignan were lost. Tilly-la-Campagne, occupied by the 89. Infantry-Division, was a position particularly bitterly fought for. After repeated attacks by strong infantry and tank units, the blood-stained rubble had to be left to the British attackers at approximately 7 A.M.

To the west of the Route Nationale, the columns of the Canadian Armoured Brigade and of the 4th Canadian Infantry Brigade also encountered difficulties in orientating themselves. The Royal Regiment of Canada pushed past Rocquancourt to the east instead of to the west, and the Royal Hamilton Light Infantry, which continued rolling to the west, pushed right through the town. The third battalion of the Essex Scottish completely lost its orientation.

The fourth column of the Canadians, the 8th Canadian Reconnaissance Regiment, was brought to a halt just short of its objective, Hill 122. Around noon of August 8 the attackers generally reached the planned objectives of Phase 1. The superior Canadian-British forces achieved, thanks to an aerial bombardment by 1,000 bombers and shelling by more than 700 artillery guns, a great success. The positions of the 89. Infantry-Division were broken through at a width of six kilometers. Without Panzers and mobile heavy antitank weapons, the infantry-division was unable to withstand this assault. The enemy was able to advance deeply along the road toward Falaise. Only the worn-out units of the 12. SS-Panzer-Division, which were not in action at other hot spots, were thrown at the enemy.

These were, on August 8, one Panzer-abteilung with thirty-nine Panzer IVs, one company of the Schwere (heavy) SS-Panzer-Abteilung 101 with ten Tigers and an antitank company. In addition, there was one battalion of Panzer-grenadiers (Kampfgruppe Waldmüller) and the escort companies of the division and the corps. Even before dawn, the divisional commander of the 12. SS-Panzer-Division, Oberführer Kurt Meyer, drove to the front line with a few messengers to determine the situation on the spot. "Panzermeyer" drove cross-country to Cintheaux where he met a platoon of Waldmüller's antitank guns. The town was under artillery fire.

On both sides of the road he noted German soldiers, retreating south in total disintegration. Panzermeyer reported:

> For the first time during the long, cruel years of people killing each other, I see fleeing German soldiers. You can no longer speak to them, they have gone through the hell of the raging battles and are stumbling, emaciated and with eyes full of fear, past us. Fascinated, I stare at the leaderless soldiers. My uniform sticks to my body, sweat caused by the fear of responsibility breaks from all pores. Suddenly, I realize that the fate of the city of Falaise and the safety of both armies depend on my decision. I am standing upright in the VW as we drive in the direction of Caen. More and more shocked soldiers come toward me and flee to the south. In vain, I attempt to halt the front, which is in motion. The terrible bomb attacks have broken the nerves of the units of the 89. Infantry-Division. Shell fire is covering the road and empties it of people; only on its right and left the flight continues in straight lines. I jump out of the car and stand alone on the road. Slowly, I walk toward the front and address the fleeing comrades. They stop short, halt, ponder me unbelievingly as I stand on the road armed with a carbine. The boys probably consider me crazy, but then they recognize me, turn around, wave their comrades over and organize the defense of the height of Cintheaux. The town has to be held at all costs to gain time for the two Kampfgruppen. Greatest speed is required.

Kampfgruppe Waldmüller was immediately set in march. The attack was to have begun at 12:30 P.M.

In the meantime, the enemy began preparations for Phase 2. The 1st Polish Armoured Division and the 4th Canadian Armoured Division advanced to the assembly areas of the infantry divisions in the morning hours of August 8. The start of the attack by these two tank divisions was set for 1:55 P.M. while the preparatory bomb attack was scheduled from 12:26 P.M. to 1:55 P.M. The 8th U.S. Air Force appeared over the target area at 12:55. The Canadian artillery had received marker shells, whose red smoke was to indicate the targets, an hour before and was able to open fire just in time.

The violent and well-aimed defensive fire of our III. Flakkorps hit the lead bomber, which had to make an emergency drop before reaching the target. This caused the following aircraft of the group to drop their bomb loads short and onto their own troops. Losses of dead and wounded occurred, guns and vehicles were lost to the attacking troops, but the confusion this brought about was much worse.

At 1:30 P.M. the Poles hesitatingly began the attack. The 2nd Canadian Corps reported that the "start line" was crossed at 1:55 P.M. by both tank divisions. Panzermeyer reported:

I meet with Waldmüller north of Bretteville-le-Rabet, and both of us drive to Cintheaux to determine what the present situation there is. The Tigers of Wittmann are standing ready east of Cintheaux behind a hedge; they have, so far, not entered into the firefight. Cintheaux lies under artillery fire while the open terrain is fairly free of shelling. From the northern edge of the town, we spot heavy tank columns north of the road to Bretteville. The tanks have assembled in groups. The same picture can be seen south of Carcelles and at the edge of the woods southeast of town. The sight of these masses of tanks takes our breath away. We cannot understand the behavior of the Canadians. Why does this overwhelming tank force not continue its attack? Waldmüller and I realize that we must not let these tank groups assault us. The enemy tanks must not be allowed to lead any more attacks. On either side of the road, an enemy tank division is ready for the attack. During the last briefing with Waldmüller and Wittmann we observe a single bomber flying repeatedly over the terrain dropping marker flares. The bomber seems to be a flying command post, and I order an immediate attack to bring the troops out of the target area of the bombs.

Once more I shake Michael Wittmann's hand and refer to the extremely critical situation. Our good Michael laughs his boyish laughter and climbs into his Tiger. So far, 138 enemy tanks in the east and west have fallen victim to him. Will he be able to increase this number of successes or become a victim himself? Without hesitation, the Panzers are now rolling north.

They cross open terrain at high speed and make use of small dips in the land for their firefights. The Panzer attack pulls the grenadiers ahead. In a widely dispersed line they are moving toward the target of the attack: the wood southeast of Carcelles with its assembled tanks. I am standing at the northern edge of

Cintheaux while enemy artillery aims destructive fire at the attacking Panzers. The Tiger of Michael Wittmann races into the enemy fire. I know his tactics during such situations, it is called: Straight ahead! Never stop! Get through and gain an open field of fire! All Panzers are hurdling into the steely inferno. They have to prevent the enemy attack, they have to destroy their schedule. Waldmüller and his grenadiers are right behind. The brave infantrymen follow their officers. An endless chain of bombers is approaching from the northwest, as town after town is being wiped out. There is only one answer: Get out into the open fields. We can observe that the Canadians, too, are being dumped on by the American bomber fleet. The last waves of the 678 four-engined bombers, which had started out fly over the determinedly attacking Kampfgruppe Waldmüller without dropping a single bomb on the Panzers. The bombers are dropping on the targets as ordered, without taking notice of the changed situation. Kampfgruppe Waldmüller approaches the wooded area and has already entered combat with Polish infantry. The grim duel of Panzer against tank is being conducted by the fighting vehicles of the 4th Canadian Armoured Division and the Tigers of Michael Wittmann. At times, the Tigers are almost impossible to make out. Well-directed artillery fire hammers the Tigers and Panzer IVs. The town of Cintheaux is being attacked from the north and lies under direct fire of the Canadian tanks. Activity by some tanks of the Wittmann group from the flank keeps the Sherman tanks away from Cintheaux. We are unbelievably lucky; the other side is not carrying out a concentrated attack. The escort company of the division reports being west of St. Sylvain in combat with the spearhead of the 1st Polish Armoured Division and has knocked out a number of tanks. The Poles no longer dare to leave the woods of Grasmesnil. The fighting has now been going on for hours. The wounded are assembled south of Cintheaux, and are being moved out under enemy fire.

The physician of the Schwere SS-Panzer-Abteilung, 101 Hauptsturmführer Wolfgang Rabe, M.D., who watched the battle of the Tigers from some distance, reported on the fate of the Tigers of Michael Wittmann's company:

"Wittmann was east of the road to Caen with four or five Tigers. I was off to the side. The Panzers came under fire, reportedly from English

15-cm guns. Some of the Tigers went up in flames. I tried to determine if anyone got out. When I did not see anybody, I thought they might have left the Panzer through the lower hatch and I tried to get closer. This was impossible since I came under fire as soon as I left the ditch in an easterly direction. We waited another hour or two for anyone of the crews to show up. Towards evening I drove over to Brigadeführer Kraemer, chief of the general staff of the I. SS-Panzerkorps, and reported on developments. He ordered me, since I was the senior officer of the Abteilung, to lead the remains of the Abteilung back, and attached me to the SS-Panzer-Regiment 12, Wünsche."

The combat historian of the SS-Tiger-Abteilung, Rottenführer Herbert Debusmann, was employed in munitions removal in this area in 1947 as a prisoner of war. He found all five knocked-out or disabled Tigers, as well as two Panzer IVs close by. The insignia of the Schwere SS-Panzer-Abteilung 101 was still clearly visible. One of the Tigers, carrying the number 007, had its turret ripped off. This was the command Panzer of Obersturmbannführer V. Westerhagen, Abteilung commander of the 101, who was prevented by illness from taking part in this battle.

With the help of local French residents, in particular the owner of the land where the wrecks of the Panzers from the fighting of August 8 were sitting, and newspapers from Cintheaux and the surrounding area, the end of the Tigers and their crews could be clarified.

The remains of the crew of Wittmann's Tiger were found near Tiger 007 in the summer of 1983 and clearly identified as those of Michael Wittmann and his crew. They were moved to the military cemetery at La Cambe where they took a dignified place of rest among many of the comrades who fell during the summer of 1944 in Normandy.

The author has received a report from a French citizen, who is known to him, and who takes a position on the various descriptions of the destruction of Tiger 007 in publications:

"I am not in agreement with the reports that Tiger 007 was knocked out by Sherman tanks. I maintain, and remember perfectly, that it received a hit by a rocket from a Typhoon fighter-bomber to the cover of the engine; the air intake grill had been ripped open. At the time, I was very interested in determining why Tiger 007 had lost its turret. The turret was ripped off by an explosion in the Panzer while the vehicle itself continued rolling until it was off its broken tracks. No shells had penetrated the turret or hull. I determined this personally, and have so recorded it in my diary."

There is a map of Cintheaux and surroundings in the pictorial section on the actions in Normandy on which the mayor had indicated the position of the knocked-out German Panzers.

The report by Sturmmann Helmut Wiese, who participated in the attack of the Kampfgruppe Waldmüller as the driver of a Panzer IV of the 5./SS-Panzer-regiment 12, offers a realistic view from a perspective that was probably the same for all Panzer crews on August 8:

After surveying our target, discussion of possible danger spots, and the best path to follow, we get inside and inform Arno, the gunner, as well as Karl, the loader, and Egon, the radio operator. This will be their first time in action. Get ready, load, "Panzer, march!" Our nerves are tensed to the breaking point, as each one of us is alone with his thoughts. It is extremely quiet inside the vehicle, only the engine is humming. Slowly and carefully we crawl up the slope toward the top. What will be at its back? The commander of the Panzer, Unterscharführer Otto Knof, is standing in his open hatch . . . "Helmut, more speed!" I gear up and step on the gas. Across the top of the hill I spot the edge of the woods and aim for its left corner. We want to get around it to see what is behind. Then, we feel a violent hammering on the outside walls, machine-gun and rifle fire, now our turret MG opens up. I recognize the sound of an enemy MG, spot flat helmets. Declutch on the right, the front MG finds the target, opens fire, everything is happening at great speed.

There, at the edge of the woods, enemy soldiers are bringing a gun into position. I report to the turret, a new target for the front MG. Our gun opens up as we are at full speed. "Stop! Stop! Back! Back! Faster!" Otto, the commander, yells this order. I know that the engine is running at the highest speed; it cannot go any faster. I look at the instruments, the tachometer is showing in the red, the clock shows sixteen minutes to four o'clock. As I look through the vision port, I am blinded by an exploding brightness. There is a bang as if a full soda pop bottle is bursting after falling onto a tiled floor. Direct hit to the front, I thought. We made it. Then the Panzer is shaken as if by the fist of a giant; brightness, screaming, braking, splintering sounds, nothing remotely human. Then, the smell of sulfur and absolute calm. "Bail out! The Panzer is on fire!," comes Otto's order. I unlock the hatch and push it upward; it opens only a few centimeters. Flames immediately come through. The skirting of the turret is blocking it. I watch as our radio man, Egon, pulls his legs through his hatch. That is the way out. Across the power train, the radio, I crawl toward the hatch, find no more air; it is getting so hot, I want to get out, I have had it!

Then, I see a face far away, and arms stretched out toward me. I hear shouts: "Helmut, come out!" I push and pull, find fresh air. Finally, I am outside, jump off the tank, and drop to the ground. Egon had come back and gotten me out—thanks, comrade! He helps me to get up, and I am on my feet again. Bullets whistling by hit the hull. We run around to the side away from the enemy. Otto is there. But where are Arno and Karl? Otto points to the turret—the side hatches are still closed—and he yells: "Both were killed immediately, I was still inside!" I cannot fathom it. Arno Eltus from Königsberg in East Prussia, my gunner, is dead. We had been together with Otto since Hasselt, always in the same Panzer. The three of us had experienced our first action together, our first successes. Now he is gone. He was left in the turret, a terrible realization.

Black smoke boils from the open hatches. We are running toward our own lines. Suddenly, I hear: "Helmut, you are on fire!" I drop and roll on the ground, as Otto and Egon help to extinguish the flames. More MG rounds are whistling past us. We run and run. Finally, on the back slope we find German soldiers and cover. A group of soldiers addresses us, but I can no longer hear and comprehend anything.

I can see but cannot recognize anything. I feel a strong burning pain. Then, everything turns black and very quiet. I realize that I am in a room lying on the ground. I cannot move, I am moaning. Someone is trying to help me; I cannot see him. Then I suddenly understand a voice saying: "Calm, stay calm. You are at our field dressing station, in safety." Everything turns black again. Then, suddenly, Otto is there and says: "At nightfall I'll pick you up and take you with us!" That makes me happy, but then all is black again. The ground trembles, engines roar, voices call: "The Panzers are taking off!" That was a deep disappointment since Otto had promised to come and get me. Daylight floods through the door. I see foreign uniforms, hear a clear voice ask: "Anyone here from the SS?" There is more infantry fire, artillery shells explode. I am quickly loaded into an

ambulance, feel terrible pain, and black out again. I experience
the field hospital in Caen and the transport by ship in a trance;
mostly I am unconscious. On August 21, in Leeds, I realize and
understand that I have been captured. From the hospital documents I see that the dressing station in France had been surrendered to members of the 1st Polish Armoured Division on the
morning of August 9.

BATTLEGROUND FALAISE ERNST STRENG,
PANZER COMMANDER OF 2. COMPANY, REPORTS

On August 9, the last Tigers of SS-Panzer-Abteilung 102 were on the
march in the direction of Falaise, having been moved from the fighting in
the Vire area. A Strong English-Canadian tank corps assembled on the
previous day for an attack on the major corner stone, Falaise. Portions of
the I. and II. SS-Panzerkorps withstood the enemy superiority in bitter
defensive fighting. In the area of the Hitlerjugend-Division alone, more
than a hundred enemy tanks were destroyed in close combat.

Our Kampfgruppe was attached to the 271. Division. In accordance
with the verbal order of the divisional commander and the Ia of the 271.
Division, which was defending a line from St. Germain to the southern
edge of Brenay to the northern edge of Fresnay to the northern edge of
Espins to the northern edge of Coisilles, our company set out immediately. We reached Martainville along the route ordered and made camp
in wooded areas northwest of Tournebous from where we could detect
any tank attacks in the area.

During the course of August 10, armored cars were fought off in the
left sector of the division. In the afternoon, forty tanks were reported
near Espins, Le Monsul, and to the west of it. Reconnaissance showed
that twelve enemy tanks and some armored cars had broken through
into the ravine southwest of Le Monsul. German infantry already ran
toward the rear without their weapons and could only be stopped with
great difficulty. The German infantryman of August 1944 was no longer
the same as in 1939, when he went into battle with an unshakable confidence in victory.

In cooperation with the Tigers, the infantry retook its old positions.
Again, Loritz set four enemy tanks on fire, whereupon the others
retreated to the north. The Tigers remained at the front until dark to
provide extra strength to the grenadiers in their positions.

After 6 P.M., the Company was advised that the area was to be
attacked by English aircraft. The regimental command post was immedi-

ately moved to Placy. The communications with the division were maintained via the battle command post of Küninger.

Our further advance was impeded by the broken and tangled terrain, so we requested grenadiers on both sides of the Panzers to guard against attacks by enemy infantry. Our highest possible concentration was required, and we searched the attack area constantly through our field glasses.

Unnecessary conversation was frowned upon inside the Panzer during an attack. Observations were exchanged in short words and phrases only. The throat microphones were sensitive enough to almost transmit the sounds of swallowing and even the quietest clearing of one's throat. All four headsets were connected through the intercom and to the receiver and transmitter.

A mountain slope some seven kilometers north of us was being hit by violent fire from our rocket launchers; an attack in coordination with the first company from across the other side in order to encircle the English tanks between us. The battle order for August 12 stated: "Defense against tank attacks in the sector of the 271. Infantry-Division."

At 7 A.M., already, our company was informed that twenty-six enemy tanks had broken through east of Barberie to the south. The company secured the roads to Espins and Fresnay with one Panzer each. We, ourselves, remained in the town as a reserve until the resupply operation was completed. Schroif pushed along the road to Fresnay and Barberie with six Panzers and reached the height at the northern edge of Zingal. He was turning east when he received news of five tanks which had broken through, accompanied by English infantry. More infantry and tanks that reported in a small wooded area.

During the course of the Panzer duel, Loritz set five enemy tanks and one reconnaissance vehicle on fire, and Rodinger and Münster one more each. The company held the captured positions until German grenadiers were brought forward to the main front line.

It was just after noon when, suddenly, salvos from hundreds of guns hit us out of the blue. The English steamroller was beginning to break up the German front line, to flatten the town and everything alive in it! Bois Halbout and the German positions adjoining to the north were enveloped in a swirling wall of smoke. The English shells hit the roofs, walls, windows, and streets like hailstones. The force and violence of the artillery fire, never experienced at such intensity before, raced through the town like a hurricane. Wounded soldiers were trapped under the rubble of crumbling roofs and walls. Helpless injured overflowed the hallways and rooms of the main dressing station. Whoever was still breathing was buried under the falling walls. Around 2 P.M. the fire slowed down noticeably, but then gunfire was heard from the north edge of the village. The din of battle came closer, machine guns rattled, hand grenades exploded, the tracks of tanks clanked.

Schroif had to round up some of his men who had been caught unaware by the heavy enemy fire before he could make further plans. The five Tigers located north of Tournebous under Loritz were ordered by radio to immediately return to Bois Halbout. Günther's Panzer retreated to the village in the face of an overwhelming superiority after knocking out three enemy tanks. At full throttle he raced through the village streets, in some of which enemy infantrymen could already be found, and reached the bush-covered ravine of a creek some 300 meters further down. Then Loritz and his Panzers, coming from Tournebous, broke into Bois Halbout at high speed and knocked out English tanks at close range. The surprised Tommies fled into the ruins and side streets where they reassembled and attacked the German Panzers in close combat.

Numerous German prisoners, mostly from the Küninger battle staff, who were being escorted by the English along roads and paths, ignorant of the real situation, also fled in panic after the English into cover.

All Panzers were recalled, without delay, to a position 200 meters southeast of Claire-Tizon for a speedy refueling operation and to take on more ammunition. This began at 5 P.M. Our wounded and dead were handed over to the main dressing station located next to the road in the ravine. Messages and orders came over the radio; messengers came and went from the division in this sector to the Panzerkorps.

Six Tigers with technical problems had to be released to the repair company by the Kampfgruppe. At 7 P.M. the rest of the company reported to the regimental field command post in Chateaux-la-Motte and remained there for the night to provide cover to the north.

During the milky gray morning of August 13, the Tigers continued their move toward the south. Just outside Falaise, at the junction of the western ring road, we were surprised by a heavy fighter-bomber attack. Rockets smashed into the road and fields, trees broke off, branches, rocks, clumps of dirt whirled in the air around the fighting vehicles. Luckily, they were able to find cover in a nearby wood.

A new battle order for the Falaise area arrived for us. Our mission was to fight off tank attacks in the vicinity of Tournebous. Early in the morning, just after six o'clock, heavy fog, both natural and artificial, covered the whole sector. Our few infantrymen were soon bypassed. Suddenly, enemy infantry faced our command post, which had shrunk to three Tigers. The waves of attacks stalled in the fire from our Panzers. The English brought up Paks and tanks in the cover of the bushes and hedges. Münster's Tiger was attacked with close combat weapons, and it soon took a direct hit to the turret, which killed or wounded some of the crew.

Schroif and Loritz set fire to one enemy tank each. Shortly thereafter, Loritz's Panzer was knocked out by hits from close range. The first hit landed on the turret and must have killed or wounded all the crew. Not one hatch was opened! Seconds later, the next shell found the engine compartment, and the fuel caught on fire. Sky-high flames burned out the German Tiger with all its crew inside, setting off numerous explosions. We felt rage and sorrow at losing one of our best; this piece of bad news gripped the whole company!

A German counterattack from the rear only reached the Panzers with some weak forces and stalled there. The English defense was just too strong. Oberhuber's Panzer, just repaired, was immediately set in march to the front by radio to support the Kampfgruppe. Five German Panthers, in action on the right, were also moved out in the afternoon. Just then, the enemy began heavy bomber attacks on the whole sector. Coming from the east, the formations dropped rows and rows of bombs on the German defensive lines, bringing death and destruction to the German front lines with a brutal violence.

In the face of this, our grenadiers climbed onto the Panzers and we retreated. At 6 P.M. we were ordered into action again on Hill 184 north of Soulangy. There, we found our own infantry running from the front line, in battalion strength, chased by twelve Sherman tanks. At last daylight, we quickly set three of them on fire whereupon the German infantry began to dig in on the hill. Slowly, the numbers of living bodies decreased in the constant, tireless fighting against numerically superior forces. When would the last German reserves be used up?

The relevant report by the German Armed Forces praised the heroic defensive fighting of our heavy Panzer-Abteilung 102.

TIGER 134 (FEY) LEFT THE REPAIR COMPANY ON AUGUST 14, READY FOR ACTION AGAIN

We sat immediately off the wide concrete Caen-Falaise road with our Tiger. Our clear order was to block this important road, which stretched in a straight line next to us. Somewhat off the road, in a good firing position, we waited for things to happen. To our rear was the town of St. Pierre and in front was Soulangy, which had been captured by the enemy the day before, August 13. Ahead of us was only a thin and patchy cover by infantry from the "Hitlerjugend" Division.

The grenadiers holding the main Falaise-Caen route had received a tank alert. The front was in motion, artillery fire rumbled. Several enemy tanks in motion were spotted ahead. They came out from behind the top of a hill, and it seemed obvious they wanted to drive a wedge across the main road between St. Pierre and Soulangy. Like green tree-frogs, jumping like goats, Canadian infantrymen found their way through tangled berry bushes and across moss-covered rocks. We could not wait without taking action, so we drove slowly along the road, which was lined by high trees. Ahead of us, Panzer-grenadiers were clearing the ditch, running bent over toward a small cottage. Submachine guns at the ready, they carefully rounded the corner, kicked in the door and threw a few hand grenades inside. Several Canadians came out, their arms crossed above their heads. Facing the muzzles of the carbines, they were searched and then brought to the rear. The enemy tanks had disappeared behind the houses of Soulangy. It remained quiet. We returned to our position next to the road with our order to hold it.

The company leader of the grenadiers approached again. He asked us to advance with the Tiger and get his men out from their foxholes, which had long since been cut off, along the Route Nationale. Despite the order to block the road near St. Pierre, our commander was immediately willing to comply. He was an infantryman himself once, and he understood the predicament of these men. He had been fighting with these troops in 1940 during the French campaign, and had marched from Poland to the gates of Moscow and back again.

After a fast drive across the fields in the direction of Soulangy, we were able to understand the situation of the grenadiers there. The company leader gave us a short briefing on the extent of the positions and then disappeared to join his men. After a short period of observation, our presence there was rewarded. Between the houses of Soulangy the tanks that had been reported showed up. We recognized ten Shermans which drove in a line, one after the other, slowly along the positions, covering the foxholes with steady fire. This really made it impossible for any man to get out, and it would have been only a question of hours until the last grenadier had paid with his life for his determination to hold out. Finally, when all ten tanks showed themselves without cover, the commander gave the order to open fire. We were only 400 meters away. In accordance with proven tactics, the commander fired first on the closest and then on the tank farthest back. The confusion over there was total. They had played this little game before without being bothered. Then, suddenly, two of them were on fire. We left them no time to gather their thoughts. The other eight were also quickly set on fire by our shells, and they barely had time to make out our position.

Just as the grenadiers, some thirty young comrades of the "Hitlerjugend" Division, were leaving their positions and retreating toward our Panzer, a column of armored personnel carriers showed up on the battlefield, this time from the other side. In the late afternoon sun, we could clearly make out the white stars on the vehicles. Otherwise, there might have been doubts whether these were not our own Panzer-grenadiers on the attack from that direction. But then, explosive shells and MG rounds hammered the lined-up and fully manned carriers in quick succession. Soon, the whole column was on fire in the open terrain. We did not have to fear any surprises from that area for the next few hours!

We then had to get back to our original position at St. Pierre to block the road again. The grenadiers, beaming with joy, climbed onto our Tiger, using up all available space, and waited for us to get going. The commander ordered: "Panzer—return—march!" But our Tiger would not move. The driver turned the starter time and again, with no success. The commander and radio operator jumped off and used the crank to get the 720-horsepower engine going.

No luck! Dripping sweat, they gave up this attempt. What were we to do next? Our own troops were nowhere near. The Canadians had already pushed past us to the northeast as we could tell from the clouds of smoke and dust on the horizon at noon.

The night was falling slowly when our commander set out on foot to the Panzer of the chief, which was reported to be sitting in the orchards on the western edge of town. In a few words he explained our situation to the chief, Kalls, who set out immediately and, as it was turning dark, towed us out of our predicament. The expected reprimand did not come about in light of our successful escapade, the burning tanks and vehicles in the valley of Soulangy in front of us were proof that our presence had been urgently required. We had barely reached St. Pierre when all Panzers were ordered to move to the Falaise road junction of the Route Nationale. During this night of August 15, we had our first open combat encounter with the Maquis (French underground) fighters, who received some bloodied heads thanks to our alert sentries.

The morning of August 15 found our Panzer in Versainville, a few kilometers north of Falaise. There, at the Abteilung command post, a repair team repaired our damage and made the Tiger ready for action again. The team was still working when our commander, Weiß, arrived and issued an urgent order for action to the Tiger. The Canadians were attacking from the northwest and had already reached the first houses of Versainville. Encirclement and certain capture threatened us. Our defenses were still holding but would have to retreat before the larger attacking force. Finally, the last bolt was tightened, and our Panzer again moved under its own power as we threw the last of the tools from the Panzer. The fate of the town, the staff in it, with medical team, repair team, radio team, and everyone else, depended on our action. Confidently, we waved at the comrades of the staff: We'll look after you! Our commander guided the Panzer under cover of the houses parallel to the direction of the Canadian attack. This would enable us to open fire on the attacking lines from the flank.

We had not left the last houses behind us when the fireworks started. Salvo after salvo came howling in, exploding between the houses of Versainville. One house after the other was turned into rubble before our eyes. The school, where the wounded were assembled, took two direct hits. Those comrades were quickly loaded into ambulances and on tractors and transported back under infantry escort. The barrage continued with only a few short breaks, an inferno that seemed to be directed by the devil himself! We tried to get out of the narrow street in order to reach an open field of fire since we already knew from previous experience that enemy infantry would be advancing behind the wall of fire.

As we maneuvered in jerks around a sharp corner, our left track fell off. That was all we needed—Satan himself had to have a hand in this! Using cables, crowbar, and winch, the commander, radio operator, and loader lifted the heavy track in record time and tried to join the two ends. Holy smokes! And all this happened under a constant hail of fragments! We were dripping with sweat when we finally secured the bolt. It was not often that we had looked forward to climbing back into the Panzer, despite the oppressive heat inside, as we did then! Then full speed ahead! Swinging wide, we finally reached the flat fields, almost behind the first waves of attack. They came across the fields upright, in great numbers; it stopped our breath! Panzer—halt! Turret MG 300— open fire! Radio operator MG—open fire!

We let go, from right to left and from left to right. It was a bloody harvest! We had caught them in the middle of their attack, without cover, in the open terrain. Only a group of three or four houses offered some safety. Many tried to reach this cover running; only very few made it. We were located so that we could fire on the terrain in front and behind these houses. The first waves crawled back into the cover of the back slope as our MGs continued hammering away in short bursts. Red flares rose and immediately the artillery fire again set in, directed to the edge of Versainville. This did not bother us since we sat in the middle of the Canadian attack area. As long as we did not see raised hands, as long as weapons were not thrown away, we could not stop our firing!

The commander let the Panzer move slowly in the direction of the houses—there had to be quite a few enemy soldiers there. We reached the road; what a picture it was in the ditch there! One next to the other, they pressed themselves to the ground, wearing their flat helmets. But before we could pay them more attention, an order from the commander directed our attention somewhere else: "Panzer—halt! Tank on the left! Antitank shell 200—open fire!" Then, "Hit" and immediately the next order: "20 meters to its right, enemy tank! Fire, as soon as the turret is fully in the gun sight!" Then followed a few seconds of silence until the two shells had left the barrel. We did not, however, find time to celebrate the lightning destruction of those two Shermans. The commander, observing the terrain, spotted turrets slowly pushing up from the back slope. Our turret was turned in that direction, and before the commander from the other side could take a good look at the terrain, his fate was sealed; a bright flash, and the turret hung on the tank at an angle! The second shell must have been a direct hit to the engine compartment since a bright flash of flame immediately rose above the tank. Our gunner let the second tank, driving along the same line, move into the gun sight. It was caught equally as unaware as soon as its turret was fully in sight. There was no time for them to fire! But then, all hell let loose near us! While we were momentarily distracted by the tanks, we had not noticed that some Canadians had closed in on our Tiger. "Lock hatches! Panzer—march! Turn the turret with engine power!" These orders were yelled at us on the intercom. Not one second too soon as the explosive charges the Canadians had attached were already going off with loud bangs. But, since the turning turret had swept the Canadians from the rear of the Panzer, they had not been able to attach the charges effectively. Only the storage box from behind the turret and the left track cover whirled through the air. We pushed back a few meters to guard against danger from behind. The radio operator's MG went into action, firing single rounds. We were totally surrounded by tall Canadians who were trying, time and again, to get into the dead ground around us. Our commander used hand grenades to prevent these extremely brave soldiers from jumping onto the Panzer. They were courageous, all right but then, what choice did they have?

We cleared out the hornets' nest at the group of houses with explosive shells. They ripped into the walls from fifty meters away and broke all resistance. In among all these Canadians we could not afford to stick our heads out of the hatches, let alone to think of taking prisoners, tempting as the thought was. Slowly, we pushed ahead to reach the road junction to Versainville. Even then, there were Canadians behind the trees, bushes, and corners of the houses, jumping at our Tiger as we drove by and attacking with incendiary hand grenades. At the road fork we turned the rear of the vehicle toward Versainville and rolled slowly backward in the direction of the Abteilung command post. Just before we reached the first houses, our commander spotted two more Canadians crouching in the ditch. The Panzer was stopped and the commander hailed the two, but they did not stir. So the commander jumped off, submachine gun in hand, and briefly nudged them whereupon they hesitantly got up and raised their hands. Judging by their map-cases and signal pistols, they had to be leaders of the attack. Of course, they had to come along! The commander made them climb in and sit to the left and right of the gun. The radio operator stood guard in his hatch, pistol at the ready, and fished some incendiary hand grenades from their haversacks. These looked like small, nicely rounded boxes. Our operator helped himself to a long, light, English cigarette from an oval package, stuck one each into the prisoners' mouths and lit them. They did not dare turn around and sat like statues with their arms crossed over their steel helmets. The radio operator tried to recall his meager school English and began making conversation. They were really sympathetic guys and quite impressed us. "How many years old are you?"—"Twenty-four years"—"And your friend?"—"He is a captain, twenty-six years"—"You are strong fighters, but we German are not wild animals!"

We reached the Abteilung command post, located at a farm, without any problems. Our adjutant, Friedl Schinhofen, took over the prisoners for interrogation. The commander congratulated us and ordered the departure from Versainville for all vehicles. Our Tiger acted as the rearguard and was to follow to Eraines as the last vehicle.

Just as we were moving out, an alarm was sounded again. Tank guns and MG fire were heard from not far away. The order came from the commander: "Panzer—march!," and we moved back into the open terrain. We were uncomfortable between the houses inside our crate. Again, the Canadians were in the middle of an attack. Four Shermans rolled across the open field from the northwest toward Versainville. That meant we had to get a move on, before these tanks could reach the cover of the first houses and ruin our planned departure.

The commander, as always, gave precise instructions:

"Panzer—halt! Radio operator MG—open fire on infantry targets! Antitank shell—tank farthest to the right—400 fire!" Our first shell whistled by wide, but the second hit the center of the rear, probably the engine compartment. After a few seconds a mushroom cloud of smoke billowed above the tank. Our shell had ripped the tank around at full speed. Its front and the gun were pointed at us, but no shell came from there. Two explosive shells stopped the attempts to bail out. The second tank was in the gun sight of the gunner. "Same distance—aim ahead of it—fire!" It, too, took the hit at full speed to the side. The third and fourth tanks stopped and opened fire on us. But as their first shells were going by us, they quickly rolled backward out of our field of vision into a gully. We fired some more on the Canadians, retreating hastily, with the turret MG and explosive shells and then joined the departing vehicles of the staff at slow speed backward across the hill just before Eraines.

In Eraines, commander Weiß, adjutant Friedl Schinhofen, our company chief, Kalls, and our platoon leader, Baral, waited for us. Our Panzer, together with the command Panzer and Schinhofen's Tiger, sat at the west edge of Eraines, guns aimed in the direction of Versainville. On the horizon, we saw columns of tanks and vehicles rolling east in the evening sun, tank after tank, with no break. This meant that the encirclement, which had been obvious around Falaise for days, was to be completed. But it was not the first encirclement we had to break out of!

Our commander wanted to drive over there and open fire on the marching columns until the last shell was fired.

Our adjutant, Friedl Schinhofen, tried to explain to him the futility of this action, but the commander replied that in the morning, when the encirclement had been closed and the chase begun, everything would be hopeless also. Only the order not to open fire during this day held back our Tiger. Our commander was called to the command post for a briefing during the night. He returned with the news that we were to await further orders and to move to the railroad station of Fresnes-la-Mer during the night.

As ordered, we moved out toward Vignats, reached the town around 3 A.M., and received directions. A heavy 8.8 Flak was in position behind a hedge to secure the ground at the exit from the town. This Luftwaffe unit had been without rations for a few days already. We made them presents of our booty: canned pudding, sardines, canned butter, English tobacco, and the ever-present cider. The Tommies always carried delicious things, which we had come to appreciate! Our crew had learned the ropes, and we knew exactly where the rations were stored in the enemy tanks. We had not had to rely on our own rations for quite a while; we were part of the Allied supply effort!

It was before noon, during a sunny morning, that enemy half-tracks started to move in through a cornfield, at a distance of 1,000 meters. The Flak swung around, and we rolled ahead in the direction of a small house at the railroad crossing, since reconnaissance vehicles had in the meantime pushed into Vignats from the rear. We took up position in the hedge behind the house, only the turret and gun stuck out. Two reconnaissance vehicles advanced toward the railroad embankment, firing from all barrels. Was this to build up their courage? A 2-cm gun, mounted above the driver, was being fired by a Canadian.

We sent one shell at the first vehicle, and it was thrown against a metal mast and stayed there. The second vehicle had its front axle ripped away; the crew jumped out and surrendered. Both were wounded, one more critical than the other. They accepted our help with thanks. After administering makeshift first aid, we put them on the Flak battery, which was moving out, for transport to the main dressing station. One of them insisted on giving his watch to our commander as a present for the rescue and the help given, but we refused with thanks. Our care was offered to the wounded enemy just as it was given to our own comrades.

The Falaise–Trun Pocket

BREAKTHROUGH AND COUNTERATTACK TO OPEN THE ENCIRCLEMENT—CROSSING THE SEINE RIVER AT ROUEN

It was August 17, 1944, and the encirclement had become obvious. The commander had canceled our order to provide rear guard security for the retreating units. Each one was to try on its own to get out of the encirclement with a general breakthrough in the direction of Vimoutiers and assembly there.

The commander wished us luck as, the ring was closed. This demanded action! The mood at the command post was gloomy. Panzermeyer was missing since the previous night, when he had left in a reconnaissance vehicle. We were on our way to Trun and stopped at a crossroads on a bald hill. We were reading the road signs, when there was a bang above us: Shrapnel fire! Pitch black clouds hung overhead, and fragments noisily rained down on the Panzer and the road. We had been spotted! Full throttle, and a short halt in the next village! A heavy barricade of meter-thick oak logs blocked our road near the church. We managed to push it aside and let it roll into the creek while two young men stood at the church portal and watched us with interest. This roadblock would have meant the end for any wheeled vehicle forced to stop. We were sure those guys had their orders, but we had no time, regrettably, to inquire! The light of dawn brought new activity. Light batteries peppered the terrain, and a feeling of apprehension was in the air! We had to get out of the encirclement as we had already taken substantial damage in the actions of the past few days. The cooling system leaked, constantly losing water. The starter no longer worked properly. The air conditioning had been damaged by artillery hits. We had to make contact with a repair team! The village was full of vehicles, low-level attack aircraft harassed us constantly, and the columns were stalled. We decided to bypass this village, St. Lambert. Then, we had to stop again as the temperature of the engine rose critically. Minutes later, our Panzer was crossing an open field

168

and received direct fire, just outside of Chambois. Our driver stopped suddenly. The commander yelled down, asking if we had gone crazy to stop there. The engine had quit, just given up!

We tried to get a tow from Panzer 001, which was traveling in the same direction. Our commander, Weiß, drove up in a reconnaissance vehicle, and standing upright, bleeding from a head wound, listened to our explanations. He ordered us to blow up our Tiger and get into 001. Towing was impossible! We were surrounded in the encirclement! Then he sped off, our critically wounded Abteilung physician in the vehicle with him. Soon after, during the attempt to break out, the ambulance half-track came under heavy fire again. The Abteilung physician died in the vehicle, and our commander, wounded once more by a shot to the pelvis area, was taken prisoner, unable to move.

The explosive charges were quickly attached. The radio operator clipped hand grenades to the dials of his instruments and ripped up the code book. Everything ready! Get out! The commander activated the main charge, and the operator the hand grenades. Let's get out, otherwise we'll be dead. The hatches flew open, and the crew members ran for their lives. The enemy had been waiting for this moment. With heavy fire from ahead and the explosion of our brave Tiger behind us, we set off in short jumps. The Tiger blew up with a thunderclap. Our Tiger, which had been successful during innumerable tests of strength with enemy tanks and uncounted other armored vehicles and Paks!

We met up in a gully. The enemy had covered the nearby town of Chambois with a dome of fire, extinguishing all life inside. The command Panzer, led by Barth, picked us up. A Feldwebel waved in desperation from a gravel pit at the vehicles racing by. His right arm had been hit by bullets and dangled uselessly in the sleeve. No one seemed to take notice of him. We stopped to pick up the comrade, and he had to be put inside the Panzer. Our radio operator got out and found room on the rear. The hills all around were full of enemy Paks and tanks that observed every movement in the valley and covered it with a hail of fire. Returning vehicles reported that the road to Trun had been cut and there was no exit from the encirclement. We wanted to get into Chambois. Then, there was a whistling across the Panzer; one shell went overhead, the other fell short. But the third one had to . . . No, we were lucky once more. We let everyone who was walking along the sides of the road climb onto the Panzer, right up to a general! When there was no more room left, others hung on to the tow cables, just to get out with us—but not for long. Our Tiger attracted enemy fire, and soon after we drove along again without passengers on the hull. Volunteers from Eastern Europe crouched next to their horses, chewing crisp bread, watching the action without understanding or emotion.

Our mood was completely depressed. No one spoke anymore, and a gloomy silence covered us. In Chambois we had to push a burning vehicle aside just to get through. Our soldiers in field gray streamed north, with dry throats and sweat-dripping faces. We stopped on a hill and contemplated the situation before setting up a small Kampfgruppe at a large farm. Our commander took over the command Panzer, and we felt better again. An Oberst of the paratroopers contributed a handful of men, and so the afternoon passed. The noise from the tanks on the road nearby got louder. This caught our interest and made us want to take some action, but we could not endanger the last Tiger of our small Kampfgruppe. So the commander and his radio operator grabbed some panzerfausts and walked toward the noise, finally creeping through the bushes to the Chambois-Trun road. Immediately ahead of them, they saw a whole column of Churchill tanks pass by. Some civilians, who had suddenly appeared, were forced by the submachine guns to lay flat on the ground and keep quiet. This order was helped by a forceful look; a "non compris" (I don't understand) would have had immediate bitter consequences in that situation! The crates rolled by, close enough to touch, with their crews inside. The tactical insignia and names were easily made out, the radio antennas were swinging. The two comrades slowly got up before the last vehicle:—thirty meters—twenty-five meters—twenty meters—and fired simultaneously. The cries of fear from the French were lost in the bang. "Betty," the last tank, drove into the rear of the one ahead, and they got tangled up. Unforgettable! Not one man got out from the vehicles. The Panzerfausts did the job. Precision work! The two tank killers came running back, at full speed, falling and tripping, to the assembly area of the Kampfgruppe. Then, a murderous fire from the Churchills in front set in, but they did not leave the road. So, August 18 ended.

Then it was time to get going. The night helped us. The Oberst was quickly informed, and he agreed that further delay would only have strengthened the encirclement. In addition, the din from the tanks came closer and closer to our assembly area. Helpful civilians could have guided the enemy vehicles to our area any time. . . . During the morning of August 19, we made it through!

We rolled for a few more kilometers and then encountered parts of the reconnaissance Abteilung "Das Reich." This confirmed we were out of the encirclement. Our commander was taken to the commanding general of the II. SS-Panzerkorps, General Bittrich, to report. At the time, Bittrich had no information on the fate of our commander, Weiß, and the situation of the encircled units.

We were to be there when the major counterattack would start the next day to break the encirclement and enable numerous units to break out. We would only be able to open small holes, because our greatly reduced numbers of Panzers ready for action would not allow extensive resistance. To the north and south of us, the attack wedges of enemy tank columns rolled, unstoppably, eastwards!

ON AUGUST 20 AT THE COMMAND POST OF THE
II. SS-PANZERKORPS IN CAMEMBERT, WITH TIGER 001

Our commanding general, Bittrich, ordered all fighting vehicles into immediate action on the road from Vimoutiers to Trun to free the encircled German Kampfgruppen to the west.

Our Panzer, although not completely ready for action, rolled back the same way, past the columns streaming eastwards. After a few kilometers, we reached the blocking defensive position. It was manned by very young soldiers of the "Hitlerjugend" and "Hohenstauffen" Divisions. These boys only had their panzerfausts as effective weapons against the advancing tanks. There we were on our own; on a mission with little hope of success! Rearguard security: These commandos were almost always lost. Their most favorable fate was to be taken prisoner. Despite this, the advancing enemy suffered substantial losses.

Near Champosoult we had the first contact with enemy tanks of the 1st Polish Armoured Division. When the first two Shermans were knocked out by our fire, the others retreated out of the field of fire. Our Kampfgruppe broke through almost to the edge of Chambois without looking left or right. We had been gripped by the fever of the hunt. We rolled, we stopped, and we fired on tanks appearing in front of us.

At full speed, we fired salvos from our MGs at the transport convoys of the enemy, joyfully welcomed by German soldiers who already had one foot in the prisoner of war camp. Our enemies stared at us with fearful faces as we broke into the encirclement of Falaise, a wild and daring chase. We experienced things we never had before, such as knocking out a Sherman that suddenly showed up from a side street, at a distance of eight meters! We had achieved our mission to open up the encirclement. The whole staff of our Panzerarmee with its commander-in-chief, Hausser, which was still inside the encirclement, was able to escape being taken prisoner! But then we had to get back if we did not want to lose contact with the withdrawal operation!

In order not to be cut off, we let the young grenadiers climb on the Panzer and drove to the rear. Then the race began to the Seine River crossings. The English and American tank units had already overtaken us in the direction of Elbeuf and Rouen.

All the Panzers and artillery had to remain on the west bank of the Seine. They were driven out of the columns, and some were blown up. Some of the Panzers that were still mobile were driven into the stream and sunk or blown up in the woods. We had dragged the Panzers, artillery, and valuable equipment away from the front for days across long distances to this river; then we had to leave them there. The crews drifted across the river without Panzers and guns. But we could not leave our Panzer so easily. We drove it to Rouen, hoping to still find a crossing. Was there still a chance to get the Panzer to the other side? Along both sides of the approach to the bridge stood long lines of gray soldiers who, having run ahead of their vehicles, were anxiously surveying the approach and the bridge. Would it all end there?

Just then a navy barge came put-putting across the Seine to solve our problem and take our Tiger to the other shore. Our Tiger with the 001 on the turret, ready for action, rolled onto the barge without problems, and we set out. Was it the 001, the number of the command Panzer, that helped us get across? We were sitting on our Tiger with anticipation and had almost reached the shore when a formation of two fighter-bombers, firing from all barrels, came flying at us across the Seine.

This meant that all possible speed was needed, and our driver started the engine before the barge reached the shore. The navy men were jumping off to secure the boat when the next attack by the fighter-bombers began. Full cover was the only answer to the well-aimed fire from a low-level attack. Before the ropes were fully fastened, the Tiger set out slowly and the tracks were already getting a hold on the harbor wall when the sixty tons of our Panzer pushed the barge away from the wall. Our 001 rolled from the deck into the Seine. The stern of the barge stuck out of the water, and there was just enough time for the crew to jump off before Tiger 001 sank into the waters of Rouen harbor like a submarine. . . .

That was the end of the last Tiger of heavy Panzer-Abteilung 102, which had reached the other shore of the Seine. With our spirits low, we reported to the assembly area of the 102 in Fleurs and waited for further developments. The remains of the Tiger-Abteilung, which assembled in

Fleurs, departed in a northwesterly direction during the following night. It was a hungry, tired group, marked by the fighting of the previous weeks! Abteilungsführer Kalls ordered Zugführer Baral and Panzer commander Fey to cross the Seine at Rouen one more time to blow up the Tigers that were stranded there, some abandoned by their crews, and render them unserviceable!

Our VW jeep took us into the city and to the harbor, and a boat of the pioneers took us across in the gray of dawn of August 31 after we had agreed on a spot where we would meet again with the driver and the boat commander. A wild chaos awaited us at the crossing point, which had been devastated by a carpet of bombs the previous day. It was covered with burning and smoking wrecks of vehicles, among them dead and injured soldiers who were left there to their own resources without any help! We comforted the moaning and begging wounded, and promised them they would be rescued, knowing full well that they would fall into the hands of the enemy, dead or alive, within a few hours. We spotted the first three Tigers, undamaged, very close to our crossing point. They had been abandoned by their crews during the panic of the bomb attack.

We pushed the explosive charges, which every Panzer carried in case they were needed, into the breech of the 8.8-cm gun, poured gasoline from a jerry can into the interior, activated the detonator of the charge, and threw a hand grenade into the engine compartment to set the fuel on fire. Then we jumped off and took full cover. The explosion followed. All this took only a few seconds, and one Tiger after the other burned out with bright flames! Stragglers who still appeared from the rubble and houses reported that more Panzers sat a few streets farther down. We walked down the silent and abandoned streets under cover of the houses and did find two Panthers, but these were no longer abandoned. Blue-white-red insignia painted on the turrets indicated that French resistance fighters had already taken possession of them. They were apparently trying to learn the secrets of their German booty through test drives and practice with the aiming and turning mechanisms. We were to quickly put an end to that! We hurriedly discussed the situation. More than enough Panzerfausts were lying about along the route of our retreat. Across walls and backyards, we worked our way into a secure firing position. Baral forced the crews to take cover with a few well-aimed bursts from the submachine gun, clearing the street, while Fey's bazookas found their targets at the shortest distance! But then it was time to get out of there. A few hand grenades, exploding with loud bangs in the narrow streets, kept our backs free from pursuers on our way to the harbor! It was high time to get across to the other side again as the agreed time of meeting the boat and the driver had long passed. We found the same scene as before: Wounded men begging: "Take us along"—"Help us." Again, we could only comfort them with the promise that they would be rescued, even as we could already hear the noise of the advancing enemy tanks and vehicles that would arrive there soon, possibly within minutes! We reached the shore. There was no boat in sight anywhere to take us across. What were we to do? Captivity? No! Our first thought, to swim across the stream, was soon dropped. We watched stragglers, who had chosen this route, sink helplessly in the middle of the Seine, shot in the back by resistance fighters. We had to get out of Rouen. The Maquis came out of hiding, like rats from their holes, expecting easy prey.

Quite a few wounded were shot by these fellows. We crept along the river until we finally found a rowboat, which took us across the water outside of the city.

On August 17, Ernst Streng, With the Remaining Three Tigers of the 2./Panzer-Abteilung 102, Was Still in Falaise

Our Panzers took part in the bitter street fighting in the city center of Falaise around the cathedral and pulled back to the lines behind the city, as ordered, only with the fall of darkness. With this, a mighty cornerstone had been broken out of the structure of the German defensive front, and the German front at the invasion coast was to completely crumble in quick succession.

In the early hours of August 18, we started a general withdrawal movement, after verbal and personal briefings, from Villy to Vignats, south of Fresnes la Mer. We reached it at 3 A.M. and took over the sector to the north in conjunction with the German assault guns positioned to our left. At noon, strong English tank and infantry forces pushed into La Hoguette upon which we received new orders, after a radio report on this to the Kampfgruppe. We left immediately and reached the railroad embankment near the junction west of Necy. Panzer #124 of the first company, immobilized there, was towed to the southern edge of Abbaye. We blocked the northwest exit with two German assault guns, which forced attacking English tanks to withdraw at 5 P.M.

After the fall of darkness we received another radio order for immediate withdrawal and report to the battle command post 500 meters east of Vignats. The immobilized Panzer was destroyed with an explosive charge and two antitank shells and set on fire.

After reporting to the command post at 12:30 P.M., a new order was immediately given. We were to break through via Vignats to Necy, with extra fuel loaded on the rear, supply the Panzers of the first company there with gas, and then retreat with them to the hill near Necy.

At 2:30 A.M. we set out on the dangerous night drive through the enemy-held terrain with two 200-liter fuel barrels strapped on. A single hit from a tracer bullet could have prevented the success of the mission and brought about the total destruction of the Panzer and its crew. We raced off at high speed and, unscathed, reached the other Panzers after one hour.

After refueling, our small Panzerkampfgruppe began, as ordered, the withdrawal to the northeast. In the first light of the day we encountered English antitank positions, dug in at the road. During the moment of first surprise for both sides, our Panzer raced by the guns and continued down the road at full speed. Schroif, behind us, opened machinegun fire on the positions we had not spotted in time and from where an English machine gun fired tracer salvos at our Panzers. Then, Schroif's Panzer took two heavy direct hits to the hull. The crew below, the radio operator, and the driver, were badly injured. The third Panzer, close behind, rammed into Schroif's stopped Panzer at high speed and could not free itself. All this happened in a few seconds. Schroif, with wounds to his head and feet, jumped from the damaged vehicle and fled in long jumps into the cover of the hedgerows and across the fields back toward the German lines. Both crews were captured by the English, except for the loader who was able to achieve the same feat as Schroif. After a few minutes, when the other Panzers did not show up, we stopped and went back slowly to determine what had kept them. But, just as we came around a bend, we experienced such fireworks that it would have been insane to continue. Pak shells hit the turret and hull, MG salvos hailed against the armor. Something had to happen! Then, clearly and concisely, the orders came from the commander: "Panzer—halt! Panzer—forward—march!" The Panzer stopped with a jerk that threw us against the walls, and then, immediately, it jumped forward, the engine roaring. Our driver, with his quick reactions in directing this sixty-ton monster, held our lives in his hands more than once!

Just before Trun, German pioneers were repairing a damaged bridge, which caused an involuntary delay. In the midst of all this confusion, we spotted the tanker truck that our repair company had sent ahead to meet our Panzers. Relieved and smiling with joy, we directed the truck to the stopped vehicles, which we then refueled as quickly as possible. We received directions that our new destination was Vimoutiers where we were to be given further orders.

Within seconds—we reacted instinctively—we saw our comrades pull back into the commander's cupola. The first fighter-bomber came at us just above the roofs of the last houses of the main street, firing rockets from its wings at our vehicles. "Watch out! Fighter-bombers!" With both hands we pulled the hatches shut, but our warning was lost in the terrible explosion and noise of a rocket that hit the front of the turret roof, causing a flash of flame to race through the dark interior of the Panzer. The glass of the twelve angled mirrors, which were mounted all around the commander's cupola, burst into thousands of small splinters and rained down on us. The pressure wave took our breath away for a few moments and hurled the instruments around inside the Panzer. The periscope fell to the floor with a clang. The ceiling light, the electric wiring, fuses, and all the clamps of the gun mount were ripped from the weld of the top armor plate. . . .

The bullets from the onboard weapons rattled across the turret and rear like hailstones, mushrooms of gray smoke stood around the vehicles, lumps of dirt and rocks hurtled through the air! With howling engines, the fighter-bombers dove on us from the back in their second attack and sent their whistling, screaming, and exploding rockets and bullets on to the field and the dirt road, which was constantly being rearranged. Salvos caused small clouds of dust, bomb craters were drilled into the ground, columns of gun smoke rose into the sky. We felt like shouting and we had to hold ourselves back, with both hands gripping something firm, from jumping out and running out into the chaos of the mushrooms made of smoke and dirt! The heaving ground threw the heavy vehicle around. The bright sunlight was veiled by a heavy cover of dust. Afterward, we could not recall if previously we had lived through such a few terrible seconds or long minutes of fear of death. We shook inside, hands shaking, our legs unsteady! Death held us by the neck, pummeled and pulled us this way and that, trying to rip us apart . . . ! For a long while no one spoke a word. Suddenly there was an unnatural silence! Our blood pumped in heavy waves through our veins. It dripped from a few faces. Glass fragments dropped from above onto the palms of our hands, where traces of the wiped-off blood showed. . . .

Using our heads and shoulders we pushed open the hatches, above us the air was as clear as before!

We waved ahead—slowly the stalled engine started again—and found cover under the roof of leaves ahead. We owed our lives only to the shallow angle of the rockets when they hit; our 30-mm turret armor showed deep dents and the roof was swept clean of any dust.

At the edge of town, just off the wide, well-kept paved road, we stopped under the rows of fruit trees and hedges. Harlander and Selonke were already there, awaiting the evening. It had become completely impossible to drive ahead in any direction! Enemy squadrons above raced up and down the streets, circling the skies in wide curves. The air around us was constantly full of the organlike sounds of the howling aircraft engines and of the bursts of the explosions. All of us stayed in the vehicles. Harlander and his crew, however, repaired the damage to the left track. Despite the fact that our vehicles sat fairly well covered at the edge of town, the second rocket attack rained down on our lined-up Panzers in the next thirty minutes. Mushrooms of fire grew beside, behind, and ahead of us with all their force. The onboard weapons hit our side armor, and the ricochets, climbing steeply into the air with a whistle or burying into the ground, left clouds of dust. Rockets exploded, forcing pressure waves into the interior of the fighting vehicles, and foul-smelling veils of smoke drifted between the thrown-up dirt. Then, this nightmare was over as quickly as it had started. Harland and two of his men lay wounded under their vehicle, blood trickling from their wounds. From the many wounds caused by small bomb fragments, blood dripped from their faces, hands, and upper bodies. One of them had a long, wide-open flesh wound on his thigh, the other had one arm and an ankle smashed up. With hands shaking from nervous haste, we wound strips of gauze and dressing around the wounds, the red and white of the dressing contrasted with the pale faces. Medics came running over to provide further care and transport. Our fingers, hands, and upper arms were covered by crusted blood. The wind drove black clouds of smoke from the road over the village.

Suddenly, a steep flash of flame rose into the sky across from us. A mushroom of smoke stood above it, and pieces of metal and debris rained down on us. The German light Flak brought one of the too-numerous to the ground. But then, as far as we could survey the terrain, German vehicles were on fire, turning into ash and rubble!

We reached Elbeuf on August 25, 1944. As had been rumored, the bridge had been destroyed by bombs on the previous day. The next possible point of crossing the Seine was at Oissel. We had to get there if we wanted to bring our heavy Tigers across the Seine at all. On the heights around Oissel, down to the river, all roads were hopelessly clogged for many kilometers. Columns of vehicles, in rows of two or three, had driven

Defensive battles in the area of
Caen–Cintheaux–Soulangy–Falaise.
August 8–11, 1944 ("Totalize")
August 14–16, 1944 ("Tractable")

up, radiator to radiator, wheel next to wheel, side by side. Thousands of vehicles—we estimated at least five to seven thousand of them—were all waiting to cross. Fortunately, a clouded sky, haze, and a veil of rain just above the river reduced the visibility. That gave us a break from the fighter-bombers! A good day for flying would have brought about terrible chaos, destruction, and disaster! There were only two bridges left to cross the Seine: the one near Oissel, and the other at Rouen, a pontoon bridge that could be used only by wheeled vehicles. The bridge at Oissel turned out also to be only makeshift, not strong enough to take the Panzers across. The army had a pioneer ferry available upstream. But then, all our concerns for our Panzer were taken from us. Kalls, who led the Abteilung, ordered it blown up. The lives of the men were still more important than a Panzer! So we silently crossed the river, on foot, via the pontoon bridge. A few hours later, a carpet bombing systematically destroyed the area of the crossing, and thousands of soldiers with their vehicles found their end!

The retreat continued into Belgium. German military police at the border inspected anyone who wanted to cross. Only units with permits were allowed to pass. The remains of the units were directed toward their assembly areas in Brussels, Leuven, and Diest in the Limburg lowlands. That was initially the end of our French odyssey. The Tigerabteilung assembled its units there. The vehicle supply unit in Brussels was able to provide us fairly well with vehicles.

We moved farther to Maastricht, rolled through the Westwall (German fortification line at the western border) where we saw the brown uniforms of the Volkssturm (militia), our last resort, for the first time. These poorly equipped soldiers would not be able to resist the pressure of the best-equipped enemy assault armies. We passed through Aachen, Düren, to Cologne. Next to our route of withdrawal, women and girls dug trenches and foxholes to provide cover against aircraft attacks. What good was that supposed to do? We reached Paderborn where the following weeks were filled with training replacements who were to fill the gaps in our ranks caused by the fighting in Normandy. We received the new Königstiger (King Tiger) and knew that our days were numbered!

Retrospective and Analysis

The combat diary of Tiger 134, kept by the radio operator Heinz Traut-mann using a few key words, reflects the fifty days of Panzer action (July 10 to August 30) in Normandy. The destruction of eighty-eight tanks during these days, not to mention the uncounted kills of Paks, armored troop transports, trucks, and half-tracks on which detailed numbers were not kept, provide an impression of the superiority of the Panzer crews and the fire power of a Tiger as an individual Panzer. These figures are representative of the other Tigers! Of course, losses of men and particularly heavy damage to the Tiger were also registered. We were facing an enemy superior in numbers, with air superiority from the very first day, and constant artillery fire from sea and land. This prevented proper deployment of our Panzer units and decimated them more and more each day. It became predictable that the lack of replacements for our Panzers would develop into defeat on this field of battle. Having to hold the strategically important hill 112 near Caen and the crossing points over the Orne River, under constant attack by tank and infantry units for twenty days (from July 10 to 31), was totally different from the original mission of the Panzer forces, whose main strengths were mobility and fire power! The Tigers of Panzer-Abteilung 102 withdrew from hill 112 on July 31 when the thrust of the Allied tank armies toward the east bypassed hill 112 to the north and south.

FIFTY DAYS OF PANZER ACTION IN NORMANDY

From the diary of Tiger 134	Destroyed	Our enemy in those days
July 10 Reconnaisance in force in Maltot	3 Cromwells	9th Royal Tank Regiment, 31st British Brigade (independent)
July 10 Hill 112 recaptured (loader Hensel killed)	5 Churchills, 3 Paks	A-Squadron, 7th R.T.R., 31st British Brigade
July 11 Hill 112, attack on wooded area	3 Shermans	The Royal Scots Greys, 4th Armoured Brigade (independent)
July 16 Maltot–Point 42, threat to the flank (gunner Christoph mortally wounded)	4 Churchills, armored personnel carriers, half-tracks	153rd R.A.R in 34th Tank Brigade (independent British brigade)
July 24 Maltot-St. André, attack on Orne bridges repelled	8 Churchills, APCs, half-tracks	7th Royal Tank Regiment, 31st British Brigade
Aug. 6 Battle area Vire–Chenedolle	1 armored rec. vehicle, 1 Pak	Fife and Forfar Yeomanry, and 23rd Hussars in 29th Armoured Brigade, 11th Armoured Division
Aug. 7 Chenedolle, breakthrough to N-158 prevented	15 Shermans, 12 reconnaissance vehicles, 1 Pak, half-tracks	23rd Hussars, 29th Armoured Brigade, 11th Armoured Division (Brit.)
Aug. 14 Soulangy–St. Pierre, N-158 Caen- Falaise, relief attacks for the infantry	3 Shermans, armored personnel carriers, half-tracks	10th Armoured Regiment (Fort Garry Horse) in 2nd Canadian Armoured Brigade
Aug. 15 Soulangy–St. Pierre N-158, attacks on Positions of I./26 repelled	10 Shermans, 6 reconnaissance vehicles, half-tracks	6th Armoured Regiment (1st Hussars) 10th Armoured Regiment
Aug. 16 Versainville, Abteilung command post of Pz. Abt. 102 encircled by Canadian infantry	4 Shermans	22nd Armd. Rgt. (The Canadian Grenadier Guards); 28th Armd. Rgt. (British Columbia Rgeiment); 4th CDnd Brig., 4th Canadian Armd Div.
Aug. 16 Versainville, withdrawal of Abteilung command post 102 to Eraines	3 Shermans, half-tracks	6th Armoured Regiment near Falaise
Aug. 17 Vignats, order to cover for withdrawal	2 armored reconnaissance vehicles	
Aug. 18 Encirclement Chambois– St. Lambert, commander H. Weiß captured, Tiger 134 damaged by hits, blown up, Tiger 001taken over	3 Shermans	1st Polish Armoured Division, 24th Lancers, 10th Armoured Brigade

FIFTY DAYS OF PANZER ACTION IN NORMANDY

From the diary of Tiger 134	Destroyed	Our enemy in those days were
Aug. 18 Breakout with Tiger 001 at St. Lambert	3 Shermans, armored personnel carriers, half-tracks	1st Polish Armoured Division, 24th Lancers, 10th Armoured Brigade
Aug. 19 Report to reconnaissance Abteilung "Das Reich'		
Aug. 19 Report to Korps command post II.-SS-Panzerkorps at Camembert to commanding general Bittrich and Oberst Pipkorn		
Aug. 20 Counterattack to open the encirclement near Chambois	2 Shermans, reconnaissance vehicles, half-tracks	1st Polish Armoured Regiment, 24th Polish Lancers
Aug. 21 Coudehart–Champosoult	2 Shermans	1st Polish Armoured Regiment, 24th Polish Lancers
Aug. 22 Moving Tiger 001 in direction Vimoutiers–Rouen		
Aug. 28 Crossing the Seine on navy barge at Rouen, after fighter-bomber attack, Tiger 001 sank in harbor		
Aug. 30-31 Ordered by Abteilungsführer Kalls in Rouen to blow up Tigers and Panthers on the south shore	2 Panthers	(Maquis, with blue-white-red insignia on turret)

The Winter Battle in the Ardennes (Code Name: The Watch on the Rhine)

The Panzer-divisions of the Waffen-SS under the command of the I. and II. SS-Panzerkorps were not ready for action in this offensive despite replacements, often from outside the divisions. Against the objections of the Supreme Commander in the west and Heeresgruppe B (army group) the leadership at the highest level would not be dissuaded from this "Ardennes Offensive." In addition, there was a catastrophic fuel supply situation which did not allow the Kampfgruppen to fulfill their objectives at the predetermined time. These shortages have been reported in detail in the divisional histories of the respective SS-Panzer-divisions. The willingness for sacrifice and courage by the Panzer crews under these conditions must be valued even more. The following reports on the battles by the Panzer commanders bear witness to their readiness for sacrifice without any expectation of glory or recognition of their efforts.

Because of contradictory reports in the media and publications that are being circulated to this day, domestically and internationally, on the actions in the Ardennes in 1944–45, we preface these reports of the Panzer commanders with a sketch of the march route and battle sites of "Kampfgruppe Peiper." Using this sketch, as well as information from the British magazine *After the Battle* and reports from the Panzer commanders of this Kampfgruppe, and in conjunction with a letter from Colonel Ellis, then the main attorney for the prosecution of the U.S. Army in the Malmedy court case, to Jochen Peiper, we want to help establish the historical truth. We pay tribute to the heroic actions of the soldiers who, under the most difficult circumstances caused by snow drifts and on narrow, icy, roads, had to carry out a hopeless mission, as the law commanded soldiers on both sides to do. "Kampfgruppe Peiper" undertook the first assault that began the Ardennes offensive on December 16, 1944. After the loss of all Panzers, weapons, and equipment, it fought its way back on foot with some 800 soldiers across the heights of the Ardennes through enemy-held territory, and reached the positions of German units near St. Vith on December 25.

THE THRUST OF "KAMPFGRUPPE PEIPER" IN THE DIRECTION OF THE MAAS BRIDGES

The Kampfgruppe had available for this mission: approximately 100 Panzer IVs and Panzer Vs (Panther), the heavy SS-Panzer-Abteilung 501 (Königstiger–King Tigers), the III.(gep) Panzer-Grenadier/2 Panzer-Grenadier-Regiment and parts of the Panzer-Brigade 150 (special unit Skorzeny), which were under the direct command of Jochen Peiper. Since Peiper did not have sufficient fuel available, maps were handed out that showed the U.S. fuel depots at Bullingen and Spa so that he could find supplies during the advance.

Another U.S. Army fuel dump north of Stavelot, which could have played a decisive role, was not shown on Peiper's maps.

Now the sequence of events:

The thrust of the I. SS-Panzer-Division and Panzer-Brigade 150 (Skorzeny) in the north was delayed because the required bridge-building material had not yet arrived on December 15. There were holdups on the road N 32 south of Losheimergraben since the railroad bridge at the German-Belgian border had been blown up by units of the Wehrmacht (army) during their previous retreats and had not yet been rebuilt.

Peiper was on the scene at 2:30 P.M. on December 16 and ordered that room be made for his Panzer columns without regard. All blocking vehicles were pushed off the road since the timetable for his attack did not allow for any delays. He located a narrow point of the railroad embankment where he could cross with his Panzers and reached the main road N 32 in the evening. The Panzer spearhead of "Kampfgruppe Peiper" reached Lanzerath at 11 P.M. on December 16 and was in Buchholz at 5 A.M. on December 17. From there it went on toward Honsfeld where Peiper found the road clogged by U.S. units flooding back.

He stopped his column, waited for a gap, and then his Panzers joined the American column. Honsfeld was the refitting position for the 349th Infantry Regiment of the 99th U.S. Infantry Division.

Peiper pushed into this refitting position with his Panzers, paratroopers mounted on them. Some GIs fled, while others were captured or killed.

Peiper learned from the interrogation of the prisoners that the command post of the 49th U.S. Antiaircraft Brigade, whose mission it was to fire at the V1 rockets aimed at Liège, was located in Ligneuville.

Some 400 U.S. soldiers served with these antiaircraft batteries in the area. Peiper ordered his Kampfgruppe to split up in order to encircle Ligneuville.

He also had to push toward Bullingen with the aim to supply his Kampfgruppe with U.S. fuel.

Based on available information, 250,000 liters were captured at this depot. A small field airstrip was located near Morschheck where he was able to destroy twelve reconnaissance aircraft on the ground. Refueling began in Bullingen at 9 A.M., and then the Kampfgruppe rolled off in the direction of Ambleve. Peiper split his Kampfgruppe south of Morschheck. One group, mostly Panthers, went south; the other group rolled on the National Road to the north in order to carry out the encirclement of Ligneuville. Peiper pushed on, without encountering any resistance worth mentioning, via Ambleve and Born to the N 32 and swung north in the direction of Ligneuville. At the crossroads at the Kaiser barracks, the jeep of Colonel Mark Devine was destroyed but he was able to escape with two other officers. The city of Ligneuville had been evacuated. A U.S. bulldozer that encountered the column alerted Captain Simon Green, located at the "Hotel du Moulin." When Green went out to confirm the report, he was taken prisoner. The only resistance came from a Sherman tank, which sat next to the hotel with damaged tracks. The Kampfgruppe lost one Panther and two armored personnel carriers to the rear guard of the 7th US Armored Division south of the city.

The commander of the 1. SS-Panzer-Division "LAH," Generalmajor of the Waffen-SS Mohnke, came to the "Hotel du Moulin" to meet Peiper there. Fortunately for them, the U.S. columns flooding back were able to cross the junction at the Kaiser barracks before Peiper could reach the N 32 near Born.

When Peiper arrived at Ligneuville at 4 P.M., he determined that the planned encirclement had failed. The U.S. units had escaped. At 5 P.M., his first Panzers began the attack on Stavelot. To reach the Maas River, Peiper had to cross the Ambleve River with his Panzers. For the Königstigers this was possible only at certain bridges, among them the stone bridge at Stavelot. A U.S. sergeant of the 291st U.S. Engineer Battalion, named Hensle, blocked the bridge with only minimal equipment: antitank mines, a machine gun, and a bazooka.

The first Panzers of Kampfgruppe Peiper arrived at 7 P.M. and stopped. There were contradictory reports regarding this bridge at Stavelot. The SS pioneers thought they had observed U.S. engineers mining the bridge in the darkness.

Other reports spoke of soldiers of the Skorzeny group who were engaged in preparations to blow up the bridge. In any case, the Kampfgruppe lost a whole night. In the meantime, during the night of December 18, the 526th Armored U.S. Infantry Regiment under Major Solis had arrived and set up barricades at the most important intersections. At 8 A.M. on December 18, Peiper gave the order to attack. Major Solis retreated with his soldiers, believing that Peiper would swing north, and planned to pursue him since the large fuel depot of the U.S. Army was located only 1.5 kilometers north on the road to Spa.

Major Solis ordered the fuel depot set on fire at the spot closest to Stavelot so as to create a barricade. He was not aware that Peiper had no knowledge of this depot and did not plan to attack toward the north but in the direction of Trois-Ponts.

U.S. Colonel Frankland, who commanded the 117th Infantry Regiment of the 30th U.S. Infantry Division, later arrived from the north (Francorchamps) at the burning fuel depot. He had the fire put out and took over the guarding of the depot. The German Kampfgruppe had to get to Trois-Ponts. Peiper split his Kampfgruppe again and directed two companies of Panzer IVs to move toward Trois-Ponts via Wanne. This route, however, was not suitable for Panzers. The lost night at the Stavelot Bridge had allowed the U.S. engineers to mine all bridges along the route of advance!

The spearhead of the Kampfgruppe reached Trois-Ponts at 10:45 A.M. The railroad viaduct was defended by U.S. Paks. One Panther was knocked out and blocked the road. At 11:45 A.M. the bridge across the Ambleve River blew up. Peiper stated after the war that he could have reached the Maas River on December 19, if this bridge had remained intact and if he had known about the existence of the fuel depot at Stavelot. The only remaining alternative was an evasive move toward La Gleize. At the same time, the U.S. leadership ordered the 291st Engineer Battalion to prepare the bridge at Habiemont to be blown up.

Peiper again crossed the Ambleve River at Cheneux. But, with improved weather conditions, the attacks by the Thunderbolt, Mustang, and Typhoon fighter-bombers started again, causing heavy losses in men and materiel. The Kampfgruppe had to move into the woods between Cheneux and the bridge to seek cover.

At 4 P.M. on December 19, the fog again provided protection from the Allied air force.

Only one bridge, at Habiemont across the Lienne River, separated the Kampfgruppe from its objective! Peiper reached the N 32 south of Froidville and swung to the right. With the falling darkness the spearhead reached Trois-Ponts where the soldiers of the 291st U.S. Engineer Battalion, under Lieutenant Edelstein, awaited it. Coincidental with the first shot from the gun of a Königstiger, the bridge blew up.

Peiper determined that the poor network of roads would not allow a further attack by the heavy armored fighting vehicles with the objective of Huy to the northwest. The blown-up bridge at Trois-Ponts forced the Kampfgruppe to move into the valley of the Ambleve on December 19, 1944, when it reached the town of La Gleize and the neighboring town of Stoumont. Since no further units were following, and the Kampfgruppe had moved far from the front line, it was left to its own devices. The Americans recognized this and cut off Kampfgruppe Peiper. Jochen Peiper ordered his men, approximately 1,300 soldiers, to defend in a circular position since fuel for the Panzers was no longer available in sufficient quantities.

The defensive fighting by the encircled Peiper groups turned more and more difficult from December 22, when the ammunition began to run out and the Panzers were completely immobilized by the lack of fuel. Using strong reserve units, the Americans were able to tighten the ring more and more. The availability of materiel to the other side made the situation hopeless.

On December 23, 1944, Jochen Peiper received the order, by radio, to break out of La Gleize. During the heavy fighting of the previous several days the Kampfgruppe lost more than 700 wounded, all of its thirty-nine Panzers, many armored personnel carriers, and twenty-five guns.

Eight-hundred soldiers, conditionally ready for action, departed La Gleize on the night of Christmas Eve, fought their way south and then east and met the spearhead of its own division (SS-Panzer-Grenadier-Regiment 1 under the command of Oak Leaves holder SS-Obersturmbannführer Albert Frey) in the small town of Wanne. Approximately thirty were killed during the breakout.

About 140 American prisoners and eighty German wounded were left behind in La Gleize.

They were handed over to U.S. Captain Crisenger before the breakout with a written agreement, while a German physician, Dr. W. Dittmann, was ordered to remain and to provide medical care to the wounded Germans and Americans.

188 ARMOR BATTLES OF THE WAFFEN-SS 1943–45

The captured Lieutenant Colonel McGowen later reported in writing to his government on the correct treatment of all prisoners and underlined the unquestionable behavior of the soldiers of "Kampfgruppe Peiper."

The chief prosecutor of the U.S. Army in the Malmedy court case, Mr. Ellis, wrote to the formerly accused Peiper in 1966: "I am certain you have always known that I had no personal feelings against you or anyone else. As you, I was a soldier also, doing my duty as best I could. . . .

"I am of the opinion that you are a fine gentleman.

"On the day your letter arrived I also read in our press of the death of Sepp Dietrich. You may believe it or not, but I had a sense of mourning as I read the fairly long obituary in the San Francisco Chronicle."

For his outstanding achievements at La Gleize, SS-Obersturmbannführer Peiper (he had tied down the majority of three U.S. divisions) was awarded the Swords to his Knight's Cross on December 28, 1944, as the 119th soldier and promoted to Standartenführer (colonel). Jochen Peiper was one of the young, intelligent, and fearless Panzer commanders of the Waffen-SS. His successes on the Eastern and Western Fronts of the Second World War were outstanding and have gone down in history. This excellent soldier was assassinated by criminals on July 14, 1976, in Traves, France.

THE MALMEDY TRIALS

In the course of the offensive in the Ardennes, a spearhead of the Kampfgruppe Peiper shot up an American truck column at a road junction south of Malmedy. It was established later that this was an observer unit without war experience. The surviving soldiers surrendered, and the spearhead continued its advance. The newly captured prisoners were given the famous hand signal "proceed to the rear" and left to their fate. Because of the difficult terrain, it was impossible to establish radio contact with the main body of the Kampfgruppe following behind. The main body, when spotting the truck column, opened fire again. This caused, regrettably, further losses.

This occurrence, described here briefly and difficult to prevent in mobile warfare, led to charges of murder against seventy-four members of the LAH from the Supreme Commander of the Army, through the Commanding General, to the loader. The accused were subjected to inhuman interrogation and investigation procedures at the Schwäbisch-Hall penitentiary. After psychological pressure lasting for weeks, with tricks of all kinds, fake court proceedings, even fake executions, confes-

The author as an SS-Unter-scharführer (sergeant).

An Sd. Kfz. 232 communications armored car belonging to the Leibstandarte SS "Adolf Hitler" (motorized) during the Polish campaign (September 1939). The vehicle commander wears the crash helmet/beret combination that was unpopular with the troops in the field and quickly replaced by the more familiar overseas caps.

The same vehicle seen in a more "warlike" pose.

An early version of the Panzerkampfwagen III escorts dismounted infantry of the SS-Panzer-Grenadier-Division "Totenkopf" in the winter of 1942–43.

This Panzerbefehlswagen III—command and control tank—of SS-Panzer-Grenadier-Division "Wiking" has just crossed a temporary bridge on the Eastern Front.

A Panzerkampfwagen III, Ausführung L of SS-Panzer-Grenadier-Division "Wiking," on the Eastern Front.

Two Panzerkampfwagen IVs of the SS-Panzerkorps on the outskirts of Kharkov in March 1943.

The crew of a late-model Panzerkampfwagen III of SS-Panzer-Grenadier-Division "Totenkopf" enjoys a quick turret-top meal on the Eastern Front in March 1943.

Marder IIIs of SS-Panzerjäger-Abteilung 1 of the SS-Panzer-Grenadier-Division "Leibstandarte SS Adolf Hitler" move through the streets of Kharkov in April 1943. The divisional antitank battalion was a welcome backstop to the SS-Panzer-grenadier when enemy armor attacked.

A Tiger I of the 13./SS-Panzer-Regiment 1 "Leibstandarte SS Adolf Hitler" examined by members of a Japanese military delegation shortly before Operation Citadel in July 1943.

A Sturmgeschütz III, Ausführung G of SS-Sturmgeschütz-Abteilung 2 of SS-Panzer-Grenadier-Division "Das Reich," moves past dug-in SS-Panzer-grenadier during Operation Citadel in July 1943.

Tiger Is of the SS-Panzer-Grenadier-Division "Das Reich" moving toward the fighting during Operation Citadel in July 1943.

An SS-Unterscharführer of SS-Panzer-Regiment 2 "Das Reich" stands in front of his Tiger I sometime during Operation Citadel in July 1943.

This Tiger I of the 13./SS-Panzer-Regiment 1 is having some maintenance or repair work done on its running gear. Eastern Front, July 1943.

SS-Panzer-grenadier of SS-Panzer-Grenadier-Division "Das Reich" riding on Panzer-kampfwagen IIIs on the Eastern Front in 1943. Although officially called mechanized infantry, even most SS-Panzer-grenadier had to rely on trucks to get to the battlefield. Few units had the armored personnel carriers, the Schützenpanzerwagen—SPW for short—to carry them into battle.

A late-model Panzerkampfwagen III of SS-Panzer-Grenadier-Division "Wiking" on the Eastern Front.

This crew stands in front of its Panzerkampfwagen III, Ausführung N, which was armed with the short 7.5-cm main gun. It was generally used in an infantry-support role. The tank belonged to SS-Panzer-Grenadier-Division "Wiking" and fought on the Eastern Front.

A Panther (Panzerkampfwagen V) and Sd. Kfz. 251 halftrack of the 5. SS-Panzer-Division "Wiking" in the summer of 1944. Panther 800 was probably the company commander's vehicle of the 8./SS-Panzer-Regiment 5 "Wiking."

An Sd. Kfz. 251 half-track, possibly that of a platoon leader, of the 5. SS-Panzer-Division "Wiking" in the summer of 1944.

A Panther and an Sd. Kfz. 251/7—the engineer version of the SPW—of the 5. SS-Panzer-Division "Wiking" in the summer of 1944.

Additional views of command and control vehicles of the 5. SS-Panzer-Division "Wiking" in the summer of 1944. Of interest is the clock painted on the gun shield on the Sd. Kfz. 251, which allowed the vehicle commander to rapidly assess the primary direction of any threat according to the clock system. Although no rank identification can be seen in this photograph, the two soldiers in the foreground are officers, as denoted by their SS version of the popular "crusher" officer cap.

SS-Panzer-grenadier of the 5. SS-Panzer-Division "Wiking" observe fighting from their Sd. Kfz. 251 halftrack in the summer of 1944.

An Sd. Kfz. 251 with Wurfrah-men—rocket launcher units—of 5. SS-Panzer-Division "Wiking" during the Warsaw uprising in September 1944. The rockets came in two sizes, twenty-eight and thirty-two centimeters, and contained either high-explosive or napalm warheads. Note the piles of the discarded wooden frames that held the rockets. Due to the extensive backblast of the rockets, the crew had to remain under cover during firing.

A Wespe 10.5-cm self-propelled gun of the 3. SS-Panzer-Division "Totenkopf" prepares to fire on the Eastern Front.

The crew of a Marder self-propelled antitank gun from a Waffen-SS unit—possibly the 1. SS-Panzer-Division "Leib-standarte SS Adolf Hitler," based on the apparent shoul-der-strap slides on one of the soldiers—making friends with the local people.

Group of SS-Panzer-grenadier observing a Panther (Panzer-kampfwagen V, Ausführung A) of the 12. SS-Panzer-Division "Hitlerjugend" in Normandy in 1944.

A heavily camouflaged Panzer-kampfwagen IV, Ausführung H of the 12. SS-Panzer-Division "Hitlerjugend" in Normandy in 1944. Note the ever-present air guard on the watch for Allied close-air-support aircraft.

A Panzerkampfwagen IV, Ausführung H of the 1. SS-Panzer-Division "Leibstandarte SS Adolf Hitler" awaits orders to continue moving through a French town in Normandy in the summer of 1944.

Tank commanders of the 1./Schwere SS-Panzer-Abteilung 101. From left to right: Fey, Egger, and Glagow.

Crewmembers of a 2-cm Flakvierling (quad antiaircraft gun) of the 1. SS-Panzer-Division "Leibstandarte SS Adolf Hitler" reading their mail.

A Königstiger of the 1./Schwere SS-Panzer-Abteilung 101 moves up to the front in France in August 1944.

Another view of the same Königstiger.

A destroyed Tiger I of the Schwere SS-Panzer-Abteilung 102 during the long with-drawal to Germany in late summer 1944.

A Marder III of a Waffen-SS unit passing Allied prisoners in the vicinity of Arnhem in September 1944.

A Königstiger (Panzerkampfwagen VI, Ausführung B) of the 2./Schwere SS-Panzer-Abteilung 501 during the Ardennes Offensive in December 1944. SS-Oberscharführer Kurt Sowa was the tank commander of Tiger 222.

This Panther (Panzerkampfwagen V, Ausführung G) of SS-Panzer-Regiment 1 was turned completely upside down as the result of a nearby explosion. The Ardennes, December 1944.

This fairly intact Panther (Panzerkampfwagen V, Ausführung G) of SS-Panzer-Regiment 1 appears to have been abandoned by its crew. The Ardennes, January 1945.

sions were extorted by the American investigating authorities. During the trial itself, the freedom of action of the defense was greatly curtailed. All this led to forty-three death sentences and thirty-one sentences to terms in prison. After the public was successfully alerted, three consecutive American commissions investigated these proceedings, in particular the methods of interrogation and investigation used at Schwäbisch-Hall. Finally, and not the least based on the extraordinary efforts of the American chief defense counsel, Colonel Everett, the court decisions were changed so that the last of these soldiers was released from prison ten years later.

Panzer commander Karl Wortmann and his Flak-Panzer formed part of "Kampfgruppe Peiper" and lived through the surprise attack. He experienced the encirclement of La Gleize and reached, after the loss of all Panzers and vehicles, the assembly area at St. Vith after a forced march across the hills of the Ardennes. Here is his battle report:

On December 15, 1944, late in the afternoon, when the armored units of the Leibstandarte had made camp close to the front lines in the woods of Hallschlag and Losheim, the leaders of the units were briefed on the impending plan to attack. Up to that time movements of troops took place very quietly and only at night, and the start of the attack was kept a strict secret. Only the soldiers of the spearheads were informed during the same day, the other units heard about it only a few days later. The Oberbefehlshaber (Supreme Commander) West, Generalfeldmarschall von Rundstedt issued the following orders of the day to the attack troops:

"Soldiers of the Western Front! Your finest hour has arrived! Strong assault armies are today lined up against the Anglo-Americans. I need not tell you anything else. You all feel it: This is the decisive action! Carry inside you the solemn commitment to offer your all and to perform superhumanly, for our fatherland and our Führer!"

The 1. SS-Panzer-Division Leibstandarte SS "Adolf Hitler," together with the 12. SS-Panzer-Division "Hitlerjugend," the 12. and 277. Infantry-Divisions and the 3. Fallschirmjägerdivision (paratroopers) were part of the I. SS-Panzerkorps that was lead by SS-Gruppenführer and Generalleutnant of the Waffen-SS, Hermann Prieß. Together with two other corps it formed the 6. SS-Panzerarmee under the supreme command of SS-Oberstgruppenführer and Generaloberst (four-star general) Sepp Dietrich. Darkness, fog, and a light snowfall marked the early morning of December 16, 1944. At 5:30 A.M., German artillery made the earth tremble from Monschau to Echternach and all of the Western Front awoke.

Thousands and thousands of soldiers on both sides watched an eerie display of fire. The Western Allies had long since thought that the military power of the Germans was broken. The concentrated sustained fire of our heavy weapons raining down on them was to change that perception. The signal for all of the Western Front was given; the hour of the attack had arrived! There were certainly only a few German soldiers at this front who did not perceive at that moment that the last large-scale battle of the Second World War had begun. That was the last attempt, the last effort, and, with an immense expenditure of men and materiel, also the last venture of the German command.

Kampfgruppe Peiper, which included a Panzer-Flak company under the command of Obersturmführer Völer, was at the point of the thrust by the SS-Panzerkorps. The following report describes the action of the Kampfgruppe:

> Eight Panzers of the Flak company were a part of Kampfgruppe Peiper, which had been set up especially for this action. The 6. Panzerarmee stood on the right flank of Heeresgruppe B (army group) from Monschau all the way to Losheimergraben. The 7. Army was the left wing of the Heeresgruppe and the 5. Panzerarmee formed the center. The attack objectives of this offensive were far-reaching and included the destruction of the enemy north of a straight line Bastogne–Brussels–Antwerp. The front line of the enemy was to be broken through at suitable points. The Maas River bridges near Liège, and securing them, were the first main objective of the 6. Panzerarmee. At the same time, a strong defensive front was to be formed to the north. Further objectives in the second attack sector were the Albert Canal and the area north of Antwerp.

It was an accepted fact that the setting of these objectives put too great a demand on the army and could have only been carried out successfully if the element of surprise, which formed part of the plan, was brought into play. The Panzer-regiment had moved into position under cover of the night and was in readiness. Long columns of Panzers and armored vehicles stood on the paths in the woods of the Eifel mountains. Four Flak-Panzers, two equipped with the 3.7-cm gun and two with the four-barrel Flak guns, were at the point of the column. The other four were located in the rear third of the group.

Daylight came slowly. A new, rough, winter day began on December 16, 1944. During the first assault units of the 3. Fallschirmjägerdivision, together with grenadiers of the 12. Volks-Grenadier-Division (people's grenadiers), overran the lines of the American units. American troops positioned there, along with their leadership, were completely surprised.

Kampfgruppe Peiper, a mixed group of two Panther companies, Panzer-Flak companies, the 3. and 9. Panzerpionier companies, SS-Tiger-Abteilung 501, the III. Schützenpanzerwagen (armored personnel carriers) battalion of SS-Panzer-Grenadier-Regiment 2, and parts of the 2. SS-Panzer-Artillery-Regiment, had as its objective, within the framework of the division, to reach the Maas River in no more than forty-eight hours. There, it was to form a bridgehead and keep the route of advance open for the division following behind. First, however, it was necessary to gain space so that the Kampfgruppe could move properly. One of the big problems turned out to be that only few of the roads were suitable for our armored vehicles. The roads were frequently clogged, which hindered the advance. Dirt roads could hardly be used as an alternative since they were soft and muddy.

After overcoming these first obstacles, the Kampfgruppe began its move, pushing speedily ahead. In the first town occupied by the enemy, Lanzerath, it encountered German paratroopers fighting there and supported these until the Americans were overcome. After this battle, the paratroopers climbed on the Panzers and rode forward.

Some Panzers drove onto mines. These had not been laid by the retreating Americans but by German units withdrawing to the Westwall the previous fall.

Snow-covered terrain lay ahead of the Kampfgruppe in the early morning hours of December 17. The crews had spent the entire night in their Panzers and armored vehicles. A path through the woods leading from Lanzerath to the railroad station, located outside of the village, showed the fresh tracks made by the armored vehicles of the vanguard. The main body followed a few minutes later. American soldiers were seen on both sides of the path. They fired machine guns and other light weapons at the moving column. A few bursts from the four-barreled Flak forced them to flee farther into the woods. Mortar shells were a little more uncomfortable as they hit the ground close to the Panzers. The powder snow, thrown up by their explosions, obscured visibility for seconds at a time. Heavy enemy antitank fire came from the railroad station. It was silenced by the Panzers at the point.

After a few kilometers without enemy contact, the village of Hons-feld lay ahead of us. Because of its narrow streets, we had to reduce our speed. The long column split up at the entrance to the village, planning to rejoin later. The first four Flak-Panzers formed the spearhead of the column and entered the village along the main street. A sharp bend forced an even further reduction in speed. Parts of two buildings, facing each other at an angle and projecting onto the road, obscured forward visibility almost completely. Suddenly, a flash!—A loud bang! The first Flak-Panzer was hit. It continued to roll ahead for a short distance before it came to a stop. At the same moment came a second shot and the shell hit the second Flak-Panzer. It, too, was immobilized after a few meters. The following vehicles were blocked. The commander of the third Flak-Panzer, Unterscharführer Karl Wortmann, saw the muzzle flash of the next shot at very close range. He tried to get by the two knocked-out Panzers and fired his four-barrel Flak in the direction of the enemy gun while moving. The firing stopped. The stalled column resumed its movement.

In the center of town a heavy firefight broke out. From skylights and windows of the upper stories the Americans fired into the armored personnel carriers of the 3. Pionier-Company, which were open at the top. Returning the fire started heavy house-to-house and close-in combat. The Americans, completely surprised, used anything at all for cover. They sought safety in stables, barns, cellars, and any rooms available in the houses. Use of the two four-barrel Flaks had the desired effect. With white sheets and hands in the air, the shaking Americans came out from the houses and their hiding places and became prisoners. The number of dead and wounded on both sides was considerable.

Only after the firefight was over did the crews of the two mobile Flak-Panzers find the time to worry about the fate of their comrades in the knocked-out Panzers. They could not make out what damage the two hits had caused and whether there were dead in addition to the critically wounded. In addition to the regular crews, the company chief, Obersturmführer Vögler, had been in the first Panzer, and the second in command of the I. Zug (platoon), Hauptscharführer (first sergeant) Schröder, in the second. Both of them, and the two crews, could not take part in the further advance.

As it turned out, the American Pak had knocked out the two Flak-Panzers from a distance of approximately fifty meters. The enemy Pak still sat there, abandoned. Only its muzzle stuck out a little from a brier hedge, pointing unmovingly toward the bend in the village street. The gun could hardly be moved horizontally and was served from a house entrance. After they had come under fire from the four-barrel Flak, the four-man crew fled into the cellar of the house where they sought cover together with other Americans. The whole house was full of Americans, many of whom tried to flee through the windows in the rear of the house.

The advance continued in the direction of Büllingen. There was another unplanned halt at the exit of the town of Honsfeld. Movements were spotted behind the big old tombstones in the cemetery to the right of the road. Were they Americans? No! Fifteen to eighteen men in American uniforms approached. They touched their helmets or chests. During the briefing on the attack plans the German soldiers were informed that groups or individual soldiers in American uniforms who make these motions as a sign recognition will be men who belong to "Operation Greif (griffin). All members of this elite German group were familiar with American customs, spoke English fluently, and were equipped with American weapons, materiel, and vehicles. They were part of Obersturmbannführer Skorzeny's Panzer-Brigade 150.

The group that had shown up here reported that they had spent the entire night cowering behind the tombstones. They rode on our Panzers to Büllingen, where the vanguard and the other half of the column encountered strong enemy resistance. Before that, a small field airstrip with a few light aircraft was captured. After the end of the local fighting, the Kampfgruppe was in a position to refuel with captured gasoline and to take on captured food supplies. American prisoners were transported to an assembly camp. Kampfgruppe Peiper continued to roll toward its objectives.

These objectives could not be reached in accordance with the timetable planned before the start of the offensive. The fighting that had occurred, the poor road conditions, and the extra use of fuel caused by having to detour around towns could not be properly predicted. Thus, the Kampfgruppe encountered strong enemy resistance just after leaving Büllingen and had to make another long detour. The conditions of the streets and dirt roads of the small villages of Schoppen, Thirimont, and Ondenva were not favorable for driving for heavy Panzers, and this caused a great loss of time.

Around noon, the Panzers at the point sighted, at a road junction, a long American column of vehicles that was moving from Malmedy in the direction of Engelsdorf. From a distance of some 400 meters, some Panzers opened fire. The shells were meant only to cause alarm and not to hit the vehicles. It might have been a column of fuel tankers, which would have been a welcome booty. Most of the shells went over the vehicles and exploded in open terrain or close to the adjoining woods, which was the direction in which a number of Americans who had hastily abandoned their vehicles ran, seeking cover in the nearby woods.

The Kampfgruppe approached the junction and turned in the direction of Engelskirchen. Some of the American trucks had rolled into the ditch or against the trees along the road. The doors of the vehicles were wide open, and the majority of the American soldiers were taken prisoner. As stated in orders from the beginning, the group of Panzers, was not to stop anywhere so that it would reach its planned objective as quickly as possible. The clearing of the towns and the gathering of prisoners were to be left to the infantry units following behind. Therefore, the assembled prisoners were virtually without guard after the Panzers had moved on. However, because of the bad roads and the chaotic traffic, the infantry could not quickly follow the Panzer unit. A portion of the prisoners took advantage of this situation and picked up their weapons again as the following German troops approached. Thus, fighting again ensued.

Only a few Americans succeeded in making their way to their unit in Malmedy, where they reported on the events at the junction near Baugnez. The Armed Forces radio station "Calais" made it into a news item and reported wrongly that troops of the Leibstandarte SS "Adolf Hitler" had shot American soldiers who were about to surrender or had already surrendered in the vicinity of Malmedy. When Oberstgruppen-führer Sepp Dietrich heard of this report on the German language enemy radio station, he immediately ordered an investigation of the event.

All the findings he received confirmed without a doubt that it had been purely a matter of combat action, and that there was no question of shootings.

The advance of the Kampfgruppe continued to Engelsdorf, where an American staff was located in a big hotel. The Americans were so surprised at the sudden appearance of the German Panzers that they abandoned everything. Some of them did not even have time to put on their jackets as they tried to flee by the rear exits of the hotel. They did not get very far before they were taken prisoner and, in their own vehicles, were taken along on the continuation of the advance.

One of the Panzers at the point was knocked out by an immobilized Sherman, which sat, unnoticed, on a side road at the entrance to the town where the winding road went downhill. An undesirable delay at Engelsdorf was caused when some of the Panzers at the point encountered strong resistance and were forced to turn around. Insurmountable road conditions also contributed to this. The only possibility left was to continue the advance through the narrow valley of the Ambleve River.

The bridge across the river at Stavelot was reached during the night of December 18. There was a question whether the old stone bridge could carry the Panzers. After some hours of bitter fighting for this bridge, the Panzers rolled carefully across it and into the city. Dangerous situations occurred in the narrow streets, and bitter close combat took place. The main objective was to open the road to Trois-Ponts, the next town, in order to continue the advance. A reconnaissance unit of the Leibstandarte, which followed the Kampfgruppe at a distance, found the bridge again occupied by the enemy. It had to be cleared once more. This bridge and the town continued to be an obstacle to the units following behind, as they were to the other four Flak-Panzers of our company.

At around noon, Kampfgruppe Peiper reached Trois-Ponts, a charming town, named after its three bridges. Behind the railroad viaduct sat a well-camouflaged American antitank gun that knocked out a few Panzers at the point of the column. At the very moment the enemy gun was destroyed, courageous American engineers blew up the bridges across the Ambleve and Salm Rivers. With this, the way to the Maas River was also blocked. Deciding quickly, Obersturmbannführer Peiper gave the order for another detour via La Gleize. For a while there was no fighting. However, when the group of Panzers pushed toward Werbomont, it was attacked, for the first time, by enemy aircraft just before the small village of Cheneux.

TWO FLAK-PANZERS SAVE THE KAMPFGRUPPE FROM SIGNIFICANT LOSSES

The foggy, wintery drab weather brightened a little and the sun could even be seen for a few moments. The column of the Kampfgruppe traveled on a narrow mountain road and stretched over more than two kilometers. To the right of the mountain road was an extensive wall of rock, to its left a steep drop into the valley. Unknown to it, the Kampfgruppe was spotted on the way to La Gleize by a Piper Cub, an American reconnaissance aircraft. When sixteen Thunderbolts attacked the full width of the Kampfgruppe from the side of the valley, the vehicles stopped, still spread out and without any cover. There was no way at all to get out. The Panzer crews and grenadiers crawled into or under the iron and steel giants, which sat without cover and defenseless in the open. The two Flak-Panzers with their four-barrel guns immediately opened fire and blasted away as fast as they could. But the "vultures of the skies" attacked mercilessly, diving, firing their onboard weapons, and dropping bombs.

To hold their own against sixteen enemy aircraft, in particular when they attacked in formation, was almost hopeless for the men of the Flak-Panzers. They could not concentrate on individual aircraft under these circumstances because too many were attacking at the same time. So they put up a general defensive fire, making the pilots uncertain, and thus prevented well-aimed attacks. The amount of explosive shells from the eight barrels was phenomenal, and the burst clouds proved it. The faces of the men at the guns were covered with sweat, fear likely in their minds, as they were attacked time and again by the aircraft. The turrets of the Panzers swung left or right at lightning speed as they tried to fight off the enemy aircraft again and again.

Some of the Panzer crews removed their machine guns from their mounts and also fired at the aircraft, which would just not give up. There were a number of wounded among the grenadiers and Panzer crews, and the medics were fully occupied. What would have been the fate of this Panzer unit if the Flak-Panzers with their four-barrel guns had not been with it? Neither the onboard weapons nor the bombs from the aircraft were able to cause very significant damage to the sixty-two vehicles.

The Flak-Panzer guns set one Thunderbolt on fire, and it crashed a few seconds later. After approximately half an hour the enemy aircraft pulled away. Obersturmbannführer Peiper thanked the men of the Panzer-Flak. He had found cover under one of the Panzers at the point. After the attack by the enemy aircraft, which had shaken up everyone somewhat, the Kampfgruppe reached the bridge across the Lienne River near Neufmoulin in the evening. It was absolutely essential to cross this bridge, which was guarded by a small American unit. Just behind it lay Werbomont where the major route of advance would finally have been reached again. The objective was within reaching distance! The guards at the bridge had to be neutralized to prevent the bridge from being blown up. The Americans were faster by a fraction of a second. When the first Panzer was a few meters from it, the bridge blew up. The way to the Maas River was blocked to Obersturmbannführer Peiper there as well. All vehicles turned around on the spot. During the night the column pulled back to La Gleize. The hope that the town was still free of the enemy came true. Many of the Panzers and reconnaissance vehicles were almost out of fuel. Some could not make it past La Gleize. The 2. Panther-Kompanie and one Flak-Panzer drove with the 3. Panzer-Pionierkompanie and grenadiers of the reconnaissance battalion beyond the town of

Stoumont, five kilometers away, to scout for a new route of advance and determine the enemy situation. Encountering strong enemy resistance and losing several Panzers, the small unit pulled back to the town and prepared for defense since wounded Germans and wounded American prisoners were housed in the nearby castle of Froid Cour.

Little by little the Americans recaptured the town. The last bastion of defense was the sanatorium on a small hill near the castle. The losses there were big. The crew of the Flak-Panzer lost Sturmmänner Adolf Macht and Heinz Scholz, as well as Feldwebel (staff sergeant) Hahn who had transferred from the Luftwaffe just before this action. He had been made an Oberscharführer, the same rank, and added to the crew of the Panzer. In the meantime, Kampfgruppe Peiper had lost all contact with units of the division; even radio contact had ceased.

On December 22 and 23, the towns of Cheneux and Stoumont had to be given up. Almost out of ammunition and fuel, La Gleize was defended. Food and sleep had become foreign words to the men. In this town, which had been completely turned into rubble by the Americans, there were still more than 200 wounded as well as about 150 American prisoners. The supplies expected by air did not arrive. In the evening hours of December 23, Obersturmbannführer Jochen Peiper decided to break out on foot with the remaining 800 relatively fit men across the hills of the Ardennes. Slightly wounded comrades who could walk were taken along. All Panzers and vehicles were blown up. Dr. Dittmann, the physician of the reconnaissance battalion, and some medics remained with the critically wounded in order to turn them over to the Americans. The American prisoners were set free.

The breakout from the encirclement of La Gleize succeeded under immense hardships. The German lines and the village of Wanne, where our supply units were located, were reached around noon on Christmas Day. The totally exhausted members of the Kampfgruppe were allowed to rest and recuperate in the villages of Ober- and Nieder-Emmels until the end of the year. Kampfgruppe Peiper was disbanded.

PANZER ACTIONS OF THE HEAVY SS-PANZER-ABTEILUNG 501 IN THE ARDENNES

During the Ardennes offensive, the Korps-Tiger-Abteilung 501 was attached to SS-Panzer-Regiment 1, which only had one Abteilung due to materiel shortages. Panzer-Regiment 1's second Abteilung had to be left behind in Westphalia. The Korpsabteilung, equipped with Tiger IIs (Königstiger–King Tigers), under its commander, Obersturmbannführer von Westernhagen, marched well to the rear of Kampfgruppe Peiper. Narrow roads were not suitable for these wide and heavy Panzers, which weighed approximately 70 tons. For these reasons they were not included with the units in the spearhead of the division. The one Königstiger that had fought its way through to La Gleize remained there. Even today it is admired by many groups of tourists.

The remaining Tigers were used individually by the division and the Korps during the recapturing of Stavelot and Bastogne in house-to-house fighting and actions in the wooded areas that caused irreplaceable losses. Tigers not lost during these difficult actions were confiscated by Generalfeldmarschall Model, who had the vehicles taken from the repair shops by his orderly officers and handed over to the infantry.

Panzer Attack in the Direction of Lüttich (Liège)

PANZER COMMANDER AND ZUGFÜHRER (PLATOON LEADER) OF 2./SS-PANZER-REGIMENT "DAS REICH," UNTER-STURMFÜHRER FRITZ LANGANKE, REPORTS ON HIS ACTION IN A PANTHER TANK IN DECEMBER 1944

The great opportunities of the Ardennes offensive were already over. Bitter fighting against the increasingly stronger American units, which were fighting back with more and more determination, dominated the situation. The few good days when an overcast sky had almost prevented all activity by the enemy air force had passed, and the fighter-bombers again took up their battle-deciding role. That was the situation at the beginning of our combat in the Ardennes just before Christmas 1944. The I. Abteilung of the Panzer-regiment of Panzer-Division "Das Reich" was located west of Baraque de Fraiture and awaited battle orders. In the afternoon of December 23, the 2. and 3. Companies received orders to march, at the fall of darkness, to the assembly area near Odeigne. The attack was to begin during the night. I led the 1. Zug (platoon) of the 2. Company. It was a hard winter. The snow was high and crunched under one's feet. Frost bit even through the winter clothing. One felt almost like he was in Russia. The route led through swampy bush-covered and wooded terrain, where we got stuck a number of times and lost a lot of time. American artillery sprinkled the area with harassing fire, and, occasionally, target marker flares hung in the air for enemy night bombers. When we started our advance, it was, regrettably, already daylight. After we were briefed and studied the maps and the terrain, we no longer thought highly of our planned action. But it could not be changed. The 1. Zug, 1. Company SS "D," which was attached to our company, was reinforced by groups of antitank fighters with Panzerfautss and "stove-pipes" and a heavy MG group for a total of sixty men.

The Zugführer, Untersturmführer Erich Heller, had the same concerns as I after the briefing. However, both of us were soldiers and bound by orders and obedience. He climbed onto my Panzer with a few men. Most of the grenadiers climbed on the other Panzers, while the rest marched behind. The route led from Odeigne through the valley of the Aisne River, deeply cut in places, to a junction where a wide valley opened up. There, the 2. Company was supposed to turn left and reach the town of La Fosse on the crest of the facing hill by way of Freineux. The 3. Company was to attack to the right via Oster toward Grandmenil. I was in the Panzer at the point of the 2. Company. Just behind the junction the road led across the small river. There, I made a serious mistake. Since we expected contact with the enemy from then on, I thought two dark spots on the bridge were mines, so we waded through the water to the left of the bridge. Later we established that there were no mines. While the river was shallow and had a firm bed, the bank on the other side was so steep that we spent a lot of time before all of the company was back on the road. The first vehicle almost turned over, and too much valuable time was lost there. It was certain that we could no longer have surprised anyone, even if it could have been possible before. When we finally all made it up the bank, the marching order had become quite upset. Without pausing, we pushed on toward the small village of Freineux, which lay directly ahead of us. We drove across open meadowland to the right of the road, which fell away toward a small stream where it was bordered by a row of trees. Our four Panthers attacked the cluster of houses, in a formation staggered to the left rear. With me was a vehicle of my platoon (Oberscharführer Pippert), the leader of the second platoon, Untersturmführer Seeger, and the company leader. The grenadiers in action with us had again climbed onto the Panzers. Untersturmführer Heller stood behind my turret and observed the terrain toward Freineux through the binoculars. At the same time, the third company had reached the junction and turned right toward Grandmenil. It drove parallel to the slope in front of us on which was the town of La Fosse. Visibility, for us, was extremely poor.

We drove toward a gently rising, snow-covered slope, which glimmered brightly in the light of the sun low above the horizon. We were looking out of the hatches in order to be better able to see. We had barely advanced 100 meters when the Americans opened fire. They fired simultaneously on us and the 3. Company whose vehicles were showing their backs to them. Then, everything happened very quickly. The Panzer of Untersturmführer Seeger caught on fire with the first hit. He was able to jump out, badly burned, but the four comrades of his crew died in the vehicle. The Panzer of Oberscharführer Pippert was stopped, after taking hits, and its gun hung down, obviously out of action. The crew bailed out. I could not make out the fate of the fourth vehicle, as it drove slowly backward, after having been hit. I noticed that the Americans also fired to our sides and beyond us. I turned my head further back and watched as Panzers of the 3. Company were knocked out from behind. In such situations, when one was almost completely helpless, a terrible rage set in. We pulled ahead a little and opened fire ourselves. Because of the heavy fire setting in, to which was added increased fighter-bomber activity, the grenadiers jumped off and found, with difficulty, some cover in the shallow ditch next to the row of trees to our right. They managed, slowly, to work their way back to the road without losses. In the meantime we were able to make out what was happening in front of us. About 100 meters, half-left ahead, a tank sat next to a pile of wood, only its barrel sticking out above. It appeared that it could not be lowered enough to aim for our hull. We turned the turret in its direction and put it out of action with a few shells. It did not catch on fire but stopped shooting. The first hits to our vehicle had been to the front. Obviously, an American Pak fired from a group of dense bushes 100 to 200 meters away. Judging by the firing sequence, we figured there were two guns. The movement of their barrels seemed to be restricted, and they fired only at our hull. So we risked turning the turret to the side. The bushes were so dense that we could not spot any muzzle flashes.

After we knocked out the tank, we immediately turned the turret back to twelve o'clock, pulled ahead a little more and tried to blow away the bushes and undergrowth with explosive shells and MG bursts so that we could make out the guns. In the meantime we took more than ten Pak hits and, for the second time during the war in a Panther, the welds of the top armor plate in front, which took most of the hits, partly ripped under heavy fire. The tracks, also, were badly damaged. Since the beginning of the Ardennes offensive, we had a new radio operator in the vehicle. An Unterscharführer from the communications Abteilung, he had volunteered to join a Panzer crew and was not familiar with what happened during heavy fighting. The impressions of this, his first, violent action overwhelmed him quickly, and he could not handle them. The immensely fast actions of the crew, the ensuing racket, and the shells that hit the vehicle mostly where he was sitting, in a fast sequence, with a piercing, hard, and penetrating bang on impact were too much for him. Then, when the radio was ripped from its mounting on the gear-box and dropped on him, he suffered a nervous breakdown. He yelled and wanted to get out; the driver could only calm him down with great difficulty. Such a loss, during moments of intense concentration, could hardly be overcome by the crew of the fighting vehicle. We lost our rhythm and were only half as effective as before. A well-functioning crew was like a living organism. Critical disruptions of this kind made extremely high performance almost impossible.

We still could not make out the guns facing us. Damaged as we were, we did not dare to just set out and drive toward the bushes. Then we took a hit somewhat higher, which ripped off the block of the gun barrel support and threw it high into the air. It landed on the front edge of the turret but, thankfully, slid down the outside. I only glimpsed something fly about when the shell hit and dropped without hesitation into the compartment. My head was already inside the cupola when the barrel support landed on the turret edge. I only took a minor knock, which made me somewhat dizzy for a while.

In the meantime we had taken twenty hits and, since we just could not locate the Paks, decided to drive back again. Slowly we rolled backward past our two Panzers, one of which was still engulfed in violent flames, until we reached the road where we had previously left it. Toward the end, our radio operator completely lost his nerve, jumped from the vehicle, and had to be taken to hospital.

At the other side of the road, a depression in the terrain converged with the road at a fairly steep angle, dropping down steeply for some three meters. At its edge stood a dense row of conifers, which cast a strong shadow that we used for cover. The other vehicle, which had pulled back before we did, was already sitting there. The main body of the company had swung wide to the left toward the edge of the woods in order to shell the town from there.

The fighter-bomber activity, directed mainly against the 3. Company, had increased in the meantime. Along the approach from Odeigne, 200 to 300 meters from the junction, was a small quarry on the fairly steep slope to the right. One of our 3.7-cm Flaks had taken up position there and immediately started to fire on the low-level American aircraft. Time and again, for hours, groups of fighter-bombers attacked this gun. Because of the lay of the terrain, the aircraft could only use a certain path to attack. The gun fired without hesitation, regardless of how many fighter-bombers showed up. An exemplary action!

Every time the aircraft approached, we felt great anxiety in our Panzers. The fighter-bombers, flying at very low altitude, had to pass right overhead and we were never sure if we might be their target. Only when they were directly overhead would we start to breathe again. The deep shadow we sat in obviously provided sufficient cover.

During the drive to our present position, we had noticed that the vehicle could hardly turn without slipping off the track. We changed a whole row of links to improve our driving capability somewhat but were interrupted time and again by the still increasing fighter-bomber activity. This toiling caused a lot of sweat to all of us in the snow. Only the gunner got off easy; he was not allowed to leave his gun.

During all this, on orders of the I./SS "D," the grenadiers had continued the attack on Freineux on their own along the road. They were able to find good cover along the way. Initially, they advanced quickly but then received strong fire from the town. A panzerschreck (bazooka) team was able to knock out a Sherman tank in the center of town (two others were spotted at the southern edge of town), but the losses were so high that Untersturmführer Heller ordered a withdrawal, taking along the wounded. He, himself, and three other men with panzerfausts stayed behind. At the start of a sudden artillery fire, this group jumped into a house. From the first floor they spotted a tank dug in 100 to 150 meters off the road and a Pak. These targets, which had to be the guns we faced in the morning and could not locate, were knocked out with panzerfausts. Then the house was hit by a shell. Untersturmführer Heller was rendered unconscious for a time by falling debris. When he came to, he found himself caught under burning timber. Men from an American scouting team who showed up soon after pulled him out with great difficulty, some of them suffering burns themselves, and moved him to a dressing station. The dead men of the SS "D" were also removed by the Americans. Untersturmführer Heller then learned that more than twenty tanks had been brought in since December 25 to defend this town.

Around noon the weather turned somewhat hazy, and snow began to fall on and off. As long as it had remained clear, I had the MG fire on distinctive markers in the terrain, such as sharp bends in the road, noticeable rises in the ground, and individual trees, in order to determine exact distances that we noted on a small sketch. It was probable that sometime an American counterattack would take place down the hill, and we wanted to be prepared for it. As soon as I had a chance I spoke to the crew of the Panzer of Oberscharführer Pippert who had bailed out. We determined that the vehicle might still have been mobile. As soon as it turned dark, the crew crept over to its Panzer and was able to drive it back after all. Apparently, Americans had been inside already.

The chief of the third company, Obersturmführer Veith, came over to us and filled us in on the development of the actions in his sector. After some of their vehicles were knocked out, they escaped from the road into the woods of the rising slope to the right of the route of advance, and were increasingly attacked by low-level fighter-bombers. I learned then who had died in the knocked-out Panzers. Some very close comrades of mine, who had been together with me for a long time, were among them. Oberscharführer Vobis was one. Our mood was very depressed. The visibility kept getting worse, and the clouds hung low. Overhead, huge formations of bombers flew in the direction of the Reich. With a heavy heart and helpless rage, we could only stare into the sky in desperation. I climbed back into my seat and watched the slope in the direction of La Fosse. Obersturmführer Veith, who would later die in the Ardennes and be awarded the Knight's Cross after his death, stood in front of my vehicle next to the muzzle brake of the gun.

Suddenly, American tanks appeared. They came down the slope from La Fosse in spread-out formation and obviously wanted to drive toward the 3. Company. I yelled at Veith to get out of the way, we had to fire. He did not hear it over the noise of the engines. In a very short time the Americans were at the points we had test fired at earlier, and we had to fire our first shell.

Despite the sad situation I could not suppress a grin when Veith's cap was blown off by the air pressure from the shot. He was completely confused for a moment until he grasped what was happening when our second shell was fired. Thanks to our preparations, we knocked out the first five Sherman tanks in quick succession despite the poor visibility. They moved at a steep angle to us, down the slope, half-right. The firing distance was between 500 and 700 meters. The other tanks then turned around and drove back. Thereafter it was quiet and dusk set in soon. We drove back, with difficulty, to Odeigne, where we inspected our vehicles in peace. The shells had ripped deep grooves into the front plates. It was surprising that they had withstood this. We had been lucky that the angle of impact of the shells had been so favorable for us.

Regrettably, we could not take part with our damaged vehicle in the following attack by our Abteilung together with the armored infantry battalion of the "DF" Regiment on Manhay/Grandmenil during Christmas night. During this assault the 4. Company, driving at the point, was particularly successful. Thus we spent our last Christmas of the war. It was tough and demanded our utmost, not offering a glimmer of hope. The approaching end and the defeat became more and more obvious.

By Christmas 1945, almost all of us sat in some prison camp, deprived of our rights, isolated and the scapegoats of the nation. Some were abused or threatened by death from starvation. Robbed of all belongings, many were without a home. But one thing no one could, even today, take away from us: the constant realization that, in good days and situations, as well as bad, we had always, without conditions and to the best of our abilities, performed our duty. The time of Christmas 1944 in the Ardennes was an example of this.

The Bold Drive of Panther 401 Through U.S. Units to Manhay

ACTION BY THE I. PANZER-ABTEILUNG/"DASREICH"
Oberscharführer Ernst Barkmann, Platoon Leader of the 4. Panzer-Company Reports

The 1./Panzer-Regiment "DR" took on the responsibility for security in a westerly direction and the establishment of contact with the neighbor on the left, the 560. Volks-Grenadier-Division (VGD).

The 4. Panzer-Company remained as a reserve in a wooded area outside of Odeigne, and the 2. and 3. Panzer-Companies carried out an attack in the morning hours of December 24 in westerly and northwesterly directions. During the advance, the 2. Panzer-Company was to reach the town of La Fosse by way of Freineux. The 3. Panzer-Company was to advance on Grandmenil via Oster.

With the 4. Panzer-Company at the point, the I. Panzer-Abteilung, together with the I. and II. Battalion/"D" and the III. (armored) Battalion/"DF," was to carry out a thrust to the town of Manhay, located to the northwest, with its important crossroads. Turning west from there, the attack was to continue to Erezée, by way of Grandmenil, to link up with the 560. VGD, which was to carry out a night attack in its sector on Erezée.

Before the attack on Manhay, the "Belle Haie" crossroads, still in enemy hands, was to be taken from the rear by the 4. Panzer-Company The start of the attack for this company was to be 8 P.M. For the remainder of the Abteilung and for the Regiment "D," it was to be 9 P.M.

I looked at my chief and wished him a happy and blessed Christmas!

We scouted the terrain on foot and walked toward the northwest until, from one of the hills, we could observe the crossroads and the course of the road running through the range of wooded hills in the direction of Manhay. Sometime later, enemy infantry fire forced us to turn around.

Difficulties in the disengaging of our valiant grenadier units of the "D" and "DF" Regiments delayed the start of the attack.

Around 10 P.M. the 4. Panzer-Company started out. The III. Zug (platoon) under Hauptscharführer (master sergeant) Frauscher was at the point. The chief was next. As Panzer commander, I stood in the turret of replacement Panzer 401. The Panzers of the I. and II. Platoons followed. Behind them, deeply staggered and spread out, came the other companies of the I. Panzer-Abteilung.

Bright moonlight flooded the Ardennes landscape covered in deep snow. The tall fir trees on both sides of our advance route carried heavy loads of snow. Above us a full moon in a clear starry night unveiled all contours far ahead. Everything was going according to the plan.

Capture of the "Belle Haie" Crossroads

Coming from the southwest, we reached the enemy-held crossroads, deployed in a double row, and opened fire with explosive shells from all Panzer guns on the enemy positions we could make out. After the surprise fire attack, there was almost no reaction from the enemy.

Hauptscharführer Frauscher signed off on the radio. He wanted to reach the main road to Manhay, along which the attack was to move ahead, with his platoon. Turning onto the road, the first Panzer took a direct hit and stopped, immobilized. The second Panzer was also hit. The platoon halted! The chief urged by radio to continue the attack. I feared for my comrade Frauscher and his crews.

The Adventurous Drive of Panther 401 Begins!

As the company chief would probably have wanted, I quickly decided to sign off by radio and went to scout the situation. Without waiting for his reply, we drove off. Taking better advantage of the terrain than its predecessors, Panther 401 reached the road without trouble. We crossed it and immediately turned toward the direction of the enemy. No incoming fire! Under cover of the elevated roadbed, we slowly advanced parallel to it in order to reach the stalled fighting vehicles of the platoon at the point and to give them covering fire.

We could not find Frauscher's Panzer. Then we learned by radio that he had moved into the other Panzer and continued his advance again. So we continued using the cover of the elevated road and, after a while, reached the edge of the woods. Under the cover of the shadows from the tall firs in the bright moonlight, we pushed along the road into the woods.

Friend or Foe?

At fifty paces distant, a tank stood to the right. Its commander, upright in the turret, seemed to be waiting for me. Frauscher! I drove up to the left side of the tank and when the turrets were parallel, I stopped, had the engine turned off, and addressed him. My opposite number, however, disappeared into his turret at lightning speed and the hatches slammed shut! The driver's hatch of my neighbor opened and closed again. I spotted ruby-colored lights from the instruments! The Panther was equipped with green lights! Then I realized it—the tank next to me was an American Sherman!

On with the headphones; via the intercom: "Gunner! The tank next to us is an enemy tank. Knock it out!" Within seconds the turret swung to the left, the long gun barrel banged against the turret of the Sherman. Gunner to commander: "Impossible to knock out! The turret mechanism is stuck!" The driver, Rottenführer Grundmeyer, had listened in, and without an order the Panzer engine started and he pulled back the Panzer a few paces. Then, Unterscharführer Poggendorf, the gunner, sent an antitank shell into the center of the rear of the enemy tank at a distance of one meter. I was still standing in the turret. From the circular hole in the rear wall of the Sherman licked a blue flame. As I took cover in the turret, I heard the explosion! We drove past the burning tank. From a clearing in the woods to the right, two more enemy tanks came toward us. We fired immediately! The first one acknowledged with black smoke, while the second also stopped.

We could not establish radio contact with the company. Despite this we continued ahead with the assumption that Frauscher's Panzers had broken through before us and that the just knocked-out enemy tanks, which had been in ambush positions along the edge of the woods, had fired on Frauscher's Panzers and were trying to rejoin their own units to the rear. However, we were to be more careful.

When everything remained quiet, we slowly increased our speed. The trees thinned out. Then, suddenly, in front of us was a large open area bordered by woods, probably a forest glade. The road swung around it in a wide S-curve and disappeared again in a clearing on the wooden slope opposite.

Nine Enemy Tanks Had Us in Their Sights!

I held my breath! In the open terrain of the meadow in front of us, I counted, next to each other and dug in, nine enemy tanks! All aimed the muzzles of their barrels threateningly at our Panzer, which had, until then, been driving unsuspectingly toward them. Grundmeyer, the driver, spotted the danger. He hesitated noticeably!

Stopping or driving back would have meant suicide. Only bluffing could have saved us. So, escape ahead! Commander to driver: "Keep going at same speed!" It might have been possible to drive around them unrecognized because they took us for one of their tanks! We drove through the curve and offered them our broadside as nine tank turrets swung with us. Their gunners had us in their cross hairs! But not a shot was fired. As soon as we reached their flank, and I could make out all of the staggered rears of the tanks, I ordered a halt. We were in the best firing position and faced practically only one enemy tank as the rest obstructed each other's field of vision! I had the turret swing to three o'clock, to the right, to let the gunner take aim, and then I did not believe what I saw! The American crews bailed out, escaping from their tanks, and ran into the cover of the wooded area behind them!

A Solitary Decision

With this, our situation changed again. I then knew that Frauscher's Panzers were behind us. I understood the orders of battle, and experienced an enemy who, at least during night fighting, was inexperienced and could be confused. We had to exploit this advantage in the framework of the whole operation. We were still unable to contact the company by radio. In a solitary decision I ordered the turret back to twelve o'clock, in driving direction, and gave the command: "Panzer—march!" We would have liked to knock out the enemy tanks, but that would have woken up the entire enemy front. Besides, that was to be done by our friend Frauscher who was following behind. According to him, the tanks were manned again. He got all nine!

Right Through the Middle of the Enemy!

We drove on in the direction of Manhay. The woods took us in again. First individually, then in groups and columns, American infantrymen rushed from the woods on the right onto the road. For reasons I could not explain, the enemy was retreating. We drove right in the middle of them without being particularly careful. For the sake of my crew, especially the driver, we had to determine what situation we were in. My boys were extremely tense but wonderfully quiet, as always during such dangerous situations. The American soldiers got out of our way, jumped to the side, swore and shook their fists at us. They did not recognize us as a German Panzer despite my standing openly in the turret hatch and looking down on them. Their helmets, covered with camouflage netting, reflected the light of the moon. Their faces were distraught.

Past an Enemy Tank Assembly Area in Manhay

The forest thinned out. Suddenly, there were houses to the left and right of the road. We had reached Manhay! We increased our speed in order to remain unrecognized. More and more houses were seen. Drawn up close to them stood tanks and vehicles. In front of a lit cafe there was brisk activity, probably a staff. Soldiers rushed about. We drove right through them as they even stepped aside for us. Then we reached the crossroads. To the left lay Erezée by way of Grandmenil, the attack objective of the company. From that direction three Sherman tanks rolled toward us! I dispensed with turning that way and went straight across the junction in the direction of Liège. We had to get out of the town!

Our plan was to turn around somewhere and join the attacking company or at least get into radio range! Not a shot had been fired until then, neither from the enemy nor from us. To start a gun battle would have been madness and our doom. The danger had not ended; it was only beginning! To the right of us, in the direction of the crossroads, stood enemy tank after enemy tank of Shermans of the heaviest type, always in groups of nine or twelve, and lined up in companies behind each other. In between them stood company leader vehicles, jeeps! The crews had dismounted and stood smoking and gossiping next to their tanks. One enemy company was lined up after the other. I gave up counting and estimated eighty or more tanks. (I later learned that this was the assembly of the 7th U.S. Armored Division, the 82nd U.S. Airborne Division, and the 75th U.S. Infantry Division whose mission it was to contain the German advance in that sector of the front.)

Past American Tank Columns

We had no other choice—we had to get by them! The U.S. soldiers jumped to the side and quickly recognized us as a German Panzer, but always only after we had gone past them. Behind us, engines roared, turrets swung after us, but, thank God, the tanks obstructed each other's fields of vision and fire. I had oval hand grenades made ready in case we had to bail out. Then I ignited a smoke candle and let it roll down the rear onto the road. The heavy smoke offered us cover behind. The situation got more and more uncomfortable.

My good loader, Karl Kreller, pulled me down gently from the turret hatch, in which I had been standing erect until then, and turned up the collar of my camouflage jacket. He pointed to my Knight's Cross and commented: "It shines too brightly in the moonlight."

He had been watching me from the dark interior all along and judged the situation by the expression on my face. A chain of MG tracer bullet belts hung by his turret machine gun.

The gunner had his eyes pressed to the periscope, which allowed him to at least see what was in his field of vision. His hand gripped the lever of the turret traverse. Suddenly from the driver: "A vehicle is approaching from ahead!" I stuck my head outside again. A jeep rolled toward us! Standing in it was a man, probably an officer, who wildly waved a signaling disk.

He wanted to stop us, ordering "Halt!" even from a great distance. The man was either brave or insane! Commander to driver: "Roll over the jeep!" My driver acknowledged. The jeep driver reacted, realized his predicament, stopped, and accelerated backward. A wild chase began. The officer no longer waved. The distance shrunk meter by meter and then, a crash. Our right track caught the jeep, and we rolled over it at high speed. Its passengers tried to jump free.

Entangled with a Sherman Tank!

Our Panther, thrown off course by the collision, ran at full speed into the closest Sherman. I was almost thrown from the turret, my headphones rolled across the turret roof and hung down the side by their cord, swinging back and forth. My cap remained as a souvenir to those outside! Our engine stalled. Our Panzer was stuck. Its right drive sprocket was wedged firmly into the track of the enemy tank. After a moment of quiet, all hell broke loose outside. Infantry bullets whistled past my ears and forced me into the cover of the Panzer turret. The driver tried, without success, to get the engine going with the starter. I pulled the indispensable headset, microphone and earphones, back inside over the edge of the cupola and contemplated the possibilities of an escape for us. Were there still any?

To bail out or defend from the turret meant virtually the same for us: either death or captivity! So I spoke calmly to the driver. He concentrated noticeably. The batteries collected more power. After misfiring a few times, the engine started and picked up speed. We heaved a sigh of relief! "Backward march!" Slowly and carefully, so that the track would not jump from the sprockets, the Panzer pulled out of the entanglement with the Sherman and turned onto the road. An ignited smoke candle drove the Americans aside. "Forward march!"

Under cover of the smoke we continued our drive. On the same road, past tank after tank, truck convoys, supply vehicles, two tankers among them, past the trucks of a medical unit with a bus fitted for operating, we finally reached open terrain. The houses of Manhay were left behind us. The way to Liège was open for us! At that moment I wanted the point of my company in my spot and my Panzer-abteilung right behind.

When I noticed that vehicles were pursuing us, the gunner turned the turret to six o'clock as we moved and sent explosive shells in their direction and into the town. After some 300 meters I had the "401" stopped, the engine switched off, and listened into the night. The noise of roaring engines and the din of tanks was heard from Manhay. We had nicely disrupted the Americans in their assembly.

We Got Rid of the Pursuers

I heard the noise of battle in a distance. Enemy vehicles, one Sherman among them, were pursuing us again. Well-aimed fire took care of them. After a few hundred meters the same game was repeated. As we were pushed farther north, I left the road and found a good, well-covered firing position in a bend with a good view of the road. There, I let my crew dismount. They stood around the turret, breathing deeply. I saw grinning faces. Everything had worked out well once again.

Our Panzer Company Approached in the Attack

As the noise of battle came closer, we heard the clear cracks of the Panzer guns. They sounded like music to our ears. Our company was attacking Manhay! The radio operator turned his frequency dial. "German Tigers! German Tigers! Help! Help!" we heard on one of the enemy channels. Our Panzer Vs were taken for Tigers, none of which were in action on that sector of the front. The enemy was hard-pressed and retreated en masse to the west in the direction of Grandmenil and to the northeast toward Vaux Chavanne. We took care of enemy vehicles, which were pushed toward us, with our Panzer gun. Many vehicles drove off the road into the open fields and got stuck in the snow.

Manhay Taken!

Manhay was taken by our forces in a relatively short time. Our "401" took part in the operation. The road to Liège lay open in front of us. We listened to the battle noise of the assault on Grandmenil, then left our firing position, and drove slowly past burning vehicles back to Manhay. We did not meet any German Panzers at the exit of the town. Instead, entangled and abandoned American vehicles stood around there. We counted almost twenty abandoned Sherman tanks in the gardens between and behind the houses.

Our Own Troops Took Us in Again!
A patrol of the III. Battalion/"DF" (9. Company) blocked our way. They initially took us for an American tank. We heaved a sigh of relief. We had made it!

The murderous artillery fire during the attack had caused particularly grave losses to the Panzer-grenadiers of the "D."

Then, we were able to establish radio contact again with the Abteilung and the battle command post of the regiment, and gave our report.

We were to report to the commander. I looked at my watch: Christmas Day 1944 had begun hours before.

REPORT OF AN AMERICAN TANK COMMANDER ON THE OPERATION AT MANHAY
Declassified per Executive Order 12356, Section 3.3, 735017. By NND, NARA, date . . .

Company D, 40th Tank Battalion
1st Sgt. Melvin Kruck and others
February 1, 1945

Tanks at Manhay

The five light tanks with Company B, 40th Tank Battalion, at Malempre, were the same five that were sent toward Fraiture in the afternoon. These tanks met strong enemy patrols, bazooka, and machine-gun fire and returned to Malempre where they were placed on the road block by Captain Wolfe, CO of Company B, 40th Tank Battalion.

Under the plan for withdrawal, these light tanks were to return to Manhay at 9:30 P.M. and join the CCA column moving north. This was an hour and a half before B/40 and 4/48 were to withdraw. The tanks left at that time and went into Manhay where the column was forming, arriving there at 10 P.M.

They lined up opposite CCA headquarters, and the tank commanders went to the battalion headquarters for instructions. The battalion referred the column to CCA. When they got there, the information was just coming in regarding the A/40 tanks and the enemy advance to the south. They were only at CCA headquarters for ten or fifteen minutes when the German tank got in the column, which was just beginning to move out, and knocked out three D Company light tanks. (The fourth was knocked out much later.) The three tanks were those that had stayed in Manhay.

First information on the enemy tank was vague. At first it was thought to be an American TD; then it was reported to be an American medium. The sergeant saw the tank, however, and although it was dark, recognized it as an enemy heavy from D/40-2.

The tank escaped and headed west. The CCA column continued to move out.

The first part of the CCA column was about 300 yards south of the Manhay crossroads when the enemy tank struck.

The author has before him a report of the U.S. Headquarters XVIII Corps (Airborne) of January 6, 1945, on the operation of Panzer commander Barkmann and his "Panther 401." This report is five pages long, excerpts are quoted here:

Headquarters XVIII Corps (Airborne), Office of the Inspector General, APO 109, U.S. Army, January 6, 1945

Subject: Report of Investigation, CCA 7 AD, Manhay, December 24–25, 1944
To: Commanding General, XVIII Corps (Airborne)

1. CCA 7 AD, consisting of 40 Tk Bn, 48 AIB, and 1 Co 814 TD in a defensive position about a mile and a half southeast of Manhay, Belgium, was attacked at 10:30 P.M. December 24, 1944, decisively defeated, and partially routed by a substantially inferior German force probably consisting of four tanks and a few infantrymen.

3.b) A withdrawal to the area Grandmenil-Manhay had been ordered to commence at 10:30 P.M. At this time the combat commander started moving his CP from Manhay to the rear to conform to the movement of his command. A German tank entered Manhay from the south, ran over a quarter-ton in the street, fell in with the CC headquarters column, and after having passed through Manhay, turned and fired back into the town, disabling a halftrack, two quarter-tons, and setting on fire a light tank in the middle of the road at 1. The hostile tank then proceeded north to the vicinity of Mont-Derrieux where it turned back south on an unimproved road. A bulldozer from C48 pulled up behind the burning light tank and was abandoned in the middle of the street with motor running.

3.d) . . . Upon reaching 2, the hostile tanks, four in number, halted and the leading tank directed its fire on the dug-in vehicles of C40. Five tanks were hit and set ablaze, and all vehicles were abandoned. The condition of the remaining four is not known. The personnel of C48 and B48, during the following strafing, evacuated their position and moved north individually and in small groups . . .

The Battle for Bastogne

A REPORT BY KARL WORTMANN, PANZER COMMANDER FLA.-ABT. "LAH."

Since the start of the Ardennes offensive, American troops had been encircled in Bastogne, a medium-sized town in southern Belgium. While the main body of the German troops had pushed past the city on both sides, other units formed a ring around Bastogne and continued the attack on the surrounded forces. They advanced only slowly to the edge of the town. The fighting during the attack and the determined defense by the Americans caused increasing losses every day. American transport aircraft with fighter-bomber cover supplied the encircled troops with war materiel, ammunition, rations, and medical supplies whenever the weather allowed it. Occasional German aircraft and the few Flak units in action there could hardly have disrupted the supply of the Americans in Bastogne, let alone prevented it.

On December 22, a German captain and three escorts went with a white flag into the destroyed Bastogne to hand the U.S. commander of the encircled city a document requesting capitulation and an honorable surrender of the city. In case the proposal was not accepted, further German fighting forces would have had to be brought in, which would have caused further destruction of the city. In addition, heavy losses among the population were feared, which could not have been in the spirit of humane treatment of the civilian population. The American commander, McAuliffe, the defender of Bastogne, answered the request with a single word: "Nuts!" In a disparaging sense this could, provocatively, have also meant "Rubbish" or "Nonsense."

Thus the battle for Bastogne grew even more bitter. The town changed visibly into a fortress behind a bastion of rubble and burning houses.

On Boxing Day, the 4th U.S. Armored Division succeeded, from the outside and after heavy fighting, in breaking through the weak German line from the southwest. Through a narrow corridor, it linked up with the forces encircled in the city. The German command was absolutely determined to capture the important town and crossroads of Bastogne. The 6. SS-Panzerarmee under the command of SS-Oberstgruppenführer Sepp Dietrich was withdrawn from the area of St. Vith and shifted south of Bastogne, partly into Luxembourg. The U.S. Air Force ruled the skies without challenge, making German troop movements during the day virtually impossible. The withdrawal had thus to take place exclusively during the night. Another delay was caused by a newly starting snowfall.

On December 30, 1944, the planned day of attack, only a few elements of the Leibstandarte had reached their assembly areas. They were mainly the remainders of the Panzer-regiment, since the 6. and 7. Companies, part of the Kampfgruppe Peiper, were able to save most of their Panzers from destruction. They were removed from the unit on December 18 and given the mission to reach Trois-Ponts from a different direction and secure the two bridges across the river in the town. This operation failed, partly because of the difficult terrain and partly because of the American resistance. The Panzers did not reach La Gleize, but they were able to withdraw and thus remained available to the force. These Panzer IVs saw action again near Lutrebois and Lutremange. It was their mission to close the ring around Bastogne again and then, if possible, push into the city. They were able to close the encirclement again, but the push into the city was given up because the insufficient forces available offered no hope of success.

The enemy transport aircraft took advantage of a temporary improvement in the weather and brought large amounts of supplies to their troops in Bastogne. For the first time, they had the opportunity to fly out some of the critically wounded. The results of this resupply and simultaneous reinforcement of the fighting strength by paratroop units were felt by the German forces after only a few hours. The push by the Americans became increasingly stronger. With the help of the paratroopers, the encircled enemy thrust out of Bastogne, broke through the encirclement at a number of locations and joined up with their own units outside the city. In between were several small German units, weakened by considerable losses, that were covered by heavy enemy fire and in danger of being overrun by the Americans. There was not a crossroads, not an open area in the terrain that was not under constant fire from heavy American guns.

A small Kampfgruppe of three Panthers and two Flak-Panzers with 2-cm four-barrel guns was put in action on January 7, 1945, to secure the most important crossroads along the major road Bastogne-Luxembourg for the retreat of our troops. They took up positions near the towns of Bras and Doncols, next to the national border. For days, the Panzer-grenadiers had lived in their foxholes in this area. Snowstorms and cold had set in again, and the Americans seemed to have detected the positions of the five well-camouflaged Panzers, aiming heavy fire at them.

The crossroads Doncols-Schleif, under constant fire, were secured primarily by the two Flak-Panzers. Shell after shell came howling in at short intervals. All day, fighter-bombers roared across at low level and were fired on by the two Flak-Panzers. Whenever they attacked, the earth trembled. The never-ending rattle of MG fire from both sides was interspersed. When the mortars joined in, and Panzers and Paks barked from both sides, one thought that an insane hurricane was moving through. The echoes of war howled a thousand-fold through the valleys and ravines of the mountainous landscape. One felt as if the whole world and the sky would collapse with this terrible bursting and racket of explosions.

During the night of January 9 to 10, 1945, the enemy fired shrapnel shells on a wide front. The men in the Panzers and the grenadiers in the foxholes twitched whenever their penetrating whistle and hum came in at them at lightning speed. The woods rustled noisily, and the tops of the trees slammed together. It sounded like a terrible thunderstorm as the innumerable steel fragments came down like heavy hail.

When another salvo of these dreaded shells came in around midnight it landed squarely on the two Flak-Panzers. Loud moaning and shouts for help penetrated the darkness. The crew of the Panzer of Unterscharführer Wortmann, in action there after the breakout from La Gleize, was hit the heaviest. The radio operator, Günter Sträter, the young loader, Gerhard Hübler, and a medic who had joined the crew were critically wounded. There was hardly any room in a house nearby. The Panzer-grenadiers, who had already taken heavy losses, had sought cover there for the night. Even in the dim light of a candle, the wide-open wound to Gerhard Hübler's back could be seen; his spine seemed to be injured. He was lying on his stomach and had lost a lot of blood. All the bandages had long been used up and still the bleeding had not been stopped. A young girl living in the house fetched additional clean cloths for the wounded. She offered hot water, made tea, and was of great help.

The closest dressing station was located some two kilometers to the rear in a small customs house. Those of the Panzer crew who were uninjured wanted to take their wounded comrades there in the Panzer despite the ongoing heavy shrapnel fire. A road junction that they had to cross was still under heavy fire. The driver, Erich Miechen, went to start the engine when he noticed to his horror that the starter had been damaged by a shrapnel and no longer worked. The engine had to be hand-cranked by two men, which seemed almost impossible! Ten, fifteen turns, the men were out of breath and began to sweat despite the cold. More than twenty turns were required before the engine caught. The crew had not witnessed, let alone gone through, such an exercise until then.

The wounded were carefully placed on the Panzer behind the turret. The commander, as always during night drives, crouched on the front of the Panzer next to the open driver's hatch. He gave directions as required, since the driver could hardly see anything through his narrow visor when it rained or snowed. The engine only shifted into first or second gear. They approached the junction with greatest caution, planning to cross it without too much danger at the most opportune moment. The small dressing station was completely overcrowded, but the critically injured were, luckily, to be transported onward before daybreak.

The other German fighting units were withdrawing. They were mostly tired and worn out grenadiers from the most advanced positions.

At daybreak the five Panzers took up positions again. The damaged Flak-Panzer moved to the rear into a clearing in the woods, where it had a good field of fire toward a hill opposite where American positions could be clearly made out. The day went as had the days before—full of events and full of flying steel and lead. The whole area smelled of gunpowder. All day we could hear the noises of American tanks, apparently getting ready for a surprise attack to capture the road Bastogne-Luxembourg, which was still being used by the Germans.

During a briefing in the late afternoon at the command post of Obersturmführer Christ of the 2. Panzer-Company, the seriousness and hopelessness of the situation in that sector of the front became quite obvious. Preparations for a possible withdrawal of the five Panzers during the coming night were discussed and a code name for it was given out. That was what finally happened! Although there were no surprise fire attacks, it was another restless night. While the three Panthers and the mobile Flak-Panzer were already on the main road, the three men of the damaged Flak-Panzer still worked away with the hand crank, trying to start the engine again. After a long delay they finally toddled off as well, still only in second gear.

They knew the road. It was the same stretch they had driven some days before, when they moved into this sector. The damaged Flak-Panzer felt abandoned all by itself on this major road in the darkness of the night. But then there were noises of tanks from somewhere and the smell of exhaust fumes. Suddenly, the outlines of the rear of a tank standing on the road could be made out. "That can only be one of the Panthers!" the crew of the Flak-Panzer speculated. They stopped, engine running, at the usual distance. After a while the commander became curious and wanted to know what the delay was and what was happening ahead.

Unsuspectingly, he walked along the stationary tanks before the relatively long column appeared somehow wrong to him. There were too many! There should have been only four. At that very moment he realized the situation he was in. Those were American Shermans in white camouflage paint, just like the German Panzers. Anxiously, he walked back the few steps to his Flak-Panzer. This required steady nerves. Ideas whirled through his head. With the noise from the tank engines, it was not easy to explain to his two comrades the situation and what had to be done.

There was not much time for contemplation. The crew was simply glad that no more American tanks had moved in while they sat there. Slowly, and without too much throttle, the Flak-Panzer pulled backward some hundred meters. On the right side of the road was a ditch with an elevated embankment, too high to get across with the damaged Panzer. So, back a little farther. The attempt to get across was made at a somewhat more favorable spot. Laboriously, the Panzer gained the edge of the embankment, tipped forward and got its nose stuck in a snowdrift. After that followed a quick departure. All three then looked for an escape route cross-country. In luck once more! At the break of dawn they came across a stuck Panther with damaged tracks. They reported on their experience with the American tank column. The damaged track was remounted using joint forces.

Those days of action with the Panzer-Flak in the battlefield near Bastogne were full of drama.

During the second half of January 1945, the Leibstandarte moved in several stages into the area Euskirchen-Cologne-Bonn. After only a few days, loading began at several different railroad stations.

The new destination was unknown.

Panzer Actions of the 10. SS-Panzer-Division "Frundsberg" in Lower Alsace

After the failure of the Ardennes offensive the 10. SS-Panzer-division was incorporated into Heeresgruppe A after refitting with materiel and personnel. The I. Abteilung of Panzer-Regiment 10 had to wait a long time for their Panthers before it left the training grounds at Grafenwöhr fully fitted. On January 15, 1945, the I./SS-Panzer-Regiment 10 crossed the Rhine by ferry near Freistett. On January 17, Obersturmbannführer Tetsch started an attack with his Panther Abteilung from Offendorf to Herlisheim. The Panzer attack faltered before reaching Herlisheim in the defensive fire of U.S. Paks and tanks. Some Panzers were rendered unserviceable by damage from the fire, and the chief of the 3. Company was wounded. The adjutant of the I. Abteilung, Obersturmführer Bachmann, took leave of commander Tetsch in order to drive at the head of his old, then leaderless, 3. Company.

Bachmann reports on his action:

I rode ahead in the sidecar of Sauerwein's motorcycle. At the entrance to Herlisheim, I encountered two Panthers of the 3. Company. Unterscharführer Mühlbradt was with them. I learned that American tanks were in the town. I wanted to scout myself. The two Panthers were to give covering fire and follow.

I rode with the motorcycle to a junction in the road, stopped, and directed the Panzers to secure one road each. I went ahead on foot along the road on the right to scout further. After some fifty meters, as I reached a bend in the road, a Sherman opened fire. I ran back to the motorcycle, picked up a Panzerfaust, and reached a house from whose window I could see the main street, which ran diagonally. I spotted two Shermans on the street. I knocked out one from a distance of thirty meters with my Panzerfaust. Then I ran back to my covering Panthers, deciding on a plan of action.

I quickly briefed the two Panzer commanders: Panzer 2 was to continue to cover the road on the right, pulling ahead to the bend and opening fire when Panzer 1 started out. Panzer 1 (Mühlbradt), with me, was to drive up the road on the left, turret at three o'clock, and immediately open fire when the junction was reached and the gunner had a field of fire on the crossing road. Everything went according to the plan. The two Panzer crews cooperated in a first-rate fashion. Panzer 2 opened fire while Panzer 1 raced into the junction and knocked out the first Sherman. More U.S. tanks were knocked out, and a white flag appeared.

I stopped the fire and walked forward. An American officer offered to surrender. I requested that his men put down their weapons in front of me. When sixty Americans had put down their weapons, twenty German soldiers who had been in U.S. captivity were added. I asked the Americans if they were the crews of the knocked-out tanks. The U.S. officer explained that they were the crews of the tanks that had not been knocked out and pointed to a farm to the left of the road where four Shermans sat, their guns facing the road. He said the other tanks were a little farther down. That was a surprise for us. We had to keep calm. I demanded speedy action. I had the American tank drivers step forward and ordered them to drive the Shermans to Offendorf, accompanied by one of the rearmed German soldiers. I felt better when the tank column set off. I advised the Abteilung in Offendorf of the approaching captured Shermans and requested more of our own Panzers to come to Herlisheim and pick up another forty-eight prisoners. The total was twelve captured Sherman tanks and sixty prisoners. I deployed my own two Panthers forward to the edge of Herlisheim. From there they covered in the direction of Drusenheim and knocked out another two Shermans on their way to Herlisheim. Thus, my two Panthers achieved nine kills. After reinforcements had arrived, I was ordered back to the Abteilung command post at Offendorf.

This bold stroke by Obersturmführer Bachmann with two valiant Panzer crews was rewarded with Iron Crosses, along with the Knight's Cross for Bachmann.

In the morning of January 19, the I./Panzer-Regiment 10 attacked from the area of Gambsheim in a westerly direction. After a short battle, Kilstett was taken, in joint action with SS-Panzer-Grenadier-Regiment 21. The attack continued across open terrain in the direction of Hoerdt-Weyerheim. The II./SS-Panzer-Regiment 10 and two battalions of SS-Panzer-Regiment 22 attacked from the Offendorf area toward the west. Heavy Pak and tank fire from ahead and from the flanks affected, in particular, the 1. Panther Company moving on the left. Its chief, Hauptsturmführer Schneider, died when his Panzer was knocked out.

Enemy fighter-bombers joined in and attacked our Panzers with onboard weapons and incendiary bombs. The artillery fire increased and stopped the attack by SS-Panzer-Regiment 10. In the evening of January 19, the decision was made at the XXXIX Panzerkorps: "Stop the attack, return to line of departure!"

The German attack in Alsace, which was carried out under the code name "Nordwind" (north wind), was stopped. The withdrawal of the 10. SS-Panzer-Division "Frundsberg" began on February 3. On February 5, the first units of the 10. SS-Panzer-Division were loaded for transport to the combat area in Pomerania.

PART III

Last Battles on the Eastern Front: Hungary, Vienna, and Berlin

Panzer Attack to Relieve "Fortress Budapest"

Alert on Christmas Day! The division was to relocate to Hungary.

Loading took place between Christmas and New Year's Day at Nasjelske near Modlin. Two days later we unloaded at Raab (Györ), and the Abteilung prepared for the attack. The assembly took place on both sides of the Danube river, east of Komaron. The "Wiking" Division was on the right, and the "Totenkopf" Division on the left. Their mission was to break through between Tata and the Danube and then jointly reach, by way of the wooded terrain of the northern Vertes mountains, Bicske-Zsamneck, which was located at their eastern edge, as their first objective. Their second objective was to be the advance on Budapest.

The attack began on January 1, 1945, at 6 P.M., without preparatory artillery fire. The paths out of the mountains were heavily mined, and numerous antitank barricades blocked the road. Despite all this, the first attack objectives were quickly reached. On January 4, Sturmbannführer Meierdreß entered the town of Dunaalmas in the third vehicle at the point of the attack. Enemy tanks of the type T-34/85 sat in the farms in town and fired at our point vehicles from only five meters away. The Panzer of the commander took a direct hit to the side of the turret. Meierdreß died immediately. He was later transported to Vienna and buried next to Novotny, the heroic pilot.

The line Bicske-Zsamneck was reached on January 5. Enemy resistance grew constantly. Counterattacks began, and our attack had to be stopped. Our neighboring division could not keep pace, covering the flanks took up too much of their effort. The defensive fighting lasted until January 6. Then we moved to the Plattensee area and drove across completely ice-covered roads to the new assembly area. The attack began on January 18. At 4:30 A.M., we encountered electrically charged obstructions and mines. The enemy defended doggedly, and our breakthrough only succeeded in the evening.

Stuhlweißenburg was captured on January 21, but our losses were high. Lischewski, Grimminger, and Kröhan were killed; Hans Eggert was critically wounded and lost sight in one eye. Having swung northeast toward Budapest, we reached the Voli River between the Danube and Val on January 25. The enemy attacks became stronger. The expected enemy tank attack deep into our flanks took place on January 29 from Vertes Aska. It started a huge tank battle near Pettend. Some 200 enemy tanks were knocked out.

The enemy attacks increased on January30 . We could no longer hold our positions and withdrew westward on both sides of the Valencze Lake.

Budapest fell into Russian hands on February 12. Sturmbannführer Lackmann, the commander of our regiment, was critically injured. The company had two Panzers left. One was commanded by Unterscharführer Reif, the other by a commander from the 3. Company. All other commanders had died or were wounded.

—Martin Steiger, Panzer commander, l./SS-Panzer-Regiment 3

PANZER-REGIMENT 5 WIKING—ADVANCE ON BICSKE, HUNGARY, JANUARY 1945

On Christmas Day 1944, the regiment was moved by fast rail transport from the Modlin area near Warsaw by way of Slovakia to Hungary. The destination was the area near Komarom, where the command post of the regiment was also located. Assembly took place on January 1, 1945 near Tata. There was a briefing from units of the Heer, which had taken heavy losses and were in positions east of Tata. Advance units made up of the I./"Germania" and remainders of II./Panzer-Regiment 5 under the command of Hauptsturmführer Flügel assembled on January 2 at 2 A.M. during a starlit night. Panzers of Großrock's point platoon lined up along the main road. Units of "Germania" attacked Agostian, the first objective. The Ivans, feeling secure, were surprised and fled, some of them out of their beds in shorts. Almost 1,000 captured Germans and Hungarians were freed. A number of soldiers of the Heer and Waffen-SS who had broken out of Budapest were found murdered in a ditch. A further advance during the day was impossible since the narrow valleys and ravines of the Vertes mountains had been mined and were blocked by Pak positions.

The next assembly during the clear night of January 2 to 3 was made difficult by mine barricades. Dug-in Paks were overrun, before we swung toward Tarjan/Vertes Tolan, which was already taken by units of "Germania" (under Pleiner). At dawn in a surprise attack on the flank, the reconnaissance unit eliminated a Pak position at the edge of the woods east of Tolan. A further advance, led by the "Kerkhoff" point platoon, along a winding road and down a steep wooded slope included tank battles at close range, from one bend to the next and always under heavy fire from the flanks. After busy radio traffic between the corps and the division staff on one side and division and the regimental commander on the other side, using strong language, the divisional commander confirmed for himself that the difficult terrain was suitable for mountain troops. Coming out of the wooded ravine, the leader of the point platoon, Oberscharführer Menner, was mortally wounded, and Obersturmführer Kerkhoff's Panzer was later knocked out. After skirmishes with dispersed enemy units and uncomfortable attacks by aircraft during the day, Russian Pak positions were again encountered near Tarjan. Support was provided by the Stuka group of Oberst Rudel.

On January 4, the I. Panzer-Abteilung under Hauptsturmführer Hein took over the point. An advance along the road, as ordered, was no longer possible due to difficult terrain. The ravines and hilltops had artillery positions and were blocked by Pak positions. The Pleiner Battalion was stalled. Five enemy tanks were knocked out west of Vasztely, and Hauptsturmführer Flügel was wounded. A briefing took place with the commander, Dorr, of the Abteilung at the point. Reconnaissance by grenadiers was to determine if the town was unoccupied and could be traversed by Panzers.

The mission for the Obersturmbannführer Darges Kampfgruppe: Attack across hill 204 toward Bicskse. Capture of the Bicske road and rail junction and the blockading of the Bicske-Budapest road. Departure late in the evening.

Because of extremely difficult and steep terrain, tanks had to be pulled up the hills by tractors. At dawn, the "Norge" Grenadier-Battalion under Sturmbannführer Fritz Vogt joined in the attack. Heavy fire increased from the flanks in the fog, especially from heavy mortars in the direction of Zsambek. The Russians, based on noises from our engines, improvised a Pak front that was wiped out before it could get established. Our booty: fifteen trucks, some of them with antitank guns still hooked up. Continued massive fire from the flanks forced the Kampfgruppe into a decision: assault on the Hegyiks estate. The Russian corps staff fled, leaving many maps behind.

A surprise attack in thick fog by five Panthers was mounted on Bicske, one kilometer west of Hegyiks, under the command of Hauptsturmführer Lichte. Halfway to Bicske, the fog lifted and two Panthers were immediately set on fire. The other three Panthers retreated toward Hegyiks, dropping smoke candles. All the men, some of them wounded, were able to get out of the Panzers. The Kampfgruppe formed a hedgehog defense on the estate grounds. Its dimensions were about 200 by 150 meters, surrounded by walls on three sides and open to the east. Its force was composed of some eighteen armored fighting vehicles, parts of a reconnaissance vehicle company, and the "Norge" Grenadier-Battalion.

Because of insufficient available forces, the objective of taking Bicske could not be achieved. Scouting patrols toward Zsambek and the supply route were fought off. The Russians increased their air reconnaissance and covered Hegyiks with heavy mortar fire. Later, the enemy concentrated all its weapons in the attack on Hegyiks during day and night, including most uncomfortable MG fire with explosive bullets to the tops of the trees. The wall was shot to pieces, partly by Stalin tanks, to make way for the Russian assaults. At night, especially, they attacked every two or three hours, often with regiment-strength forces and managed to enter the estate grounds. Our own assault groups defended with submachine guns and panzerfausts, cheered on by the "Hurra" shouts from all the encircled men. Because of the darkness, friend and enemy were hard to tell apart at times. Tank attacks were repulsed, inflicting heavy losses on the Ivans. More than twenty Russian tanks were knocked out. Captured functioning enemy Paks were pressed into service where possible.

Supplies of food and ammunition were brought in, despite enemy resistance, by Panzers we had repaired again, and the wounded were taken out on them. Obersturmführer Hohenester and Stabsscharführer Schnier worked without rest. During the hand-to-hand combat of the night, Hauptsturmführer Hein, among others, was critically wounded by Russian hand grenades.

The morale of the encircled men, including the Norwegians, was excellent. We observed the enemy assembling in an endless column on the Zsambek-Budapest road. A decisive disruption of the enemy supply faltered due to our own insufficient forces, and the heavily defended town of Bicske could no longer be captured.

After six days and nights of the heaviest defensive fighting, the Panthers were pulled out to take on new missions. The remainder of the Panzer IVs and the assault guns under Obersturmführers Bauer and Weerts, together with "Norge," stayed on the estate.

The Russians did not let up and continued to attack the hedgehog positions without success. After three more days, a breakout was ordered and executed with negligible losses during the night. Observers of the neighboring "Totenkopf" Division then sent a radio message to the "Wiking" Division:

"The Wiking Kampfgruppe has ceased firing after heroic resistance."

SS-PANZER-REGIMENT 5 "WIKING" IN THE SECOND ATTACK TO RELIEVE BUDAPEST
Hungary January 20, 1945, Report by the Holder of the Knight's Cross, Obersturmführer Karl-Heinz Lichte

Attack on Sarosd. We assembled early in the morning. My 5. Company (Panthers) attacked, together with pioneers, a farm located on the crest of a long slope covered with corn. The farm was taken and great numbers of prisoners came toward us. Then, tanks rolled out of the depths of the Russian positions in a counterattack and set the farm on fire. The heavy smoke that developed cut our visibility. We pulled away from the farm. When the wheeled vehicles were outside of firing range, the 5. Company began the Panzer battle. A number of "Josef Stalin" tanks were spotted. The numerically vastly superior enemy bypassed us and attacked our flank. Then, the first of our Panzers was knocked out. The Panzer of the administrative officer of our II. Abteilung, who filled in as Panzer commander, was hit and on fire. By radio, I ordered: "500 to Company, pull back to the edge of town!" At the same time I grasped a smoke grenade, pulled and threw it to obstruct the enemy field of vision of our withdrawal. That very moment, there was an immense bang. I saw a bright flash, then darkness. . . .

The smoke grenade fell on the grating of my Panzer. Thick smoke rose from it. The Ivan who was firing at my vehicle must have thought he had scored a hit and no longer fired at it. That was lucky for my crew and me. But I did not take any of this in. I was wounded by the first hit to the turret and lost consciousness. . . .

When I came to, I was hanging, head down, over the first gunner's seat. I noticed someone grasping me by the collar, pulling me up a little, and then dropping me again with the remark that it was useless. Then he disappeared. I was in severe pain and semiparalyzed. Cold sweat covered my brow as I ripped the wire of the throat microphone that was throttling me. Using my last remaining strength, I dragged myself out of the hatch.

My winter-issue pants got hung up on the turret handwheel. I watched the Ivan come closer, kneel, and take aim at me. This is it! the thought flashed through my mind. Instinctively, I let myself drop, like dead, into the snow. The Almighty must have been watching and taken a hand in this. My friend Fred Großrock, leader of the 6. Company, also saw me and came racing up with his Panther, firing the MGs at the Russian infantry. He loaded me behind the turret and drove me directly to the field dressing station where our good Dr. Kalbskopf looked after me immediately.

Panzers as Rear Guard Near Stuhlweißenburg

SS-PANZER-REGIMENT 5 "WIKING" IN HUNGARY
Report by Unterscharführer Siegfried Melinkat 2./SS-Panzer-Regiment 5
March 16, 1945—At the edge of the town of Stuhlweißenburg on Lake Balaton. As the commander in Panzer IV "201" with a shot-off drive sprocket, behind a road barricade.

Our infantry, a mixed bunch of supply and administration units, was running back to the edge of town. The Russians fired at them, and many did not get up again. We sat outside of town in front of the houses with two Panzer IVs and one assault gun and waited for developments. Suddenly, concentrated artillery and mortar fire set in as the Ivans fired from all barrels. Clouds of dust in front of us completely blocked our vision. Driving in reverse, we pulled back to the edge of town. I drove through the barricade and positioned my Panzer between the houses at the road block. I kept the engine running and the radio on receive. All hatches were locked. My friend Hannes Immen, commander of the other Panzer IV, drove up the street a little farther and disappeared from sight. The air around us was filled by red dust from shot-up roofing tiles and bricks. My gunner, a Fleming, anxiously fidgeted in his seat. "Stay calm, son, as long as the Ivans are hammering us, they will not attack," I said and he nodded. Enemy Pak fired in the direction of the arterial route, and I could see the shells whistling by. Then the fire died down slowly. Now they will attack, I thought. We drove forward and took up position behind the barricade. There was an explosion immediately next to our vehicle. Bricks from the barricade hurtled through the air. "Power only on one track, the vehicle is turning about," I heard Georg, my driver, say.

"Get out and determine what happened," I shouted back on the intercom. Damn it, that was all I needed as the Ivans were coming down the road already. "Drive sprocket shot off," Georg reported. My thoughts raced feverishly. "Turret to three o'clock, open fire!" The Fleming rained

MG fire on the road and forced the Ivans into cover. But that did not last long; they came at us, jumping from house to house. "Eugen," I yelled at my radio operator, "run as fast as you can and tell Hannes to come quickly and give us a tow." Eugen looked at me with wide eyes, and then was gone at lightning speed. "Georg, drop the track and hook up the tow cables," I ordered the driver. Georg got out and started to work on the track. In the meantime, the Ivans had come threateningly close. "Aim lower," I yelled at the gunner, " the shots are way high!"

"Impossible, Unterscharführer, the gun barrel is already resting on top of the barricade." For crying out loud, we could no longer fire at them with the turret MG. "Keep firing," I ordered him. Even if the MG fire did not find its mark, it had a deterrent effect. Then the Ivans approached to within sixty meters. Our own infantry, three or four men, fired a few more times and then took off. We sat alone behind the barricade. "201 to Luchs (lynx, code name of the leader of the Kampfgruppe), 201 to Luchs, am sitting with shot-off drive sprocket behind the barricade. Our own infantry has withdrawn. The Russians are within fifty meters. Need a tow immediately," I radioed. "Luchs to 201, maintain radio discipline!" came the reply. I answered for a last time, citing the well-known line of Götz of Berlichingen, to "kiss my behind," and shouted at the Fleming: "Hand me the submachine gun and hand grenades!" The gunner and the loader complied immediately. Their faces were ashen. It was just in time as the closest figures were already within throwing distance. I dropped a few oval hand grenades among the Russians. Then I held the MPi 40 (submachine gun) on them until the magazine was empty. Some of them were hit, while the others jumped into cover behind the houses. At the same time, a Panzer IV came racing down the road. Thank God, it was Hannes in his vehicle. Right at our Panzer, his driver pulled the vehicle around 180 degrees and stopped. Eugen and Georg immediately threw the tow cables crosswise over the towing bar and jumped back on.

Hannes took off immediately. He pulled our vehicle by the rear behind his. Shells from Paks whistled overhead but much too high to hit us. The Ivans probably just fired blindly in our general direction. As we set out, we fired the turret and radio operator's MGs at the barricade and the houses next to it. That way we kept our backs clear. Behind a bend in the road, we were out of sight of the Russians. The tension subsided. We silently smoked cigarettes. Hannes towed us slowly from the main front line to the repair shop. We had made it once again.

The Battle for Vienna

The ensuing battles during the withdrawal from the Stuhlweißenburg area were dictated by the superior Soviet Armed Forces, which were pushing west with armored spearheads to capture the city of Vienna. The Panzer units of the 6. SS-Panzerarmee, which had been patched up with inexperienced reserves from the homeland war effort and members of the Luftwaffe and Navy since the Ardennes offensive, suffered increasing losses that could no longer be replaced.

Difficulties with the transmission of orders in Armeegruppe Balck were anything but a good omen for a successful operation.

A documentation by the chief officer of the General Staff of the 6. Panzerarmee, SS-Obersturmbannführer Georg Maier, "Drama Between Budapest and Vienna," published by the Munin-Verlag, offers detailed information.

The Panzer units saw organized action only rarely. Actions by companies and platoons on their own became the rule, the Panzer commander and his crew were often left to their own resources and fought to the bitter end.

Here follows a report on the action of the SS-Panzer-Abteilung 501:

> During the ensuing fighting in Hungary and the Gran bridgehead, as well as the assault on Fünfkirchen, the Abteilung was again attached to the SS-Panzer-Regiment 1 ("LAH"). It was successful in destroying numerous JS tanks, but it quickly decreased in strength since there were not enough vehicles available to tow damaged Panzers during the rapid withdrawal. Only few "Königstiger" (King Tigers) were knocked out during the fighting. Most of them had to be blown up by their own crews. This situation was probably the same for the Panzer units of the other Panzer divisions of the Waffen-SS. The author had access to only few reports from Panzer commanders in this theater of war.

The last reports of Panzer commander Ernst Barkmann of the Panzer-Regiment "Das Reich" are probably indicative of the other Panzer crews in similar battle situations:

"The division was shifted to the left flank of the Heeresgruppe.

"The Panzers of the division reached Vesprem under their own power and were loaded in Herend, a small town west of Vesprem on the rail line Para-Raab."

THE LAST ONES ARE BITTEN BY THE DOGS!
Ernst Barkmann reports on the "odyssey" of the 4. Panzer-Company/"DR"

The 4. Panzer-Company was securing the loading of the II. Panzer-Abteilung "DR," with minimal fuel left in the tanks. The Russians pushed across the rail line to the north at that moment, and the company, as the last unit to be loaded, found itself in a trap without fuel.

With great difficulties we secured the required fuel from the closest airfield and reported to the nearest Heer Armeekorps with the ten Panthers of the 4. Panzer-Company.

During the same night we were sent into a counterattack together with an armored unit of the Heer and lost two Panthers during the withdrawal. The unit of the Heer was annihilated during this counterattack. Left to our own resources, we forded a shallow river, crossed a railroad embankment, and pushed through the enemy spearheads to establish contact with the 1. SS-Panzer-Division "LAH," engaged in rear guard action, and reported to the Panzer-regiment.

Obersturmbannführer Peiper wanted to take over our eight Panzers. His entire regiment consisted of only ten Panzers ready for action. He had plenty of crews without Panzers. We were supposed to fight our way to our own units without our Panzers. He was dreaming! We would not hand over our Panzers. Then he lectured us that he usually treated his guests gently, but in this situation he could not show us any special concern and we would get to know the fierceness and morale of his unit the hard way. My company leader, Untersturmführer Knocke, nudged me.

During the next days, until March 28, we proved to our good Obersturmbannführer Peiper that the fighting spirit of the Panzers of "Das Reich" was not second to that of the "LAH" and we became close friends. We were then securing the withdrawal to the left and right of the main route, always engaging the enemy, and unbelievable and dangerous situations occurred. We held positions on hilltops during the day, were written

off and forgotten, and had to fight our way back through towns occupied by the enemy in order to link up again with our troops.

When one platoon became bogged down in a firefight, the other came to its aid and helped it to fight its way out. During an attack by nine T-34s in the early dawn, enemy tanks pushed past us to the left and right and attacked us from all sides. The bravest T-34 broke through us right on the main route and rammed one of our Panthers before my gunner blew its turret from the hull. We were successful in knocking out all nine T-34s. All antitank action took place without support from the infantry; we were the firefighters. Despite a damaged gun barrel, we knocked out a Josef-Stalin tank from a position on a back slope and towed two of our Panthers, which had taken hits from it, from the battleground. The enemy pushed back the "LAH" northwest of Lake Neusiedler in the direction of the Vienna woods.

After two Panthers, my own included, were disabled by direct hits, we blew up both in sight of the enemy. We said good-bye to Jochen Peiper and reached Panzer-Regiment 2 "DR" in the Esterhazy area on March 28, 1945. We had long before been written off.

NEW SOVIET CAMOUFLAGE MEASURES
Oberscharführer Ernst Barkmann reports

Hauptsturmführer Matzke, commander of the I. Panzer-Abteilung "DR," gave me the order to conduct reconnaissance toward Großenzersdorf north of the Danube River. The pioneer platoon of the regiment, under Hauptscharführer Carsten, with armored personnel carriers, was attached to me. We reached the edge of the terrain across which the enemy advance was taking place and spotted a column of troops moving westward in our direction. I positioned my Panzers and advanced with Carsten's armored personnel carriers to scout further.

Russian units had joined or followed along behind an immense mass of unarmed Hungarian Honved troops.

A firefight ensued near a railroad embankment after the Red Army soldiers realized that their camouflage was no longer working. I ordered my Panzers to advance, while I played grenadier and fired the MG 42 from the command vehicle of my friend.

The Russian advance had thus reached Großenzersdorf. A blocking force of units, which were urgently needed in Vienna, was put into place. During the withdrawal across the Reich Bridge, the order reached us to secure in the direction of the Prater amusement park. The famous ferris wheel had long since been damaged. The amusement park was held by the Russians who had infiltrated from the east.

In the morning of April 13 I drove my Panther in the direction of the Florisdorfer Bridge and, due to steering problems, ended up in a bomb crater from which no one could pull me out. From this involuntary cover, we defended our Panzer, and when that was no longer possible, Horts blew it up with a panzerfaust from the window of a neighboring house. We were forced into the cellar by enemy infantry fire. Using another panzerfaust, we blew a hole into the cellar wall and escaped to freedom through the next cellar. Lucky one more time! We reached the bridgehead south of the Florisdorfer Bridge after a few hundred meters. The situation there was catastrophic and getting worse by the hour. Below the huge span of the bridge, units and staffs piled up.

Critically wounded soldiers, fairly safe from further harm, lay next to each other right to the shore of the Danube. All the enemy fire was concentrated on this small section. Our grenadiers fought grimly and tenaciously in the hail of shells from Russian artillery and mortars and established a last blocking position before the enemy. One Panzer IV of the 6. Panzer-Company was still in action but was knocked out soon after.

The small bridgehead had to be held until the fall of darkness.

PANZER REINFORCEMENTS FOR THE BRIDGEHEAD?

Standartenführer Lehmann called me over. He asked whether I thought I could manage, despite my injuries, to get across the bridge and carry an order to Obersturmführer Boska, chief of the 6. Panzer-Company, to bring his remaining battle-ready Panzers from the north shore of the Danube to reinforce the bridgehead.

I felt I could do it and took my crew along. One of us would get through. So we jumped from column to column across the Florisdorfer Bridge, through the violent hail of the bullets, and found Boska and his Panzers.

The chief of the 6. Panzer-Company started out with three Panthers. All three Panzers were knocked out as they rolled across the bridge, Boska in the lead, just short of his objective, at the southern end of the bridge. He jumped from the turret of his Panzer and sprained his leg. Another critically wounded commander was rescued from the middle of the bridge, under a hail of bullets, by the equipment specialist of the 6. Panzer-Company riding a motorcycle with sidecar, and taken back. The spirit of comradeship proved itself during every moment of the fighting.

The commanders of the division and the regiment tried to make the battle commander understand that it was madness, as ordered by the Führer, not to blow up the Reich Bridge, which would thus have fallen undamaged into the hands of the Russians. The bridge would have given them the opportunity to attack the flanks or the rear of our forces north of the Danube, while, on the other hand, fighting "to the last man" was to have taken place at the Florisdorfer Bridge. However, the battle commander could not be influenced. He stood, unmoved, in the heaviest fire, without steel helmet, wearing his forage-cap, a hand grenade clipped to his belt. We sensed that he was finished with life and wanted to die under enemy fire because he saw no other option.

General von Bünau, battle commander of Vienna, had sent his Ia to the Supreme Commander of the 6. Panzerarmee, Generaloberst Sepp Dietrich, to report on the situation at the bridgehead and request new orders.

The Supreme Commander shared the opinion of the commander of the SS-Panzer-Division "DR" that the bridge should be blown up after dark and after all the wounded had been rescued. He issued the order to blow up the Florisdorfer Bridge, for which the commander of the city of Vienna was responsible by order of the Führer, to the commander of the "DF" Regiment, Obersturmbannführer Otto Weidinger. He trusted that Weidinger would know best when the last man of his regiment had crossed the bridge. The withdrawal began with the fall of darkness. The regimental commander waited for another hour after the report that the last man of the III./"DF" had crossed the bridge before giving the order to blow it up. Ignited electrically, a portion of the center span blew up. At least there the enemy could not cross with heavy weapons, and the division had some breathing space. The units of the II. SS-Panzerkorps left Vienna on April 14, saving the city from total destruction.

The Last March of
SS-Panzer-Regiment 3 ("T")

MARTIN STEIGER, 1./SS-PANZER-REGIMENT 3 ("T")
We crossed the border between Hungary and Austria at Lake Neusiedler and followed the withdrawal to Lanzenkirchen, south of Vienna Neustadt. There, the supply company with all its units was ordered into infantry duty. We took up positions at the canal together with the cadets of the Officer Candidate School in Lanzenkirchen. Around early afternoon of Easter Sunday, the Russians broke into Lanzenkirchen. We could not hold the position and withdrew to Vienna Neustadt.

The last resistance was mounted from the foothills of the Alps via St. Pölten to Krems. The division had taken up positions in the Krems area. The exhausted troops finally got some rest.

The gaps were partly filled by giving Panzer training to members of the Luftwaffe. Then there was a shortage of Panzers. Unterscharführer Reif was also wounded so that Oberscharführer Steiger represented the 1. Company as its last commander in the newly formed Kampfgruppe under Obersturmführer Neff. Kampfgruppe Neff with five Panzers, two of which were Panthers, represented the last remains of Panzer-Regiment 3. A Flak platoon, with four-barrel guns mounted on American tank hulls, was attached to the Kampfgruppe.

The remaining Panzers were moved from Rohrendorf to Krems to take up positions on the banks of the Danube. In the early morning hours of May 8, heavy Russian artillery fire ripped us out of our sleep and was probably meant to be a peace salvo. Neff and Lumitsch were at the battle command post and read the last regimental order to the remaining Panzer commanders: "Germany has unconditionally surrendered. We have been ordered to secure the withdrawal of the division and prevent a possible crossing of the Danube by the Russians until 5 P.M."

We left Krems at 5 P.M. and were to join up with the supply units on May 9 in Neumarkt. When we arrived there, we learned that they had already pulled further back to the west. The bulk of the division stopped at Prägarten near Linz. There we encountered American troops who refused to let us cross. In the meantime, the Russians had caught up with the kilometer-long column of the "T" Division and demanded the handing over of the division. The commanders of the amassed divisions ("T." Division, "Großdeutschland," and a Luftwaffe unit) negotiated with the Americans and Russians for two days.

An order by the Allies spelled out that all German troops who found themselves in Russian-occupied territory on May 8, 1945, were to start their trek into Russian captivity. All German troops located in the American-held territory were to be taken into American custody.

Brigadeführer Becker addressed the division one more time and mentioned that his personal fate was sealed. It was in the hands of the Russians. Despite his greatest efforts to hand over the division to the Americans, they had refused acceptance and referred to the order of the Allies.

Thus, all of the "Totenkopf" Division, with its commander Becker, was to be abandoned to the Russians. The consequence of this decision was that a mass escape to the west began during the night of May 12 to 13. It spread and turned into panic during which people were trampled and driven over. But only a few managed to get through the American lines. Most were stopped by American tank units and handed over to the Russians.

Eyewitnesses reported that a march of misery to the east, which lasted for weeks, decimated the last brave men of our division. Those who were able to escape to the west evaded this cruel fate and were saved from a slow death. But captivity, internment, denunciation, treachery, hunger, and misery awaited them also.

Powerless, we faced these facts. Without a home, ostracized, betrayed, our hearts torn into pieces, we returned back to Germany after six years of war.

Last Battles for Danzig– Gotenhafen–Arnswalde

OPERATIONS THEATRE ARNSWALDE–KÜSTRIN– GOTENHAFEN–DANZIG, FEBRUARY–MARCH 1945

After receiving the last thirteen Königstigers on January 25, 1945, the heavy SS-Panzer-Abteilung 503 began to load for transport to the Eastern Front on January 27. Regrettably, it never saw action as a complete unit, as even while still in Berlin it was split into two groups. The first group, under its commander Obersturmbannführer Fritz Herzig, set out with twelve Königstigers for the area of Arnswalde-Pomerania, while the second group was diverted into the area Landsberg-Küstrin.

The first group under commander Herzig was encircled, from February 4 on, in Arnswalde together with a Panzer support battalion, some 1,000 soldiers who had been removed from the trains taking them on leave to form units ready for immediate response, and some five-thousand civilians. The Königstigers of Panzer-Abteilung 503 could certainly have broken through the encirclement, but this would have meant abandoning the other units and the civilians to the enemy. After bringing the III. (germanic) SS-Panzerkorps to the edge of the encirclement, Operation "Sonnenwende" (solstice) was commenced with the objective of freeing the encircled in Arnswalde. A further thrust was to take place in the Landsberg-Küstrin area to attack the flank of the Russian front (the 2nd Guards Tank Army and the 61st Army) at the Oder River.

During the first day of the attack the German assault wedge reached Arnswalde. Through the narrow corridor it had opened, which was defended by the Königstigers against the ferocious attacks of the enemy, the transport of the wounded, the return of civilians, and the supply of the troops began.

On February 15 and 16 the Russians had only a few tanks available there, but they had a strong antitank front. On February 17 the 2nd

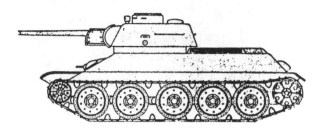

Tank T-34 (76) with 7.62-cm gun L/41,2

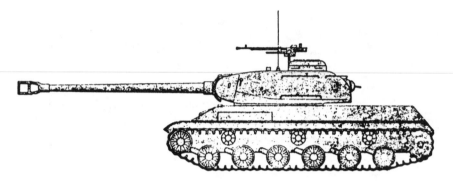

Tank JS-II with 12.2-cm gun D-25 L/43

The main Soviet enemies

Soviet Guards Tank Army brought numerous heavy Stalin tanks into combat, bringing to an end operation "Sonnenwende."

The action spots in the Danzig-Gotenhafen area changed almost daily and became the crucial test to prove the worth of the Königstigers, mostly operating on their own, which fought there to the bitter end and perished. Representative of the appreciation for all these Panzer crews was a laudatory mention in the report of the Armed Forces of April 10, 1945:

"In the spirit of the battle of Gotenhafen, SS-Untersturmführer Karl Brommann, company leader in the heavy Panzer-Abteilung 503, has been particularly outstanding. Despite being wounded three times, he, together with his crew, destroyed sixty-six tanks, forty-four guns, and fifteen trucks."

The decimated remains of the heavy SS-Panzer-Abteilung 503 in the Danzig area began to load on March 30 and managed to reach, by sea and the harbor of Swinemünde, the Berlin theatre of battle. Parts of the Abteilung remained in Danzig and were used as infantry. They set out on their way into captivity from Schievenhorst on May 9. Many did not return.

Six Königstigers of the heavy SS-Panzer-Abteilung arrived in the Berlin battle area. They became the decisive support for the tenacious grenadiers and tank destroyer teams that fought against the tank units of the Red Army during the final battle for the capital of the Reich, Berlin, and in the breakout in the direction of the Elbe River.

WITH THE KÖNIGSTIGERS IN THE PANZER BATTLES FOR POMERANIA
Fritz Kauerauf, SS-Untersturmführer and Panzer Commander in the heavy SS-Panzer-Abteilung 503, reports

On February 7, having completed a company commander's course, I crossed the Oder River at the only crossing still open near Stettin and reached Zachan by way of Stargard. There I was able to establish radio contact with my unit, which was encircled at Arnswalde. I was given orders to take over three operational Königstigers, out of the seven at the repair shops in Stargard, and break through to Arnswalde via Reetz.

During the night the three combat-ready Panzers were handed over, and we set out in the direction of Reetz. Just before reaching Reetz, which had in the meantime been captured by the Russians, we were directed by our corps toward Jacobshagen. The Russians were already reported to be marching in the direction of the Baltic Sea, and there was danger that the streams of refugees from Pomerania fleeing in the direction of Stettin would be cut off. We reached the command post of the I. Abteilung of SS-Panzer-Regiment "Hermann von Salza" of the SS-Division "Nordland" while it was still dark.

At dawn on February 8, 1945, I, Fritz Kauerauf, then a twenty-two-year old Untersturmführer of the heavy SS-Panzer-Abteilung 503 (Königstigerabteilung of the III. germanic SS-Panzerkorps), was given orders at the command post of the Panzer-Abteilung "Hermann von Salza" to report to its commander, Obersturmführer Paul-Albert (Peter) Kausch. "Take one Königstiger and the three assault guns of Oberscharführer Wild and drive with them across the Ihna bridge to Ziegenhagen and Klein-Silber and there cut off the reported Russian advance!"

After issuing this order, Kausch accompanied me outside and introduced me to Obersturmführer Wild. Then he said good-bye, wishing us all the best on our mission.

I took over the Königstiger and crew of Unterscharführer Lindl, whom I personally knew very well. Lindl came with us part of the way but then had to remain behind.

From the command post, located south of Jacobshagen behind the hills west of the Ihna River, we drove to the crests of these hills and, in full daylight, observed the dire situation. We saw an endless Russian column advancing across the line of hills east of the Ihna, stretching from south to north, with tanks, artillery, vehicles of all descriptions, even horse-drawn units. Oberscharführer Wild, who had been attached to me as a specialist in successful Panzer attacks and who had been awarded the Knight's Cross by Field Marshal Model in Kurland in 1944, agreed with me that something had to be done immediately since, "if they continue to advance, they will reach the Baltic Sea and might cut off our corps coming from Kurland," which had not yet been completely moved by sea to Stettin. Since we were much too weak, with our four Panzers, against the obvious enemy superiority, I sent Wild back to bring reinforcements for our attack. He managed, within a very short time, to indeed bring up two more Königstigers under Obersturmführer Kaes and some ten more assault guns of the I. SS-Panzer-Abteilung "Hermann von Salza" as well as a company of paratroopers. With these forces, which were joined by the assault guns of the assault gun Abteilung 11 (Nordland) under Sturmbannführer Schulz-Streek, we started to move in the direction of Ziegenhagen around noon. We had to stop, even before reaching the Ihna River, to wipe out some antitank positions at the edge of the town of Ziegenhagen. The paratroopers advanced along both sides of the road across the small Ihna Bridge toward Ziegenhagen.

We followed, with two assault guns at the point and our Königstigers behind, across this bridge and entered Ziegenhagen together with the paratroopers. A battle from house to house began, but we were able to advance relatively quickly after a bend in the road to the left until we reached a right curve. There, the two assault guns fighting at the point were stalled in heavy antitank fire. This fire came from a Russian antitank gun next to a church, approximately 150 to 200 meters away. The road we were on joined the route of the Soviet advance to Groß-Silber at that point. A violent firefight between our assault guns and the Russian antitank gun ensued during which neither was able to score a hit due to an elevation in the road between them. The shells from both sides fell wide. The attack was stalled.

In this situation it was up to me, with the greater height of our Königstiger, to get the attack going again. I asked the commander of the assault guns to brief me on the position of the anti-tank gun and then, during an arranged pause in the firing, we came around the corner so quickly that we managed to knock out the surprised Russian gun with a high explosive shell. We continued to advance immediately, followed by the two Königstigers of Kaes and Wild's assault guns. The success of the operation was in our hands alone. But we were stalled again, stopped by a visible row of mines across the road between two houses facing each other. The Russian rifle fire on our tanks increased drastically. One noticed that immediately when throwing out empty shells. The paratroopers had fought their way up to our position along the street from house to house, and we gave each other cover. The town itself was still in Russian hands.

My request for pioneers to remove the blocking mines was without success. Finally, I was supposed to get out myself and clear them away. Easily ordered but poorly thought through. But help came from an unknown comrade, in dress uniform and possibly on his way back from the hospital, who jumped past our Panzer into the cover of the house to the right of the mined strip. He carried a duffel bag full of explosives. One would not have though it possible, but jumping back and forth, he blew up one mine after the other, by placing hand grenades or explosive charges on them. There were between five to ten of them. This was an admirable feat, which no one who witnessed it will ever forget.

This unknown Untersturmführer, whom we covered as best we could with our machine guns, managed something else that had a deciding impact on the further course of our attack. He identified a threat to our Panzer advancing behind the house and drew my attention to it by wildly gesticulating and repeatedly pointing to the street and the fork in it. I ordered the loader, Tuschkewitz, to change shells. He took the 1.20-m-long explosive shell out of the barrel and replaced it with an antitank shell. Thank God for this, because a muzzle brake that could only belong to a Josef-Stalin tank already appeared at about half the height of the house, and the Russian monster tank rolled directly toward us from approximately fifty meters away. "Twelve o'clock, antitank shell 50, Josef-Stalin, aim between hull and turret, fire!" Fritz Lukesch fired. The Russian tank stopped immediately—its hatches were thrown open—and our crew cheered. But since its barrel was still pointing at us, I yelled down at the top of my lungs: "Have you gone crazy! Fire again!" And then one more time: "Fire again!" The Josef-Stalin tank stood in bright flames before us, its ammunition exploding constantly. But then we spotted something else. To the left of the knocked-out Russian tank, two more of the same type showed up. Their crews had probably received a bad shock, for they bailed out and ran away. We did not fire on these tanks with their guns pointed upwards. Obviously, they had not expected us and probably had never seen a Königstiger from such close proximity. The paratroopers waved at us joyfully, and we received congratulations by radio. But we had to press on! After the fire in the Russian tank giant had died down a little, we forced our way past it and entered the route of the Russian advance, pushing them off the road to all sides. The road belonged to us then, to our paratroopers and the Panzers and assault guns, with Oberscharführer Wild, behind us. We fought our way forward, accompanied by the paratroopers, knowing full well that success had already been achieved. We took two or three more hits that ricocheted, but the Russian advance to the north had been smashed. Toward the evening we reached the southern exit of Klein-Silber in the direction of Reetz and took up defensive positions there with our three Königstigers.

We only had some seven paratroopers left with us, too few to take turns manning two machine-gun positions. The paratroopers had an enormous effort behind them and were totally worn out. Despite that, they continued with determination.

During the night Kaes and I tried to make our way by foot to the command post, which had also moved forward, but that was impossible. There was still chaos in the town behind us. We learned that the unknown Untersturmführer who had blown up the mines and warned us had been killed by a shell. We were quite shaken by this since we felt he deserved the Knight's Cross for his feat. Later during the night a supply vehicle reached us and delivered one barrel of gasoline, 200 liters, per Königstiger. We had no food, but then we were not hungry either. Refueling from the barrels was extremely hard work. Throughout the night, Russian stragglers and horses with carts but no drivers crisscrossed the terrain. To get some rest we tried to find the most comfortable positions in the narrow interior of the Panzers. One of us kept watch in the commander's cupola. With retreating Russian artillery constantly pounded the town, we hardly got any sleep.

Toward the morning the order was given to take the remaining part of the town toward the east. To do this, we had to pull back approximately 100 meters. A misunderstanding made us, despite an agreement to the contrary, the point Panzer yet again. The situation did not look promising for a successful continuation of the Panzer attack; the terrain could be dominated by other means, as indeed happened later. Since we had no infantry with us, as the paratroopers the day before, to cover the

Panzers in close combat, I requested by radio that "sand rabbits" (code name for infantrymen) be sent. Instead of an answer, however, we were given more and more urgent orders to attack. Finally, I shouted down to the driver: "Menke, should we go or not?" The answer from the crew came in unison: "Untersturmführer, we'll go." Since the transmitter was open by mistake, our conversation was listened to, as I learned later, by the Steiner staff (then SS-AOK 11) where our and the Russian radio traffic was monitored. This brought about praise for our crew, however they did not learn about it.

I then sent a radio message: "Regenbogen (rainbow) from Adler 1 (eagle), I am advancing toward the exit of town, please follow!" and to our crew: "Panzer, full speed ahead, to the exit of town!" Menke drove forward. It was only some 500 to 600 meters, and I hoped that the Panzers and assault guns would follow behind us so we could do it without infantry support. We found ourselves at the edge of Klein-Silber without anyone else. Constant attempts to establish radio contact were in vain and even my ultimatum to move in behind us or we would have to pull back went unanswered. We just could not believe that they had not followed us. Only later, while in the hospital, I found out that the Königstiger of Obersturmführer Kaes, which was immediately behind us, was set on fire by the Russians and blocked the road for the following assault guns. Luckily, Kaes and his crew were only shaken up. Sitting at the edge of town, we gave ourselves another quarter of an hour since we could not hold out any longer than that. When no one had arrived by then, we backed up very slowly, occasionally firing our machine guns at the Russians. We only managed to get back halfway; the Russians had in the meantime erected a roadblock, using a rack-wagon and some farm equipment, which blocked our route of withdrawal. We tried to drive around the roadblock slowly but slipped with the left rear into the ditch so that our gun pointed at the sky. A defense with the front or turret machine guns was not possible. The Russians immediately closed in and climbed onto the Panzer, leaning ladders against it. We were momentarily helpless. I ordered Menke, our driver, to pull forward back onto the road under full power and, through a gap between the farms on the right, out of the town. This seemed, initially, to be successful. But we had not quite made it out of town when there was an immense explosion and a flash of flame. The Panzer stopped immediately. "Get out and away!" I yelled down and jumped from the cupola as the turret took a second direct hit, which smashed up my left shin. It took a third direct hit as I jumped off the Panzer. I saw one comrade run off, but in reality two got away.

They had picked the right direction and reached our defensive position of the previous evening. An assault gun sat there behind the road embankment as well as our third Königstiger, which was immobile due to the failure of the electrical system. It could only fire its two machine guns. Our paratroopers of the previous day were also still there. All this I did not know as I fell down next to our knocked-out Panzer. During the fall, in the face of the nearby Russians, I yelled loudly and threw up my arms. Once on the ground, I pulled my pistol from the pocket of my pants. The Russians, however, did not pay me any attention at the time. The spectacle of the burning Königstiger was more interesting to them. In it died our comrades, gunner Fritz Lukesch, a seventeen-year-old Saxon from Transylvania, and Bruno Tuschkewitz, the loader who believed to the last that he would recapture his home village in Pomerania. Their Königstiger became their grave! Beißer, the radio operator, whom I had seen running away, and Menke, the driver, only suffered burns. The front of our knocked-out Königstiger and its gun were visible from the assault gun which our two men had reached. I was quickly spotted from there. When I began to crawl toward an animal pen, consisting of two shacks connected by a wooden gate, both our assault gun and the Russians in the farm became active. The assault gun started to fire explosive shells into the farm and around the stable where I was lying, but always at a distance that the shrapnel would not hit me. The Russians were forced into cover. Meanwhile, using the cable from my headset and a piece of wood, I tried to apply a tourniquet to my left leg, from which my foot and its twisted boot were still hanging painlessly in my tattered pants. I then lay on my stomach and waved in the direction of the assault guns. Suddenly, there was a pain in my right and left thigh. Behind me stood a Russian who fired a machine gun at me from his hip. The first two bullets had hit me, then he could not hold the gun steady as the salvo pulled it to the left.

I turned around and shot him with my pistol and fired on another who was looking around a corner. The Russian I had shot was pulled around the corner of the stable by his feet. I then lay on my back, watching only the two corners of the stable. No one else came, but a hand grenade was thrown at me and landed on my lower body. I was able to grab it and throw it away. It was just out of my hand when it exploded and a four-to-five-centimeter-long strip of metal cut through my lower lip and got stuck in my lower frontal teeth. I was able to pull it out right away. Again, I had yelled loudly after the explosion in the hope that the Russians would think I had finally had it. In the center of the small stable, a Russian appeared again, the second one I was able to shoot. No one paid him any attention. I suddenly saw, as must have the Russians behind the two stables, three men from the assault gun at the edge of the farms along the street working their way toward us. They made it to the next farm and were almost within shouting distance when they turned around and disappeared at the assault gun. I was totally depressed but then crawled up to the wooden gate between the two stables and saw a Russian machine gun immediately behind there, with the round magazine on top and two men behind. With the loud noise from the fighting all around, I did not attract any attention. I had long since put the second magazine into the pistol. Then, as I held it close to a crack in the gate to fire at the two Russians by the machine gun in touching distance, I reminded myself to save one bullet for me, but it turned out differently. I aimed, fired, aimed, fired, and aimed again, could not see anything anymore and fired, but the pistol jammed! It's all over! Throw the pistol away, far away! No, it was not over! Crawl, crawl, and more crawling. Crawl to where my comrades had made it before, I ordered myself, and made it! I disappeared under a hill of potatoes. As I got angry at being unable to pull the smashed leg into cover also, I blacked out.

I remembered, later, seeing a Russian Rata (fighter aircraft) swinging through the clouded sky and a paratrooper standing at my feet, firing an assault rifle into the farm. Two of our men in leather uniforms shouted at me: "Untersturmführer, where can we grab you?" And I joyfully yelled back: "Grab me by the shoulders and let's get out of here!" On the run, without stopping, they dragged me across the field for 200 to 300 meters in a straight line to the assault gun. Only when we had reached it did the third man, our paratrooper, run back. The commander of our third Königstiger came over to the assault gun and reported to me the total failure of his Panzer. I ordered him to blow up the breech of the gun and set the Panzer on fire. This was done. I do not remember who all rode on the assault gun, but in any case they delivered me to the main dressing station around 9:30 A.M. I was later able to identify one of my rescuers. His name was Leonard Theunissen, and he did not return from the fighting for Berlin. Someone found his paybook and sent it without comment or return address to his parents. His last letter reported that his Panzer had to be blown up at Klein-Silber and that all his belongings were burned in it. "God be with you" was his last wish for his parents.

When I was carried from the dressing station to the ambulance, some of the men of Panzer-Regiment 11 were standing there, and one shouted in my ear: "Untersturmführer, we saw the whole thing, all the best!" I learned in the hospital that the grenadiers of the "Nordland" Division took over the terrain we had captured and that this made it possible to relieve the encircled Arnswalde about a week later. Some of the Königstigers of our heavy SS-Panzer-Abteilung 503, which made it out of there, were even brought by train to Danzig for its defense.

During the breakthrough to Arnswalde, Oberscharführer Philipp Wild, holder of the Knight's Cross, was also shot and brought to the hospital badly wounded.

Regarding the dramatic attack which Kausch, Wild, and I had initiated, I was told after the war, toward the end of 1945, in the Ratzeburg hospital at the Below barracks (SS hospital guarded by the British), by a Hauptsturmführer of the staff of the SS-AOK 11 (Steiner) in Pomerania, the following: While monitoring Russian radio traffic, enormous excitement was noted on the Russian side, causing great joy and relief to our staff, when our Königstiger at the point destroyed the three Josef-Stalin tanks and our Panzer column pulled across the Russian route of advance.

Felix Steiner wrote about it on page 317 in his book *The Volunteers, Idea and Sacrifice* (Die Freiwilligen, Idee and Opfergang), which was published in Göttingen in 1958 by Plesse Verlag K. W. Schütz, from his vantage point as a general of the Waffen-SS at the time:

"The 'Nordland' division attacked and destroyed, on the move, a long Soviet column which had broken through. Now the front was firm. The refugees were now able to cross the Oder River."

Between the Oder and the Elbe, 1945

KÖNIGSTIGERS IN HIGH-SPEED TRANSPORT
TO THE ODER FRONT

After the action in Normandy the heavy SS-Panzer-Abteilung 502 was refitted at Sennelager/Paderborn and received the Tiger II. Heavy air attacks on the Henschel assembly plant in Kassel delayed the delivery of the full complement so that the Abteilung could only be moved to the Eastern Front on the Oder at the beginning of March with twenty-nine Königstigers out of the required forty-five. We reached Stettin, where the Abteilung was unloaded, by express transport on March 11. Panzer commander and platoon leader Ernst Streng, 2./schwere SS-Panzer-Abteilung 502, who had already distinguished himself in Panzer-Regiment 2 "Das Reich" and in Normandy, kept the war diary of his company and reported from the commander's cupola of his Tiger on the last actions of the Abteilung on the Eastern Front and in the Berlin area.

We had spent the weeks of late fall and winter 1944 to 1945 in Sennelager near Paderborn, refitting our Abteilung and training the young replacements with theoretical lectures on many topics, breaking in our new Tigers, firing practice, and, not last, with the inevitable duty on foot of the German soldier.

Every evening we dropped into our beds dead tired. We never had the shameful feeling of spending time far away from the war since we knew only too well that the strict duty in Sennelager had only one objective: To harden us and make us as efficient as possible for the final battle of the next months!

Thus, the winter in Westphalia went by very quickly. On one of the last days of February 1945, the time had come. An order came from Berlin to start the Abteilung immediately on its march to the Eastern Front. The exact destination was initially kept a secret, but the Abteilung had to be loaded within forty-eight hours on twelve or more transport trains and on the move!

A bustling activity set in. The Panzers of the 1. Company rolled to the loading ramp at the Sennelager station. Our vehicles were loaded at Neuhaus and Paderborn. We worked all night by the light of our flash-lights to steer our giants onto the flatbed cars and tie them down. At five o'clock in the morning our heavy transport train set out, and then we learned our destination was Stettin, where we were to join the battle for the large harbor, the center of shipping to the front in Kurland.

ATTACK NEAR SACHSENHEIM

It was the area west of the bend of the Oder River between Frankfurt and Küstrin. There, the western Russian front followed the bend in the river. Its line lay roughly from Lebus via Sachsenheim, Seelow, Gorgast, through the Oder marshes back to the stream. Two days' march to the west lay Berlin, the core of Germany, with the military and political lead-ership and its four-and-a-half million inhabitants. In this bend of the Oder River, the Red Army, during its victorious advance of the fateful days of January and February of the same year, had established a bridge-head and a position from which to begin further operations.

Large numbers of troops had been moved in during the previous days and weeks to oppose this Russian position with its critical threat to Berlin and the German Eastern Front. An SS-Panzerkorps was formed. Numerous army and Panzer divisions were brought up and reinforced the defensive line along the hills west of the low ground.

The daily numbers of casualties were in direct relationship to the numbers of troops amassed there. The completely encircled old fortress of Küstrin, one of the cornerstones of the Eastern Front, was in the last stages of its battle against the constantly attacking Soviet regiments. An incomparable concentration of Russian artillery, Paks, and tanks in the small space seemed to safeguard the Red Army and the confidence in victory of its soldiers from any surprise and threat. Around 3 P.M. the chief was ordered to the Abteilung command post. He came racing back in his car.

"All commanders report for a briefing immediately—Get the Panz-ers ready!" Using the map, the chief explained the attack ordered for that night. It was to start at the middle of the enemy bridgehead near Sachsenheim and split it open, in cooperation with a division of para-troopers and the entire Panzer-Abteilung. We were to push right through to the Oder, through completely unknown terrain and the expected enemy resistance, in the dark of the night.

We looked at each other with deep concern, and we all had the same thought. We did not hold back our misgivings and objections since we knew with some certainty that such an operation by our side was sure to fail. On the other hand there were some weighty reasons for it, such as the large concentration of enemy artillery, which, it was hoped, could be destroyed during the night when chances of being observed were reduced, as well as the numerous antitank positions.

Well spaced, we made our way toward the boiling front along winding dirt roads, through valleys and across hills, trailing long plumes of dust. Hidden behind the last range of hills was a rotating searchlight, installed as a marker for the Luftwaffe support, which had been promised for that night. Our most advanced positions were reported to be not far from the opposite edge of town. The Panzers faced the enemy, but the front line was still quiet.

It was a few minutes before midnight. Our platoon was at the point; the other Panzers were following in a column along the road. Messengers bustled to and fro with shouts inquiring after units, names, and answers.

Suddenly, there was the bang of a discharge, a bright flash. Other guns from Schroif's platoon joined in. Artillery, mortars, Panzers, the whole machinery of death and destruction was activated.

The noises of digging spades, the rattling of metal mess kits were joined by the howling of heavy engines, the din of the tracks, and bestial yelling. Almost nothing could be made out in the dark; only the radio provided clues on what was happening. Groups of bleeding soldiers darted backward past us along the road. Ahead, explosive shells and MG salvos hammered the closest farm held by the enemy.

Around one o'clock the first enemy position was taken. The flat terrain was already lit by the red glow of burning farms and tanks. Our column advanced slowly. To our left an enemy tank blew up with a bright bluish flash. Tracer bullets whistled in long rows at the Panzers, ricocheted to the side and upwards.

Our Panzers then faced the second enemy line, lit from behind by burning farms that were visible as sharp silhouettes. We were ordered to the right to secure the side of the most threatened flank. All of us were completely in the dark. We got stuck in bomb craters or at other obstacles and only the flames from the exhausts of the neighboring Panzers showed their positions.

Dawn slowly arrived. The ghostly shapes of trees and hills took on form and color. The platoons formed up. The most advanced parts of the regiments gave hand signals to show their positions, and the units began to deploy and regroup.

Then a barrage burst forth from our machine guns and cannon, firing precisely over the heads of our charging soldiers; in front of us brown clusters of men hastened back across the field and were immediately swallowed up in the fog. Ten, twenty, thirty barrels hurled tracer salvos into the enemy rows and into the milky gray background. In disarray, the Russians retreated in visible haste to other prepared lines of defense. Suddenly, however, a heavy hail of enemy mortar shells came down on the advancing attack like a thunderstorm, forcing the well-spaced rows down, hammering the bodies pressed into the ground. They were hurled up in the air, dropped back, ripped open by hot shrapnel. Shouting and moaning was heard everywhere.

Far ahead, numerous enemy antitank guns were seen racing over from the right, taking up positions at a back slope and digging in to form a widely drawn line of fire.

Immediately, we opened fire with the guns of four Panzers at 1,200 meters distance on the enemy battery. Our other Panzers were still in cover behind the estate. Two, four, eight, ten barrels fired from behind the hill at us, and their shells fell ever closer to our Panzers out in the open. The duel of the guns lasted for minutes. Then, the first and a second Pak were covered with explosive shells and destroyed. Almost simultaneously Schaubinger took a direct hit to the turret; seconds later we were hit in the front and the tracks. Hellwig reported his turret hit and damage to his gun, and then there was one hit after another. Schaubinger pulled back into a depression in the terrain. Before we could notice it, Hellwig also pulled back. The hail of enemy shells immediately concentrated on our vehicle. The loader was overcome by exertion and the fumes from the powder, and dropped unconscious to the floor. The gear shift lever for reverse was knocked out of position by a hit. It took long and anxious seconds before the driver noticed the minor hit, but each new second could have brought the fatal direct hit. Schroif's platoon, then only consisting of two vehicles, was unable to open fire from the left of the road.

Only Schroif and our vehicle were left facing the enemy and kept fighting. We had pulled in an infantryman as a replacement loader.

All the other Panzers were far back near Sachsenheim with various damage. The Abteilung command post sent the first company in at that time to provide relief and carry out a counterpush. At full speed, widely drawn apart, its first platoon came racing up to us, stopped to fire, and began its attack on the Pak position. We were, regrettably, unable to draw the attention of its platoon leader, Baral, to the real danger, as his company was using a different frequency for its radio traffic. He was fatally wounded in later fighting.

A number of black bugs crawled toward us from far ahead to the left along the poplar-lined road. They were identified as enemy tanks. At 1,000 meters from us they blew up in flashes of flames, even before they knew what was happening and from where the shells came. Like factory chimneys they blew oily dark clouds of smoke from their insides, sitting in the terrain like burning torches.

Around eleven o'clock the Abteilung commander ordered our remaining Panzers back to Sachsenheim. The whole attack sector was handed over to the first company. All its vehicles had been rendered immobile by enemy fire, and it was only during the night that they were towed back and salvaged. We assembled outside Sachsenheim and set out through the town and then to the right along the country road toward Seelow.

Along this road we received supplies of fuel and shells and were able to repair the most critical damage. On our right track alone, eleven links had to be replaced. Then followed a briefing by the commanders, reports on the numbers of successes, and a discussion on the factors that caused the failure of the attack. It had been thanks to the foresight and quick reaction of a small number of Panzer commanders that the whole thing did not turn into a fiasco.

Schaubinger and Oberhuber were let go to the repair company. The staff Panzer was assigned to us as a temporary replacement. Since Hellwig had been ordered to take up a firing position just behind the most advanced line near a farm, Schmidt took over the sector on the right, well forward at an estate. We drove over near a battalion command post and set up position just to the left of the road. We were at the same time the relay station for orders of the company command post during the hourly radio exchanges. Ahead of us, on and behind the railroad embankment, parts of an assault gun brigade had set up positions as the initial German antitank defense.

Well over twenty burned-out enemy tank wrecks, knocked out in a very small area, sat behind the embankment in the German lines. They bore witness to the massive bitterness of the previous defensive battles. No Russian tank, despite concentrated action, had managed to push through the German front lines.

We sat on the roof of our camouflaged Panzer in the garden of the farm until dusk and took over the first watch where we had to relay or answer the evening reports and requests by radio. Just in case, our gun was aimed at the embankment and the road ahead of us 800 meters away. The men of the Kampfgruppe command had brought straw into the cellar and set up beds down there. The soft light from white candles flickered in the cellar and was reflected by the shining weapons. Hand grenades and ammunition boxes, telephones, map tables, and steel helmets stood about or hung from the walls.

The watch on the roof of the turret was taken in a two-hour rotation. No one was allowed, in case of an alarm, to move outside of shouting distance. There was no thought of sleep in any case, as constant disruptions by incoming and outgoing messages, supplies of food, requests and orders by radio, checking the sentries, and observation kept us awake. All our senses were tensed. We listened toward the front and to the multitude of noises, magnified by the night, in our forward front sector.

The night passed slowly, an hour at a time.

Night Attack to Relieve "Fortress Küstrin"

Discussions and briefings between Schroif and the chief took up all afternoon of March 26. Hellwig, who had been reinforced the previous evening by Schaubinger, set two Russian tanks on fire. The verbal order to pull out arrived the same afternoon. All Panzers were to assemble by 8 P.M. at the departure position at the company command post. If possible, the departure was to take place unnoticed by the enemy and at different times. Further briefings took place during the following issuing of orders. These orders were to be given verbally. After each individual commander had reported in, the Panzerkorps, as ordered, would commence an attack that very night on both sides of Gorgast with all available Panzer forces and two Jäger divisions, supported by a Volksartillerie Korps, to relieve Fortress Küstrin.

An additional order from the Abteilung came in:

"The 1. Company, followed by the 2. Company, will begin the attack from Gorgast at 1 A.M. in cooperation with the attached infantry units, one armored reconnaissance battalion, and pioneer units. The 3. Company will attack one kilometer to the right, along the main road, together with one Panzer-abteilung. The assault gun Abteilung will take over the left sector. The creek from Gorgast in direction of the Oder will mark the dividing line."

For weeks, the Soviet push from the east, south, and north had been stalled at the completely encircled Fortress Küstrin. The circle of the defenders had begun to show breaks; it had retreated farther into the fortress and closed again. However, since a few days before, the defenders were amassed in a very small area and could only hope for relief from the outside. Otherwise, their total destruction in a very short time was foreseen.

All available forces inside the fortress were to attempt to break out that night.

"Let's go!" With engines roaring we rolled down the elevated village street toward the houses. The first greetings of the enemy artillery exploded at the near edge of the village. Ahead of us there was one delay after the other, what was going on? Cursing, the commander drove back in his armored reconnaissance vehicle, had everyone pull over sharply to the right, and got himself stuck in a shell crater. The village offered a picture of destruction, much like Sachsenheim. Without gunning the engines and in low gear, we were to pull ahead into the pastures to the right of the road. The 1. Company, led by Knight's Cross holder Kalls, was already facing the first enemy trenches in battle formation. All engines had been turned off. There was dead silence all around us, as if the low fog setting in was swallowing all sounds. So, we got back into the crate and put on the headsets. We did not have to wait long for the blessings from the artillery. The Panzers at the point started their engines. They roared, and the other Panzer engines joined in with primeval force. Ten, fifteen well-spaced Panzers set out forwards. Violent MG fire was heard from the point. The German MGs could be recognized by their high rate of fire. The attack had begun, and the Panzers began to take part. Guns, mortar explosions, and hand grenades increased the noise of the battle. White flares brightened the darkness for moments. The meter-long flames from the exhausts blinded us more than they lit the dark for us. We seemed to be moving ahead at walking pace. The mass of the attack, concentrated not long before, spread out through the vastness of the terrain. Half-left, rifle fire still flickered from the first overrun enemy positions in the stands of beech trees.

The Panzers at the point had long since rolled past these. Russian tracer salvos whistled at the approaching front of steel. We could not return fire in the dark without seriously endangering our own men. The main Russian position was supposed to be one kilometer ahead. There was a general halt. The rifle regiment seemed to be redeploying. We heard thumping feet, companies running by, shouts, curses, fragments of conversations. Then we assembled again. Seconds later came an emergency call to all, repeated three times: "Attention—attention—mines—mines!" and a little later the position of the minefield. Three Panzers of the 1. Company sat immobile in the minefield, their tracks ripped apart. The attack stopped again, there was a general halt. Pioneers had to first open up a path through the mines for the vehicles, and valuable time was slipping away.

If a strip of mines there could have already stopped the attack, how many such strips were in front of the enemy trenches?

The 2. Company, with Schroif's platoon at the point, was guided through the open path by the command vehicle to continue the attack. Our platoon took over securing the flank to the left. Dawn was already breaking in the east, but ground fog greatly reduced visibility.

At that time the 3. Company should have reached the main trench on the right flank, but it, too, was stalled by mines. One Panzer was knocked out by a bazooka in the barbed wire and burned out. Another one was stuck in the minefield.

Then, they seemed to want to force a break through the Russian main line by using an armored reconnaissance vehicle company and pioneers. At high speed, dropping numerous smoke grenades as camouflage from the enemy, single personnel carriers raced from out of the depth of the minefield on the right. Under cover of this fog, the others followed in a row. In a daring drive the phalanx of steel raced up against the barbed wire obstacles and disappeared like ghosts into the sea of fog. The success of our attack was on razor's edge. Schroif passed through the path opened by the pioneers with all his vehicles and, together with the following infantry, faced the barbed wire entanglement. However, the enemy defenses, in particular the invisible machine guns on the flanks, were too strong. They forced the charging lines to the ground. Death-defying groups of infantrymen rose up again, charged into the raging fire and tried to reach the enemy trenches and sank, hit, one after the other to the ground. Machine guns hammered incessantly from the barbed wire.

Defensive fire from enemy artillery began and concentrated on the sector of the attack. The assault companies sought cover in the plentiful craters. The vast brown fields lay empty and abandoned, quickly turning into a landscape of craters, plowed time and again.

Enemy tanks surprised us, rolling, under cover of a farm behind the opposite lines and from an adjoining row of bushes and trees, to within 500 meters from us. Schroif took the first hit through the hull. With lightning speed all vehicles on the same frequency reacted to his alarm call. Seconds later the first enemy vehicle blew up in a flash of flames after all the Panzer turrets had swung toward the new targets.

The second one tried to move on under cover of the explosion of his neighbor, but it suffered the same fate. The flashes of fire followed each other so quickly that no one could claim the kill for himself alone with any certainty. We kept a very careful watch on this dangerous corner with our field glasses. By afternoon, four Russian tanks had burned out with oily black plumes of smoke in this deadly hideaway. The same was true for the Paks. Ten, even twenty times, the brave Red Army soldiers tried to crawl to their abandoned guns. But our gunners were on their toes, shooting them down on the spot. Still, the stoic determination of the Russians to reach their goal was admirable!

Based on the arriving radio messages and orders, the attack seemed at least to have stalled, if not broken off. Other enemy tanks were forced back or knocked out even as they left the opposite edge of town. Numerous columns of flames indicated successful Panzer battles. But this did not at all mean, despite the fact that the Panzers in the section to the right finally made progress against the defense, that the attack was successful until the main trench was crossed and the advance continued in the direction of Küstrin. To achieve this, we needed a path cleared by the pioneers through the mines since five vehicles were already stuck in a heap.

The fighting went back and forth throughout the morning. In the afternoon our armored reconnaissance platoon under Lieutenant Justus was requested to evacuate the critically wounded. He boldly raced up, dismounted his troops and arranged a security belt on the left flank.

Again, our machine guns hammered the Russian lines to provide cover for the operation. Then, the Panzers sitting in the minefield were to be towed out. We did not have enough power to pull the vehicles, which had rolled off their tracks. They had first to be put back on the tracks, which could only be done under cover of darkness. The gunners who bailed out to attach the heavy tow cables were a picture of courage and boldness. Around 3 P.M. all mobile Panzers, except for three that were left to continue to provide cover, were pulled back. During this, Schaubinger ran onto a mine and got helplessly stuck.

Hellwig and Oberhuber were attached to us to help with providing cover. This could be done only after all damaged vehicles were recovered.

Then, finally, darkness came. Under its cover the promised salvage platoons were to come forward.

After urgent requests from Schaubinger we finally gave in and tried to pull him from the minefield or at least tow him onto his track so that he could get free under his own power. But the fates were not with us. We were only a few meters to the side when there was an explosion that threw everything about in the interior. The next mine had blown up under our track. None of the men standing around were seriously wounded despite having been hurled to the ground with full force. One of the wheels was missing, and some of the links were half ripped off.

Would they hang together while we pulled out to safety? Driving slowly we moved out of that damned sector and rolled back at walking speed to the village behind us.

At the entrance to the village, we quickly fixed our tracks. Or at least we tried, since we were bombarded for hours by constant waves of enemy planes dropping flares, a rain of phosphor and explosive bombs.

Feverishly, we banged away with our hammers, inserting the missing links, so that we could under all circumstances get out of there before morning.

When the final pin had been driven in, it could not have been long until morning. We sought the cover of the steel walls, exhausted, and ready to sleep forever.

Schroif's vehicle was sitting off to the side of the road; it had rolled from its track. Food was handed out. A new day slowly dawned behind us as we spooned the cold food from the mess kits. The whole plain was still covered with thick ground fog. During the previous night another attack had been set into motion on the left flank to support the forces of the few thousand men breaking out of Fortress Küstrin to the main German front lines. After initial successes by the Panzers, which had been moved in from other spots and by the assault gun brigade, the attack stalled. Mines and the increasingly determined resistance negated all their bravery. The fighting spirit of the Red Army showed itself at a high level; it hung on to its old positions with the will for victory.

A dispatch rider brought an order from the chief: "Take the vehicle immediately, follow the dispatch rider, and salvage Harlander's Panzer in the left attack sector before the fog has cleared up completely!"

Without pious thoughts, the order was carried out with cursing and grumbling, caused not by the mission itself, but by the immense strain it put on one's own vehicle. Often enough, Panzers that towed others had returned with damage to the driving gears, the tracks or the engines.

Good Lord, what a situation we found up front! The Panzer had rolled off the track and sat on soft black dirt. We did not have very much hope to salvage it. Still, we tried quickly to pull the track into position and tow the vehicle onto it. But we gave that up very soon as the ground fog was already lifting and the Ivans had figured out our plan. Salvos from MGs whistled by above us, pistols and hand grenades were heard.

So we hooked up the crate as it was and hit full throttle! The wire cables, hooked up crosswise, tightened and jerked. One of the steel brackets ripped apart with a sound like an explosion. We hooked up the spare cable to the bottom of the hull to pull it up also. After 10 to 20 meters we stopped for a moment. A meter-deep, wide rut marked the track only too well. Only the bottom of the hull prevented further sinking into the soft ground. Then we had made it behind the cover of an elevation in the terrain. We took a break and let the engine cool off. The next leg took us behind the long stretched-out brick stables, which had been turned into a command post and an assembly point for the wounded. From there the Panzer could be towed away by regular means.

We departed for the company command post and reported back to the chief. At the same time we asked him to have our repair team come over to us with the required spares to replace our worn-out front sprocket wheels. Our firing position at that time was 400 meters to the left, behind and away to the left from a farm. We had not closed our eyes for sixty hours, were overtired, hungry, and thirsty. But first we had to care for our vehicle, refuel, load ammunition, clean the weapons, make sure the engine was all right, and repair some damage. The third night set in with cool temperatures.

We thoroughly inspected a Stalin tank which sat close by, ready for action and mobile. We were greatly impressed by its 12-cm gun, its robust equipment, the cast parts, and diesel engine.

CHANGE OVER TO DEFENSE

Schroif scouted the areas of action indicated on the map on April 3, determined the respective firing positions with good fields of fire, and arranged to have them dug out by parts of our supply and staff companies.

Our departure was to take place the next morning at nine o'clock. However, a few minutes before, a hail of heavy-caliber shells set in on our Panzers. Our departure became questionable. We sat behind walls and trees as flashes and explosions of the shells were all around us, waiting for a pause in the fire so that we could escape into the Panzer. We just wanted to get out of that corner, but we had to pay with some wounded. We did not have to go through the briefing and distribution at the rear edge of the town of Litzen.

From one day to the next the long predicted major offensive was announced. New safety measures, which made our sleep during the nights difficult, showed up. As a first step, all use of gasoline was drastically reduced. Our rations were brought forward in horse-drawn carts, dispatch riders were on foot. The available supply of ammunition, in particular of explosive shells and with a small reserve thrown in, was handed out for the days of fighting. Readiness for action at any minute, especially in the morning, had to be assured. Thorough cleaning and repairs of the interior equipment, the radio, weapons, ammunition, the sight, and engines took turns with inspections of the uniforms.

The daily reports from the Armed Forces sounded threatening. The English and Americans were advancing toward the Elbe River, through all of southern and central Germany. The Russians had victoriously raced toward Vienna, captured it, and continued their march toward St. Pölten. This caused great anxiety, in particular to our friend Rodinger and the other comrades from Austria.

Every one of us realized with great seriousness that the fighting would probably come to an end within four weeks at the latest, one way or another.

The Major Russian Offensive on Berlin, April 16, 1945

April 16, 1945!

It was four o'clock in the morning. Those of the crew who had preferred spending the night in the warm straw in a small crater next to the Panzer rather than in its interior suddenly found the ground below them vibrating. The Russian artillery sent its first salvo, followed immediately by the rolling echo of the second. The men, coming numbly out of their sleep, could hear the explosions of the next salvos, the following echoes merged with the explosions of the shells.

The major Russian offensive, expected for weeks by the German troops on the Oder, had begun and with it the last great battle in Germany. It was as if the curtain had been lifted on the last act of a terrible drama when barrages of unimaginable ferocity and violence commenced in the slow dawn of the morning. The Russian batteries were lined up for kilometers in width and depth, literally one gun next to the other.

Pulling our blankets behind, we crawled hastily out of our hole, not noticing the cold of the night, climbed breathlessly up the wall of the Panzer, pulled open the heavy steel hatches and sank, heaving a sigh of relief, into its interior. With quick fingers we mechanically buttoned up our uniforms and leather jackets, put on microphones and headphones, grabbed our pistols and field glasses.

The night should still have been dark, but in the angled outside mirrors we saw the eastern sky in flames. From the plains along the Oder, from the hills near Lebus and Reithwein all the way to Seelow, the whole country seemed to be on fire. All around us, everything was under a deadly storm of steel. Thousands of enemy guns threw their iron loads in a racing whirl of fire onto the land. Heavy artillery fired across the Oder; the explosions had to be heard for dozens of kilometers. One after the other, ten, twenty, thirty black shadows from aircraft darted across the roofs and ruins of houses, dropping bundles of heavy phosphor and explosive bombs into every parcel of woods, every town, deep into the country.

In the smoke and glow of the fires, behind us and ahead, we glimpsed trees, bunker roofs, barricades, pieces of guns, and dirt whirling through the air. Ahead of us and half to the right were exploding bunkers and houses.

The quiet hum of the transmitters and receivers came in on the headphones, while the flanks of the Panzer trembled with the roar of the heavy engines. The loader prepared antitank shells, readied the machine guns, and stowed duffel bags and blankets in the fighting compartment. The gunner checked the electrical firing mechanism, the sight, and the intercom.

Outside, the German batteries had entered the battle, firing everything they had as fast as they could. From the barrels on our side of the front flashed the lightning of uncounted batteries and calibers. Grenade after grenade rose from the mortars and traveled eastwards in immense barrages. Bright walls of fire from the explosions were built into the sky toward the rising sun. Gray-black banks of smoke drifted from the plains of the Oder across the positions in the surrounding hills of the Harden Mountains to the west.

For the last time in the Second World War, the German front-soldier rose from his foxhole after hours of barrages to fight back the assault of the Red Army.

From the closest foxhole to the trenches in the rear, hundreds of thousands waited for this deciding hour behind their machine guns, in the command posts, behind their guns' sights, and at the map tables. Reserve troops were alerted and moved into their assembly and defensive positions. From the most advanced infantry battalion back to the German headquarters near Zossen one radio message chased the other; report and reply. Then, formations of German fighters and bombers joined the broiling battle. The air trembled with the howl of engines and propellers on top of the explosions. Bundled tracer salvos drilled into aircraft bodies, which broke apart, dropping to the ground with mushrooms of fire growing into the sky. Heavy guns and automatic antiaircraft guns from numerous air defense batteries deployed across the whole sector put up dense curtains of fire in front of the long-barreled German guns that were being attacked from the air.

There were terrible losses on both sides.

The large hand of the watch moved right ever so slowly. It was five o'clock, six o'clock. The sun rose, blood-red, over the Oder marshes. It penetrated the darkness of the bands of fog only with difficulty.

The core of the German Oder front was gripped by the strangling fist of the enemy. The reports from the defensive positions of our infantry grew fewer and fewer; most likely the communication wires were ripped apart.

It turned seven o'clock, eight o'clock.

Up til then, our Tiger company, which was attached to the Kurmark Division on the right front sector of the bridgehead, had not received orders to join the fighting. For half an hour before, we heard the pulsating noise of infantry fighting. The staccato hammering of the machine guns seemed to be moving closer.

The wall of our soldiers two to three kilometers ahead of us seemed to be withstanding the overwhelming assault of the Soviet regiments sure of victory. Nowhere could a withdrawal by our troops across the heights be observed. But, a breakthrough of entire groups of Russian tanks had to be expected at any moment. Judging by the time, the battle had reached its peak. We sat silently in our fighting vehicle and listened, everyone of us deep in thought, contemplating the fate of our comrades out there in the foxholes at the front lines. How often, during the years of war, had we ourselves been in the middle of it at the front, together with those who were facing hell out there, hands grasping the safety of the ground. Having to wait, helplessly, was so terribly difficult.

Around 8:30 the enemy artillery fire seemed to weaken. We constantly searched the burning villages and battle sectors covered in smoke with our field glasses for the reported enemy tanks. Without thinking, and not really hungry, we forced ourselves to eat the sandwiches that the radio operator had prepared.

Finally, at a few minutes before 9 A.M., we felt quite confident and believed that our own front lines had held together against the overwhelming onslaught. While the chief rushed ahead of the Panzers in his jeep to scout the terrain, Schaubinger led the company into position.

As the engines roared and the camouflage dropped off, our Panzer tracks pulled us out of the craters and the meter-high dirt walls onto the village road. In a wide detour the giants rolled backward, separated into platoons and well spaced, out of the village into the flat country. Some 300 meters further we were caught in a heavy bombing attack, but none of the vehicles was damaged.

All along the roads and country lanes, armored reserve units clanged their way to the front in deeply spaced marching columns. The commanding general of the II. SS-Panzerkorps, Obergruppenführer Kleinheisterkamp, himself on the way to the front, received our report on our orders and wished us much luck on the way. The company reached the regimental command post in the right sector of the division by way of

Dolgelin and Falkenhagen at 1 P.M. We were to begin a counterattack on Schönfließ, held by the Russians, in two hours, together with an officer cadet battalion.

To the left and the right of the elevated railroad embankment east of Schönfließ, the remnants of the bravest fighting troops had dug into the ground, on the flank of the breakthrough, and thus cushioned the first push, just like a bridge pillar surrounded by a brown flood.

According to the briefing by the chief, we were to push into Schönfließ first, together with an assault party of officer cadets, then push the company ahead by radio, and, together with the battalion which was to have moved forward by then, carry the attack ahead to the railroad embankment. Because of the obstruction to the field of vision and the narrowness of the village street, action by the vehicles in formation was out of the question. It was now 2:30 P.M. Time was getting short, and we only had a few minutes left to discuss details of the attack with Schaubinger.

The time had come. Our steel giants broke out of the path through the woods in a long line into the sloping open fields and wound their way under cover of depressions in the terrain past deeply staggered positions, our Volkssturm men waving at us from their perimeters. A kilometer-long veil of dust whirled above us across the plain. In the wooded area to the right of Schönfließ, the infantry battalion, assembled for the attack, was waiting. It provided an assault team to come along with us. Without stopping we continued our way to the entrance of the village, flanked to the left and right by officer cadets of the war school.

We broke into the occupied village through a dangerous, narrow gorge, which offered room only for one Panzer at a time. The din from our tracks running over the tangle of telephone posts, bricks, and roofs, which had been blown off by the pressure waves of explosions, echoed deafeningly from the ruins opposite us. The stink of hot oil rose as our Panzer hammered its deadly load into the gardens and house ruins. Occasionally, we spotted the brown uniforms of Russians among the rubble. Explosive shells and machine-gun salvos drove them from their positions. To the right and left of us dirt-brown men rose from cover and ran, bent over, toward the exits of the town. Blue clouds of smoke from the hand grenades of our infantry rose behind them, submachine guns rattled around the corners of houses. Many Russians jumped up, threw up their arms, and fell back. Others were hurled backward by unseen blows and did not rise again. Slowly, we made our way past the antitank barricade at the end of the village. The soft ground along the path welled up under the weight of our vehicle. Then, the barricade was behind us and we climbed from the valley into the open fields. Behind us, the officer cadets finished clearing Schönfließ with bold, daredevil actions.

The brown-green pasture land ahead was in full view, and it rose toward the railroad embankment, our real objective, some 1,500 meters away. We had to be prepared for antitank fire from there, at least for heavy artillery fire, but maybe even a tank attack. Up until then there was no movement in the dug-in positions along the embankment, halfway up.

While Schaubinger, as agreed, swung to the right we continued to roll ahead along the uphill path through the fields toward the underpass in the embankment. Two-hundred meters farther on we were stopped by trenches crossing the path at a right angle from which Russians appeared and immediately attacked us from the sides with bazookas. We barely managed to fight them off with hand grenades and submachine guns. Schaubinger, off to the side, faced the same situation. We agreed by radio to halt and wait until our company could rush up to our uphill positions. Since the Russians were cut off from any chance of escaping by our machine guns, they defended their trenches with utmost determination.

Shortly, our other vehicles pulled up at the edge of town and set up a firing line. The infantry battalion, too, had moved up through Schönfließ. The continuation of the counterattack was ordered. Regrettably, we could not overcome the trenches with direct fire, and, however often our daring assault teams attempted to break into the trenches from the sides, they were mowed down from above or smashed inside the trenches by barrages of hand grenades. In limitless exasperation we forced our way with our Panzer past the trenches, almost to the linesman's cabin. But we were immediately greatly threatened by approaching antitank teams, which we were barely able to hold off with hand grenades and submachine gun salvos. As long as our other Panzers did not follow, we could not remain up there by ourselves, so we pulled back to the line of the others. Schaubinger's Tiger received damage to the tracks and had to be released from action. We started out again to leave the trenches behind us.

While Harlander gave covering fire, Kuhnke rolled his Panzer across the fully manned trench, his tracks digging into the ground of the crumbling walls and the compressed bodies. It was always the same, terrible game.

The bitter, terrible fighting for the trenches went back and forth for hours. No decision could be brought about. Our own reinforcements were brought in, and we suffered severe losses.

At exactly four o'clock in the afternoon an immense barrage set in again on the defense sectors to the left. It lasted for one and one-half hours, then the attack from across started again, wave after wave. When the reports were released in the evening, they said: "We were able to still hold the front together. Deeper breakthroughs could be cut off." The demands for help from the threatened sector read: "Send us men, send us ammunition!'

The chief drove back to the regimental command post in the rear. He wanted to bring up artillery support, but it did not work out—no ammunition.

In the evening our driver reported damage to the steering mechanism. Laboriously, we drove backward and forward and finally managed to bring our vehicle to our own firing line.

It was only around midnight that our battalion succeeded in retaking, one after the other, the bitterly fought-for German trenches. As our own infantry told it, the trenches were a picture of horror. They were literally filled with hundreds of dead Russians.

A German lieutenant arrived later from the railroad embankment ahead and to the left, requesting us to open fire with our Panzer on the linesman's cabin, which was full of Russians. Since we no longer had a proper field of fire, we passed the request on to Oberhuber's Panzer by radio. Despite the fact that we had been sitting in firing position only a few hundred meters away from the cabin for all of the afternoon, we had been unable to determine whether it was held by our own troops. The Russians had been particularly lucky. What had confused us was that white flares had constantly been fired from about 150 meters to the left of it. They indicated the forward sectors of trenches held by us. The fighting had also been made extremely difficult for us Germans by the fact that entire units of the attacking Red Army were equipped with German uniforms, steel helmets, and weapons. In accordance with the orders of the army of the same day, German units had to roll up both sleeves in order to be recognized, but this hardly made the fighting any easier. As unbelievable as these reports sounded, we saw hundreds of Russians in our field-gray uniforms who brought confusion and disaster into our lines.

Meanwhile we were in an upbeat mood. If the front had held elsewhere as well as it had in our sector, the Russians would score only minor successes, if any, the next day also.

We were ordered to have Hellwig's Panzer tow ours to the rear. The battlefield was to be cleared by dawn. Hellwig towed us back through the valley and across the plain. Around us, the night was silent. Thick clouds of dust from the arid ground swirled above us. The stars faded. The morning of April 17 slowly replaced the darkness of the night.

After reporting back to the chief, our own Panzer was handed over to the repair company. In the meantime we were to take over Kuhlmann's Panzer and be ready for action, together with Hellwig, with the left-most regiment of the division. The main front line was to be moved back to the positions at the Hardenberg hills. The end to our forward positions had come. It was possible that we would be able to hold the Hardenberg positions, which were stretching across the more easily defended heights along the Oder plains.

Just after dawn we reached the wooded area, marked on the map and situated on a hill approximately one kilometer from the regimental command post. It was located in a farm and to the right of the road running from Falkenhagen to Lebus.

Approximately 300 meters from the woods Hellwig ran off his left track, as he started out from a gully, and sat immobilized until the evening.

The commanders were called by dispatch riders to the regimental command post at 9 A.M. for a briefing. For more than one hour we waited in vain for radio communication with the company.

We had barely reached our Panzer again when a tremendous barrage from the Russian batteries started. Shells rained into the woods to our left and right, in front and behind. Their explosions threw up mushrooms of smoke and dirt, which blocked out the sun; shrapnel smacked against the walls of the Panzer.

On the other side of the embankment, some three to four kilometers away, heavy traffic by tanks and columns could be seen. Our advanced artillery observer was only able to get a few salvos laid on them since the artillery in the sector and the ammunition were only to be used for confirmed enemy attacks. Fifteen-cm mortars hurled their heavy shells across with visible success, and for a long time after a bank of black smoke stood over the blowing veils of dust. At 5 P.M., alarm! All available Panzers were deployed to the far left sector of the division where the Russians were reported to have begun an attack with great masses of infantry and tanks. After a verbal briefing by the chief, we were to roll to the main road immediately, together with the remaining vehicles, and follow him.

While our Panzers were engaged in hard and bitter defensive fighting for each hedge, each trench, and each farm, the fields were once again covered with dead and wounded. Schaubinger and crew members from various vehicles were critically wounded by bombs from Russian planes. He died during the following night at the main dressing station.

During the same day we received our own Panzer back, ready for action. To reach the company before evening, we immediately started the drive back to the front.

In the town of Falkenhagen we stopped for a short while with Harlander whose vehicle was being repaired by our own repair company at a farm. The farmers very kindly and considerately offered us coffee and cake after we had cleaned up in their washhouse. Terrible lamenting set in when the local German command ordered the town immediately evacuated. Quite a few harsh and bitter words could be heard.

The avalanche continued its advance on April 19. While the German defensive lines held along the Oder on both sides of Frankfurt, the Russians moved into threatening proximity to the outer suburbs in the north near Oranienburg and to the east of Berlin. To the south, their strong tank forces penetrated deeply into Lusatio; the fighting there was particularly bitter. One more time the German soldier tried to hold off the advancing Russian masses.

In Berlin the rumor of a liberation army was being spread at this very time.

WITHDRAWAL MOVEMENT TO THE WEST

When we requested further orders from the Abteilung command post near Fürstenwalde, we were told soon after: "Immediately deploy the company to the north exit from Berkenbrück." We set out and reached the town after a fast drive of twenty kilometers past extensive dark woods of pine trees. The Panzers were supplied with fuel and ammunition from the remaining reserves of the supply company. There were no army supplies available at all in Elsbruch, which was located on the other side of the railroad embankment and some one and one-half kilometers north of the town.

After hours of work we had cleaned the 6.5-meter-long gun barrel of powder residue and oiled it, filled up with 800 liters of fuel, and stowed the 22-kilogram shells in the interior of the hull. Suddenly, the din of new fighting echoed across from Neuendorf and from Steinhöfel, in the middle of the woods. Panzer-grenadiers of "Großdeutschland" fought bitterly in the woods to hold on to a small bridgehead east of Fürstenwalde, which had already been entered by Russian tank forces twenty-four hours before.

Armored personnel carriers full of pale, bleeding, and moaning wounded rattled in a steady stream along the paths through the woods to the rear. At the edge of the woods the wounded were first given medical attention and then transported onward. Armored assault teams took on the Russians slowly advancing on the trails through the woods, while parts of our 1. and 3. Companies set out to face the Russian tanks on the road Demnitz-Steinhöfel. They had to pull back, however, since the enemy infantry constantly outflanked them. A four-barrel antiaircraft gun was brought forward as a last resort, but it soon took a direct hit from a Pak. The guns of our antiaircraft platoon were mounted on heavy tractors and were just too visible in the open terrain. All our Panzers, except our own which was still ready for action, had suffered damage to the tracks, engines, or guns and were sent to the repair company at Saarow. The commander walked from Panzer to Panzer, deep in anxious thought and with knitted brow, reissued well-known directives, and asked about this or that.

An order had been issued for the bridgehead to be defended under all circumstances until midnight of the following day to keep the highway Frankfurt–Berlin open for the masses of troops flooding back. The responsibility and concern for more than 1,000 men and the priceless Panzers rested heavily on the commander's shoulders.

Shortly after the fall of darkness, all available Panzers of the Abteilung were again moved and thrown against a Russian tank attack between Steinhöfel and Demnitz. It was repelled after fifteen enemy tanks were knocked out. Cold and moist veils of fog hung over the wet fields. They were later blown away by a rising wind. We pulled our heavy overcoats tightly around us, shivering, and put our heads down as soon as the din of fighting stopped for a while to grab an eyeful of sleep. A reconnaissance patrol from the Abteilung in a Volkswagen demanded immediate action at the railroad embankment to Ketschendorf since some enemy tanks were reported advancing from the town of Fürsten-walde. Violent MG fire rained on the embankment and into the German positions from the long buildings of the army supply camp and its many-storied warehouses. We could still make out the German MGs in the racing whirl of fire. Deafening explosions of heavy mortar shells and the thumping noise of the hand grenades increased the din of the fighting. Our most advanced line had to be over there; there also had to be an elevated spot from where we could observe while the Panzer would follow the VW driver to the road.

In long jumps we raced down the right side of the road past a 5-cm Pak, across the embankment which was under fire and a plowed field. The bullets whistled by us. We dropped into a shallow depression between the embankment and the field to get out of the strings of fire from the enemy machine guns. The roar of heavy tank engines could be heard from a group of bushes near the road, barely fifty meters away. Occasionally, the black bodies of the monsters could be spotted by the flashes of firing guns. Rifles and MGs constantly hammered from hedges and bushes. We looked across the edge of our ditch for a second. The closest Ivans were only thirty meters away, and we could sometimes hear their hoarse shouting. The most advanced MG positions had been abandoned. We had to move it if we did not want to get involved in hand-to-hand combat, which was not part of our mission.

So, back along the same route, we fumbled our way across the trenches and the embankment to the road, raced by car toward the Panzer, got in, and pulled up to the edge of the woods.

A heavy enemy tank rolled toward us along a tree-lined road on the left. It was stopped by our first shell at 400 meters in a blue-red flash of flame. Black, oily smoke welled up from the interior while its ammunition blew up like fireworks to one side. After a third antitank shell a flash of flame rose up straight into the blue night sky from a second Soviet tank and the black cloud remained sitting over the land for hours just outside the city. A third tank burned brightly less than 300 meters away, giving off black smoke. Its glowing steel walls blew apart with a hissing and cracking noise, the burning fuel setting the nearby hedges on fire. Steel fragments were hurled through the air all around. Minutes later our own hatch lid was blown off by a hit. The angled mirrors were in pieces, but no one on the inside was injured by fragments. An infantry lieutenant again requested Panzer action in his sector of the trenches.

Together with Rodinger, we tried to determine just how far the threat to our left flank had advanced. Without a sound we crept through the undergrowth between the tree trunks to the railroad embankment where two infantrymen were dug in at the slope, all by themselves.

Starting at midnight, only some six hours from then, the bulge in the German front north of the Spree river would have served its purpose to secure the highway for the withdrawal of the 9. German Army to the south and would be evacuated.

The major highway bridge twelve kilometers east of Fürstenwalde was to be blown up by German pioneers at three o'clock in the early morning. By then, all vehicles were to have been withdrawn across the Spree River.

Outside of town Russian fighter aircraft roared above us. These IL-2 ground-attack aircraft were terrible machines. They looked like fire-spitting balls thrown at the earth by the sun when they dove on us in formation. The dirt clouds from the exploding bombs stood above the woods. We rolled off the road and, crushing telegraph posts and hedges, found cover in the woods. On the other side of the bridge, along both sides of the highway, all our tractors and recovery tanks were ready to tow any damaged Panzer across the bridge during the course of the night. We were soon sent to the repair company at Bad Saarow to have some damage repaired.

Artillery salvos were already howling across overhead; some of them exploded on the concrete surface of the highway. During the same night our repair team at Ketschendorf took a direct hit from a shell, which critically wounded Wiefel, Seckes, Marx, and Roth. Just before sunrise we reached Bad Saarow at the northern tip of Lake Scharmützel, a popular destination for Berlin excursionists. Military police collected the thousands of stragglers there and directed them to the closest assembly point. The roads were filled with agitated people, among whom the soldiers moved on toward the west. The end had become obvious everywhere. Terror and despair were written in the faces of the women, old men, and children.

For the first time in days we met Schmidt, the leader of the staff Panzers, again at the western exit of the resort town. We were greeted with joyful shouts of welcome by our comrades, who found themselves together with the men of the staff Panzers in a house close to the road. Then the door opened, and our Panzer guard led Schroif, the I. orderly officer of the Abteilung, inside the room. All mobile Panzers were ordered to immediately move to the Ketschendorf area north of the highway. An attack at dawn was to throw the Russians crossing the Spree River back to its north shore. The Tigers had to be ready in time. Within a few minutes all commanders had left.

Outside, the heavy engines roared, and the black monsters rolled from the woods onto the road. The lake glittered like silver in the light of the moon. From a distance the never-ending rumble of the front could be heard in a wide arc from the east to the north and toward the west near Berlin.

The ribbon of the road became visible again in the light of dawn. It followed the lakeshore in the direction of Storkow. Before we could move on, we had to take on a supply of gasoline. By way of Reichenwalde, along the northern shore of Lake Storkow, we rolled to the northern outskirts of Storkow. Stragglers and wounded soldiers piled up again at the major crossroads. Depending on their division, they were directed into this street or that and then transported onwards. The surrounding woods were filled with columns of cars, supply units, staffs, and medical units, which already incorporated fleeing girls and women.

Around 5 A.M. we drove on the road toward Prieros, as the rear Panzer. Within the town's farms and narrow lanes, army supply vehicles were already being turned over to the populace.

Equipped with sacks, baskets, bags, and handcarts, young and old strained to carry off their treasures of soap, canned goods, chocolate, and crisp bread. The ground was covered with pages of directives, pamphlets, and secret files. The soldiers, amazement showing in their eyes, put some of the goods in their mouths and some in their pockets as they listened to the guns in the distance and continued running through the village. They followed the road to the west, which had been churned up by wheels and tracks, by columns of trucks and towing vehicles. The beaten army moved in the direction of Königswusterhausen-Luckenwalde-Magdeburg.

The immense woods behind Prieros seemed to absorb the endless stream of the fleeing and the traffic of columns from the armed forces flooding back. The two- or three-fold ribbons of vehicles passing or bumping into each other continued from morning to evening, even into the night. At the edge of the woods, immediately behind the wooden bridge across the Dahme River and surrounded by large lakes, our repair company had been working since the early hours of the morning to fix damaged Panzers as quickly as possible. They were all supposed to be ready for action by evening. An attack by bombers during the evening did not damage the bridge, but explosions, only 10 meters away from our Panzer, in the surrounding houses turned walls and apartments into huge piles of rubble. Right at the lakeshore the craters were large enough for a farmer's cabin and its roof to find room inside. We dug through the ruins for a long time in the hope of hearing signs of life from those possibly buried alive. But we did not find anything.

On the road from Prieros to Königswusterhausen, the steady stream of vehicles, assault guns, radio cars, tractors pulling guns or trucks, and Panzers, intermingled with ambulances, supply and ammunition units, horse-drawn carts, and self-propelled guns, flooded across the bridge into the thick woods in a westerly direction. In among them were people—hundreds, thousands, some of them with horses and carts, others with bicycles or handcarts, wheelbarrows, prams—on their way to anywhere in the west, just as long as it was away from the Russians.

Since the narrow corridor was broken by a Russian tank wedge during the night, the stream moved back along the other side of the road in the hope of being able to get through somewhere else.

Leaflets were dropped on Berlin: "The Wenck Army is on its way and will bring you liberty and victory." And the Berliners, as well as the soldiers, believed once again.

After reporting to the chief at the regimental command post, we were to advance immediately into the left sector of the division to support Kuhnke. However, by the time we had been briefed on the map, a radio message had arrived making our action unnecessary. A significant proportion of our Panzers was under repair because of damage from hits or other mechanical problems so that those still at the front were in constant action. Even before midnight, Walter came to the front with our daily rations. He told us of his daring escape, after English troops had marched into Paderborn, through central Germany to the Eastern Front. Walter was in charge of a remaining team of the Abteilung in Hövelhof at the supply depot. He brought us the last letters and greetings. Most of us had been without news from our families for three months. The mail we wrote was taken out, but replies were no longer received.

To escape the deadly encirclement, which was threatening at any time, in the left rear of the division, the army ordered the withdrawal of our Kurmark Division during the night of April 19 to 20 to a position behind the main road Fürstenwalde-Frankfurt, next to the regiment holding the sector on the right and along the front line at the Oder.

Until then, this valiant division had succeeded, in holding the beleaguered line since April 16, despite the immense thrust of Soviet soldiers and materiel, and allowed only minor breakthroughs. Since the Russians had broken through near Küstrin and Seelow in the north, masses of Red Army tanks and infantrymen flooded through this gap into the open country and threatened the German Panzerkorps at the Oder with a deadly encirclement. First, huge supplies of weapons and materiel fell into the hands of the victors, and, while we were embroiled in chaos, the way to Berlin was open to the Red divisions.

Throughout the night our troops withdrew to the rear into the positions as ordered. Our Panzers remained in front of the regimental command post as regimental reserves until 5 A.M. Thick fog still covered the dark fields, and the outlines of our withdrawing infantry could barely be seen in the milky-white gray.

Our Panzers were ordered to begin withdrawing so that before dawn they would be out of sight of the enemy and the withdrawal movement could be completed. We rolled along the road to Frankfurt by way of Falkenhagen back toward the east, pulled off to the right into deep woods, and held ourselves available to the division. By the time supplies were issued, the weapons cleaned, and contact established with the divisional command post, the sun was long shining brightly from the cloudless sky of April 20. The German Supreme Command of the Army sent its own last combat reserves from Zossen into action; 250 men against hundreds of Russian tanks and aircraft. This was the most dangerous thrust on Berlin at that time; 400 tanks approached from the south. There were no further reserves available.

Our work done, we tried to get a couple of hours of sleep. We were so terribly tired. We had been on our feet, almost without a break, since April 16 and were existing only by using our bodies' last reserves. In the early afternoon a radio message arrived from the Panzerkorps directing the immediate deployment of the company into the area east of Fürstenwalde to await orders from the Abteilung there. We set out immediately. Even as we rolled through Falkenhagen in a westerly direction, Russian batteries opened a fierce bombardment on the town. Soldiers and columns of vehicles moved along the country road Wilmersdorf-Falkenhagen. The floods of vehicles piled up at the tank barricades at the exits of the town. It was a mixture of excited men with horses and carts, cursing soldiers, and helplessly crying mothers yelling at each other. We got out and tried to untangle the mess, a difficult job, by either using threats or common sense.

Just before Fürstenwalde we pulled our three combat-ready fighting vehicles off the road to the left and right into woods of firs. We set up the company command post in a cabin at the railroad line Frankfurt-Fürstenwalde-Berlin. The two-tracked line had been blown up by our pioneers at many different spots a few hours before, an action that made it useless for weeks to come.

We met with comrades from the other Panzers in the living room of the cabin, which was lit only by a flickering oil lamp. We had so much to tell each other about the experiences of recent days. It calmed us wonderfully to know that our comrades understood us and empathized with us.

It had turned completely dark outside. Unnoticed, but quickly, the time was approaching midnight when there was a loud shout from the sentry outside.

Almost immediately, the chief of the 2. Company, Kurt Neu, who had been led through the dark by a sentry, entered the light of the warm, smoky room. With a few short words he told us that he had just returned from the Abteilung command post where the immediate action of our Panzers in the Heinersdorf sector had been demanded. Guides from the staff company were waiting at the road ahead, asking us to speed it up. While we said good-bye to our comrades, we stuffed our pockets full of cookies and chocolate, pushed dozens of ration packs into our leather coats, and ran, wine bottles pressed under the arm, up the path through the woods. Quickly, we climbed up the front, up the gun barrel into the turret, and slipped on headsets and microphones. With the engine roaring, the wide tracks ground their way from the path in the woods onto the road and into the black night. After the fork in the road near the mill at Demnitz, there was noticeably less traffic under way. Our defensive lines along the southern flanks of the Russian tank armies advancing on Berlin were barely ten kilometers to the north. There was a lengthy delay at the antitank barricades at the exits from Demnitz. The drivers of vehicles and of horse-drawn carts all fought, with much cursing, to get through first. The road to Steinhöfel was completely empty. We passed the castle and the estate, the few houses of the farm workers, and then stood, perplexed, at the northern fork in the road to Heinersdorf. Even our guide from the Abteilung in his Kubelwagen was lost in the dark. We had just gotten out to look for the way on the map in the light of our flashlight when Kalls, the chief of 1. Company who was returning from Heinersdorf, arrived and directed us to the castle where we were to stand by for further orders. By the time the Panzer was positioned under the wide branches of chestnut trees along the driveway, and the sentries posted, it was three o'clock in the morning. We finally lay down inside the Panzer to sleep until dawn.

After barely half an hour of sleep, we were shaken awake. A dispatch rider stood outside. We were to report to the chief immediately. We climbed up the wide outside staircase and walked down corridors and stairs to the cellar built of massive stone, where, in the flickering light of candles, our command post was set up.

It was terribly cold down there. The commander was bent over a map as we reported in. He looked up and motioned us over to the map, which was covered with red and blue arrows. Since the Russians had attacked toward the south from the areas of Marxdorf and Müncheberg, by way of Heinersdorf, and an unbroken line of defense no longer existed, we had to expect enemy tanks to show up in town at any time. Staff Panzers and a few Tigers of the 3. Company sat in firing positions one kilometer southwest of Heinersdorf. Some of these positions were given up the previous night after all shells had been fired. Our Panzer was to go into a firing position immediately, just outside the northern edge of Steinhöfen, 500 meters east of the Tempelhof woods.

Around six in the morning, the fog began to lift. A Panzer came roaring up on the road to Heinersdorf and stopped alongside. The order from the chief: "Follow it immediately with your own Panzer in the direction of Heinersdorf."

Two heavy buses with trailers of the Berlin transit commission sat along the road to Heinersdorf; one was burnt-out, the other driven into the ditch. After a drive of half an hour we reached the position as ordered by Schroif and were directed by Rodinger, who had been awaiting us, to a spot 300 meters left of the road, between Tempelhof and Heinersdorf, and facing in the direction of Müncheberg. Next to us, a brown-uniformed Volkssturm company, which had made its way through the Russian lines during the previous night under cover of darkness near Müncheberg, set up its makeshift line of defense. They were mostly older men, digging their foxholes in the wet earth next to our vehicle. Untrained and poorly equipped they were to be easy prey for the Russians. Just before ten o'clock we were ordered by radio to move to the hill of the Heinersdorf mill southwest of the village. Hellwig had sustained damage to his gun and had to be replaced immediately. Swinging wide to the rear, we drove onto the road where Schroif was waving at us, laughing. His own Panzer sat, badly damaged and abandoned, at the back slope to the left of the road outside the town where he had stopped all enemy attacks. We rolled slowly up the hill and reported to the chief for a verbal briefing. We urgently requested a supply of fuel soon, since a certain reserve had to be available for each vehicle because of the constant withdrawals.

We set up our firing position on the rear slope of the hill, which towered over the village, some 200 meters from the Heinersdorf mill. Our view to the east was open and unrestricted across many kilometers to Litzen Forsten. To the right we could see Marxdorf and Falkenhagen and all the way to Arensdorf to the south. From the wooded hills to the east came a steady stream of horse-drawn vehicles pulling guns of the Russian divisions, followed by large columns of tanks. Next to them, past Heinersdorf and by way of Müncheberg in the direction of Berlin, Russian infantry regiments were on the march. Entire divisions of the Red Army marched, before our eyes, toward the west into our rear. That obviously meant our defeat. What was to happen then?

We could have predicted what was to come at us next. Russian mortars and batteries laid fire ever closer to the crests of the hills. The enemy shells over there rose into the air like heavy fishes, flipped over, and tumbled into the clayish ground, exploding to our left and right, in front of us and behind, causing streams of chunks of earth to hurtle through the air, and throwing up dark columns of dirt. The ground began to boil and shake, and the trembling caused our vehicle to vibrate gently. The sky sunk onto the hills with smoke and thunder. It turned dark around us. Shrapnel and fragments ricocheted whistling and humming off the steel walls. We had closed all hatches tightly and moved the vehicle backward 100 meters down the slope as it had become impossible to see anything. The top of the hill continued to be the center of flaming explosions and more than half an hour went by before the defensive enemy fire ended. Slowly, we drove our tank forward again into firing position. The enemy targets over there were clearly visible in the light of the sun, tempting and close enough to almost touch. Unconcerned with previous experiences, the Russians assembled behind a wooden shed and the batteries sat in the open fields.

And again, our shells hissed into the enemy troops, among the burning vehicles. The Russian advance, visible from our position, stalled. A few minutes later, however, further enemy artillery barrages enveloped the heights of the Heinersdorf mill. Their explosions danced across the slopes like will-o'-the-wisps. The blue powder smoke drifted slowly past the mill toward the road where other Panzers of the Abteilung were engaged in a heavy firefight with Russian Paks.

At 2 P.M. an order arrived from the chief by radio: "Discontinue the engagement. Report to me!" The Abteilung command post had ordered immediate action by our Panzers at the western edge of Steinhöfel in the direction of Neuendorf. We drove around the partly marshy pastures arid fields to the south of the Heinersdorf mill and reached Steinhöfel by the road through Hasenwinkel.

We took up covering positions to the west of the Steinhöfel castle gardens against Russian tanks, which had been reported, our guns aimed toward Buchholz. The chief's vehicle sat in the sand off the road to Neuendorf. Shivering, we stood under the tarpaulin and peered at the woods, some 1,200 meters away, through our field glasses. The rain-soaked plains ahead of us lay abandoned. No humans could be seen. Again, we reminded the chief of the urgent need for fuel supplies. They were promised very soon.

Just before 4 P.M. a messenger from the Abteilung command post brought a verbal order to move the Tigers immediately to Hasenfelde and be available for antitank defense in that sector. At the command post the Panzers of Hellwig, Oberhuber, Kuhlemann, and Münster, who had followed us from the repair shops, joined us. Under cover of the large farms, we drove in the direction of the enemy and took up positions south of the town and the railroad station. To the east of the expansive village, our own infantry trenches, manned by weak Volkssturm companies, stretched across the hills near Heinersdorf and through flat terrain all the way to Arensdorf.

Over to the east the same activity as during the morning hours took place. Strong Russian tank and infantry forces, coming from Dolgelin, were on the march through the woods near Litzen toward Heinersdorf tank after tank, followed by foot soldiers and horse-drawn carts. Kurt Neu and Oberhuber opened fire on the widely scattered enemy columns. The brown masses ran back into the woods, up the hills, and into an outwork ahead of the hills.

Our explosive shells quickly followed, thrusting through the brick and wood walls, their violent explosions dispersing the masses of Russians who had sought cover behind it. Some 400 men raced back up the heights, together with their horses and carts, constantly pursued by the explosions from our explosive shells. Unbelievable, but true, there was not one single German artillery battery available anymore in the entire sector. It would have been much more successful in decidedly stopping the Russian advance on Berlin.

"Dislodge the enemy from the hills near the Heinersdorf mill!" was our next order. Until our own platoon was complete again, Kuhlemann and Oberhuber were attached to us. While Oberhuber stayed behind as a reserve, we drove together with Kuhlemann to the top of the hill into our old firing position of the morning, south of Heinersdorf. Without warning, and with bright explosions, our shells dropped among the enemy guns, self-propelled guns, trucks, and horse-drawn carts assembled in the valley. Within a few minutes, flames were bursting from the hit vehicles. The confusion and chaos over there increased with every shot. A messenger from our 3. Company, whose fighting vehicles stood at the road to Heinersdorf 300 meters north of us, urgently requested our help in towing away an immobilized Tiger. Otherwise it would have had to be blown up.

At the same time we received a radio message from the chief's Panzer, which did away with all our doubts of possibly offering assistance. It ordered the immediate return of all Panzers to a position south of Hasenfelde. Just before reaching the town a second message ordered us to set out toward Arensdorf. There was, at most, one hour left before dusk. At full speed the heavy Panzers rolled toward the nearby railroad station, following in the tracks of the Panzers ahead. A gap was left where we had been pulled out, and there, too, we would hardly be able to prevent the collapse. We used up almost all of our fuel during these trips from one sector to the other. The fact was that the thin lines of our worn-out infantry needed help everywhere. We only saw expressionless faces, without hope in their eyes, only despair, nothing else. There was no more room for questions; the only thing left was to fight.

We joined up with the company even before the entrance to the town.

Grenadiers of an SS-Kampfgruppe were defending Arensdorf against an overwhelmingly superior force. All they had left was their determination, their valor, and experience. Inside and outside of the village was the din of ripping metal and the thunder from the explosions of the Russian artillery shells. The regimental adjutant briefed us, and the loaders pushed antitank shells into the barrels. Noisily, we rolled through Arensdorf, past the regimental command post. Russian tanks were reported to have advanced to the edge of town, so we disappeared into the turret and the interior. Wooden beams, paving stones, and chunks of concrete rained down on the Panzers. Swinging to the left, we broke with our platoon, Oberhuber on our left and Hellwig to the right, through the gardens to the northeastern edge of town. Trees, walls, and wooden beams in our way splintered and broke under us. Neu took over the sector along the road to Falkenhagen, to the east of the village. A wave of hot air rushed at us, raced across our faces. Artillery, mortars, tanks, the whole machinery of hell raged all around us. It rolled across the German soldiers just outside of town who were crouched in their foxholes like mummies, wounded, unmoving, and shrunken in size. It passed the German positions like spirits from hell. The rattle of tracks, the iron din of the Russian tanks was close to the edge of town as we broke through walls and fences with the even greater thrust of our heavy Panzers, into the firing positions and sent our first antitank shells into the massive black bodies of the enemy tanks. Flashes of flames rising high into the sky showed the immense explosions in the light of the dying day. Showers of oil came down on our positions, whole turrets were whirled through the air by the force of the explosions, and tracks hurtled about through the bright flames. We had long since stopped counting our victories.

Completely surprised, the enemy tanks and assault guns retreated. They fought back desperately from under their heavy armored skins, until the deadly direct hits knocked them out.

But all hell also broke loose where we sat at the edge of town. Russian Paks, tanks, and artillery had spotted and located their dangerous enemy, and we experienced new heights of horror. Sky and earth stood still. We were afraid to breathe.

In wild haste the Russians sent their shells across the burning terrain into the ruins of the houses and the German Panzers next to them. But these Panzers that dared to repulse Stalin's attack so close to its objective, and to set fire to so many of the attacking armored vehicles, the Russians were not prepared for!

Without pause we hammered the heavy shells into the enemy positions. Once we took a heavy hit to the thick front armor plate. A weak flash sprang through the interior of the fighting vehicle and knocked us about. Chunks of walls dropped with loud bangs onto the roof of the turret. We were engaged in a merciless tank battle, which demanded all of our knowledge and instincts.

At a distance of 800 meters another one of our shells scored a direct hit on the dark body of an enemy tank, and seconds later it was enveloped in flames. We counted eleven blazing torches of knocked-out enemy tanks.

We worried about our empty fuel tank as night crept across the plains. Our lines had held, but for how much longer? Half of the Kampfgruppe had probably been lost. The burning tanks were still glowing among the ruins of the destroyed town.

A bloodied group of men crept from the ruined trenches back into the village. Oberhuber's vehicle provided cover to the right of us. There were a few quiet minutes in our sector, the noticeable restlessness before the gathering storm which was to come before long. Flares rose into the sky from everywhere in the Russian lines of attack encircling us. These stars bursting into the sky were the sign for us of a renewed Russian assault on the bitterly defended town of Arensdorf.

More and more salvos howled through the air and burst into the ruins, streets, and foxholes with immense explosions, an endlessly raging inferno of steel and iron ripping into the hard ground. Helplessly exposed to the invisible onslaught, one wanted to yell. Our insides trembled and shuddered, but not because the earth was shaking. No, death itself was holding us by the neck and shook us to and fro. We wanted to get out of this hell! No one spoke anymore as we listened to the outside through the closed hatches. Our antenna, hit by a shrapnel, was bent toward the ground. Explosions from heavy-caliber shells forced hot air into the interior of the vehicle.

If we would have had to bolt from there, it would have looked bleak for us because we would not have gone one kilometer on our remaining fuel. We had to have fuel, otherwise we would have been lost. Only after some urgent calls could we establish radio contact with the vehicle of the chief. We reported our present situation and requested an immediate supply of fuel. We ordered all Panzers to open fire with their guns and machine guns on the terrain in front of us where the Russians had already come very close to our positions. Our tracer salvos hammered into the forefield like strings of pearls, crossing the salvos of tracers from the other Panzers. Our explosive shells left our gun barrel with long tails of fire and raced into the darkness. Enemy discharges roared very close by. Our German positions outside the village lay silent, and no defense was put up from the trenches. Were they all dead in there or buried alive?

Our crews became nervous and restless from the never-ending hail of shells. Their radio messages came faster and faster. In addition, there was the pressing concern for the missing fuel. Hellwig reported damage to his gun and returned to the regimental command post on his own. Kuhlemann's Panzer no longer answered at all. What might have happened over there in the right sector?

With a terrible howl the shells whistled across above our heads. Forty concentrated guns to the east created a flaming comet's tail almost close enough to touch, and threw heavy shells into the village.

Next to our vehicle an infantryman crawled through the craters and the debris back to the village. Leaning far out of the turret we yelled at him: "Who is left at the front? Why are you no longer firing?" Our questions came one after the other. He stopped for a moment in his crawl to catch his breath and shouted, painfully: "Other than the dead and wounded there is no one left in the demolished trenches!" Then he continued his crawl through the garden. So we were all on our own. Those in front of us had finished suffering. With an urgent report on the situation to the regimental command post, we requested immediate close support by the infantry. It was impossible for a Panzer crew to make out enemy infantry in the dark, so we ordered fire from all weapons of the other fighting vehicles. Then we took a hit, which knocked out our turret MG. Red tracer salvos raced out into the open terrain, and the artillery fire into the village stopped completely.

In the left sector of the town hand grenades exploded in close combat. Not 100 meters away, Russian machine guns hammered their slow fire into our trenches, ricochets buzzed through the night. Then, yelling, animal-like howling, an advancing wave: Uraa, Uraa. They had to be close! We got our hand grenades and submachine guns ready. The noise of infantry fighting in the village grew louder. We broadcast a radio message to all that at any time Russians could be expected to attack our Panzers. Kuhlemann reported a critical hit by Pak. His tall blond radio operator from Memmingen was dead, the others severely injured. The crew abandoned the Panzer and fled to the regimental command post. The Panzer fell into the hands of the advancing Russians. We opened all hatches and readied submachine guns, flares, and hand grenades on the turret roof, ready for anything. Our headsets pushed back, we listened into the oppressive darkness. Oberhuber reported that the first Russians had broken into the village between the house ruins. It was high time to retreat to the center of the town before the vehicle was blown up. Right away, we established radio contact with the chief's vehicle and demanded an immediate decision. Oberhuber was ordered to withdraw behind the antitank barricade.

Our radio operator hammered short bursts from his MG into the darkness. To our left and right we spotted movement, disappearing again into the dark after a quick burst from our submachine guns. The Russians bypassed our Panzer without further action. Slowly, their battle cries died away behind us in the village. Full of suspicion, leaning far out of the turret, we listened to the fading shouts and yells. Had they forgotten us? We were helpless in the darkness.

Finally, after terribly long minutes, we received the answer from the regimental command post: "Withdraw and report at the regimental command post with the other Panzers immediately!"

So, withdrawal in stages. When we were in the village street, we passed the order on to the others but only Oberhuber and Müster acknowledged.

Start the engine, backward march! Our driver pushed the starter button. With the engine howling wildly the Panzer rolled out of the garden. Suddenly, the engine died. A few more powerless revolutions, but the engine remained still.

There was no doubt, the fuel tanks were completely empty, at a moment of greatest intensity and decision on life or death! While our loader bailed out to get a few liters of fuel from the regimental command post, we sent an emergency message to all requesting immediate help. Oberhuber reported being in the village street at the barricade already. We lay on the back of our vehicle, our pistols in our right hands, and unscrewed the fuel tank cap in preparation. Time went by terribly slowly. Would he make it, or was it too late? That would mean the bitter end for all.

Panting under the heavy burden, our loader came running out of the dark and threw two jerrycans of twenty liters each onto the rear. The fuel ran gurgling into the empty tanks as the loader shouted his report that the Russians had pushed already into the northern part of the village and had cut off most of our route of withdrawal there. All scattered units of the regiment and the wounded were to assemble immediately at the regimental command post east of the railroad station. The fuel came from Rodinger who had driven out in his Volkswagen half an hour before. There were no other reserves of fuel. But then our engine sang its old melody. Rolling backward along a parallel route, we reached the town center and made our way through craters and across debris to the command post.

"Assemble immediately at the road fork in front of the command post! Attention! The village has been captured by the Russians!" Our operator radioed to all vehicles. The large farm building behind the road fork, where our command post was located, was dimly lit by the fires all around. Leaning against its walls and in the ditch lay the last surviving wounded infantrymen who had escaped hell. In the wide yard some twenty Volkswagens and Schwimmwagens sat next to the Panzer of the chief, awaiting departure. Oberhuber was still missing. All the other Panzers took up covering positions along the main street of the village. Our commander bailed out and reported to the chief at the command post, which was inside a cellar at ground level. The officers stood around the regimental commander, all obviously waiting for a report. While the last actions of the battle were taking place in quick succession outside, the company chiefs and officers nervously smoked their cigarettes.

The cellar echoed with heavy explosions every few seconds. This was the rhythm that would command the future.

Our question as to what would happen next was answered with a shrug. If we could not find any more jerrycans, we would have to blow up the vehicle after the next 500 meters. On orders of the commander, the adjutant, Willy Winkelmann, came out into the yard with us and ordered all drivers to immediately hand over to us all jerrycans.

Then we crawled with Rodinger, dragging the cans behind us, across the path that was under fire, to our vehicle. Despite the fact that we were convinced the order could not be carried out, Oberhuber was to drive to the old position with his vehicle and somehow destroy Kuhlemann's Panzer. But it was much too late for that.

It was completely clear to us that we would attempt to break out in our own vehicle, even if it was on our own responsibility.

It was after midnight. The last fires from the houses and German vehicles still glowed with a red shine in the east and north. Long columns of Russian soldiers stumbled through the night in front of the fires and disappeared as they had shown up. Our concern was only how to get out of the encircling ring. Oberhuber came back because the road on which Kuhlemann's Panzer sat was already swarming with Russians. From the direction of Falkenhagen, Russian tanks rattled and roared on their way toward us. The wind carried the noises through the mild night as if they were only 100 meters away. Suddenly, Russian machine guns barked again in the northern sector of town. Red-glowing bullets buzzed across the path and ricocheted off the walls and rocks. Shouting hoarsely, the Russians tramped through the houses. There was nothing we could do for we had to save ammunition. We had already fired all our MG ammunition, and we would only use explosive shells on definite targets. From the other side of the ruins, the battlefield of the evening, the flaming and howling comet's tails of the Russian rocket launcher salvos again climbed into the sky. We dropped down next to the wall immediately, and, as we gripped the earth with our fingers and fought for breath, huge mushrooms of smoke and dirt grew all around us. The ground shook to its very foundation; rocks and chunks of dirt hit the hard earth during the breathless silence. They had mounted the disgusting guns on their tanks and brought them close to the village under cover of darkness.

The officers finally stepped into the yard from the lit command post. We were to move out. The Kampfgruppe, our Tiger at the point, was to push across the embankment to the left of the railroad station toward Wilmersdorf. We were to open fire only in the most urgent cases. Our wounded and the stragglers stomped into the yard and climbed onto the Panzers. They were the remains of the German soldiers, the front line.

We took the point of the wedge, which was to break through during that night. Behind us were three armored reconnaissance vehicles and a long column of Schwimmwagens. Our Tigers, again, formed the last group. Our path took us across breaking trees, falling walls—even a barn was run over—into the open terrain to the east of the railroad station.

Then our column disappeared into the cover of the woods. As a reaction to the inhuman tension and concentration of all one's powers, the soothing feeling of regained freedom and safety caused a sudden collapse of the body's strength. We could have fallen asleep just where we stood. During a lengthy halt outside Wilmersdorf, Rodinger distributed the daily rations to the crews. There were cookies, chocolate, cold food, and schnapps. It was 3 A.M. on April 23 when the column stopped in the main street of the village. All the infantrymen we had brought along were collected there and taken to newly built and fortified positions. Poor souls!

After the last major briefing on the situation at the Führer headquarters in Berlin, attended by the representatives of the state, party, and army, Hitler admitted defeat for the first time. While Russian shells exploded in the streets of Berlin, Generalfeldmarschall Kesselring was given the supreme command, and the responsibility for all government affairs in the southern part of the Reich. Großadmiral Dönitz received similar powers, applicable for northern Germany. Hitler wanted to stay in Berlin. Only a few people knew what was the real situation facing our fatherland at that hour.

The reports of the quick downturn in our situation spread through the woods and the withdrawing columns like wildfire.

Our 9. Army under General Busse had again urgently requested, in a radio message to the Führer headquarters, permission to withdraw toward Berlin in a northwesterly direction. The army had been encircled by Russian troops for days and was without any supply possibilities. It was being fiercely attacked from the rear and threatened with destruction.

Hitler, however, refused this request from the commander of the army for the second time. The morale of the troops dropped to zero. It was the same picture everywhere. Many of the old Volkssturm, poorly armed, trained, and equipped, convinced of the absurdity of further fighting, left their positions, often before even weak assaults, and returned to their wives and children in the cellars of their houses. The Hitler youths, on the other hand, these fourteen-, fifteen-, and sixteen-year-old boys, fought everywhere with the same recklessness the best German soldiers had shown during the daring campaigns of this war. Mobile tank hunter teams, together with brave soldiers, achieved great successes, chasing down and destroying a significant number of Russian tanks that had broken through. Many of the brave boys showed great heroism in the battle for their homeland. The troops themselves, what few were left, also fought bravely but suffered from a shortage of weapons and ammunition. The worst, however, was the lack of able-bodied soldiers in the defensive positions, which became more noticeable by the hour. Irrational and contradictory orders confused the situation of the individual units, right down to the company in its position. Only very few of us got any rest that night. The alarm messages constantly jolted the men in the woods awake.

In the early hours of April 24 or 25—we did not know exactly since the concept of a calendar day, even of time itself, had become irrelevant—we only barely heard the rumble of the front. On this day, too, the Russian avalanche continued to roll into the heart of Germany.

Long since without contact with our neighboring corps, the army, then being attacked from all sides, stood far behind the Russian front lines. The defensive fighting became increasingly bitter. The commander ordered all Panzers that were still ready for action to form their own Kampfgruppe under the command of Klust and move north of Prieros to reinforce the defensive sector there. The five fighting vehicles set out immediately on the road in the direction of Storkow by way of Prieros, then to the left through sparse pine woods, and set up camouflaged positions at the edge of a moor. According to reports received by radio, Russian tanks attacking from the north had pushed into Wolzig and were seriously threatening our Panzers, in position outside of Storkow, from the rear. Thorough reconnaissance and reports from our soldiers indicated vastly superior tank forces, assault guns, and Pak positions. In addition, we faced the disadvantage of the broken, uneven, terrain that rose slowly toward the town occupied by the enemy.

Our Panzers were immediately redeployed to the other side of the bridge near Prieros. During the morning it was readied by a pioneer demolition team to be blown up at the first sign of approaching Russian tanks. Our infantry reported Russian tanks approaching from the north, from Wolzig, along the Dahme River toward the town.

While only few of our soldiers marched on the road to the west, we set up defensive positions against the reported enemy forces on the eastern river bank at the edge of the village.

The hallways and cellars of the houses were full of desperate women, innocent children, old men, and despondent soldiers, awaiting the impending arrival of the Russian infantry. A terrible, endless stream of refugees from the east had already moved through, telling of atrocities against defenseless German women, of murder, pillage, robbery, and rape. Unbelievable misery and horrible destitution moved into these cities as the German troops withdrew. The people did not beg us to hold on. The defeat and dissolution of the German Army had become inevitable and obvious to everyone. But their dejected eyes asked what horror the coming hours would bring.

Then, our soldiers reported Russians crossing the northern branch of the river westward in rowboats they had found. We sat at the center of the bridge and swung the turret over the railing, sending explosive shells among the boats. The explosions threw columns of water high into the air. Our bridge trembled every time a shell was fired. Two of the boats sank, the others disappeared under some willows hanging over the river-bank.

We had to get back. At any moment, the Russian tanks that had been reported could have broken out of the woods and opened fire on our Tiger, which sat on the elevated wooden bridge.

As we rolled off the bridge, the order to withdraw from the eastern bank came over the radio. All Panzers were to be withdrawn immediately and assembled in the woods to the south. An order of the previous day from the army stated that all units had to blow up their vehicles, except for the fighting vehicles, regardless of their loads or use. This was based on the fact that no more supplies of fuel could be expected. The only other exceptions were the field kitchens and ambulances, which were indispensable. The remaining fuel was to be collected from the tanks of the vehicles and made available to the Panzers.

The road was lonely and abandoned. The masses that had moved along the ribbon of the road to the west not long before had fled into the woods near Zossen and Königswusterhausen. The road itself became the battleground.

The ring of the encirclement was tightened more and more by the incessant attacks of the Russian infantry and tank forces. In the east, west, and south, our soldiers withdrew in quick succession to supposed lines of resistance. The complete destruction of our division could have only been a matter of days. The end was as certain as night follows day.

While the main body of our 9. Army held the Oder front line near Frankfurt, and despite the fact that the Russians had advanced well over 100 kilometers behind us, Hitler had rejected any suggestion to withdraw the Army to Berlin for the defense of the capital of the Reich. And then, there was the lack of fuel, the lack of almost everything we needed.

Finally, Klust radioed the order to move our vehicles immediately into the woods located south between Prieros and Märkisch-Buchholz. There was a general sigh of relief as the engines began to roar and the Panzers rolled, in file, from the road to the center of the woods.

Our driver shifted gears as always to catch up with the Panzer ahead. Then, a knock from the gearbox, and we stopped. Transmission damage! We were able to continue using the emergency transmission—available gears were one to four—at walking speed. But at least we were still moving.

Near the stone bridge, which was almost destroyed by bombs, across the Seenge River, we got onto the paved road leading to Märkisch-Buchholz, but left it again after only two kilometers and turned onto a path through the woods. We were constantly trying to establish radio contact with the company in order to get information on its position. But every time you needed such contact, an order for radio silence, was in effect or something else prevented it.

In one wooded area after the other, we asked our way to the Abteilung. As soon as we caught up, the repair team of our company began working on the damaged transmission. We were terribly tired and worn out but could not sleep. Not only were there the hammering of the work at the front of the hull between the driver and the radio operator and the bright flash lights and the interior lights, but we were also tortured by the concern and sorrow about everything that was going on all around us. Fortunately, we were held by the unbreakable bond of comradeship, hardened in battle and need, the ribbon of spiritual harmony.

Hitler ordered an attack for April 25 by Army Wenck, which was assembling on the east bank of the Elbe River, south of Magdeburg, in the direction of Potsdam to relieve Berlin. On April 27, one more time, the Germans broke through the Russian encirclement, which was moving in from the south to the area west of Berlin.

But this German attack petered out after joining up with the Reimann Corps. Of the nine divisions of the 12. Army, six existed only on paper. Only three divisions (one corps) were ever set up, and these divisions were poorly equipped and armed. The front north of Berlin and south of Stettin, in the sector of the 3. German Army, had virtually collapsed, according to a radio message on April 25. A relief attack by the army under the command of General von Manteuffel from the Oranienburg area also collapsed after an initial success of two kilometers was achieved under the leadership of SS-General Steiner.

Münster, Hellwig, and Mahler, whose fighting vehicles had assembled with us in the meantime, were to refuel and get ready for action. The fuel reserves, which had been brought in barrels, were not enough to fill the tanks of any of the Panzers, and further reserves were not available anywhere. What was to happen? Our salvage team had towed in the immobilized vehicles during the night. Those not in battle-ready condition were to be blown up. Schmidt's command vehicle had already been blown up the previous evening during the withdrawal from Storkow.

None of us could hide his nervous anxiety anymore in the face of our uncertain fate in the threatening destruction.

Meanwhile, the rest of the company assembled on the path in the woods. Comrades joined by despair and battles got on the small tractor and the field kitchen. For many, this was to be good-bye forever. We could only look with sorrow and anxiety on the adventure that was to take us through the Russian lines for 100 kilometers. First came a private from the Panzer-division, then Kuhlemann. Both wanted to ride with us in the Panzer. We did not want to refuse them but could not let them obstruct us in the fighting compartment. So they crawled under the gun. Then, hell broke loose. As the masses of vehicles and soldiers assembled all around in the woods, the Russians opened harassing fire from their mortars. We switched our radio to receive mode. It was probably just before 7 A.M. when the commanders were ordered to the Panzer of the chief by a messenger. Waiting for the next explosion, we ran forward and climbed into Neu's Panzer. We had to wait for Kuhnke, who dropped through the loader's hatch a few minutes later. Then we stood around the gun and studied the map, which was spread out and lit by the ceiling lamp.

After the long-delayed order for our army to fight its way to the Wenck Army had been issued on April 27, an order arrived for all encircled troops to break out that night, past Berlin to the south and through the province of Mark Brandenburg.

With our Panzers at the point, we were to push to the right of Märkisch-Buchholz, right through the woods toward Halbe. After Halbe we were to reach the highway Cottbus-Berlin and to break through, in the general direction to between Baruth and Zossen, under cover of the vast woods until we had reached the Wenck Army, which was stretched from Potsdam to Magdeburg. Assembly was to be in fifteen minutes at the latest. Time check: 6:50 A.M.

Infantrymen from the officer cadet regiment of the Kurmark Division were to ride on the Panzers of the company as support. The attacking column was not to stop for anything. Any resistance was to be broken with all available means. The continuity of the advance had to be ensured. We were in the point platoon. All of us appreciated the difficulty of our mission: to break into the Russian lines with the point platoon, to face such a superior, prepared and concentrated enemy defense. Never before did Panzer commanders have to carry out such a mission. Never during the previous years had the lives of thousands of soldiers and civilians depended on the action of so few Panzers!

As we jumped off Neu's Panzer, a salvo of shells exploded among the Panzers at the point. We briefed the other commanders with a few words on the situation, demanding the greatest vigilance and keeping up with the Panzer ahead under any circumstances. Other instructions were to be sent by radio.

Behind us we heard the stomping of thousands of boots. The soldiers moved through the woods into the assembly areas. Quickly, we slipped on the headsets and microphones. The driver started the engine. Swaying, the Panzer started on its way forward. The woods echoed with the noise from all the Panzer engines. More and more soldiers streamed out of the woods by the thousands and stood around our assembled vehicles. The last orders and directives were issued. Generals and colonels tried to bring order into the rows of the assembled divisions. The young sergeants of the Kurmark Division, with whom we had been in action on April 16 at the Oder, climbed onto our Panzers in groups. All conversation centered on the impending breakout. Would we get through, and how?

Just before 11 A.M. on April 27,we were ordered to the chief, who briefed us on the combat sector that ran along the road. It was imperative that the edges of the woods were held, mostly by the infantry, until evening. There was a possibility of tank attacks. Radio frequencies that would be used were confirmed. We were to be part of the 2. Platoon, initially as reserves. The 1. Platoon, ahead of us, was to be lead by Kuhnke. We returned to the tanks and backed them off the road into the woods. One-hundred meters deeper in the beech wood, the Russians lay in their foxholes behind the road whose asphalt surface showed through between the glades and rows of bushes. Ten minutes might have passed when we received a jolt and cowered down into the cupola. During the next minutes one salvo after the other hit the earth near us and shook it.

We slammed the hatches closed as all around us it rumbled and thundered. For minutes, the ground of the path boiled and trembled. Dark columns of dirt and smoke rose into the sky. We were crouched at the visors in the interior of the Panzer, observing to all sides. The vehicle shook as did the ground below. The biting odor of sulfur was forced into the Panzer from the outside.

That day was supposed to be April 28. Men of an SS company assembled just after 3 A.M. behind the fighting vehicles for a counterattack. They then stormed with battle cries of "hurra" through the canopy formed by the treetops, pulling forward into battle with them all who fell behind or were doubtful of their own bravery.

The blue balls of smoke from hand grenades danced ahead of the attackers. The shouting of the advance was drowned out by the staccato of machine guns. Soon, many of them came staggering or crawling back along the path of the attack. Most were seriously wounded, filled only with hope and yearning for help from another human. Without rest, the doctors and medics worked, set splints, put on dressings, operated, and comforted. But what was to happen to the badly wounded who were left out there? It was unbearable even to think of them.

Rodinger brought hot food at 6 P.M. and said that we were to get going that night. One more time we filled ourselves with sweet rice pudding. Some hastily took last drags from their cigarettes. The engines still hummed in idle, full of force, and only a few seconds were left to the start of the attack.

The commander ordered us to line up. The time to attack had arrived. It was to decide the life and fate of tens of thousands of German men.

We set out. Slowly, our roaring giant climbed up to the road, halted for an instance, and then, its automatic weapons hammering, broke into the woods opposite. After the deep despair of destruction, a roar of relief came from the throats of the thousands and thousands, a shout affirming life, as the men stormed forward, next to each other and one row after another, into the Russian lines. Anything that resisted was destroyed, trampled, run over, wiped out.

One more time the critically wounded lifted their heads from the blood-soaked ground, looked at us with eyes growing dim, and then looked toward the sky, which began to fill with smoke and dust behind us. Before our fierce determination to break through, the Russian resistance fell apart.

Like the flood from a broken dam, the stream of tens of thousands pushed forward behind the smashing force of our Panzers, passed us in their wild advance, and grew to a width of a few hundred meters, with an endless depth, toward Halbe.

The 9. Army in the Halbe Pocket

The defensive fire from the enemy always centered on the Panzers. Vehicles to carry the wounded were supposed to follow in the column. Next to us, and among the wrecks of burnt-out trucks and tractors blocking the way, the pressing masses of soldiers pushed and shoved. Everything was concentrated in such a small area; what craziness! They all wanted to walk behind the Panzers as if the bodies of the steel monsters would offer them safety and cover. Just before a railroad crossing and to the right was a sawmill where the divisions assembled during a lengthy halt. The small town lay frighteningly quiet. We had hardly any time to glance at it because there was so much left to be clarified, discussed, and prepared. Night fell and fires brightened the darkness. Not a shot was fired.

Scouting teams we had sent ahead reported a roadblock and anti-tank barricade 300 meters away at the exit to the highway to the west, in between opposite houses. The general ordered an immediate attack on the city. We drove ahead in our Panzer. The chief's Panzer followed at a distance while the other Panzers closed in.

We requested an infantry assault team as we sat 30 meters from the barricade and were unable, due to the narrow, tree-lined road, to drive around it or to fire. Only the Panzer at the point was able to fire. Along this narrow front a bitter battle began from house to house, backyard to backyard, ditch to ditch! The road was covered with dead and wounded soldiers. The tractors and trucks, loaded with wounded, were wedged in between the Panzers. The houses were catching on fire. Red flames flickered across the roofs and from the windows, loud explosions echoed through the darkness. The Russian defensive fire got stronger by the minute, especially from the terrible mortars. From the mowed-down rows of the wounded covering the pavement of the street and the sidewalk came painful shouts for help.

Phosphor shells exploded with white-glowing spray; we had come under fire from enemy tanks. It was getting serious! While it was difficult to make out the muzzle flashes of the enemy guns, our Panzers sat as dark silhouettes in front of and behind the blazing fires. We had no way to get away to the right or the rear. The general's Kubelwagen, which had been sitting behind us, drove away. Panzer stood behind Panzer, and it was in this situation that we suddenly took a direct hit. A blinding white flash, and within seconds the vehicle was engulfed in flames and glistening white light. As Ott yelled into the intercom: "Vehicle on fire!" we all ripped the hatches open in panic, dropped headfirst from the turret hatch onto the pavement, and hit it hard. Ott fell on the metal covers above the track and sustained a contusion to his ribs. We jumped away from the Panzer, ran down the street, and turned around one more time. At that moment we realized what had happened. In the middle of the debris of broken telegraph posts, shingles, and branches of trees stood the dark mass of our Panzer, lit by the blazing fires. Then we realized that it must have been an incendiary shell. We jumped back, one following the other, and climbed into the fighting compartment. In the middle of the confusion surrounding us, the moaning driver slumped over his steering wheel and thought that he could no longer drive. But he had to drive, he just had to! We begged and scolded that he could not give up. The vehicle and crew depended on him alone. Our hastily transmitted words were stopped by other messages.

Kuhnke no longer answered. What had happened? The commander ordered the immediate withdrawal of the fighting vehicles to the crossroads just in the nick of time. It was impossible to get through there, and the only thing left to do was to pull out of the tight noose with the fewest possible losses.

As he was turning around, Kuhnke's Panzer was set on fire by an antitank shell. A Tiger, which had pulled up next to us—because of the darkness and haste we could not determine if it was one from our platoon—was about to back along the sidewalk when its tracks caught the front of a heavy truck. It pushed the front end and the motor under the rear of the Panzer. The flaming gases from the exhaust of the Panzer set the fuel from the tanks of the truck on fire. The flames immediately engulfed the truck and the Panzer in a sea of fire. The critically wounded who were riding on the turret and the rear of the Panzer, as well as the crew, dropped to the street like human torches with wild yells of pain. Who was to look after them? We all had to look after ourselves! We started out immediately. The burning Panzer next to us threatened to set our Tiger on fire. Kuhnke's Panzer blew apart with a bright flash of flame. Among constant explosions the ammunition sprayed across the glowing walls of the Panzer into the darkness of the night. The street to our rear was already cleared. Blinded by the brightness of the fires, we slowly rolled the vehicle backward into the dark cover of the trees. The tracks of the Panzer caught the mangled dead on the street who were being run over for maybe the tenth time. For some minutes, the middle of the street was under antitank fire from the barricade.

We turned our Panzer 180 degrees on the spot and rolled back down the street. During these anxious seconds a frightening feeling grasped the men, a feeling that slowly crept up one's cold spine. At any moment an enemy antitank shell could have hit the rear of the vehicle, and we fully understood that it would have penetrated our relatively weak armor there without any problem. When we finally turned into the crossing street, we felt a deep gratitude to the fates who had allowed us to live through the heavy fighting.

Our movement led us right across a main street where Kuhnke was waiting for us. He hastily reported on the loss of his Panzer. We went on, from the town up into the woods where our Panzers and thousands of German soldiers had preceded us. First we were the point, and then we were one of the last vehicles to roll off the street. We were worried about maintaining contact with the column, which swung south and then, under cover of the woods, to the west. Only a few houses were to be seen along our way out of the town. Its streets turned into roads of death and were covered, according to later counts, by the bodies of four to five thousand dead soldiers.

Hundreds of soldiers, walking individually or in groups next to the road, led the way, which took us into a ravine at the edge of a wood that was under heavy Russian fire.

Everyone fled into cover of the slowly moving fighting vehicles. Up ahead where the Panzers of 1. Company had taken over the point, the column stalled and once more our infantry suffered terrible losses from the fire of the Russian machine guns. Again, we had to leave our wounded where they fell. Whoever was still able to walk or crawl was carried through the night toward the west by the stream of thousands.

There was no end in sight to this horrible night. Harlander's Panzer was knocked out by tank-hunter teams. The commander died, but the other crew members were able to bail out. Läbe climbed into our Panzer as temporary relief for our completely exhausted loader.

Just before dawn, the point, consisting of five Panzers, rolled right into a Russian battery position, and shells from its guns, fired directly, exploded in the trees and on the armor of the Panzers. For the second or third time the wounded who were riding on the vehicles suffered more injuries from the shrapnel raining down on them. Since every commander was intent to get past the battery as quickly as possible, but because the point halted for unknown reasons, the vehicles behind got stuck once more. It was almost impossible to spot the individual enemy guns in the clearing in the woods to the left. After each discharge a bright flash could be seen for only a second.

But we all calmed down again quickly. Without delay the turret was swung to the left, and while the loader pushed an explosive shell into the breech, the gunner aimed the barrel at the firing positions. Shell after shell left the Panzer and smashed the enemy. Red and white flares rose, lighting the terrain brightly for a few seconds. These seconds were long enough to allow the individual Panzers to make out the enemy. The radio operator's and the coaxial MG hammered tracers into the enemy position, which became deadly silent within minutes, and our way was open.

The group of Panzers stopped again 200 meters further. This time it was a joyful message that was passed from man to man. The highway Berlin-Cottbus, our first objective that we had fought for with so many sacrifices, was directly ahead. Slowly, the dawn of the new morning rose behind us in the east. Scouting teams were sent ahead to find the best crossing and to secure it. As the pale light touched the tops of the trees, ground fog still covered the pastures, which might have been hiding quite a few unwelcome surprises. Then came the report from the point that the bridge was open and the crossing secured. While the night gave way to the day, our Panzers rolled across the bridge into the woods on the other side where we were to wait until the main body of our division had arrived. Infantry was sent out to secure the area, and the Panzers pulled off the path. Then, another concern filled our hearts with apprehension. Our fuel reserves were dwindling drastically. In the heavy terrain our gasoline would be completely used up after another ten kilometers.

Then what? Then it would have been all over for the tens of thousands of soldiers following us, as well. Captivity would have been the only option left. Again we drew the chief's attention to this danger. The further success of our breakthrough depended only on gasoline. Terribly wounded soldiers lay next to the Panzers on the wet ground in the woods. Medics and comrades put on dressings. Who was to look after those we left behind? Our path was marked by thousands of dead and probably three times as many wounded who all perished without care and human help in the woods. What a desolate picture this thorny road of our 9. Army was!

For our breakthrough to the Wenck Army, everything depended on that army holding on to the positions they had captured.

The commander of our Panzer-abteilung ordered one Panzer on the path through the woods against Russian tanks, which blocked the main body of the division east of the highway.

The Panzer group, in the meantime, waited at the edge of a moor. Again, infantry were sent ahead to secure. They captured a few Russians. We were ordered by the chief to carry out the order received by radio. So the critically wounded were unloaded immediately. Again, we reminded the chief of the low reserves of fuel, which would make it impossible to even reach the other side of the highway. The argument went back and forth. It was clear to everyone that the Panzer carrying out that order would have been lost. First, fuel had to be found. Rodinger, who was wounded at Halbe, had been bedded by his driver Stinzel behind our Panzer. He was to be loaded into our fighting compartment. But where were we to put him? There was no room inside and to ride outside would have meant his certain death. His hair was tangled, and his face was pale as he lay on a brown, blood-soaked blanket. A black-edged hole gaped in his back. In his Viennese dialect he said to me quietly: "Take my love to my wife and my boy. I'll soon be gone. Just don't leave me lying here, take me with you!" We calmed him and told him not to worry.

Suddenly, the continuation of the march was ordered. The Panzers of our 1. Company rolled out of the woods into the moor. Into the gaps between them pushed tractors, trucks, cars, motorbikes, radio trucks, self-propelled guns, and antiaircraft guns. While the wave of the fighting vehicles rolled into the sunlit moor, we were still looking for a way to take Rodinger along. Almost at the rear we stopped an ambulance armored personnel carrier whose doctor, after our earnest entreaties, agreed to take Rodinger along despite the fact that the vehicle was already full of wounded. We quickly loaded the feeble body on a stretcher, covered our deliriously moaning comrade with blankets, and propped the stretcher, since there was no other room, across the thin steel walls of the personnel carrier.

For the last time we pressed the lifeless hand of our Hans. His further fate remained unknown to us.

Our spearhead was stuck once again at the railroad embankment between Baruth and Zossen. Sharpshooters hidden in the trees and Russian machine guns, of no danger to our Panzers but inflicting all the greater losses on our infantry, blocked the way and prevented further advance for hours. Since our engine might have run out of fuel any

moment, we again contacted Neu. He, however, had no other advice but
to blow up the Panzer if it became necessary. Walking along the stopped
column, we asked every driver if he could spare a few liters of gasoline
for the Panzer, reminding him at the same time of the verbal order from
the general that all fuel reserves had to be handed over to the Panzers.
This dire need, which could determine life or death for tens of thousands of German soldiers, was appreciated by all, and we were able to
add a total of 140 liters to our tank.

Breaking Through the Russian Encirclement

As always and everywhere, the last positions were defended by an elite. Toward evening most of the ambulances returned after having searched for hours in vain for field dressing stations. The seriously wounded, who had already suffered so terribly, were still loaded. To be wounded was probably the worst possible fate then. All serious cases were hopelessly lost. After the fall of darkness, we buried our dead. The graves were leveled. Only a sketch of their location and the address of the closest relatives were noted for possible later notification.

Ground-attack aircraft dove into the withdrawal movements, circling above the tops of the trees and forcing the men into foxholes. The entire wood came alive again with shooting everywhere. Every group of bushes, every crater, every ditch was filled in no time with masses of humans looking for cover. Onboard weapons hammered away without pause, shrapnel bombs exploded, and vehicles raced about and went up in flames. Shouts for the medics echoed through the trees. Then, the nightmare was over; the aircraft circled over another wooded area. We jumped from the Panzer and looked after our boys. Two soldiers were killed in the sudden attack, and quite a number were slightly wounded by the shrapnel. We took the paybooks and identification tags from the dead and buried the bodies right there.

Another approach by fast fighter aircraft drove us back into the Panzer. Leaflets floated from the sky: "Soldiers of the 9. Army, surrender and hand over your weapons! Come over to our side! Death or captivity!" Shell after shell left the glowing barrels. Fire, the howling flight of the shell followed by the explosion, fire—explosion, fire—explosion! Without pause. And in between we heard the thinly yapping fire from rifles and machine guns, more and more persistent, closer and closer. A motorcycle dispatch rider came racing up, crusted with dirt and wet through and through, with the driver of a Tiger who reported the total loss of his vehicle and the rest of the crew by a direct artillery hit. Our

301

losses were particularly high in the concentrated enemy artillery fire and the continuous air attacks, which we could no longer beat back.

Then came more low-level air attacks, rain, retreating infantry. We sat in the closed-up Tiger, maps on our knees, and listened to the last reports from the Supreme Command of the Army, which described the course of the fighting in the capital of the Reich: heavy street battles in Köpenick, the spearheads of Russian tank forces at the Alexander square! Russian troops were advancing from the north on Frohnau by way of Oranienburg. It was all over! We all knew it, but no one said it because the last chapter for us was just beginning, and we were determined to live through it. As long as Russians were in front of us, there was to be no surrender. Time crept painfully slowly as we waited. We had no idea whatsoever about our situation; the Russians might have appeared at any time from the broken, wooded terrain. Finally, the motorbike dispatch rider came racing up, yelling as he drove by: "Everyone get ready, we're going!" The order, based on the decision of the 9. Army to assemble for the breakthrough, had been issued. Seconds later the first engines roared. Dark figures rose from ditches and foxholes all around and stumbled quickly through the dark to their vehicles. Like primeval monsters, our Panzers crawled down the wide, rutted path through the woods to the group at the point, which had already assembled. The sand crunched under our tracks. The infantrymen hung on to the smooth steel in thick bunches. Here and there, their daring faces were lit by the glow of hastily smoked cigarettes.

Messengers hurried through the night to their companies. The infantry was on the march. Spades, weapons, and equipment clanked in monotonous rhythm.

Noiselessly, they pushed along the paths, helmet next to helmet, group after group, regiment behind regiment, hundreds, thousands, more and more battalions and the last of the regiments. In between them were horse-drawn carts covered with tarpaulins, masses of refugees, field kitchens, and guns with their wheels grinding through the deep sand, sinking and pulled from the soft ground with curses. The departure took place with robotlike precision. Only quiet orders were heard, and the rattle from the vehicles at times drowned out the humming of the engines and the marching sound of the infantry. Flares lit the dark night sky in increasing numbers, and through the mangled, whispering woods drifted the breath of an army preparing for its breakout, its last battle.

We drove our Panzer past the tightly closed columns to the secondary road, lined by woods of high fir trees, whose pale asphalt surface led to the Russian lines, and found our place with the Tigers of the point group.

Then, white flares rose, the signal for the attack. Instinctively, our hands once more checked the weapons and uniforms. The order to start out came by radio. Once again we broke into the Russian positions, the defensive, fire-spitting front. Flares climbed into the sky without pause. The guns of our Panzers barked sharply as we rolled, firing from all barrels, across trenches and barricades in order to open up the way for the infantry. Red tracers from Russian machine guns drew countless glowing patterns in the sky. Shells from Paks whistled in front of our Panzers, causing us to instinctively pull in our heads. Suddenly, the artillery was silent, and hoarse shouts of victory indicated that the enemy had been driven out. We stopped to let the infantry climb on and then set out again. "Get on, start the engine!" a voice yelled and immediately flashes of flame thundered from the exhausts of the Panzers. The heavy engines roared. The tracks started to move with a jerk, and our column was in motion. The old fever came back. The often-experienced passion of the hunt made the blood in our veins race. Were we to be the hunters or the prey?

At good speed we approached a town into which infantry was pushing from all sides. The population there had lost everything. Beds, furniture, boxes, suitcases, and household effects of all kinds were strewn about, mangled and burnt. We did not see any civilians and pushed ahead anxiously. In the distance, blood-red clouds of smoke were seen over the route of our advance. We continued to advance, but for how much longer? Were there Russian tank units rolling toward us through the night to block the road? Was the vastly superior enemy force crushing the huge encirclement like an empty bag and attacking the rear and the flanks of the units behind us?

A few kilometers ahead the next town was on fire. Again we ran up against a barricade. The Ivans on the other side knew that the beaten remains of the 9. Army were moving west along this road in endless, decimated bands and immediately threw their fighter-bombers into action. We heard them approaching and hastily tried to make out their direction. Everyone hung from the vehicles, ready to jump into the bushes and find cover. The throttled engines droned threateningly above the treetops as the aircraft flew slowly, searching. Then our four-barrel Flak began to bark, rifles and machine guns pointed skywards, and a storm of fire raced toward the attackers. Parachute flares floated from the sky, lighting the crowded road. The column stopped, and the aircraft dropped their bombs.

Immediately, vehicles were on fire and painful shouts for the medics rang out.

Our mission appeared hopeless. In our Panzers, at the point, we might have been able to fight our way through, but the blind herd behind would have run into certain destruction. There was only one chance; remain, at all costs, at the point, right up front. To be where our forceful Panzer wedge would rip open a gap, to break out fighting. All the others who avoided the fighting at the point, because it faced the most concentrated resistance, broke apart in the massive enemy fire. The last survivors to escape the barrages from heavy weapons stumbled toward the Russians in the light of dawn, their hands raised.

The engines of our Panzers roared again. The steely tracks kept advancing. Hundreds of our wounded lay among the glowing timbers from the house ruins and in the yards, yelling for water and medics. Supporting each other, they dragged themselves with difficulty up to the tracks of the vehicles: "Comrades, take us along, don't leave us lying here. Comrades, help us, help!" But no one could help anymore. All vehicles were already overloaded, and even the smallest car had soldiers hanging from it like bunches of grapes.

Our Tiger was at the point. Its 700 horsepower pushed the remains of burnt-out vehicles, crashing and splintering, in front, thrust them together, and whatever was not run over by this roaring assault was thrown to the sides into the ditches by the heavy tracks.

Batteries of rocket launchers, the dreaded Stalin organs, sent their howling projectiles at us from the woods, and the earth around us trembled with dozens of brightly flashing explosions that ripped through the black darkness. As in a daze, only one thought flashed through our feverish brains: it's all over, finished, this is the end, it has to be the end! This wall of fire ground everything into the dirt. One had to live through this tornado in order to comprehend it.

This paralyzing terror was followed by the lightning-fast action and reaction of the battle-hardened soldier. After all, everything was routine, a matter of experience and instincts.

Daylight came, almost imperceptibly. We rolled ahead slowly, expecting an attack by Russian tanks at any moment. The loud din of battle had ebbed off. The quiet after the storm of fire of the merciless night sank upon us like a nightmare, since we sensed silent danger all around us. In the weak light of the morning the extent of the destruction on the road littered with wrecks became apparent. Wherever one looked there were terrible scenes beyond description.

Based on our experiences of the events during the previous night, we were able to establish an approximate picture of our situation. Russian tank units were chasing us from the rear, increasing fire attacks were reported on the flanks, and the rattle of Russian submachine guns was often heard threateningly close by. We really had not achieved much of a victory, but our courage and confidence had returned.

We were still stuck in the broken wooded area south of Berlin and had to turn directly west if we did not want to collide with the Russian troops attacking toward Berlin.

We had put almost twenty kilometers behind us during the previous night. How much suffering and death we had seen, how many Russians barricades we had broken through during our action. And what was still waiting for us, on our way to the west through the Russian masses?

We had to keep going, to get across the embankment. As we started to roll, a Russian tank appeared over the top of the embankment and came racing at us at full speed, firing from all barrels. We reacted immediately. With lightning speed the Panzer turret swung its barrel toward the embankment. Fire! And immediately there was a horrible bang. Something black and smoking blew apart and threw pieces of ripped metal above the treetops. After the smoke had blown away, we found that the explosion had been the Russian tank, which had shaken the air. Our shell had hit the ammunition storage and the fuel tanks from barely thirty meters away. Explosions went off inside the wreck of the tank as the remaining ammunition blew up piece by piece.

Total silence set in for a few minutes. Then we took over security and had the vehicles roll on. The first Kubelwagen started out toward the embankment, raced up the slope with the engine howling, and got stuck between the railroad tracks. At the same moment a Russian MG opened up and hammered its bullets across the embankment and tracks from the flank. Wounded soldiers staggered from the roof of the vehicle and fell down, moaning.

Two of our Panzers rolled slowly toward the embankment from the edge of the woods and climbed up the slope, their guns pointing steeply into the sky and then sinking back to the horizontal. Under the safe cover of the massive Panzer walls, some fifty soldiers, women, and children jumped across into the woods on the other side. We only hoped that those who had remained behind could make it through.

The armored personnel carriers of the Division "Großdeutschland" secured the flanks for the next groups to cross the embankment. Our Panzer spearhead continued its drive from the embankment to the west through a wood of beech trees. After we had poured two jerrycans of ether into the tank, our engine suddenly quit and could only be restarted and kept running with great difficulty.

Hellwig came over from the railroad embankment and reported that he was forced to blow up his vehicle. So we lost one Panzer after the other due to the lack of fuel. How were we to fight our way through the Russians without fuel?

The Tigers broke onto the plains in a long line. Once more they presented the picture of an immense thrusting force. For a time, not a shell was fired. But soon we made contact with the enemy and as the Russian tanks suddenly fired, the guns of our Panzers rumbled also.

The Russian tanks, hidden in wooded parcels, exploded with loud bangs. The force of the explosions hurled black, smoking, and flaming pieces of steel above the treetops, and for a long time after, columns of flames and smoke rose from the dark pines into the blue evening sky. It had all worked out that time, and the attack rolled forward again. The soldiers came out from behind our Panzers with laughing faces, their courage renewed. These mixed groups of soldiers raced behind the advancing Panzers with their weapons at the ready. Our objective was a wood of beech trees ahead of us where a Kampfgruppe of ours had been fighting off the Russians for days. Suddenly, Russian MGs again hammered our right flank. Our soldiers hastily sought cover behind the walls of the Panzers. On the move, we sent our shells and MG salvos into the tops of the pines. Far behind us, oily veils of smoke from burning vehicles drifted above the black body of our steely column.

In a large open stand of low fir trees we found the reported German Kampfgruppe whose soldiers jubilantly welcomed us with waving arms. With tears in their eyes, these brave men surrounded us. Once again, they felt hope for a rescue from their despondent situation. Their gratitude knew no bounds. They were no longer alone; their determination had paid off.

Many wounded were bedded down on stretchers. Their hopes, too, were obvious: hope for a bed, hope for a roof over their heads, hope for care. These hopes were to be smashed less than a half hour later when they had to be left behind. What was to be their fate? Slowly, the Panzer column rolled on. The Russians had set up defensive gun positions at the crossroads. They were crushed by our tracks, ground into the dirt. Bloody bundles of humanity lined the road. The last of the brown shapes fled into the dark cover of the fir trees, their faces distorted by fear. Our path was fought clear and, like a narrow flow of lava, the ribbon of thousands flowed along the roads toward Luckenwalde.

The generals and commanders ordered the thousands of soldiers to assemble in accordance with their original divisions, outside of the city, so that a chain of command over the leaderless masses could be established. The divisions lined up in marching formation in rows of twelve or sixteen. One division still numbered one thousand men, the next barely one hundred: the remains of the "Oder Army."

The loud orders from the newly detailed officers echoed through the woods.

What was left of our Panzer company immediately took over the point of the column again. Behind us followed the 1. Company with its three Panzers. In the growing darkness, we could barely see the outlines of the trees.

As ordered by Neu, we pulled our vehicle into the lead, ahead of the chief's Panzer and the other vehicles, and swung to the right until we reached the edge of the woods. There we switched off the engine.

"Pass the word to the rear quietly: extreme silence, put out cigarettes, the enemy is close by!" This message was passed on. Damn it, it was getting interesting.

A slim Oberst (colonel) with a Knight's Cross and an officer from the general staff of each of the divisions crawled into our Panzer with us to examine their maps in the light of our electric bulbs and to discuss the situation. The Oberst received a thorough briefing from the other two on the reported enemy situation. We overheard as they discussed that, according to that day's Armed Forces report, our own troops had reached this town or that. It showed that even the command staffs had to rely on reports from the Heer, which were outdated and hardly represented the situation at the time. What had happened to the relief forces who were supposed to help in breaking open the all-encompassing stranglehold of the enemy?

And on top of all that, the sword of Damocles in the form of the shortage of fuel hung above our heads. Out there, at the front, everything was still quiet, so quiet that we could hear the wind gently blow through the trees. Only from a very considerable distance came a nimble as if tanks and guns were rolling down a bumpy path through the forest. The time was a few minutes after midnight. A ranking SS officer joined the group, which was deep in deliberation. Right away, an agitated dispute began. We opened the hatches and listened to the loud voices.

Except for the SS commander who insisted on it and wanted to carry it out himself, all the others were opposed to an immediate attack in view of the forces of the enemy. Finally, they agreed on immediate assembly.

When that order was issued, a low grumble set in. The soldiers moved without any enthusiasm. None of them were in a hurry, and the officers had to snap loudly at the men in the woods, just to get them off the ground. Most of them tried to stay in the middle, hoping to slide through this shit unharmed.

We started the engines and rolled without haste from the forest onto the gray plains. Slowly, the column behind us began its move.

Not a shell was fired, not a sound could be heard except the rumble of the Panzer engines and the rattle of the tracks. Scattered widely across the fields, the soldiers trotted in line alongside our Panzers.

The silhouettes of the first houses became visible in the gray haze, less than 800 meters away.

Up to that time there was no movement. Had the Russians left the village? Then, however, a sickening jet of fire whizzed from the town and we ducked down in the cupola. Above us whistled a shell, barely missing our vehicle. Long snakes of fire flew from the gun of our Panzer, and our shells exploded in the village. Then we heard the Panzer guns behind us firing, and the walls of the houses ahead were blown apart. We could hear the yelling of those hit on our side. The Russian defensive fire from the edge of town became concentrated and effective.

As we rolled along the road toward the village, our shells burst into the main street and the tracer salvos of the MGs ripped into the walls and trees. The ground beneath us, the air around us, everything trembled. Once they had overcome the first shock, the soldiers hugging the ground rose and formed into a mass, which ran after the Panzers. After the deep despair of dying, the liberating shouting and battle cries rang like a song of victory across the plowed fields. Once more eyes shone bravely; a desperate fighting spirit thrust even the hesitating ones toward the front. Once more the wounded stood up, filled with a last readiness for death.

Swinging from the left we rolled toward the center of the village. Our explosive shell blew a Russian antitank gun into pieces with a loud bang and threw the mangled metal fragments along the street. The walls of the houses blew apart and were hurled into the air. Black fog from smoke and powder began obstructing our vision. Yellow sheaths of flames licked along the ridge of the roofs and illuminated the neighboring trees and houses. Even before we reached the center of town, the hold was broken and there was nothing left to stop the Russians from running. Their guns stood abandoned along the street. They were mangled by our tracks and thrown up in the air. Window panes rattled, the explosions from hand grenades died down, and the sputter of the machine guns became weaker. The infantry came jogging up to our vehicle.

Behind the village the terrain to the right of the asphalt road rose slowly toward a fir wood. The fields to its left dropped off in the direction of a dimly glittering lake. Then it got ticklish. Two, three long flashes of fire jumped from the edge of the forest half-right; antitank guns were barking harshly. Suddenly, a massive hit shook our Panzer. We were hit in the hull next to the radio operator, and the metal track fenders fell to the road with a rattle.

We could not make out any details. The edge of the wood was still 300 to 400 meters away. Then, our Panzer gun roared toward the woods and bright explosions hurled trees and branches through the air over there. Like a flash of lightning the second hit illuminated the interior of our fighting compartment. With an immense force, the shell had hit the right side of the hull and been deflected straight upwards.

From the turret MG the strings of pearls of our tracers hammered into the dark woods, and ricochets hummed to the sides. Four or five muzzle flashes were spotted at the edge of the forest.

Another shell whistled by just above our vehicle. Long flashes of fire were thrown from our barrel, and, at times, the Panzer was completely enveloped by a sickening powder fog.

Then came a terrible bang. Instinctively, our hands held on to whatever was there, and our teeth clamped together. It was as if we were being blown up.

It was a massive hit to the right side of the turret. The entire vehicle and the ground below us were lifted in the air. "Driver, pull hard left, full throttle, march, march!" the intercom yelled. The vehicle reared up and then tilted down the slope into the field, dropping toward the lake. In this manner we managed to get out of the direct enemy field of fire. Just before the lakeshore we swung right and rolled across the soft shore, parallel to the road, toward the Panzer of the chief, which had also withdrawn there from the fire along the road.

After barely 50 meters, the engine stuttered, then quit. The driver pushed the starter button. The engine caught immediately and then died again. A second and third try ended in the same result. No more gasoline! This realization made our ears feel hot. Ott reported businesslike that the tank was empty. Terrible, we were sitting in deep s . . . ! Was it all to be over there and then? The Panzers of the 1. Company came racing out of the village. Their shells roared into the enemy line of defense until it was put out of action and fell silent. The main resistance was broken, the way past Luckenwalde open for thousands of German soldiers.

Widely staggered, the Panzers, trucks, and tractors rolled down the road between the lake and the forest, among the soldiers on foot.

The commander ran to the chief's Panzer, which also sat by the lake without fuel. "Blow up the vehicle!" was the terse order. This had to be done within a few minutes since we wanted to stay with the column at all costs.

While we threw the duffel bags and handguns from the hatches of the condemned Panzer, the crew lifted out the wounded into the open. Pape set the explosive charges and joined the fuses at the charge.

After a long hesitation the commander gave the order to blow up the Panzer. Pape pulled the cord and jumped away. We ran to the closest crater and dropped flat into the wet grass. Holding our breath we counted the seconds. Thirty, forty, sixty seconds, and no explosion! We waited for five minutes. There was no doubt anymore. Pape had not removed the cardboard cover that protected the charge from moisture. But then we had our doubts about destroying the vehicle after all. We had to find fuel somewhere, at any cost.

Ingenious infantrymen searched the village for fuel for our Panzer, and one of them yelled that a full tanker truck was sitting in the Russian positions. This was our chance, but it could have also spelled our death.

We collected all of the crews who could still walk. Infantrymen joined us; anyone who could came along to form an assault team on the enemy position just outside the forest. A young girl cowered freezing in a haystack. She wanted to wait there for us to pick her up on our way back. Widely spread, with pistols, hand grenades, and submachine guns ready, we crept, our heads low, from the road toward the woods. Among explosions from hand grenades and salvos from the MPs, we entered the positions from which the Russians had fled. We found a tangle of cars, humans and horses, wood, steel and flesh, dead and wounded. Shells still lay next to the guns, which had been ripped and thrown about by our own shells. Strong arms lifted a full gasoline barrel onto the pasture and rolled it into the open from out of the pines. German hand grenades were thrown in a wide arc into the chaos, salvos from MPs rattled again, and then we hurried back across the fields to the road. One more time everyone lent a hand, and the 200-kilogram barrel was lifted onto the rear of our vehicle from where the gasoline gurgled into the tanks.

These 200 liters would be enough for twenty to twenty-five kilometers at the best. But they were a ray of hope, nevertheless.

A white ground fog formed dew on the pastures and hung on our clothes. We began to feel cold from hunger and exhaustion. But we were to go on soon.

Just as we were climbing into the Panzer, a terrible bang ripped apart the silence. As if gripped by an invisible fist, we were slammed to the ground with full force. As we caught our breath, shock and fear paralyzed our limbs for seconds. We could collect our thoughts only very slowly. Trembling, we ran our hands across our heads and bodies and felt for our feet. Everything was still there. In a daze I pulled up my feet and pushed up my body with my arm. A burning pain raced through my body, and the cold sweat of fear crept up. The shell had come across the lake from an enemy tank, half-left. It took aim at our Panzer, glimmering dimly in the light of the moon, just as we were climbing in.

Carefully, the men lifted the commander onto the rear of the vehicle and pushed him through the open ammunition hatch into the fighting compartment where they bedded him down on coats and blankets. As Pape and Läbe put on dressings, they found black, burnt holes with pieces of red flesh gaping in the commander's right upper arm, right shoulder, and right thigh. A sweat ran from his brow in pearls.

"Läbe will immediately take over the Panzer and catch up to the main column!" Shortly, the morning was to dawn in the east. Then, the first gray light came through the open hatches into the interior. Shaking, the Panzer rolled down the paths and across obstructions. It was a strange feeling to be lying helplessly in the fighting compartment and not knowing what dangers were lurking around us.

Finally we stopped. Läbe had caught up again. The pale morning light entered through the rectangular loader's hatch. On the orders of a staff officer, all wounded were collected under the direction of the doctors and medics. Dressing stations, which were to be turned over to the Russians later, were set up.

After a few hours of rest our commander had recovered and climbed back into the turret. The white, blood-soaked dressings were in strange contrast to the black uniform.

All other wounded had to be unloaded. Two Lieutenants of the infantry, who had been in the vehicle since the night at Halbe, had to be lifted out on orders from the chief. Wringing their hands, these poor guys begged us to let them stay in the vehicle, but we could not help it, they had to leave.

We continued our advance; scratched, worn out, half crazed. The chief of the 3. Company, Friedl Schinhofen, and Fink drove from vehicle to vehicle in a captured American jeep to bring fuel. At the road ahead of us sat a heavy Russian gun next to a wooden barricade. Dead and wounded Russians lay in front of it. On another road to our right was a tangle of Studebaker trucks, which had been driven into each other. We rolled on. For a while, the chief of our former staff company, Hauptmann (captain) Hans Graalfs, rode in our vehicle. Night fell again. A loud babble of voices brought us back to reality. The column had stopped. We clearly made out the individual voices out there. Apparently the chief's Panzer had broken down.

Then we got going again. To the left and right enemy shells ripped open the pavement. We were again under heavy fire. During the course of the night the Russians had barricaded and reinforced their troops along all roads and possible paths to the west. Every meter had to be fought for. Again, we heard the roar of heavy aircraft engines as the planes darted across the road. And behind us followed the kilometer-long line of German soldiers, individually and in groups, a gray mass with horror showing in their tired eyes. Their only hope of getting through were our Tigers. We then rolled downhill into a forest.

It had turned silent around us. We were thirsty, hungry, and thirsty again. All our canteens were empty. How long had it been since we last ate? During the previous days we never had thought of it, but at that time the hunger caused us pain. This "National Labor Day" which we had formerly celebrated became a day of severe suffering for us.

It was after 8 A.M. when it appeared that we had reached a position just outside Berlin. The vehicle was again crowded with our own wounded. Whoever was able had to leave the Panzer. The loader could not move, and combat-readiness had to be maintained in the interest of all. As so often before, the wounded hanging on to the outside of the Panzer had been swept off by deadly MG salvos. And yet, the vehicle was again covered with more wounded.

At short range we set a number of Russian T-34s on fire. The Russians retreated into the woods to the left and right. We continued to roll past burning tanks and cars, dead and wounded. Soon after we sat immobilized on the road because the left track was ripped apart. It was a miracle that it had lasted until there. It would have taken at least twenty minutes to repair it.

A little later our Abteilung commander joined us with a one-ton tractor loaded with wounded. Everyone who was not wounded was busy outside putting on the track when Schuller suddenly received a bullet right through his thigh. "Russian snipers!" Stinzel yelled and sought cover inside the vehicle. He had taken a bullet in the stomach. Where were these snipers hiding? Ahead of us and to the right, a windmill stood in bright flames.

Black-yellow banks of smoke drifted slowly across the fields. Our Panzer spearhead had shrunk to two Tigers. There was not one among our crews who had not repeatedly suffered wounds or burns during the previous days. We looked awful with black burn blisters on our arms and faces and our bloody dressings. Neu returned from a briefing with the commander. Then, Milker, our replacement driver, was also wounded and lost to us. The former platoon leader of the repair company, Öhls, took over his spot. The intercom failed. The wounded of the previous few hours lay listlessly and resigned to their fate below the gun. There were no doctors who could have offered help.

The spring sun shone brightly on the land. It was about 10 A.M. We were somewhat hopeful because some time that day we were to reach the German defensive lines of the Wenck Army. Slowly we rolled along the road toward Beelitz. The soldiers came out from the woods widely spread out and formed marching columns behind the Panzer on both sides of the road, which was lined by fields of asparagus. We picked up speed quickly. If only we could have communicated better. With the hellish racket inside the vehicle, every order had to yelled below individually. The Panzer stopped again. At the side of the road sat an enemy Pak, which was blown away with an explosive shell. How many Paks, how many tanks was that? No one counted anymore, it had become so irrelevant.

Half-left stood another Russian tank. Antitank shell! Slowly the turret of our Panzer swung left. Fire and hit! Clouds of smoke obscured our visibility. Suddenly there was the sound of metal breaking at the rear right side of the hull; a long-drawn hissing. Blinding white sparks flashed around us. We were hit from the right. There was a deadly silence for a few seconds. Then a loud whistle and hum burst from the interior, and a bright, hot, glowing flame took our breath away.

Instinctively, our eyelids closed tightly. Our hands and arms enclosed our heads, as if these automatic movements could have averted and suppressed the demoniacal force that had been let loose. A white ball of smoke filled the interior, and the heat dried our throats. The Panzer was on fire. Glowing flashes of flame burned into the unprotected skin of the hands, the upper body, and the face. Heads and bodies collided, hands grasped the hatches, which promised safety. Depleted air built up in the lungs, the pulse raced in the neck and brain, and a purple darkness, interwoven with green flashes, grew before the eyes. We let ourselves drop headfirst from the three-meter-high turret and pushed our bodies away from the hull with our hands. From the edge of the road we fell down the embankment into the sand. Then we jumped up and staggered a few steps further. Immediately ahead of us the burning and reeling figure of the radio operator jumped off the rear of the Panzer. Hartinger, Neu, and Öhls ran past us. Two more burning figures tumbled from the operator's hatch and rolled down the embankment. They both held their bleeding hands and faces toward us, hair in flames, uniforms ripped open. We closed our eyes to this spectacle. The first men from our Panzer reached the commander's tractor, which then raced into the near-by forest. The rest of us returned to reality. We jumped back, quite instinctively. Smoke rose from the hatches of our Panzer. We pulled the blankets from the box on the rear, took the fire extinguishers from their clamps, shoveled dirt into a bucket, and managed, slowly, to put out the smoldering fire. Within view of the German lines we saved the Panzer one more time. It was to have taken us the last piece of the way to the rear positions. We breathed more freely when we heard the familiar hum of the engine and rolled on along the road to the west, toward Beelitz. The hill on the other side was covered with a dark forest, which touched on the bushes and pastures of the plain.

The point group, widely spread, reached the plain. Was there to be an open gap in the front through which the German lines could be reached?

Suddenly, guns from Russian tanks roared, and bright flashes of fire and black balls of smoke appeared among the most advanced lines. Unnoticed by most, three Russian T-34s had driven out of the woods on the left into the open fields and hammered their shells into the helpless bunch on the slope.

Anyone who was able ran back and leaped into the cover of hedges and trenches. We left the road at high speed and swung right in order to gain the most promising firing position. Our few antitank shells had to find their target. Anyone still hanging on to our Panzer had to jump off. The Russian tanks were so preoccupied with their action that they paid no attention to us, or maybe they did not expect any more German Panzers from that direction. Another 400 meters, 300 meters, then we were there. "Panzer halt! Aim at the tank furthest right—300—Fire!" And the first antitank shell left the barrel—hit! "Next target—the tank on the far left—Fire!" Again, the shell did not miss its target, no wonder at that distance and with stationary targets. Then, the third and last T-34 was also in the gunner's sight; fire and hit! As long as only the first Russian tank was smoking, we kept firing on the other two. Explosive shells and short bursts from our MGs prevented the crews from bailing out. Finally, heavy clouds of smoke confirmed the end of the Russian tanks. The stream of our soldiers flowed on. They appeared from everywhere, from trenches and behind bushes. We rolled down the road again, past the smoking T-34s. The soldiers waved at us. The mood inside our Panzer was joyfully excited. We had almost reached the goal we had so longed for.

Then it came down on us; two massive hammerlike blows crashed into our rear. Our Panzer jerked forward a little farther and then stood still. A flash of flames, which illuminated our fighting compartment bright as daylight, indicated that our fuel tank had been hit. There was no time to observe or defend if we did not want to blow up with the Panzer. We pulled our wounded out of the loader's hatch, under cover of the mushroom of smoke billowing above the rear of the Panzer, and then ran away from it. It burned intensely, and there was no chance to save it once more.

We rushed onward. From the near edge of the woods behind us the Russian tank guns hurled their shells into our helpless group. Then we heard the sharp bark of a 8.8-cm Panzer gun. That was probably the last Tiger of our Panzer spearhead, following behind, taking on the Russian tanks that had suddenly appeared. Behind us we heard a heavy thud, a penetrating banging, and the exploding of our shells. Our vehicle had blown up, the 18-ton turret was lifted and hurled skyward. There were to be exploding shells and MG belts for hours and, finally, a slow dying down of the glow.

Ahead of us stretched a pasture into the valley. There were no bushes, not even high grass, to offer us cover. We passed limping and crawling soldiers when the whistle and bang of shells forced us to drop down once more. Bent over, we finally ran toward a near-by hamlet. An antitank shell splashed us with mud. We raced on, our lungs threatening to burst. We were lucky. The shooting died down, and the MG in particular seemed to have given up. Completely worn out, we staggered toward the closest farm, where a young German boy came forward and led us up a wide staircase into the large living room. A German doctor and a medic cut the half-burnt pieces of shirts from our upper bodies and the ripped leather pants from our legs. The farmer's wife fetched a jug of water from the cellar and handed it to us. Greedily, we slurped the reviving liquid. Suddenly, the young boy came running up the stone staircase and shouted into the room that the Russians had come within 200 meters of the hamlet. That was the signal for the doctor and the others, who then stormed from the room into the yard. A Schwimmwagen started up outside, and, even before we reached the staircase, it drove off at full speed.

Russian tanks and guns occasionally rumbled in the distance across some country road. Finally, the noise of marching boots and shouts was heard from the edge of the hamlet. Numerous figures appeared from the darkness and assembled. The first of the groups, quickly thrown together, disappeared row after row into the dark and the fog which enveloped everything. Silently, anxiously, we listened into the night. Some soldiers still lay on the ground, leaning against a wall, dozing.

Then as the order came for the wounded to also begin to move, the usual grumbling and complaining started. But one after the other got going, between two o'clock and three o'clock in the morning. With their feet stomping and shuffling they dragged themselves through bushes and ditches, up and down, on and on. We marched in a platoon, noiselessly, like ghosts chasing through smoke. Occasionally, someone dropped from the file, but we went on without stopping. Dawn came slowly, and we could again make out the country around us. An elevated road appeared from out of the morning fog. We stumbled across the embankment and disappeared in the bushes on the other side, just in time! Behind us heavy tracked vehicles rattled and rumbled by—Russians! Daylight came. We followed a creek and found our way out of the woods, exhausted. Ahead of us lay an expansive, wet pasture. Greedily we slurped the icy swamp water down our feverishly hot throats. The seriously injured were lifted across the creek one after the other. About 400 meters farther on, a small village church, half collapsed, pointed the stump of its steeple into the morning sky. Someone said we had reached the German lines. This did not bring about any feelings of joy. This return had been paid for all too bitterly with the bodies of an entire German army.

That was also the end for the soldiers of the heavy SS-Panzer-Abteilung 502 whose journey terminated between the Oder and the Elbe. Who was to count the fallen, the wounded, and those who would not return from captivity? During the years after the war some 150 comrades were found from the over 1,000 soldiers who had been transferred to this Panzerabteilung of the II. SS-Panzerkorps in Argentan on April 1, 1944.

The Final Battle for Berlin— Königstigers in Their Last Action

During the final battle for Berlin, the 11. SS-Freiwilligen (volunteer) Division "Nordland," with the Königstigers of the heavy SS-Panzer-Abteilung 503 and a French grenadier battalion of the "Charlemagne" Division, became the central point of the last resistance against the Red Army. It was only a small number of Königstigers that became the fire brigade and the backbone of the defenders of the government quarter, the "Zitadelle" (citadel).

On April 26, Generalmajor Dr. Kruckenberg reported six Königstigers and assault guns ready for action on the routes leading to the "Zitadelle." They were to defend against the Russian attack units and to provide reinforcement to the grenadiers in this hopeless battle. The concentric attack by the Russian forces began on April 29 with the bombardment of the east-west axis. Two Königstigers blocked the Avus (major road) and the Kurförstendamm (major Berlin thoroughfare), while other Königstigers sat in the Tiergarten (a central park), ready for action at the trouble spots.

At the Halensee railroad station, the commander of a Königstiger, Unterscharführer Bender, was wounded after having knocked out several T-34s. When the Soviet tanks began their assault on the "Zitadelle," the two Königstigers of commanders Turk and Diers entered the action and were able to destroy Russian T-34s and JS-tanks on the other side of the Spree River. The Königstigers commanded by Schäfer and Körner formed the bulwark of the defense at the Kurfürstendamm and prevented any breakthrough. During April 29, the men of the Henri Fenet Battalion were involved in extremely heavy defensive fighting in Puttkammer Street and, with their Panzerfausts, stopped the tanks attacking along Hedemann Street and at the Belle-Alliance Square. Burning wrecks of tanks in Saarland Street bore witness there also to the action of the French volunteers and of the other tank hunter teams against the Soviet tanks attacking time and again. The Königstigers and the assault guns received their battle orders from the command posts of Panzer-Regiment "Nordland" (commander P. A. Kausch) in Tiergarten street and of the heavy SS-Panzer-Abteilung 503 (commander Friedrich Herzig). On April 30, the Russian assault units once more threw everything they had into the battle. They wanted to report to Stalin the capture of the capital of the Reich on May 1. With their Stalin tanks and T-34s the Soviets ran up against the nests of resistance and the ever-dwindling number of defenders. They suffered heavy losses in men and materiel. On April 30, commander Turk received the order to drive his Königstiger to Potsdam Square. He had been able, the day before, to fight off, together with commander Diers, all attacks in this sector at the bridges across the Spree River and the Schloß Island. His Tiger had sustained massive damage from enemy fire. The Königstiger of commander Stolze knocked out five Soviet tanks at the Halensee railroad station during that day.

According to available reports, five Königstigers and six Panzer IVs and assault guns were ready for action on May 1.

In the government quarter the soldiers of the Fenet Battalion and the tank hunter teams of the close-combat school "Charlemagne" under Obersturmführer Weber formed the heart of the defense. Their lines drew ever closer to the Reichschancellery. After knocking out his thirteenth Soviet tank, Wilhelm Weber was critically wounded in the shoulder on April 29 and evacuated to the makeshift hospital in the Reichschancellery. Standartenjunker (Waffen-SS officer cadet) Will Fey took over his place and held his tank hunter team together until the bitter end and the breakout. In the meantime the negotiations on the surrender, which was to take effect on the morning of May 2, had begun. During the night from May 1 to 2, the assembly of small Kampfgruppen began. They were to attempt a breakout before the capitulation would take effect in order to avoid certain imprisonment in Soviet camps. During the night of May 2, absolute chaos reigned in Berlin. Commanders Körner and Stolze with their Königstigers joined a Kampfgruppe, which planned to break out. The heaviest fighting of those days, including heavy losses, took place during the dawn of May 2 at the Spandau Bridge. The Russians had set up a strong barricade there and controlled the sector around this bridge with infantry and antitank weapons as well as artillery. The third Königstiger, still mobile under commander Diers, set out around 3 A.M. and with its gun elevated, broke, through the antitank barricade at the Weidendammer Bridge. Behind it rattled the other armored and wheeled vehicles, followed by a great number of soldiers and civilians. There was no immediate reaction from the Russian side, but then a sudden hiss came from the right at the intersection of Ziegel Street. The Königstiger was shaken by numerous hits and picked up speed until its wild race ended at the next antitank barricade. The armored personnel carriers following behind were knocked out. The carrier with Albert Kausch, the critically wounded commander of Panzer-Regiment "Nordland," on board was buried by a collapsing wall, the commander injured once more. The accompanying medical officer, Dr. Bartak, transported him to the emergency hospital at the Adlon Hotel and operated on Kausch as best possible.

Around 10 A.M. the Russians came, and his captivity began. After the hospital was moved to Frankfurt/Oder and after two unsuccessful escape attempts, Kausch's long trek through many Russian camps during eleven years of captivity began. He returned home in 1956.

Another group was formed by Generalmajor Mummert to attempt a breakout across the Schulenburger Bridge in Spandau. The two Königstigers of commanders Lippert and Schäfer joined this group, driving up to the bridge and providing covering fire. As soon as the long 8.8-cm guns of the Königstigers opened fire, the fire from the Russians died down. Under the cover of this fire, the spearhead of the attack rolled across the bridge. The Panzers, armored personnel carriers, and self-propelled guns took up positions on the other side and hammered the enemy positions from all barrels. The Russians withdrew from their positions near the bridge, and the Königstigers took over securing it. It was a time-consuming and laborious operation. Only when the Königstigers fired could a group of vehicles, soldiers, and civilians cross the bridge. Finally, the breakout group could continue on its way in the direction of Heer Street. A few hundred meters before reaching southbound Heer Street, the Königstigers encountered Russian infantry and tanks. A JS tank was the main obstacle, and commander Schäfer moved to the point to knock out this obstruction. As he opened fire on the Stalin tank, he received a direct hit from 120 meters away, fired from a German 8.8-cm antiaircraft gun that had been captured by the Russians in the meantime. Two soldiers of Schäfer's crew could not save themselves. The other three bailed out, seriously wounded, and dragged themselves to an emergency hospital on Seeburger Street. Commander Schäfer was terribly burned and lost consciousness. He survived and, after many years and a period of temporary blindness, his serious wounds healed and he regained his memory.

A larger group, with Generalmajor Mummert and the commander of the heavy SS-Panzer-Abteilung 503 (Königstigers), Sturmbannführer

Herzig, broke through to the area of Ketzin on the Havel River on May 3. There, the group was encircled during the evening and decimated by Russian fire. Some were able to reach the Wenck Army and thus cross the Elbe River, but most fell into Russian captivity. Commander Herzig made it through and across the Elbe River. He died in a car accident in 1954 in Aalen.

The Panzer crews of Panzer-Regiment "Nordland" and of the heavy SS-Panzer-Abteilung 503, through their actions right until the hour of the surrender, set an example of carrying out the duties of a soldier in a hopeless situation and have added a glorious chapter to the history of the German Panzer forces.

HEAVY PANZERABTEILUNG 503—THEY FOUGHT AND THEY DIED
A Report by Fritz Kauerauf, SS-Obersturmführer
SS-Panzer-Abteilung 503

Many of the units that were set up during the last months of the war did not receive a detailed, documented history of their actions in the form of the normal large volumes with photos. However, these battalions performed extraordinary feats. They did not often enter action as complete units but were sent in smaller groups, dictated by the many emergency situations, into action wherever they were most needed at the time, often without the regular routine of assembly and without sufficient arms and personnel strength. Improvised solutions, which were outdated within hours, led directly to disaster. The survivors of such units reported on their histories in notes after May 8, 1945. The following report, put together from fragments of documents, is a realistic, living history of war, as the ancient Greeks might have told it.

These documents on the actions of the heavy SS-Panzer-Abteilung 503 in the final battles from the end of January to May 1945 in Küstrin, in Pomerania, near Danzig, Stettin, and Berlin, are proof that these men were fighters. Almost no Panzer escaped the fate of being knocked out. It was too large a target, it was generally in the center of the action, the enemy fire was aimed at it automatically, and it was often without cover from the infantry. The crew knew only what the commander told it, whether it was the direction of travel to the driver or the distance from the target to the gunner and the radio operator who were at the gun and at the two machine guns, one of which was coaxially mounted with the gun. The loader, responsible for the ammunition and without whom no Panzer could be successful, could not see anything at all. These circumstances required a crew that could react at lightning speed and was able to grasp situations at the same time and to act decisively. A crew that possessed the highest virtues of the soldier, such as a high fighting morale, steadfastness, and a spirit of sacrifice. These virtues were exhibited time and again during the constant state of having to depend on each other.

This was the only way a Panzer unit could function. It had to search out success, be constantly mobile, and use its immense firepower intelligently, otherwise it could not carry out its mission. The heavy SS-Panzer-Abteilung 503 with its forty-two Königstigers was such a unit. After a thorough period of training of one year, its considerable efforts and feats helped large numbers of the threatened population in the eastern part of our homeland to escape a terrible fate.

Toward the end of February 1945, I had overcome the danger to my life caused by injuries to my head, burns, and the amputation of my left lower leg after being knocked out on February 9 in Klein Silber/Pomerania. I reported this to my unit by letter. My unit then sent my possessions, which had been put together for my parents, to the reserve hospital at Uetersen/Holstein where I had been moved. On July 17, 1945, after the fighting had long been over and I had suffered through yet another operation, English soldiers arrived with two armored reconnaissance vehicles and an ambulance and took me prisoner in my bed. Oddly enough, they were quite friendly and brought my possessions, which had fallen into their hands in a postal bag in Hamburg. The package contained my paybook, watch, fountain pen, and correspondence. These soldiers exhibited a certain friendliness and esteem toward me not only because they could see my personal fate but also because they had a letter to me from Obersturmführer Max Lippert. It fell into their hands with the same mail, and they knew its contents. They let us know that we were closer to them than their "allies" against whom we had fought. One could not be fairer! Such events, too, occurred, and they were typically British.

What Max Lippert wrote in his letter was really a war diary of the 1. Company:

Dear comrade Kauerauf! OU April 12, 1945
    Returning from hospital yesterday I found your letter of March 5. As I see, the amputation of your left foot was necessary, but after you have gotten over the worst and considering your young age, you will be able to come through with no problems. My best wishes for a speedy recovery!

Now to the events: Menke is not dead, you are wrong there, he is long since back in action. The dead comrades of the company are: Near Arnswalde: Schall, Jäger, Schlachta, Ludwigs, Knorr, Belda, Thies, Krenn(?), Martin Peter, Franz R. The repair team had to take on infantry duties twice. Near Danzig in March: Heinrich, Nolte, Dietzen, Jeserer, Klünder, Kremann, Müller G., Melzer, and Fürbacher. Missing are Kofler and Grupe. Not yet back from Küstrin: Allmer, Fell, Fischer, Möller, Nottrott, and Sturm. This is a list which will likely grow. The dead leaders are Kaes, König, Grimminger; wounded: Meinl, Schäfer, Johannigmayer, Bellé, and myself. The Abteilung is now in two parts, one in Danzig and the other at the Oder, but will soon be reunited. Brommann has sixty-six victories—was named in yesterday's report of the army—has lost an eye.

Our effectiveness was pretty high, but it could have been much higher if the tactical actions had been different. But the fragmentation that had been there from the beginning stayed on our heels as our doom seems never-ending. Superfluous to state that not one vehicle made it out of Danzig. Instead of my brave 1. Company, I now have a mixture. Only my own and the crew of Bender are left with me. It is so sad that one cannot even think of it.

It is quiet right now. We are on guard here until they grab us by the tail. Haake got married, got out of Küstrin, but has not arrived here yet. He could at least have sent word. I remain with my best wishes for a speedy recovery.

Your comrade, M. Lippert.

This letter was a report on the situation of the unit at the time it was written. It was all the more important since it turned out that the fate of the fallen wounded and missing soldiers could not be followed up along the normal official lines. Obersturmführer Max Lippert died a soldier's death a few weeks later in Berlin.

Following my discharge from the hospital, after having been moved a number of times while in British custody, I handed over all dates and facts known to me then on the fates of members of our Panzer-Abteilung to the German Red Cross, which used them in its tracing service.

The German Red Cross deserves thanks, and it must be emphasized here that this organization, with all its branches and under difficult circumstances, accepted without reserve the Waffen-SS as a part of the army and never, not even internationally, questioned the fact that we had been soldiers. There followed an intensive correspondence with members and repatriated soldiers. The second report, below, came from the then-young Panzer driver, Sturmmann Lothar Tiby, who is today a graduate engineer and manager in a well-known industrial enterprise. Tiby provided it after his return from Russian captivity, where he had carried these notes for years with him. Tiby's precise report is, naturally, centered on his personal experiences in a Panzer of the 1. Company.

January 25, 1945

Acceptance of thirty-six Panzers, type Königstiger, at Sennelager near Paderborn and loading for transport east. (Six training Panzers had already been available.)

January 28, 1945

Unloading of parts of the Abteilung in Pomerania in the Wedell area. Other parts of the Abteilung were directed toward Küstrin and Gotenhafen. Action by the Abteilung as a complete unit did, thus, not take place.

January 31, 1945

Attack with four Panzers from our company (under Obersturmführer Lippert) together with paratroopers. Our own crew: commander Unterscharführer Löchner, gunner Unterscharführer Klöckner, driver Sturmmann Tiby, radio operator Sturmmann Horak, loader Sturmmann Unkel.

The objective of the day, Regentin, was reached without tank engagement. Russian losses: eighty antitank guns and great numbers of infantry.

Our own losses: one commander by bullet to the head, no losses of Panzers. Approximately thirty percent of the paratroopers wounded or dead.

February 1, 1945

Attack with tank engagement. Our own Panzer was at the point, rolled onto a mine, and sustained damage to track. Chief's Panzer took over the point to provide cover while track was changed. Heavy Russian mortar fire on both Panzers during the repair of the track.

Our own losses: Löchner, wounded in the back; Horak, wounded in the thigh; Unkel, wounded in the leg; the driver of the chief's Panzer, Öchsle, wounded in the head (blind). All four transported to the hospital. Klöckner and Tiby not seriously wounded, ready for further action.

The new crew: commander Grünhofer, gunner Klöckner, driver Tiby, radio operator Breitenstein, loader Badke.

Attack achieved the objective of the day, a further ten kilometers were behind us.

February 2, 1945

Another advance of five kilometers, then withdrawal to avoid encirclement.

February 3, 1945

Visit to the repair shop in Neu-Wedell for minor repairs. Strong Russian reconnaissance team destroyed at the outskirts of town. Moved to new front sector Arnswalde.

February 4, 1945

Attack with four Panzers of our company from Arnswalde to a town five kilometers from Arnswalde where German infantry was encircled. Strong Russian tank and antitank gun resistance. Three of our own Panzers lost because of damage. Lippert as commander in our vehicle, still ready for action, two enemy tanks knocked out. Our Panzer sustained direct hits, no penetration, immobilized. A second attack by four more Panzers of our Abteilung relieved the infantry and had us towed back.

February 6–20, 1945

Our own vehicle was at the repair company in Stargard. The Abteilung was encircled in Arnswalde, relieved from the outside on February 18.

February 21–March 14, 1945

Our own vehicle in Berlin-Tempelhof for repairs. They would take a few months. Took over another vehicle with minor repairs in Berlin.

March 15, 1945

Return to the central sector at the Oder. The Abteilung consisted of only ten Panzers.

March 20, 1945
Our wounded radio operator Horak returned to action in our vehicle. New commander Bender.

April 1–15, 1945
Assembly in Frauenhagen.

April 16, 1945
Marching orders to Strausberg by way of Angermünde.

April 18, 1945
In position along the road from Bukow, waiting for Russian tank spearheads advancing on Berlin. Twelve Russian tanks knocked out by our vehicle. The ten Panzers of our Abteilung knocked out a total of sixty-four Russian tanks.
Our own losses: one Panzer. A few Panzers sustained minor damage, our own Panzer with damage to the track tension adjuster and the gun laying mechanism.

April 19, 1945
Breakthrough by the Russians toward our repair company and encirclement. Two Panzers there were repaired immediately. During the first breakout attempt, one Panzer was knocked out. During the second attempt, two Russian tanks were knocked out by our vehicle. Set out in the direction of Berlin with the repair company. Two more Russian tanks were knocked out by us outside Berlin.

April 22, 1945
While our Panzer was being towed to the repair company, our radio operator Horak was once more seriously wounded and transported to the hospital.

April 24, 1945
The Russian ring around Berlin was closed. The remaining Panzers of our Abteilung were distributed throughout Berlin. Our first action was at Mecklenburgische Street, four tanks knocked out.

April 25, 1945

New action at Heer street railroad station.

April 26, 1945

Action at Halensee railroad station.

April 28, 1945

Abteilung commander Obersturmbannführer Herzig and four more commanders of our Abteilung were awarded the Knight's Cross by Hitler in the Reichschancellery.

April 29, 1945

Commander Unterscharführer Bender wounded in the stomach outside the Panzer. New commander Semik.

April 30, 1945

One Russian tank knocked out at Helensee railroad station. Commander Semik seriously wounded outside the vehicle by mortar round. New commander Oberscharführer Stolze.

May 1, 1945

Five more Russian tanks knocked out at Halensee railroad station. This was the last tank engagement. A total of twenty-eight Russian tanks were knocked out by our Panzer.

May 2, 1945

Attempt to break out from Berlin in westerly direction with the two last Panzers of our Abteilung. Our vehicle with commander Lippert, the second Panzer with the holder of the Knight's Cross Schäfer of 3. Company. The heavy fighting against a vastly superior force lasted all day. There were very high losses of vehicles, infantry, and civilians on our side and very high losses of personnel carriers and infantry on the Russian side due to action of the two Panzers. During a renewed attempt to break through, Schäfer's Panzer took a direct hit, two men dead, the rest seriously wounded. A further attempt to break out was no longer possible. Our vehicle, the last Panzer of the Abteilung, was destroyed.

May 3, 1945

During an attempt by Obersturmführer Lippert to make his way west as an infantryman, he was killed by a bullet in the head. The high losses of our Abteilung during the action of only three months were exemplified by our Panzer crew. In action were six commanders, three radio operators, two loaders. Only Klöckner and Tiby were in action from the beginning to the end. (signed) Tiby

Reports similar to the one above could have come from any of the Panzers of the Abteilung even if they were not continuously in action. It must be reiterated that the heavy SS-Panzer-Abteilung 503 was doomed during its action in the final battles. These biggest and strongest of the German Panzers, wherever they appeared, were the last hope and a certain support for the soldiers, commanders of the troops, refugees, and the population in the struggle to stem the flood of the superior Russian strength. For the men of the Königstigers, this meant fighting to the last Panzer and being a shining example until the final destruction.

It was in that spirit that Max Lippert wrote: "It is so sad that one cannot even think of it."

Finally, in this sense, the letter from the mother of our killed orderly officer, Adolf Grimminger, should be quoted here. This letter, an answer to my note reporting his death, is dedicated to all our soldiers who risked their lives in the loyal performance of their duties.

Schwäbisch Gmünd, January 23, 1947

Dear esteemed Mr. Kauerauf,

We have received your letter of December 30 and are grateful for it. The sad news of the death of our dear Adolf had been passed on to us at the time by two comrades. It was very sad for us that our dear son had to die so close to the end, after he had been in the heaviest action for such a long time with such fervent devotion. We did not receive any official notification since his death took place during the sorrowful time of the collapse. We had to sacrifice so much; of four children we had to part with three.

On September 23, 1944, our son Walter was killed during the heavy fighting for Arnheim, in action as battery commander of his assault gun Abteilung. He is buried at Bocholt near the German-Dutch border.

Our only daughter died giving birth to her fourth child in April 1945. She, too, was a victim of this unfortunate war. All this was too much for my nerves. I had a brain seizure. With God's help I have recovered, but the loss and the yearning for my dear children will not let me feel cheerful ever again. The Lord puts a burden upon us, but He also helps us carry it, as I have experienced time and again. It often hurts me bitterly that our soldiers who did their utmost and sacrificed everything with sincere hearts should now be despised. They were heroes in the true sense of the word, those who died and those who are still alive. They gave their best for the fatherland and their fellow men. I often think that my son would have suffered very badly because of the sad and hopeless end.

Dear Mr. Kauerauf, I thank you sincerely for your sympathy. I wish you all the best for your future and send you cordial greetings as Adolf's mother.

Mrs. Eugenie Grimminger
Schwäb. Gmünd, Olgastr. 59

I bow my head with reverence to my comrades of the SS-Königstiger-Abteilung 503 and their families.

Fritz Kauerauf

THE END IN BERLIN, 1945
A report by Unterscharführer Georg Diers, Panzer commander in the heavy SS-Panzer-Abteilung 503

April 19, 1945—Coming from the Seelöwer Heights, we assembled in Buckow near Straußberg/Müncheberg. Damage to the track, hits to the cupola and turret from JS-II. Previously, thirteen tanks knocked out in some nineteen minutes.

April 20, 1945—Back into the repair shop at Hönow near Altlandsberg to fix the track. As the turret was being welded, a fire broke out. The sight and weapons in the fighting compartment were damaged by the Tetra fire extinguisher fluid.

April 21, 1945—Alarm during the night, breakthrough by the Russians. Retreat to Berlin, towing another Panzer, via Marzan, Lichtenberg to Biesdorf to the firm of Krupp & Druckemöller.

April 22, 1945—Early in the morning from Biesdorf via Köpenick and Oberschöneweide/Spree to Neukölln across the Teltowkanal Bridge. One JS-II knocked out on the bridge. This was the most accomplished kill by the gunner yet since only a small part of its left track was visible. This was the commanders forty-ninth kill. The intercom had failed, communication with the help of a piece of string. We secured the antitank barricade on the left at the Sonnenallee, in the direction of the bridge. Last rations issued by Oberscharführer Taube. At noon, return to the command post at the courthouse of Neukölln. Received order for action in Neukölln, in the direction of Berg and Richard Streets, in front of the Hertie department store on Berliner Street, across from the post office. The daily report of the Supreme Command stated that the Köpenick railroad station had been recaptured.

April 25, 1945—The battle of Neukölln began. The Russians tried to cross the Berg and Berliner streets. Another Panzer, dug in outside the main post office in Neukölln, was completely shot to pieces. The commander of our own vehicle was wounded in the afternoon. He lay immobile in the Panzer, one eye ripped out. The crew drove the Panzer back to take the Obersturmführer to hospital. He was loaded onto a truck and I have never heard from him again. Where to get another commander quickly? On the sidewalk stood an officer in Panzer uniform, he had been in a Berlin hospital, wounded. He took over command of the Panzer. The vehicle immediately returned to the front for a counterattack since the Russians had broken through across Berliner street. We conducted the counterattack from the Hasenheide, together with the French legion "Charlemagne." We succeeded in throwing back the Russians, returning to the previous positions and knocking out several tanks. Later, however, there was a breakthrough across Richard Street into Neukölln which was in Russian hands.

After knocking out three tanks near Jahn street, an area our present commander knew very well, we returned to Hertie square.

April 26, 1945—Order for withdrawal in the direction of Hermannsplatz (square). The Panzer had been damaged during the night; we continued on to the divisional command post. During an artillery attack by Stalin organs (rocket launchers) the commander was seriously wounded. We took him to the hospital at the Anhalter railroad station and continued to Potsdamer Platz. The command post was no longer there, it had been moved into the House of Labor on Potsdamer Street. We reported to commander Kausch and commander Herzig. Hauptsturmführer Dr. Cappell ordered the old commander, Diers, to take over the crew again. Finally, orders to drive to the repair shop, which had been moved to Uhland Street (Kurfürsten Damm). We were looking forward to our first night of sleep.

April 27, 1945—Departure for the central subway station, securing of the corner Linden Street/Kommandanten street in the direction of Belle Alliance Square.

April 28, 1945—The Russians attempted, without success, to break through to the right of the Luisenstadt church with the help of flamethrowers.

April 29, 1945—Withdrawal to Potsdamer Platz, facing Saarland Street and Anhalter Platz. The Turk's Panzer was on the opposite side of the street. The Russians concentrated heavy artillery fire on the Potsdamer Platz and the government quarter. They tried to break through with tanks from the Anhalter railroad station, however, without success. Among others, we knocked out a JS-II coming from behind hotel Haus Vaterland and a number of T-34s so that Saarland Street was blocked.

April 30, 1945—Orders by radio to move to the Reichstag (parliament building) in the afternoon. Turk's Panzer remained at Potsdamer Platz. During our drive we noticed increased Russian radio traffic. They had probably listened in when we received the order. The Reichstag building was already badly bombed, the plenary hall burned out. At the front of the building we looked over to the Kroll Opera building, and saw a large number of T-34s sitting to our right, about thirty of them, their gun barrels pointing at the Reichstag building, at us. After a thorough briefing of the crew, we dared to race around the corner and opened fire on this large number, with success.

May 1, 1945—Area of operation: Reichstag building, Brandenburger Tor (gate) to the Siegessäule (victory column). Counterattack along the central axis near the Kroll Opera. In front of the Kroll Opera, Russian tanks were in position, inside there were still German wounded. We were able to keep the square in front of it open. Our radio operator, Alex Sommer, was injured by an overhead trolley cable.

The Russians broke into the Reichstag building with an assault team during this day and were able to hold its center. They fired down the air shafts and spiral staircases on German soldiers. A few of our MGs were still firing from the top floor of the building, but they fell silent one after the other. A German command post was located on the lower floor. A counterattack with our support achieved only a few extra holes in the walled-up windows. The order to break out arrived around 7 P.M. We took on ammunition at the Göring Villa on Wilhelm Street. I had been ordered to the

Reichschancellery, where I had to run along numerous hallways and came into the open down a wide staircase, which was covered with a large plate. I then had to go through this building and saw, at an inner yard near the wall, attempts to burn something (the body of Adolf Hitler) by throwing gasoline on it. With every attempt, a cloud of smoke rose and the Russians immediately fired with mortar or artillery. Then, two mines were put under it and detonated. Goebbels gave me the order: "Assembly at the Friedrich Street railroad station, Weidendammer Bridge. Breakthrough of our forces there. Three to five more Panzers may join. Breakthrough in the direction of Oranienburg, join up with the Steiner Kampfgruppe, and continue on toward Schleswig-Holstein. There, join up with the Canadian forces and prepare for a counterattack towards the east." I learned there that Adolf Hitler was dead, that he had married Eva Braun in the meantime, and that those were the bodies of Hitler and Eva Braun outside. We arrived at Friedrich Street in front of the Weidendammer Bridge at around 9 P.M. A column of comrades willing to risk the breakout assembled slowly behind us. There were three or four Panzers, assault guns, and some armored personnel carriers, but mostly trucks. The Weidendammer Bridge, ahead of us, was secured with an antitank barricade. I walked down the stairs into Friedrich Street once more and talked with a number of ranking SS officers. Among other things I was told that the commander of the Panzer-regiment, P.A. Kausch, was above, lying severely wounded in the armored car, which was parked in front of the hotel. When I was back in the Panzer, a number of uniformed men reported to me and requested to be taken along. They climbed onto the rear above the engine. We began our breakout at midnight or just before midnight.

A high-ranking officer joined us. His insignia could not be made out since he wore an overcoat. He was obviously respected by those around and asked to be taken along. He, too, climbed onto the rear. We had to break through the antitank barricade during the breakout since the passages were too narrow for the Königstiger. It was reported to be either on the Weidendammer Bridge or directly behind.

At the first street from the right, Ziegel Street, as I later learned, we received murderous fire, not so much from armor-piercing weapons as from artillery, infantry, etc. Everything on the outside of the fighting vehicle was shot off, the track cover, towing cables, and so on. The intercom inside failed, the driver kept going at high speed. Ahead of us was a large crater in the street toward which the driver was headed. Through the gunner I was able to get the driver to steer around it on the sidewalk. Doing this, we ripped down quite a number of lampposts on which the overhead power cables for the streetcar were strung. A little further on we came to the barricade. As I opened the commander's hatch, a peaked cap appeared at the side. I could not accurately make it out in the darkness and took the pistol in hand immediately, but then I saw the death's head. It was an Unterstürmfuhrer. He stated that he was the driver and second adjutant of Goebbels. He knew his way around the Berlin streets. He told me that he had jumped onto the track cover on the left when the Panzer had started out and had held on to the turret since he knew that there was fairly violent firing at Ziegel Street. To the question as to what had happened to the people on the rear, he said that they had been ripped apart. There were only pieces of cloth and flesh left. We untangled ourselves from the cables and drove on slowly after having gone around the barricade. He was well informed and told me that the last one to join us was Martin Bormann. None of the three on the rear had survived the fire. He then guided us on between Züricher Street and Schönhauser Allee where all was quiet. There were almost no Russians around. We passed a fairly large column on the left but could not determine what it was. Some women were drawing water from a fire hydrant. We stopped the vehicle and asked who that was on the other side. We were told they were also Germans. We drove on and then reached the so-called second Russian ring at the Schönhauser Alley. There, General Bärenfänger was attempting to bring some order into the chaos, and he requested us to drive to the other side of the street through a subway underpass and to take over the point. After a short drive we ran onto German mines. General Bärenfänger came back immediately, and I reported to him that we were immobilized at the moment but would be ready for action again in one hour. General Bärenfänger said to me then: ". . . my boy, see to it that you blow up your Panzer and, most important, that you get your boys home safely. We have lost the war." I informed him of the orders I had received from Goebbels. He then said: ". . . I have spoken with General Krebs who conducted the negotiations with the Russians. We have totally lost the war. Everyone must try to get home unscathed." We blew up the fighting vehicle; it was a sad sight. We had been able to knock out thirty-nine tanks in Berlin. They had been set on fire by us. Whatever else we may have knocked out, we were unable to register accurately.

    May 2, 1945—All this happened around 7 P.M. under the subway line, which ran elevated near the station at the Schönauer Allee. Despite the chaos I still had my crew with me and had been able to persuade the driver of an Opel-Blitz truck, after quite a while of talking, to race it across this wide street, which was under heavy Russian fire. Only the first car would have a very good chance to get across. The others behind would be lost. Once the driver had agreed I collected my crew and filled them in on the plan. They were supposed to hang on to the left side of the truck and then try to find their own way on the other side of the street after we got across. At the same time, masses of soldiers and civilians were also trying to cross the street. However, the dead bodies kept piling up and this wave, too, was thrown back. This was not easy since those in the rear could not see what was happening in front and kept pushing forward. The Opel-Blitz then started out, succeeded in crossing, and came to a stop on the other side. It had been shot to pieces.

My crew had not dared to jump on and remained behind. I, myself, made it across. I was wounded, however, and traveled the next few kilometers limping, until I came across an Adler Cabriolet car. Our loader, Alex Sommer, had received a bullet in the stomach during this chaos and is still missing today. The gunner was slightly wounded and went into Russian captivity together with the loader and the driver. I drove on with the white Adler car and came across another group breaking out with five assault guns and a very large column of soldiers and civilians on trucks and ambulances loaded with wounded. Our breakout was in the direction of Nauen-Oranienburg. We traveled through towns, often under murderous Russian fire. Anyone wounded had to be left behind. Many of them begged for a hand grenade or a bullet in the head. We could only give out hand grenades as long as there were any left, to help these boys. An ambulance driving ahead of me, a former truck with two or three rows of stretchers, was hit. The wounded clung to the sides, screaming. It was a terrible sight. We drove on across fields, again through villages captured by the Russians, and finally into the woods where we disbanded. I managed to get through, by way of Neuruppin and the direction of Wittenberge, to Havelberg. We started out with five men, toward the end there were only two, then I was left as the only one. We had our weapons with us and ready at all times since SS men were generally bumped off as soon as the blood group tattoo was detected. I had seen this repeatedly with my own eyes, and I did not want to arrive up there without bringing company.

On June 17, 1945, I was, without warning, taken prisoner by the Russians after the chief of the German militia in Havelberg, whose granddaughter I had saved from drowning in the Havel only four days previously, handed me over to the Red Army. The interrogations were very tough, but the shootings were no longer quite so frequent. Subsequently, I was sentenced to death twice, once in Havelberg and once on the estate of Count Itzenplitz in Stüdenitz. I avoided the first sentence by my own actions, and the second one by lucky chance. I then spent time in Brandenburg as a prisoner of war and was released on Christmas Day, 1949. The very same day I found my gunner and driver who had been taken prisoner together. The gunner had worked in a mine near Stalino, the driver near Stalingrad. They were released the same day, and thus ended the history of the Panzer and its crew.

The crew of Königstiger 314, 3./heavy SS-Panzer-Abteilung 503, were commander Georg Diers, gunner Wolf-Dieter Kothe, loader Alex Sommer, driver Willi Kenkel, and radio operator Bodo Hansen.

WITH TIGER AND PANZERFAUST—THE FINAL BATTLE FOR BERLIN
Henri Fenet, commander of the 57. Battalion of the French volunteer division "Charlemagne," reports

In Berlin, there is a Französische (French) Straße (street) and a Französische Kirche (church). They are memorials to the Huguenots who fled religious persecution, moved to Prussia at the turn of the seventeenth century and helped build the capital. Around the middle of the twentieth century, other French had come to defend this capital, which their forefathers had helped to build.

On April 25, just before noon, the 57. French Battalion, still 300 men strong, crossed Berlin from west to east, from the Havel River to near Hasenheide, close to Tempelhof. These volunteers, riding in some dozen trucks, sang and waved cordially at the Berliners who returned the greetings with warmth, their faces lit by smiles. On the day before the attack the Berliners appeared, to us, as full of life as ever, without a trace of panic, confusion, or despair.

On April 26, the battalion and the Panzers of the Waffen-SS-Division "Nordland" attacked from the direction of the Neukölln city hall in order to drive back Russian units, which already threatened the center of Neukölln. We advanced approximately one kilometer before the Russians reacted. Then, however, their resistance stiffened, and they attacked violently our neighboring sectors where they broke through our lines. Around noon, the battalion command post, which had been set up in the city hall, was, to its great surprise, under Russian machine-gun fire. An immediate counterattack cleared that quarter of town, however. We held it firmly until the evening when our messenger arrived and reported that the Russians had reached Hermannsplatz (square), some 900 meters behind us. There was no longer any contact to our right or left. The encirclement was beginning to close behind us.

Night fell as we reached Hermannsplatz by the last open street. The assault guns of the "Nordland" Division, set up behind a barricade of paving stones, held off the Russian tanks and knocked out an impressive number of them. Around midnight the guns had to be withdrawn due to lack of ammunition. We finally reestablished contact with the division and spent the night in the "Thomas-Keller" beer hall near the Anhalter railroad station. After this first day I began to ponder the real situation of the defense of Berlin. There were strong points as well as weak ones, in particular the shortage of material and ammunition. There was no way of maintaining contact except through messengers who were often held back by the intensity of the bombings. The units were mostly on their own, and each made the best of its few remaining resources in cooperation with its immediate neighboring units. Two thirds, or even three quarters, of the fighters were Hitler Youths or Volkssturm without any training, armed and equipped with whatever was available. Despite this, the Hitler Youths distinguished themselves and destroyed a great number of tanks with Panzerfausts. I received a detail of Hitler Youths as reinforcement in Neukölln. The boys fought well throughout the day. The regular units of the Army and the Waffen-SS were at a strength of less than 20,000 men, less than 100 Panzers, and the artillery was almost completely out of ammunition.

Despite all this, they fought with an unbelievable vehemence. The enemy acknowledged this with fairness: "I have the impression that a damned heavy battle lies ahead of us," Stalin said before the battle of Berlin. Marshal Konjew, wrote in his memoirs that the Soviet army lost 800 tanks in Berlin, equivalent to four or five tank divisions. General Popiel, chief of staff with Zhukow, said: "We had a lion sitting on our back." And General Tschuikow stated: "All I can say is that this last nut was the toughest we ever had to crack." This same Tschuikow said to Zhukow, who was badgering him on the telephone: "I cannot advance any faster because of SS units with their Tigers, fighting bravely."

These Tigers and the soldiers of the Waffen-SS who held up Tschuikow's advance were a mere 3,000 men: Germans from the Leibstandarte of the Lichterfelde barracks, stragglers from SS divisions who had made their way there, 300 men from the staffs of the Waffen-SS,

Finns, Danes, Swedes, and Norwegians of the 11. SS-Panzer-Grenadier-Division "Nordland," men from the Panzer-Regiment "Hermann von Salza" and the heavy SS-Panzer-Abteilung 503 of the III. SS-Panzerkorps (with eight to ten Königstigers, under the command of Obersturmbann-führer P.A. Kausch which knocked out 480 tanks in twelve days) 300 French from the "Charlemagne" Battalion who destroyed sixty-two tanks with Panzerfausts, Latvians, Spaniards and Hungarians. All of Europe was there during this last rendezvous.

But one did not have to be in the SS to fight with greatest determination. The 18. Panzer-Grenadier-Division, the artillery of the division, and the Panzer-Regiment 118 under the command of major Neuer destroyed 100 tanks in one day just outside Berlin. The legendary acts of heroism of Generalmajor Bärenfänger have already been told numerous times. During the first days, the "Zitadelle" sector in the heart of Berlin was the hardest piece of Tschuikow's nut. We French held our positions in close cooperation with our Scandinavian comrades, the Panzer-Grenadiers of "Nordland" Division under the command of Sturmbannführer Ternedde, and the tank hunter teams under the command of Weber and Fey.

The intensity and the vehemence of the fighting grew by the day. In the evening of April 27, we were in action between the Belle-Alliance Platz and the entry gates to the Reichschancellery. Two famous streets in the center of Berlin were in our sector, Wilhelm Street and Friedrich Street. We were under a deluge of artillery fire, day and night, almost without pause. We were attacked by tanks firing at the positions we were holding and by Soviet infantry, which tried to drive us out with flamethrowers. There was fighting everywhere, in the backyards behind the houses, on the roofs, with assault rifles, with hand grenades, and with bayonets.

The houses were on fire, collapsing. Immense clouds of dust rose to the sky. The smoke and dust almost choked and blinded us. We could only see for half a meter. Our tank hunters were constantly on the alert. Not one tank made it through. Wilhelm Street was littered with burning tanks, their ammunition exploding and their fuel tanks blowing up in flames.

There was neither day nor night, we could barely see the sky. It was just a cover of heavy haze, which reflected the threatening flames. We heard the din of the bombardment, the crackle of the firestorms, and during the nights, very close, the wailing and the howls of the women. This chilled us and made us shiver more than did the explosions and the firestorms. According to the former social-democrat lord mayor Ernst

Reuter, 90,000 women were raped by the soldiers of the Red Army drunk with success. Fighting from ruin to ruin, we found ourselves in the evening of May 1 in the cellar of the headquarters of the secret service. Above us, everything had been demolished. Some 100 police officials were attached to me for the following days. They fought as regular soldiers, very bravely. As a Hauptsturmführer, I was in command of all these Sturmbannführers, Obersturmbannführers, and Standartenführers. It was admirable how they went on the attack, rifle in hand.

During this first evening of May, we had at least one satisfaction. The Russians had announced that they would capture all of Berlin on May 1, but we were still there.

Our neighbors to our right were still fighting bitterly for possession of every piece of ground. In order to see in the dark we had stuck candles into yule candleholders. In the flickering light of the wax candles down there in the cellar, I handed out the last Iron Crosses.

We were then already beyond hope or fear, almost beyond time itself. We felt an inner joy, the joy of being united in the comradeship of battle, and of the feeling of boundless trust we had for each other. Those who were decorated felt immensely proud. I would never forget their shining eyes, which looked at me so sincerely, and their handshakes. Right from the beginning they all had only had this one thought, to be awarded the Iron Cross. Some days previously I had taken up position at a window with a Panzerfaust. My men pulled me back, saying: "Let us earn our Iron Cross!"

In the morning of May 2 we were in the building of the Air Ministry. All of the sector was quiet when several cars flying white flags approached. In the cars were Russians, accompanied by German officers. The Soviet soldiers, men and women, came over and invited us to surrender. A major of the Luftwaffe said to me: "It is over. The capitulation has been signed. There is no choice but to surrender." My men and I decided quickly. We would set out for the Reichschancellery where our divisional command post was located. Avoiding Russian troops, we advanced along the subway tunnels. At the Kaiserhof station it became obvious; the streets were filled with Russian trucks, incessantly blowing their horns. The walls of the Reichschancellery remained silent.

Not much later we were taken prisoner in a hiding place under the bridge of the Potsdam railroad station in Berlin where we had wanted to wait for nightfall and then make our way to Potsdam town. There we had hoped to join the Wenck Army.

Captured! The whole world seemed to break apart inside us. Our guards treated us without brutality, but all around us reigned the ecstasy of victory, an ecstasy that was dangerous to the vanquished. One of my noncoms, at my side, was killed by a bullet in the temple before our guards could prevent it.

We were crowded into an area near the damaged Brandenburg Gate and watched, with heavy hearts, the great victory parade, hundreds and hundreds of red-draped tanks. We felt crushed, broken. It was an absolute catastrophe, the feeling of being wiped out, the fall into nothingness, into the blackest night.

I remember the stages of my imprisonment, the inner yard of Moabit prison, buildings of red brick, my first night as a prisoner, sitting on the ground leaning my back against a tree. There I heard the news of Hitler's and Goebbel's deaths. The next day I was moved to Siemensstadt. It was abandoned, all the furniture had been thrown from the windows. A few days later I arrived in the camp at Finow. I had been wounded in the foot on April 26 and could hardly walk. The Russians took me to the city hospital where I got to know firsthand the legendary care offered in German hospitals and provided, in my case, by a head nurse who was a little surly and two young nurses, Gerda and Irmela. I was surrounded by friendship and human warmth.

When the Russians moved the camp to the east, they decided not to take me along, so I returned to France. "You will suffer the fate that traitors deserve!" Such were the slogans with which I was greeted at the border. During my court case, a year later, the prosecutor asked me: "Do you regret what you did?" My answer was: "If the war had ended differently, would you really believe that I regretted it? If I told you now that I regretted it, I would be a liar or a coward." The jurors, almost all communists, were not angry at me. Their sentence of twenty years' hard labor instead of the death penalty was a sign of esteem as my attorney was told later.

Three and one-half years later the prison gates opened for me. I worked with a group of prisoners outside, in a lodge belonging to the Ministry of Justice.

On the day of my release the administration officials were present and offered me champagne. The priest of the city had come up in his small Citroën car and waited for me at the gate. After the formalities were looked after, one of the officials drove me to the nearest railroad station. They were all sincerely pleased to see me set free. My own joy was increased by experiencing such human warmth in my own fatherland. The joy of freedom washed away the hardships endured before.

BERLIN 1945
Karl-Heinz Turk, Unterscharführer in the heavy SS-Panzer-Abteilung 503, reports

After having been in action constantly at different locations in the city, such as the Schloßbrücke (castle bridge), Gertrauden Bridge, the Reich bank, Wall Street, Spittelmarkt, and others, I received an order, on April 29, to drive across the Potsdamer Square toward the Anhalter railroad station and there engage Russian tanks. This turned out to be extremely difficult because of the rubble, debris, and overhead wires hanging down. We did not reach the Anhalter railroad station since we encountered enemy Paks and tanks firing on us even as we drove toward it. I ordered to open fire and had the Panzer pull back slowly. We took up position at Prinz-Albrecht Street. We managed to keep the enemy tanks at a distance and set some of them on fire. In the meantime it had become dark and we reduced our fire in order not to waste our shells. We were not certain if we would be able to get more ammunition. The fire from artillery and infantry continued. Since we had to constantly fight off enemy infantry, our two MGs were never silent.

During the night we heard loud tank noises from Saarland Street and expected a surprise from the Russians at daybreak. We were not wrong. At dawn the guns of the Russian tanks began to roar. They had towed away the knocked-out tanks during the night and brought in others that were ready for action. We fired as fast as we could, but an enemy hit ripped apart our right track. After an hour's battle the Russian tanks and Paks fell silent, but we were no longer mobile.

After discussing the situation with my crew, I set out on foot, under heavy artillery fire, to the Tiergarten to get a recovery Panther. I was lucky that the commander of the sole remaining recovery Panther was my former gunner Leo Piller. We drove to the Potsdamer Square in the Panther where Piller and I hooked up the Königstiger and the shot-off track under heavy fire for the tow to the vicinity of the Reichschancellery. After three hours we had repaired the track and drove forward again to the Saarland Street. We had difficulties driving, however, since the Panzer could only be steered with one track. We took up our old position on the right side of Saarland Street. Shortly thereafter, two officers of the Luftwaffe showed up and requested that I come with them to the Reich Air Ministry building where our command post was located. Radio contact had been lost quite some time before. After some time we arrived there, having worked our way through the ruins of the bombed houses. The fire from the artillery continued to rage, and we spent more time in cover

than we spent running. The commander of our Abteilung, Sturmbannführer Herzig, wanted to know why I had pulled back my Panzer for
about three hours. After filling him in on the details I ran back to my
Panzer. I had been ordered to find a suitable position at Potsdamer
Square and to prepare for defense in all directions. We positioned the
Tiger in front of the entrance to the Potsdamer Square subway station;
behind a barricade thrown up to provide cover from shrapnel. This provided us cover to the side but still allowed us to fire in all directions by
turning the turret. From this position we fired on anything we could
make out. The machine guns had to fire repeatedly on lifting sewer lids
from where Russian infantry crawled out time and again.

On May 1 we began to seriously run out of ammunition, and we had
no idea where we would get more. The artillery fire suddenly died down
in the afternoon. Since there was no longer any system of exchanging
messages, I walked into the subway station. To my surprise, the station
was filled with civilians who stared at me frightened and asked timidly
whether the war was over. After some searching I found an army captain
whom I asked for a report on the present situation.

It turned out that he was a dispatch rider who was only wearing his
superior's coat. He was able to provide me with the requested information, and I learned of the death of Adolf Hitler. I also learned that the
remains of a Waffen-SS pioneer platoon were in position nearby, reinforced by groups of Volkssturm and Hitler Youth. I sent off the messenger to bring the leader of the pioneer platoon and to send home the
Volkssturm and the Hitler Youth. The messenger did as I had ordered,
and the Oberscharfürer of the pioneer platoon arrived with a few of his
men.

They had some more news, also of the attempted breakout at the
Weidendammer Bridge. The Oberscharführer reported that two armored
personnel carriers, ready for action, sat at the Reichschancellery. We managed to get one of these vehicles going and drove off in the direction of
the Weidendammer Bridge.

During our fast drive during the night, which was lit only by the burning fires, we failed to notice a shell crater into which we ran with the carrier. It was impossible to get it going again. After the loss of our Tiger,
which we could no longer steer, we had also lost this armored carrier.
Among the soldiers who had joined me and my crew was a native Berliner
who took over guiding us. Along a subway line, and from there through
water half a meter deep, we arrived at the Weidendammer Bridge.

As I recall, the breakout began on May 2 at around 12:15 A.M. A Königstiger drove at the point, and large numbers of soldiers and civilians ran behind. Immediately after the antitank barricade we ran into heavy enemy fire, which caused numerous dead and wounded. An officer of the Luftwaffe and I were able to jump across the bridge without being wounded. Since we did not consider it possible to get through any further at the time, we sought cover in the Berlin urban transport building. We spent all of the next day and the following night in this building. Meanwhile, we had been able to secure work clothes and then started out on foot in the direction of Frohnau.

After being taken prisoner in Berlin, and again at Steutz on the Elbe River, I swam across the Elbe and Mulde Rivers near Rosslau (Kornhaus). After four weeks on the run through Russian- and American-occupied territory, an American military police patrol nabbed me near Leuna. I was sent to an American prison camp and later to the Rhine into French hands until I finally ended up in the internment camp at Darmstadt.

At the end of the war, the valiant Panzer units were deployed at all sectors of the front, from north to south, in their last action against the advancing Red Army.

On the day of surrender they laid down their weapons and began their long and bitter way into captivity from where there would be no return for many of the comrades.

On May 8, 1945, the commanding general of the II. SS-Panzerkorps, general of the Waffen-SS Wilhelm Bittrich, delivered his last address to the leaders and soldiers of his combat staff, the corps security company, and the army corps communications Abteilung 400, which was always attached to the staff, east of Linz:

My comrades!

We are faced with the most hopeless day for any soldier, capitulation as ordered by the Supreme Command, and we look into each other's eyes for the last time. As low as our spirits may be, we have to carry out this duty.

The path for all of us leads into an uncertain future. The bitter fate of imprisonment, maybe even deportment, lies ahead of us. I have tried with all my means to bring the mass of the Korps to the Americans. This was possible as parts of the corps were in action against the Americans near Linz. I thank you for your fighting spirit in action, your loyalty, and for your admirable discipline, which I would beg you to prove again on your way through the darkness that lies ahead of us.

For many long years, decades, our national anthem will not sound in our ears, the words Germany and fatherland will not be spoken during the coming time. But in the world of our hearts they have to maintain their sacred and important significance for future generations whom God may provide the gift of a better fate and of freedom.

Long live Germany, our fatherland!

PART IV

Appendices

Das Reich Panzers

by Miles Krogfus
San Diego, USA

The striking power of "Das Reich" was initially augmented by armor when a Sturmgeschütze battery of ten assault guns, commanded by Obersturmführer Eberhardt Telkamp, entered combat in June 1941 against Russia. It was not, however, until the spring of 1942, when refitting and retraining in France, that the division was assigned a Panzer-regiment, whose equipment arrived throughout that summer and fall. Its first, third and sixth companies received Panzer IV Gs, its second, fourth, fifth and seventh companies Panzer III Ls, its eighth company, led by Hauptsturmführer Grader, was supplied with three platoons of Tigers and one of Panzer III. The assault gun battery expanded to a battalion with Hauptsturmführer as its commander.

"Das Reich" Panzers played a key role in the Charkow campaign in early 1943. At the end of January, the division entered combat southwest of that city. Included in its armor strength on February 1 were sixty-six Panzer IIIs, sixty Panzer IVs, and four Tigers. The Panzer-regiment's commander was Sturmbannführer Herbert-Ernst Vahl, its Ist Battalion CO Sturmbannführer Albin von Reitzenstein, its IInd Battalion CO Sturmbannführer Christian Tychsen. Reitzenstein took over command of the regiment on February when Vahl became CO of the division. In mid-February Hauptsturmführer Grader was killed, and briefly Hauptsturmführer Herbert Kuhlmann, then Hauptsturmführer Fritz Herzig took over the Tiger company. On February 19, thirty-three Panzer IIIs were fit for combat. Just after 9:15 A.M. on February 22, 150 kilometers south of Charkow, Hauptsturmführer Karl Kloskowski in Panzer III #431 seized a bridge across the Woltischia River on the western outskirts of Pawlograd, in the process destroying 3 T-34s and a number of Paks. Soon assisted by Unter-scharführer Paul Egger's Tiger, the two panzers held the bridge until reinforcements arrived, allowing "Das Reich" Panzer-grenadiers to secure the town less than two hours later. For this action Kloskowski was awarded the Knight's Cross in July.

Eleven Panzer IIIs remained fit for combat on March 4. At 2 P.M. on March 14, Hauptscharführer Karl-Heinz Worthmann in Panzer IV #631 raced ahead of Kampfgruppe Harmel to storm hill 209.3 near Wossyschtschewo, thirteen kilometers southeast of Charkow. He destroyed twenty-seven heavy Paks, two artillery pieces, and numerous machine-gun nests, driving the Russians from a strongpoint that was helping to prevent the complete encirclement of the city. After Charkow fell to the SS Panzerkorps, "Das Reich" tanks were involved in the seizing of Bjelgorod during the third week of March. The division knocked out a total of 292 tanks and SUs in the Charkow-Bjelgorod campaign and lost seventy-seven tanks and assault guns. For his brilliant leadership of its IInd Battalion during this period, Sturmbannführer Tychsen received the Knight's Cross on the March 31, as did Worthmann.

In April, Obersturmführer Karl-Heinz Lorenz, recipient of the German Cross in Gold as CO of the 2nd Panzer Company, joined the IInd Panzer-Abteilung staff, while Hauptsturmführer Herbert Zimmermann took over the Tiger company. Worthmann was promoted to an Untersturmführer and became CO of the 6th Panzer Company. Kloskowski transfered to the 7th Panzer Company, becoming the leader of its third platoon. The majority of the Ist Battalion's personnel traveled west to train on the new Panther tank, and did not return to Russia until after Operation Citadel. Thus, to bolster "Das Reich's" lone remaining Panzer battalion for Kursk, the IInd and captured T-34 tanks were formed into a company (its 9th). The 5th and 6th Companies had Panzer IVs for the upcoming battle, but the former's strength had to be filled out by a platoon of Panzer IIIs, most were left over from the Charkow campaign.

On July 4, "Das Reich" had forty-eight Panzer IIIs, thirty Panzer IVs (one quarter with short barrels), twelve Tigers, eight Panzer III command tanks, eighteen T-34s, thirty-three Sturmgeschütze, and ten Marders combat ready. On February 5, the first day of Citadel for the division, its Tigers knocked out twenty-three tanks in some six hours of heavy fighting near Beresoff and hill 233.3 to the north. On the 6th south of Lutschki I, Tigers destroyed ten tanks of the 2nd Guards Tank Corps, but Pak fire killed the 6th Panzer Company's commander, Untersturmführer Worthmann. After being awarded the Iron Cross First Class as a company CO in I/"Langemark," Hauptsturmführer Dieter Kesten took over the 6th Panzer Company. By July 13, Untersturmführer Hans

Mennel in Panzer IV #621 had knocked out twenty-four tanks during the campaign. Although from July 5 through 16, "Das Reich" accounted for 448 Russian tanks and SUs, losing a total of forty-six Panzers and assault guns destroyed, Army Group South failed to completely break through to the final Russian defense line south of Kursk. On July 28, before it departed for Italy, the "Leibstandarte" handed over to the "Das Reich" nine Tigers, thirty-nine Panzer IVs and four Panzer IIIs. "Das Reich" already had thirty-three Panzer IIIs, seventeen Panzer IVs, two T-34s, and two Tigers fit for combat.

After being transferred south to oppose the Russian counterattack across the Mius River, and destroying 391 tanks and SUs from July 30 to August 21, "Das Reich" moved to the outskirts of Charkow, where it was involved in even heavier fighting. Its Panther battalion first saw combat on August 22, around Starja-Ljubotin and Kommuna, knocking out fifty-three Red tanks. The next day twelve kilometers west of Charkow, the platoon of Untersturmführer Karl Muehleck (Panther 211) broke up a Russian tank assault. Muehleck himself destroyed seven tanks. On the 24th, Hauptsturmführer Kesten's 6th Panzer Company, newly supplied with side-skirted Panzer IVs, battled sixty T-34s between Udy-Bogens and Orkan, just southwest of Charkow, which had fallen to the Soviets on the previous day. Kesten's panzers knocked out twenty-nine of the sixty tanks. Muehleck and Kesten later received Knight's Crosses for these actions. In battles around Charkow from August 22 through September 2, "Das Reich" scored 463 armor kills. On August 27, it had four Panzer IIIs, thirty-one Panzer IVs, six Tigers, and six command tanks fit for combat, plus one Panther company. The other Panther companies were briefly attached to other divisions.

"Das Reich" Panzers moved to the Walki area in early September. On September 13, some sixty kilometers southwest of Charkow and twenty kilometers west of Walki, over seventy T-34s attacked "Das Reich's" reconnaisance battalion. From their reserve position, Hauptsturmführer Friedrich Holzer (in Panther #101) led seven tanks of his company to the rescue. In a forty-minute battle, the Panthers destroyed 28 T-34s. In two days, seventy-eight Soviet tanks were left burnt out in the long grass of the steppes. Throughout September, "Das Reich" Tigers scored heavily against Russian armor. On September 23, Untersturmführer Alois Kalls (Tiger S31) received the Gold Cross in Gold for adept leadership of his platoon during the late summer. His assistant platoon leader, Hauptscharführer Johann Reinhardt, was posthumously awarded the Gold Cross in Gold on September 25. At the end of the month, "Das Reich" moved to the Dnjepr front, having destroyed 268 tanks around Walki.

On October 29, just outside of Khodorov on the western bank of the Dnjepr River, some seventy-five kilometers southeast of Kiev, twenty T-34s pierced "Das Reich's" defense line after 5 A.M. Quickly advancing to this dangerous breakthrough, Hauptscharführer Willy Simke in Panzer IV #531 and his third platoon, 5th Panzer Company, fired upon the T-34s from twenty to thirty meters, and knocked out seventeen of them. In the same area on November 1, the Russians tried to secure their bridgehead over the Dnjepr. Sturmbannführer Tychsen's IInd Battalion was on the right flank of "Das Reich's" position. When enemy tanks and infantry attempted to outflank his unit, Tychsen led his Panzer-battalion HQ and an engineer platoon to the attack around hill 188. Three T-34s appeared over a rise. Tychsen's Befehlspanzer (command tank) III knocked out two, then his swiftly advancing force destroyed six more and drove off the rest of the enemy. That same day in a Tiger, Hauptscharführer Hans Soretz, I zug leader 8/Panzer-Regiment "Das Reich" scored the 2,000th armor kill for the division in 1943. Its Panzer-regiment had accounted for some 1,100 of these to its own losses of over 250 tanks. On September 11 in Slavia, Tigers shot up more than a dozen Russian tanks. Prior to becoming an Obersturmführer (on September 18), Alois Kalls was wounded after taking over as acting commander of the Tiger company. On the morning of September 13 near Bolschaja Grab, Soviet infantry assaulted the IInd Panzer-Abteilung headquarters. Obersturmführer Karl-Heinz Boska, its adjutant, led five Panzers in a counterattack that destroyed twelve Paks and two infantry guns and killed over 300 troops. That same day, the Panzer-regiment's commander, Obersturmbann-führer von Reitzenstein, received the Knight's Cross for the efforts of his unit during the summer and fall. Soon afterward, charged with off-duty misconduct, he committed suicide on September 30. Tychsen assumed command of the regiment. On November 26, "Das Reich" had nine Panzer IVs, two Tigers, Panthers, and two command tanks fit for combat.

In mid-December, most of the division was ordered to France to resupply and retrain. A kampfgruppe remained behind, its depleted Panzer force formed into a battalion of only two companies, one led by Obersturmführer Schomka, the second led by Obersturmführer Kloskowski. The acting battalion CO was Hauptsturmführer Willi Ende-mann. six Panzer IVs, four Panthers, and five Tigers were fit for combat. From December 25, 1943 through January 18, 1944, the battalion destroyed only twelve tanks, fourteen SUs, and twelve Paks. Three of its Tigers were knocked out on March 4 east of Semjalintzy. Untersturm-führer Teghoff and Standartenjunker von Einboeck were mortally wounded. A handful of "Das Reich" tanks fought on until April. The

Tiger company was disbanded that spring, its surviving personnel distributed among the three companies of the forming 102 SS-Panzer-Abteilung (most "Das Reich" veterans went to its first company). In all, "Das Reich's" Panzer-Regiment scored 1,200 armor kills by April and lost approximately 300 tanks in combat against the Russians.

When the Allies landed in Normandy, "Das Reich's" Panzer-Regiment had not completed refitting and retraining. Its commander was Obersturmbannführer Tychsen, its Ist Abteilung CO Sturmbannführer Rudolf Enseling, its IInd Abteilung CO Sturmbannführer Kesten. It traveled from the Toulouse area in southwest France, arriving southwest of Caen in late June. Taken from reserve during the first week in July, its strength was twenty-six Panthers in the Ist Abteilung and fifty Panzer IVs in the IInd Abteilung.

The 5th and 7th Panzer Companies were attached to the 17th SS-Panzer-Grenadier-Division along the Périers to Carentan Road, the 6th Panzer Company was attached to I/"Deutschland" and the rest of the Panzer-Regiment was positioned south of Sainteny. On July 7 and 8, the 5th and 7th Panzer Companies, which had formed a defense line running from Les Landes to Lemondiere, were attacked by the U.U. 83rd Infantry Division. On July 9, along a road near le Désert, a company of the U.S. 743rd Tank Battalion, in pursuit of two Panzer IVs, was ambushed from the flank by Obersturmführer Kloskowski's 7th Panzer Company. In fifteen minutes, nine Shermans were destroyed, three damaged (and abandoned). The next day, II/Panzer-Regiment "Das Reich" clashed with American armor near Sainteny and Château de Bois Grimot. From the Périers area, I/Panzer-Regiment "Das Reich" attacked northeast toward Sainteny, running into the 3rd Armored Division. By dark, "Das Reich" had scored ninety-eight armor kills in eight days. On July 12, 600 meters west of Château d'Auxais, the 3rd and 4th Panzer Companies battled U.S. armor and infantry while the 5th Panzer Company was engaged near Bois Grimot. The division scored some thirty more kills by July 13. On July 15, Oberjunker Fritz Langanke in Panther #211 spotted five Shermans coming up the road near Saint Denis. His tank cut across the road and wheeled around to fire on the Shermans, knocking out four. The fifth backed away into a thicket but was soon sighted and destroyed. A month later, Langanke gained the Knight's Cross for this and other tank-killing feats during July.

"Das Reich's" Panzer-Regiment had eight command tanks, thirty-five Panzer IVs, and thirty-five Panthers combat ready on July 23. Having retrieved his Panther #424 from the workshop on the morning of July

27, some ten kilometers northeast of Coutances, Unterscharführer Ernst Barkmann drove along the road to Saint Lo in order to intercept a force of Shermans. In the melee that followed, he knocked out nine of them. His own Panther was so badly damaged by tanks and fighter-bombers that it had to return to the workshop. For the entire month of July, Barkmann scored twenty-five armor kills. On July 28, Oak Leaves holder to the Knight's Cross Obersturmbannführer Tychsen, having two days earlier assumed command of the division, was killed in his Volkswagen just northeast of the village of Cambry. Thus died "Das Reich's" greatest high-level panzer commander.

Just after midnight on August 7, the Avranches counterattack began, with "Das Reich" overruning Mortain, its Panzers striking farther west, as well as southwest toward Saint Hilaire. A week later, the attack was completely smashed, and many German divisions began to be cut off in the Falaise pocket. On August 19, some tanks from the 1st Polish Armored Division took up defense positions on hills 262 and 239, about two kilometers west of the Mont Ormel ridge. The next day a mixed group of Panzer IVs and Panthers advanced to hill 239, then from its heights, shelled hill 262 a kilometer away, destroying five tanks, and allowing some German units to escape the closing Falaise noose. On August 23, Sturmbannführer Enseling received the Knight's Cross for his leadership of the mixed Panzer group during that action. Twelve days previously, Obersturmführer Karl Kloskowski had become the third of only six company commanders in the whole Panzertruppen to be awarded the Oak Leaves to the Knight's Cross. During the battle for Normandy, his company led "Das Reich" Panzer IV companies in kills. Untersturmführer Adolf Reeb, the 7th company's leading ace, received the Knight's Cross on August 23. During seven weeks of combat in France, "Das Reich's" Panzer-Regiment knocked out over 200 Allied tanks to a combat loss of some seventy-five tanks plus thirty more abandoned around Falaise as a result of mechanical problems or a lack of fuel.

Kloskowski left "Das Reich" in the fall, and Obersturmführer Horst Gresiak took over command of its 7th Panzer Company. Wilhelm Matzke was promoted to Hauptsturmführer and went from command of the 3rd Panzer Company to that of the Ist Panzer-Abteilung. Obersturmführer Johann Vieth assumed command of the 3rd Panzer Company. Obersturmbannführer Enseling was then CO of the Panzer-regiment, with Sturmbannführer Dieter Kesten remaining as IInd Panzer-Abteilung CO. When the Ardennes offensive began, "Das Reich's" Panzers (twenty-eight Panzer IVs, fifty-eight Panthers, twenty-eight assault guns, and some twenty Jagd-Panzer IV/70s) were held in reserve to be used to exploit any significant German breakthroughs in its battle sector. This was slow to occur, so on December 23 the 7 Panzer Company (it and the 8th had Panzer IVs, the 5th and 6th Panzer Companies had Sturmgeschütze) was attached to II/"Der Fuhrer" and an assault gun company to III/"Der Fuhrer," and given the task of seizing the important crossroads at Baraque de Fraiture. Obersturmführer Gresiak in Panzer #701 led eight Panzer IVs north to the crossroads just after 4:20 P.M., battling a platoon of Shermans from the U.S. 3rd Armored Division, knocking out two and losing two Panzers to the Shermans and two more to a howitzer. Some of the panzers then approached from the east, finished off the Shermans, and overran the crossroads by 6 P.M. Gresiak's company claimed a total of seventeen armor kills for the day. Seriously wounded the next morning, he received the Knight's Cross a month later.

On December 24 around 10 P.M., U.S. 7th Armored Division tanks and other vehicles were retreating northwest of Baraque de Fraiture to the moonlit Manhay crossroads. Hauptscharführer Franz Frauscher in Panther #431 and another Panther of his platoon slipped unnoticed into this column. On the ascending S-curve on Highway N15 just south of the town, the Panthers swung out of line and shot up the column and some partially dug-in Shermans, scattering the American armor in confusion. Nine Shermans were destroyed. During the takeover of Manhay, the 4th Panzer Company's CO, Hauptsturmührer Ortwin Pohl, was wounded, and early the next day (December 25) Obersturmführer Reeb in Panzer IV #711 was killed.

The following few days saw "Das Reich" futilely trying to continue its advance against regrouped and reinforced American units. For Enseling's Panzers, the rest of December and early January 1945 became a battle of attrition in which Obersturmführer Veith, the killed commander of Panther #301, was posthumously awarded the Knight's Cross. In the period December 23 through January 15, "Das Reich" claimed 224 armor kills to its own loss of sixty-eight panzers, including thirty-four Panzer IVs and twenty-eight Panthers.

By mid-February, the Panzer-regiment had been transported to the Bakony Forest in Hungary. It had thirteen Panzer IIIs, eighteen Panzer IVs, eight Jagd-Panzer IVs, and twenty-three Panthers on strength. The regiment advanced from the northwest to the northeast of Lake Balaton to where on March 6 it became engaged in combat southwest of Budapest. On March 9, Das Reich Panzers, reinforced by III(gep)/"Der Führer" overran hill 159. On March 12, fierce combat raged in the Külsö,

Püsköp, and Myr areas. Hauptscharführer Emil Seibold in Panzer IV #831 scored his sixty-fifth kill that day. "Der Führer" then advanced with the division's remaining Panzers to Heinrich Major. In that area on March 17, one day after the Russian counter-offensive Operation Vienna, Oberscharführer Barkmann's platoon knocked out five T-34s, scoring the division's 3,000th armor kill since the start of 1943.

Driven back south of Komaron during the third week of March, "Das Reich" personnel claimed to have met the JS III for the first time in combat. On March 28, "Das Reich's" Panzer-Regiment had five Panzer IVs, two Jagd-Panzer IVs, two Panthers, and five Jagd-Panthers fit for combat as it retreated northwest toward Vienna. On the morning of April 2 north of Baden, Sturmbannführer Kesten, CO of II/Panzer-Regiment "Das Reich," was killed. Assaulted by the 5th Guards Tank Corps from the northwest and the 9th Guards Mechanized Corps from the south, most of "Das Reich's" Panzers were backed up against the Donau Canal just north of Vienna during the second week of April. The division's last significant tank battle was fought there on April 13.

Early that morning, Oberscharführer Barkmann's Panther was put out of action, not by enemy fire, but by driving into a bomb crater and damaging its steering. In the vicinity, near the west end of the Floridsdorf Bridge across the Donau Canal, a lone 6th Panzer Company Panzer IV fought on but soon was silenced. Obersturmführer Karl-Heinz Boska, CO of that company, rounded up three Panthers on the other side of the bridge and led them toward the dwindling German bridgehead. The three tanks made it halfway across the bridge before they were knocked out and Boska wounded. "Das Reich's" Panzer force had virtually ceased to exist.

Its Panzer-regiment collected twenty Knight's Crosses and seventeen German Crosses in Gold during some 111 weeks of combat, knocking out over 1,730 tanks, SUs and tank destroyers against its own combat losses of 500 Panzers. Its kill ratio on the Eastern Front was about four to one, on the Western Front two-and-a-half to one. Although "Das Reich's" Panzertruppen had good leadership on the higher levels, Tychsen was its sole great battalion or regimental commander. The greatest strength of "Das Reich's" Panzer force was the superb leadership that it received on the platoon and company levels. Kloskowski was its outstanding company commander, and numerous platoon leaders, such as Worthmann, Kalls, and Mühleck, showed exceptional verve and resourcefulness. A number of graduates of "Das Reich's" Tiger company went on to become leading aces of the 102/502. SS-Panzer-Abteilung (Tigers). Ernst Barkmann was

"Das Reich's" outstanding Panther ace, scoring over sixty kills. Emil Seibold was in some ways its most spectacular ace. While commanding only T-34s and Panzer IVs, he managed to score sixty-nine kills.

The author has no reports on the battles from SS-Panzer-Regiment 9 "Hohenstaufen."

The area of action of this SS-Panzer-division, which was attached to the II. SS-Panzerkorps in 1944 and 1945, was the same as that of the 2. SS-Panzer-Division "Das Reich," and it was given credit in the reports on the action of SS-Panzer-Regiment 2 ("DR").

SOURCES OF THE PHOTO MATERIAL

Archive, Munin Verlag, Osnabrück
Heimdahl Verlag, Bayeux
Private collections, R.H. Wüst, S. Varin, W. Theffo
Time-Life-International, London

It is my wish that this book on the Panzer troops of the former Waffen-SS, through word and photo, will contribute to keeping the battles and the dying of these young Panzer soldiers alive in the memories of later generations. This, we owe to our fallen comrades!

It may also fill the painful gap caused by the fact that, to this day, there are no memorial stones for the Panzer-divisions of the Waffen-SS in the honor grove in the grounds of the Kampftruppenschule in Munster to bear witness to the fighting and sacrifices that these Panzer units offered to our fatherland!

A WORD OF THANKS

For their loyal support with photos and battle reports, a special thanks goes to the authors of the divisional histories, of the 1.SS-Panzer-Division "Leibstandarte," the 2.SS-Panzer-Division "Das Reich," the 12.SS-Panzer-Division "Hitlerjugend" and to the Panzer commanders Streng, Isecke, Kauerauf, Lichte, Langanke, Melinkat, Dr. Renz, Diers, Turk, Hein, Barkmann, Wortmann, and Bachmann for their reports on the hot spots in the east and west. Included in this appreciation, with credit to their cooperation through photos, town maps, and information that helped explain certain events during the invasion battles in 1944, are, in particular, the French contributors and witnesses of events. Messrs. Paul Samson, Rene-Henri Wüst, Serge Varin, and William Theffo offered a valuable contribution to the Panzer book of the Waffen-SS.

Register of the Panzer Units of the Waffen-SS

Heer: 1.–27. Panzer-Divisions
(army)   116. Panzer-Division
       233. Reserve-Panzer-Division
           Panzer-Lehr-Division (training division)
           Panzer-Division "Feldherrnhalle"
           Panzer-Division "Großeutschland"
           Panzer-Division "Hermann Göring"

Total: 33 Panzer-Divisions
         11 Independent heavy Panzer-abteilungen (Tigers)
           1 Jagdtiger (tank destroyer) Abteilung 512 (Tigers)
         13 Independent Panzer-brigades (101–113)

(In 1944, the Heer established independent Panzer-brigades, which saw action with the designations 101–113. Parts of these brigades were used mainly to reinforce Panzer and Panzer-grenadier-divisions until the end of the war.)

Waffen-SS: 1. SS-Panzer-Division "Leibstandarte Adolf Hitler"
            2. SS Panzer-Division "Das Reich"
            3. SS-Panzer-Division "Totenkopf"
            5. SS-Panzer-Division "Wiking"
            9. SS-Panzer-Division "Hohenstaufen"
         10. SS-Panzer-Division "Frundsberg"
         12. SS-Panzer-Division "Hitlerjugend"
            SS-Panzer-Regiment 11 "Nordland" (Berlin combat area)
            SS-Jagdtiger Abteilung 561

Total: 7 SS-Panzer-Divisions
            3 Heavy SS-Panzer-Abteilungen (Tigers):
               Heavy SS-Panzer-Abteilung 101 in the I. Panzerkorps
               Heavy SS-Panzer-Abteilung 102 in the II. Panzerkorps
               Heavy SS-Panzer-Abteilung 103 in the III. Panzerkorps_
               (In 1944, they were renamed to 501, 502, 503 and
               equipped with Königstigers.)

These listings and structures are given here to provide the readers of the post-war generation and in foreign countries with a general overview. They do not lay claim to absolute accuracy in types and numbers of allied tank production. There were variants and special types of the standard tanks, which are not included in the definition of fighting tanks.

Detailed and complete information on all tank vehicles can be found in the specialized literature from the following:

Podzun-Pallas-Verlag, 6360 Friedberg 3, Postfach 314 (Scheibert); Motorbuch-Verlag, 7000 Stuttgart 1, Postfach 1370 (W. J. Spielberger); J. F. Lehmanns-Verlag, 8000 München 60 (von Senger and Etterlin)

Combat Panzers that saw action during the World War II can be seen in their original, mobile state in the following museums:

Germany: Kampftruppenschule II der Bundeswehr, 3942 Munster
            Wehrtechnische Studiensammlung, 5400 Koblenz,
            Mayenerstr. 1
            Panzermuseum Sinzheim, 7573 Sinzheim
France: Tank Museum Saumur, Loire

Tank Types of the Enemy in the East and West

In the theaters of war in the east, the German Panzer units faced the following fighting tanks of the enemy:

KW-1	48 t	7.62-cm gun	(KW = "Kliment Woroschilow")
KW-2	52 t	15.20-cm howitzer gun	
T 34/76	26 t	7.62-cm gun	
T 34/76	28 t	7.62-cm gun	
T 34/76	30 t	7.62-cm gun	
T 34/85	32 t	8.50-cm gun	
JS-I	45 t	8.50-cm gun	(JS = "Josef Stalin")
JS-II	46 t	12.20-cm gun	
JS-III	46 t	12.20-cm gun	

(In addition, Sherman, Churchill, and Cromwell tanks through the Lend-Lease Agreement)

In the western war theater (Normandy, the Ardennes, inside the Reich), the German Panzer units faced the following fighting tanks of the enemy:

Great Britain:
Churchill I–XI   38.5–40t 4.0–7.5-cm gun, 9.5-cm howitzer
Cromwell I–VIII   26.5–28t 5.7–7.5-cm gun
Shermans of U.S. production in variants and special editions

USA:
Medium M 4:   The U.S. production used the name "Sherman"
The British production used the name "General Sherman"
The Canadian army used "RAM," with minor variants
Operational weight: 30.2t–35t, with 5.7-cm, 7.5-cm, 10.5-cm guns
From 1944 (Normandy), the French and Polish divisions were equipped with Shermans from the U.S. production.

Canada:
See U.S. tanks, which also were the equipment of the French and Polish tank divisions.

The **USA** produced, during World War II, approximately:	88,400 fighting tanks
Great Britain produced:	24,800 fighting tanks
Soviet Union produced:	52,000 fighting tanks
(Based on experiences with Russian practices of secrecy, these figures are low.)	

Total	165,200 Allied fighting tanks

In accordance with the Lend-Lease Agreement, which became effective on March 11, 1941, and was originally valid for Great Britain but, by agreement of the U.S. Senate on October 23, 1941, also included the Soviet Union, the United States of America provided 7,056 tanks and Great Britain 2,400 tanks, among other war materiel, to the Red Army.

The armored personnel carrier "Bren Carrier," which saw action in many roles and under numerous other names with the western Allies, was provided to the Red Army in the framework of the Lend-Lease Pact and became more and more noticeable in 1944–45. In many special variants, this armored universal vehicle served as a carrier of machine guns, guns, and bazookas and primarily as an armored reconnaissance vehicle, tractor for Pak, fog and flamethrower, as well as serving in large numbers as personnel carriers with the motorized infantry. We did not experience one attack in Normandy in which these Bren Carriers did not take part in the roles described. They were noted in the reports of successes as "Karretten" (small carriers) and, because of their large numbers, detailed counts were not kept. They were easily knocked out by explosive shells to the tracks or set on fire by shells to the engine compartment. The drive and track system was so highly thought of that it was used for the German "Maultier" (mule) halftracks.

German Panzer production

German Panzer production: 38,821 fighting tanks
The German Panzer production composition:
Panzer III: 15,350; Panzer IV: 8,121; Panzer V (Panther): 5,508;
Panzer VI (Tiger I): 1,355; Panzer VI (Tiger II): 487 = 30,821 Panzers

The "Zimmerit" antimagnetic mine paste on the Panthers and Tigers became mandatory at the beginning of 1944. Its only purpose was to prevent magnetic mines from being attached. Because of the large areas of dead ground around them, the heavy tanks faced the danger of being destroyed by individual soldiers. It has not been shown that Zimmerit would catch on fire from hits. It did break off after being hit by shells, but it had no other detrimental effects. Its composition must have remained unknown to our enemies since it did not show up on any enemy tanks. Instead, the Allied tanks in the west increasingly added safety features such as sand bags, track links, and additional armor plates against the 7.5-cm and 8.8-cm guns of our Panzers as protection against their high tank losses.

Panzer-Kampfabzeichen

The Panzer-Kampfabzeichen (tank assault badge) was created by the Supreme Commander of the Heer, Generaloberst von Brauchitsch, on December 20, 1939, to be awarded, in silver, to crews of the armored fighting vehicles. It was initially named "Panzerkampfwagenabzeichen" (tank badge). In accordance with the regulations issued by the Heer Supreme Command, the badge could be awarded, as of January 1, 1940, to officers, noncoms, and crews of the Panzer units. They were required to have been in action three times and on three different days as Panzer commander, Panzer gunner, Panzer driver, or Panzer radio operator, and to have actively taken part in the fighting.

On June 1, 1940, the Supreme Commander of the Heer, Generaloberst von Brauchitsch, created the Panzerkampfwagenabzeichen in bronze "in recognition of the spirit shown during the many assaults by all units of the Heer and as an incentive for the greatest efforts by every individual man." This badge could be awarded to the members of the rifle regiments and the motorcyle-rifle battalions of the Panzer-divisions and to the armored reconnaissance units under the same conditions as required for the badge in silver. With the same order, the Panzerkampfwagenabzeichen was renamed to Panzer-Kampfabzeichen.

The awarding of the badge began after May 10, 1940.

An order from the Supreme Command of the Heer on June 22, 1943, stated that "in recognition of the constantly proven fighting spirit of the members of the heavy weapons branches attacking with their Panzers, the Führer has approved the introduction of higher levels of the Panzer-Kampfabzeichen." From then on, the badge could be awarded, in silver to the Panzer crews of the Panzer units and in bronze to the Panzer crews of the armored reconnaissance units after:

25 confirmed actions, the II. level
50 confirmed actions, the III. level
75 confirmed actions, the IV. level
100 confirmed actions, the V. level

During the further course of the war the previously issued regulations were repeatedly modified and changed. The Supreme Command of the Heer ordered on December 1, 1944, that the Panzerjäger (tank destroyer) units equipped with Jagdpanzer 38, Jagdpanzer IV, Jagdpanther, Jagdtiger, and Sturmgeschütz (assault gun) III and IV, would receive the badge in silver.

Insignia of the Seven SS-Panzer-Divisions of the Waffen-SS

1. SS-Panzer-Division
"LAH"

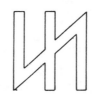

2. SS-Panzer-Division
"Das Reich"

3. SS-Panzer-Division
"Totenkopf"

The Leibstandarte changed its insignia frequently; its last presentation is not shown here. It consisted of a double line; here it is only single. The insignia of the Panzer-Division "Das Reich" also changed a number of times. However, "wolf trap" marking remained to the end.

The 3. SS-Panzer-Division, too, had a number of different insignia. Primarily, however, and until the end, it was the "death's head."

5. SS-Panzer-Division
"Wiking"

9. SS-Panzer-Division
"Hohenstaufen"

10. SS-Panzer-Division
"Frundsberg"

The 5. SS-Panzer-Division "Wiking" used the Nordic symbol of the sun wheel, either in yellow or in white color.

The 9. SS-Panzer-Division "Hohenstaufen" initially showed a sword pointing down; toward the end, however, it pointed upwards. This division used a total of three different insignia over the years.

The insignia of the 10. SS-Panzer-Division "Frundsberg" symbolized the awarding of the Oak Leaves to its commander. It, too, used four different insignia. This one was the most commonly used, and the last.

12. SS-Panzer-Division
"Hitlerjugend"

The insignia of the 12. SS-Panzer-Division remained unchanged from its inception to the end of the war.

Tank Types of World War II

TECHNICAL DATA ON THE BEST-KNOWN PANZER
AND TANK TYPES OF WORLD WAR II

Germany:

Kampf-Panzer III J			*Panzer IV H*		
(J=long barrel)	Weight	23.3 tons	*(H=with skirts)*	Weight	25 tons
	Length	5.52 m		Length	5.89 m
	Width	2.95 m		Width	3.29 m
	Height	2.51 m		Height	2.68 m
	Armor	57 & 20 mm		Armor	80 mm
	h.p.	300		h.p.	300
	km/h	40		km/h	38
	Range	175 km		Range	200 km
	Crew	5		Crew	5
	Armament	1 gun, 50 mm		Armament	1 gun, 75 mm
		2 MGs, 7.92 mm			2/3 MGs, 7.92 mm

Kampf-Panzer V G		
(Panther)	Weight	44.8 tons
	Length	6.88 m
	Width	3.44 m
	Height	3.00 m
	Armor	120 & 80 mm
	h.p.	700
	km/h	46
	Range	177 km
	Crew	5
	Armament	1 gun, 75 mm
		2 MGs, 7.92 mm

Kampf-Panzer VI I E (Tiger I)			*Kampf-Panzer VI B* (Königstiger)		
	Weight	55 tons		Weight	69.7 tons
	Length	6.21 m		Length	7.26 m
	Width	3.73 m		Width	3.75 m
	Height	2.86 m		Height	3.09 m
	Armor	110 & 102 mm		Armor	185 & 150 mm
	h.p.	700		h.p.	700
	km/h	38		km/h	38
	Range	100 km		Range	110 km
	Crew	5		Crew	5
	Armament	1 gun, 88 mm 2 MGs, 7.92 mm		Armament	1 gun, 88 mm 3 MGs, 7.92 mm

Enemy tanks on the Eastern Front:

Soviet Union:

Battle tank KW-1 B (Kliment Woroschilow)		
	Weight	48 tons
	Length	6.75 m
	Width	3.32 m
	Height	2.75 m
	Armor	110 mm
	h.p.	550
	km/h	35
	Range	335 km
	Crew	5
	Armament	1 gun, 76.2 mm 3 MGs, 7.6 mm

Battle tank KW-2			*Battle tank KW-85*		
	Weight	52 tons		Weight	46 tons
	Length	6.80 m		Length	6.80 m
	Width	3.25 m		Width	3.35 m
	Height	3.25 m		Height	2.80 m
	Armor	110 & 75 mm		Armor	110 & 75 mm
	h.p.	550		h.p.	550
	km/h	26		km/h	43
	Range	250 km		Range	330 km
	Crew	6		Crew	5
	Armament	1 howitzer gun, 152 mm 3 MGs, 7.6 mm		Armament	1 gun, 85 mm 3 MGs, 7.6 mm

TECHNICAL DATA ON THE BEST-KNOWN PANZER
AND TANK TYPES OF WORLD WAR II

Battle tank T 34/76 C			*Battle tank T 34/85*		
	Weight	30 tons	*(from 1943)*	Weight	32 tons
	Length	6.07 m		Length	6.07 m
	Width	2.95 m		Width	2.95 m
	Height	2.65 m		Height	2.72 m
	Armor	75 & 60 mm		Armor	75 & 60 mm
	h.p.	500		h.p.	500
	km/h	53		km/h	50
	Range	400 km		Range	300 km
	Crew	4		Crew	4
	Armament	1 gun, 76.2 mm		Armament	1 gun, 85 mm
		2 MGs, 7.6 mm			2 MGs, 7.6 mm
Battle tank JS-I A			*Battle tank JS-I B*		
	Weight	44 tons		Weight	45 tons
	Length	6.77 m		Length	6.77 m
	Width	3.07 m		Width	3.07 m
	Height	2.73 m		Height	2.75 m
	Armor	160 & 100 mm		Armor	160 & 100 mm
	h.p.	550		h.p.	550
	km/h	37		km/h	37
	Range	150 km		Range	150 km
	Crew	4		Crew	4
	Armament	1 gun, 85 mm		Armament	1 gun, 122 mm
		3 MGs, 7.6 mm			3 MGs, 7.6 mm
Battle tank JS-II			*Battle tank JS-III*		
	Weight	46 tons	*(new from 1944 to 1945)*	Weight	45.8 tons
	Length	6.77 m		Length	6.67 m
	Width	3.07 m		Width	3.20 m
	Height	2.75 m		Height	2.44 m
	Armor	160 & 100 mm		Armor	200 & 120 mm
	h.p.	550		h.p.	550
	km/h	43		km/h	40
	Range	190 km		Range	190 km
	Crew	4		Crew	4
	Armament	1 gun, 122 mm		Armament	1 gun, 122 mm
		1 MG, 12.7mm			1 MG, 12.7mm
		3 MGs, 7.6 mm			1 MG, 7.6 mm

(From 1942 on, shipments from US and British productions were in addition.)

Enemy tanks on the Western Front:

Great Britain:

Battle tank Churchill	Weight	39 tons	*Churchill VII-VII*	Weight	40 tons
(series I-VIII)	Length	7.45 m		Length	7.45 m
(data for Mark III-VI)	Width	3.25 m		Width	3.46 m
	Height	2.74 m		Height	2.74 m
	Armor	88 mm		Armor	152 mm
	h.p.	350		h.p.	350
	km/h	25		km/h	20
	Range	140 km		Range	200 km
	Crew	4		Crew	5
	Armament	1 gun, 57 mm		Armament	1 gun, 75 mm
		1 MG, 7.92 mm			1 MG, 7.92 mm
Mark V	Armament	1 gun, 7.5 mm	*Mark VII*	Armament	1 howitzer, 9.5 mm
		1 MG, 7.92 mm			

Battle tank Cromwell	Weight	27.5 tons	*Cromwell Mark VII-VIII*	Weight	28 tons
(series I-VI)					
	Length	6.35 m		Length	6.35 m
	Width	2.89 m		Width	3.05 m
	Height	2.49 m		Height	2.49 m
	Armor	76 mm		Armor	101 mm
	h.p.	600		h.p.	600
	km/h	43		km/h	52
	Range	265 km		Range	265 km
	Crew	5		Crew	5
	Armament	1 gun, 57 mm		Armament	1 gun, 75 mm
		2 MGs			2 MGs
Mark IV	Armament	1 gun, 75 mm	*Mark VIII*	Armament	1 gun, 9.5 mm
		2 MGs			
Mark VI	Armament	1 gun, 95 mm			
		2 MGs			

TECHNICAL DATA ON THE BEST-KNOWN PANZER
AND TANK TYPES OF WORLD WAR II

USA:

Battle tank M 4
(Sherman + RAM)

This tank was produced in a great number of variants for Canada and Great Britain. Engines and armament varied greatly. It was also largely used in the Red Army.

Weight	30.5 tons
Length	6.23 m
Width	2.67 m
Height	2.96 m
Armor	105 mm
h.p.	450
km/h	42
Range	161 km
Crew	5
Armament	1 gun, 75 mm/76.2 mm

The M 3 "Stuart" tank was used, in large numbers, with all Allied units as an armored reconnaissance vehicle.

Series Stuart I-VI
Stuart I

Weight	12.3 tons	*Stuart VI* Weight	15 tons
Length	4.46 m	Length	4.84 m
Width	2.30 m	Width	2.28 m
Height	2.47 m	Height	2.30 m
Armor	43 mm	Armor	43 mm
h.p.	250	h.p.	2 x 121
km/h	57	km/h	64
Range	112 km	Range	270 km
Crew	4	Crew	4
Armament	1 gun, 37 mm	Armament	1 gun, 37 mm
	5 MGs, 7.6 mm		3 MGs, 7.6 mm

Waffen-SS Service Ranks

SS-Rank	Wehrmacht
SS-Schütze	Schütze
SS-Sturmmann	Gefreiter
SS-Rottenführer	Obergefreiter
SS-Unterscharführer	Unteroffizier
SS-Oberscharführe	Feldwebel
SS-Hauptscharführcr	Oberfeldwebel
SS-Sturmführer	Hauptfeldwebel
SS-Standarten-Oberjunker	Fahnrich
SS-Untersturmführer	Lieutenant
SS-Obersturmführer	Oberleutnant
SS-Hauptsturmführer	Hauptmann
SS-Sturmbannführer	Major
SS-Obersturmführer	Oberstleutnant
SS-Standartenführer	Oberst
SS-Oberführer	—
SS-Brigadeführer and Generalmajor der Waffen-SS	Generalmajor
SS-Gruppenführer and Generalleutnant der Waffen-SS	Generalleutnant
SS-Obergruppenführer and General der Waffen-SS	General
SS-Oberstgruppenführer and Generaloberst der Waffen-SS	Generaloberst Generalfeld-marschall also Feldmarschall

U.S. Deliveries to U.S.S.R.

DELIVERIES FROM THE USA TO THE USSR
FROM THE BEGINNING OF THE LEND-LEASE PACT
TO SEPTEMBER 30, 1945
(Twenty-First Report to Congress on Lend-Lease Operations, p 25)

Aircraft	14,795
Tanks	7,056
Jeeps	51,503
Trucks	375,883
Motorcycles	35,170
Tractors	8,071
Guns	8,218
Machine guns	131,633
Explosives	345,735 tons
Building equipment valued	$ 10,910,000
Railroad freight cars	11,155
Locomotives	1,981
Cargo ships	90
Submarine hunters	105
Torpedo boats	197
Ship engines	7,784
Food supplies	4,478,000 tons
Machines and equipment	$ 1,078,965,000
Noniron metals	802,000 tons
Petroleum products	2,670,000 tons
Chemicals	842,000 tons
Cotton	106,893,000 yards
Leather	49,860 tons
Tires	3,786,000
Army boots	15,417,000 pairs

Index

Note: Page references in *italic* type indicate illustrations.
The denotation "*P*" followed by a number indicates
a plate in the series following page 188.

The author poses with his Knight's Cross at his home in Germany in 1994.